Alan Jacobs is a retired businessman and art dealer, and has been interested in mysticism and comparative religion since an early age. He has made an extensive study of the teachings of GI Gurdjieff, J Krishnamurti and Douglas Harding and is at present Chairman of the Ramana Maharshi Foundation UK. He is also a poet and is published regularly in the magazines *Reflections* and *Self Enquiry*.

THE ELEMENT BOOK OF
Mystical Verse

edited by
Alan Jacobs

ELEMENT

Shaftesbury, Dorset • Rockport, Massachusetts
Melbourne, Victoria

© Element Books Limited 1997
Introduction and selection © Alan Jacobs 1997

First published in Great Britain in 1997 by
Element Books Limited
Shaftesbury, Dorset SP7 8BP

Published in the USA in 1997 by
Element Books, Inc.
PO Box 830, Rockport, MA 01966

Published in Australia in 1997 by
Element Books
and distributed by Penguin Australia Limited
487 Maroondah Highway, Ringwood, Victoria 3134

Cover illustration J Catt
Cover design by Slatter-Anderson
Design by Roger Lightfoot
Typeset by Footnote Graphics, Warminster, Wilts
Printed and bound in the USA by
Courier Westford, Inc., Massachusetts

British Library Cataloguing in Publication data available

Library of Congress Cataloging in Publication data available

ISBN 1–85230–875–3

To the pilgrims of all religions
who seek to tread the inner way
to the city of God

Contents

PART 2: *Fourth Century to Thirteenth Century*

PART 3: *Fourteenth Century to Fifteenth Century*

Part 4: *Sixteenth Century*

Part 5: *Seventeenth Century*

PART 6: *Eighteenth Century*

PART 7: *Nineteenth Century*

PART 8: *Twentieth Century*

Acknowledgements

The editor and publisher gratefuly acknowledge the following for permission to use poems in copyright.

Coleman Barks: for extracts from 'Naked Song' and 'Lalla', published by Maypop Books 1963 (196 Westview Drive, Athens, Georgia 30606, USA).

Bloodaxe Books: for 'Kyrie' from *Mass for Hard Times* by R S Thomas.

Carcanet Press Ltd and Alfred A Knopf Inc: for 'The Coming of Light' and 'Keeping Things Whole' from *Selected Poems* by Mark Strand. Copyright © 1979, 1980 by Mark Strand.

Mark Cohen: for translations by J M Cohen, reprinted in *The Rider Book of Mystical Verse*, edited by J M Cohen. Copyright © The Estate of the late J M Cohen.

Constable Publishers: for 'Business Men', 'Valley Wind', 'Taoist Song', 'A Gentle Wind', 'The Scholar in the Narrow Street' and 'On Trust in his Heart' from *170 Chinese Poems*, translated by Arthur Waley.

Jeff Cooper: for 'He' from *The Sale of Saint Thomas* by Lascelles Abercrombie (Oxford University Press).

Gerald Duckworth & Co Ltd: for 'God' from *Collected Poems* by Harold Munro.

Faber & Faber Ltd: for 'The Garret', 'Ortus' and 'Ballad for Gloom' from *Collected Shorter Poems* by Ezra Pound; 'The Day' from *Day by Day* by Robert Lowell; 'Crag Jack's Apostasy' and 'The Perfect Forms' from *Lupercal* by Ted Hughes. Faber & Faber Ltd and Harper Collins Publishers Inc: for 'Fire-Eater' from *Selected Poems 1957–1967* by Ted Hughes. Faber & Faber Ltd and Random House Inc: for 'Prime' from 'Horae Canonicae' and 'Anthem' from *Collected Poems* by W H Auden, edited by Edward Mendelson. Copyright © 1951, 1972 by W H Auden. Faber & Faber Ltd and Harcourt Brace & Company: for 'Mind' from *Things of This World* by Richard Wilbur. Copyright © 1956 and renewed 1984 by Richard Wilbur. Faber & Faber Ltd and Alfred A Knopf Inc: for 'An Ordinary Evening in New Haven' (VII), 'Credences of Summer' (VI, VII, VIII), 'Design' and 'To the One of Fictive Music' from *The Collected Poems of Wallace Stevens*. Faber & Faber Ltd and Doubleday, a division of Bantam Doubleday Dell Publishing Group Inc: for 'The Waking', extracts from 'Meditation at Oyster River', 'The Minimal', extracts from 'The Lost Son', and 'The Right Thing' from *The Collected Poems of Theodore Roethke*. Copyright © Beatrice Roethke, Administratrix of the Estate of Theodore Roethke. Faber & Faber Ltd and Harper Collins Publishers Inc: for 'Black Rook in Rainy Weather' from *The Colossus* by

Sylvia Plath. Faber & Faber Ltd and Farrar, Straus & Giroux Inc: for extracts from 'Lightenings', 'Seeing Things', 'Settings' and 'Squarings' from *Seeing Things* by Seamus Heaney. Copyright © 1991 by Seamus Heaney. Faber & Faber Ltd and Harcourt Brace & Company for 'Little Gidding, IV' from *Four Quartets* by T S Eliot. Copyright 1943 by T S Eliot and renewed 1971 by Esme Valerie Eliot.

The editor also wished to include extracts from T S Eliot's 'The Rock' and 'Ash Wednesday'; however it was T S Eliot's wish that only parts IV and V from the *Four Quartets* could be used in anthologies, after his death.

Suha Faiz: for extracts from 'The City of the Heart' from *Yunus Emre's Verses of Wisdom and Love* (Element Books, 1992).

A E I Falconar: for 'Diving' from *Gardens of Meditation* (Colin Smythe, 1981).

George Allen & Unwin, an imprint of Harper Collins Publishers Ltd: for material from *Rúmí: Poet and Mystic* by Rúmí, translated by Reynold A Nicholson.

Golgonooza Press: for 'Self', 'Night Sky', 'Natura Naturans', 'To the Sun' (4 parts) and 'The World' from *Selected Poems of Kathleen Raine* by Kathleen Raine.

Harvard University Press and the Trustees of Amherst College, and Little, Brown & Company (for No 827): for 'He Fumbles at Your Soul' (No 315), 'Our Journey Had Advanced' (No 615), 'The Only News I Know' (No 827), 'I Taste a Liquor Never Brewed' (No 214), 'Safe in their Alabaster Chambers' (No 216), 'Heaven is What I Cannot Reach' (No 239), 'Read, Sweet, How Others Strove' (No 260), 'We Thirst at First' (No 726) and 'Bring Me the Sunset in a Cup' (No 128) from *The Poems of Emily Dickinson*, edited by Thomas H Johnson, Cambridge, Massachusetts: The Belknap Press of Harvard University Press. Copyright © 1951, 1955, 1979, 1983 the President and Fellows of Harvard College.

David Higham Associates Ltd: for 'The Child' by W S Merwin from *The Penguin Book of American Verse*, edited by Geoffrey Moore (Penguin, 1989); for an extract from 'Faust's Confession' from *Goethe's Faust*, translated by Louis MacNeice (Faber & Faber).

Kanvashrama Trust: for 'Bridal Garland of Letters' by Sri Ramana Maharshi, translated by Sarvatma Chaitanya and Om Sadhu.

Krishnamurti Foundation of America: for extracts from 'The Song of Life' from *From Darkness to Light* by J Krishnamurti (Harper, 1980).

Liveright Publishing Corporation: for 'Meditation', 'Hieroglyphic', 'The Hurricane' and 'Atlantis' (40 line excerpt) from *Complete Poems of Hart Crane*, edited by Marc Simon. Copyright 1933, copyright © 1958, 1966 by Liveright Publishing Corporation. Copyright © 1986 by Marc Simon.

James MacGibbon: for 'The Airy Christ' from *Collected Poems of Stevie Smith* by Stevie Smith (Penguin Twentieth Century Classics).

Harold Morland: for 'For Kathleen', an extract from 'The Unquenchable Fire' and an extract from 'The Elements of Life' from *Collected Poems* (Harold Morland).

Motilal Banarsidass Publishers and A J Alston: for *Devotional Poems of Mirabai (Poems 190–198)*, translated by A J Alston (Delhi, 1980).

Mountain Path, Tiruvannamalai, India: for 'Inquiry Into the 'I'' by Oleg Mogilever, translated by Nadhia Sutara and 'The Song of the Poppadum' by Ramana Maharshi, translated by A W Chadwick.

John Murray (Publishers) Ltd: for extracts from *From the Persian Mystics* by Attar, translated by Margaret Smith.

New Directions Publishing Corporation: for an extract from 'Poetry, A Natural Thing' from *The Opening of the Field* by Robert Duncan. Copyright © 1960 Robert Duncan.

W W Norton & Company Ltd: for 'I thank You God for most this amazing' from *Complete Poems 1904–1962* by E E Cummings, edited by George J Firmage. Copyright © 1950, 1978, 1979, 1991 the Trustees for the e e cummings Trust and George James Firmage.

Hugh Noyes, for Alfred Noyes Literary Estate: for 'Creation' by Alfred Noyes.

Oxford University Press Ltd: for poems from *The Poetical Works of Robert Bridges* (1953).

Oxford University Press Inc: for 'The Eclipse' from *Collected Poems 1930–1976* by Richard Eberhart. Copyright © 1976 Richard Eberhart.

Penguin Books Ltd: for 'Sunflower Sutra' (from 'Howl'), reprinted in *Selected Poems 1947–1995* by Allen Ginsberg (Penguin Twentieth Century Classics, 1997). Copyright © Allen Ginsberg, 1996; for extracts from *The Upanishads*, translated by Juan Mascaró (Penguin Classics, 1965). Copyright © Juan Mascaró, 1965; for extracts from *Tao Te Ching* by Lao Tzu, translated by D C Lau (Penguin Classics, 1963). Copyright © D C Lau, 1963; for poems from *The Penguin Book of Hebrew Verse*, edited and translated by T Carmi (Penguin Books, 1981). Translation copyright © T Carmi, 1981. Penguin Books Ltd and The Ecco Press for 'Revelation' from *Selected Poems* by Zbigniew Herbert, translated by Czeslaw Milosz and Peter Dale Scott (Penguin Books, 1968). Translation copyright © Czeslaw Milosz and Peter Dale Scott, 1968.

Laurence Pollinger Ltd and Viking Penguin, a division of Penguin Books USA Inc: for 'The Song of a Man Who Has Come Through' and 'The Ship of Death' from *The Complete Poems of D H Lawrence* by D H Lawrence, edited by V de Sola Pinto and F W Roberts. Copyright © 1964, 1971 Angelo Ravagli and C M Weekly, Executors of the Estate of Frieda Lawrence Ravagli.

Princeton University Press and Motilal Banarsidass Publishers: for material from *Poems to Siva*, translated by Indira Viswanatha Peterson. Copyright © 1989 Princeton University Press.

Ramakrishna-Vivekananda Center: for poems from *The Gospel of Sri Ramakrishna*, as translated by Swami Nikhilananda and published by the Ramakrishna-Vivekananda Center of New York. Copyright © 1942 Swami Nikhilananda.

Ramana Maharshi Foundation UK: for poems by Robert Goslin, published in *Self Enquiry*.

Random House UK Ltd: for poems from *Selected Works: Volume 2: Poetry* by Rainer Maria Rilke, translated by J B Leishman (Hogarth Press, 1960); for 'Bereft' and 'The Trial by Existence' from *The Poetry of Robert Frost*, edited by Edward Connery Lathem (Jonathan Cape).

Editions du Seuil: for 'Meditation' from *On Love* by Pierre Teilhard de Chardin. Copyright © Editions du Seuil, 1967.

Shanti Sadan: for extracts from *Songs of Enlightenment, Poems of Swami Rama Tirtha*, translated by A J Alston (Shanti Sadan, London, 1991); for extracts from *Indian Mystic Verse*, translated by Hari Prasad Shastri (Shanti Sadan, London, 1984; 3rd Edition).

Colin Smythe on behalf of the Estate of Diarmuid Russell: for 'Krishna' and 'Unity' by George William Russell.

The Society of Authors as the literary representative of the Estate of John Masefield: for an extract from 'The Wanderer' and Sonnets: XII, XIII, XXVIII, XXXII, XXXIII from *Collected Poems* by John Masefield. Mrs Nicolette Gray and The Society of Authors on behalf of the Laurence Binyon Estate: for extracts from *The Divine Comedy: Paradiso* by Dante, translated by Laurence Binyon.

Sri Aurobindo Ashram Trust: for three sonnets and passages from *Savitri* by Sri Aurobindo.

Sri Ramakrishna Math: for 'Hymn to Annapūrṇā' from *Self-knowledge* by Swami Nikhilananda.

Sri Ramanasramam: for 'Arunchala', 'Be Still', 'The Dance', 'Death' and 'The Few' by Arthur Osborne from *Those With Little Dust*, and 'Ramana the Magician' by Muruganar from *Homage to the Presence of Ramana*.

Lucien Stryk: for poems from *The Penguin Book of Zen Poetry*, edited and translated by Lucien Stryk and Takashi Ikemoto (Penguin Books, 1981).

Threshold Books (RD 4 Box 600, Putney, Vermont 05346, USA): for quatrains from *Unseen Rain: Quatrains of Rúmí*, translated by Coleman Barks, and a selection from *This Longing Poetry, Teaching Stories and Letters of Rúmí*, translated by Coleman Barks and John Moyne.

Visva-Bharati, Santiniketan, India, on behalf of the Estate of R N Tagore: for poems from 'Gitanjali' and others from *Collected Poems and Plays* by Rabindranath Tagore (New York: Macmillan, 1937).

A P Watt Ltd on behalf of Anne and Michael Yeats: for 'The Lake Isle of Innisfree', 'The Secret Rose' and an extract from 'Sailing to Byzantium' from *The Collected Poems of W B Yeats*; A P Watt Ltd and Simon & Schuster Inc on behalf of Shree Purohit Swami and Michael Yeats:

for an extract from *The Ten Principle Upanishads*, translated by Shree Purohit Swami and W B Yeats (Faber, 1970); A P Watt Ltd on behalf of The Trustees of the Maurice Baring Will Trust for 'The Heart of the Lily' by Maurice Baring.

The Wylie Agency: for 'Without God I Cannot Live', 'Other Verses with a Divine Meaning', 'The Soul Aflame', 'Verses Written after an Ecstasy of High Exaltation' and 'Song of the Soul in Intimate Communication and Union with the Love of God' by St John of the Cross, translated by Roy Campbell. Copyright © Roy Campbell 1951.

To Jane Adams with grateful thanks for her continual support and encouragement in compiling this anthology.

The editor and publisher have made every effort to secure permission to reproduce material protected by copyright. They will be pleased to make good any omissions brought to their attention in future printings of this book.

Preface

A Poet's affair is with God, to whom he is accountable,
and of whom is his reward.

Robert Browning in a letter to Ruskin

Alas! who was it that first found
Gold hid of purpose under ground;
that sought out pearls and dived to find
Such precious perils for mankind!

Henry Vaughan from *Obriscarus*, 165

Pearls lie not on the seashore,
If thou desirest one, thou must dive for it.

Oriental Proverb

Life is a pure flame, and we live
by an invisible Sun within us.

Sir Thomas Browne

The life and power of poetry consists in its ability
to step out of itself, tear off a fragment of religion,
and then return into itself and absorb it.

Friedrich Schlegel, *Philosophical Fragments*, Ideas 25

True poetry springs only from
the calm heart's clarity which followed
the elimination of the ego
by inward search and finding out
that none of the five sheaths is I.

Garland of Guru's Sayings No 140 (*trans* K Swaminathan)

Bhagavan loved to listen to readings from the Bible, Shakespeare,
Milton, Wordsworth, Keats and so on. He enjoyed them all,
and brought out their inner significance by a few words of comment
at once apt, penetrating and revealing.

From *Muruganar*, K Swaminathan

Would we with ink the ocean fill,
Were every blade of grass a quill,
Were the world of parchment made
And every man a scribe by trade,
To write the love
Of God above
Would drain that ocean dry;

Nor would the scroll
Contain the whole
Though stretched from sky to sky.

Meir Ben Isaac Nehorai

Lord, my first fruits present themselves to thee;
Yet not mine neither; for from thee they came,
And must return. Accept of them and me,
And make us strive, who shall make a gain:
Theirs, who shall hurt themselves or me, refrain.

George Herbert

An empty book is like an Infant's Soul, in which anything may be written.
It is capable of all things, but containeth nothing. I have a mind to fill
this with profitable wonders. And since Love made you put it into my
hands, I will fill it with those Truths you love without knowing them: and
with those things which, if it be possible, shall shew my love; to
you, in communicating most enriching Truths; to Truth, in exalting her
beauties in such a Soul.

Thomas Traherne, *Centuries I(1)*

Introduction

In 1917 the *Oxford Book of English Mystical Verse* was published. Now out of print for many years, the time has surely come for a second major anthology on the same theme. This new compilation has undoubtedly benefited from the recent impact of Eastern mysticism upon the Western world.

Mysticism is often described as the Soul's journey from the darkness of worldly confusion to the blissful light of that experience when the seeker and the Self are known to be One. As Evelyn Underhill has written: 'The poetry of mysticism might be defined on the one hand as a temperamental reaction to the vision of Reality: on the other, as a form of prophecy. As it is the special vocation of the mystical consciousness to mediate between two orders, going out in loving adoration towards God and coming home to tell the secrets of Eternity to other men; so the artistic self-expression of this consciousness has also a double character. It is love-poetry, but love-poetry which is often written with a missionary intention.'[1]

Many are the signposts on the way, and the records of different voyages. Each has his own emphasis and angularity, speaking from a certain standpoint on the pilgrimage, in the language and cultural setting of his day. The poet is perhaps the best placed to express these experiences – if they can be adequately expressed at all.

The compiler of this anthology has tried only to give a flavour of certain poets in literature, often omitting those authors and classics that are all too familiar. The reader may well be encouraged to delve deeper in a direction which speaks to his own particular taste and inclination.

The order of the poems is broadly chronological and thematic. Literary translations from different religious traditions have been included. The extracts are by no means comprehensive; one volume cannot possibly contain more than a fragment of this magnificent library.

To some degree, the selection reflects a personal quest, but all the poems are universal in character, and may appeal to many from different backgrounds who are interested in this vital field of enquiry.

Alan Jacobs
London

---

[1] From *Introduction to Songs of Kabir* Evelyn Underhill (*trans* Tagore)

PART 1:
Pre-Fourth Century

RIG-VEDA (*trans* F Max Muller)

The Song of Creation

Then was not non-existent nor existent: there was no realm
    of air, no sky beyond it.
What covered in, and where? and what gave shelter?
Was water there, unfathomed depth of water?

Death was not then, nor was there aught immortal: no sign
    was there, the day's and night's divider.
That one thing, breathless, breathed by its own nature:
    apart from it was nothing whatsoever.

Darkness there was: at first concealed in darkness, this All
    was indiscriminated chaos.
All that existed then was void and formless: by the great
    power of warmth was born that unit.

Thereafter rose desire in the beginning, Desire, the primal
    seed and germ of spirit.
Sages who searched with their heart's thought discovered the
    existent's kinship in the non-existent.

Transversely was their severing line extended: what was
    above it then, and what below it?
There were begetters, there were mighty forces, free action
    here and energy up yonder.

Who verily knows and who can here declare it, whence it
    was born and whence comes this creation?
The gods are later than this world's production. Who
    knows, then, whence it first came into being?

He, the first origin of this creation, whether he formed it all
    or did not form it,
Whose eye controls this world in highest heaven, he verily
    knows it, or perhaps he knows not.

ANCIENT EGYPTIAN (*trans* anon)

God

is One and Alone,
and there is none other beside Him.
GOD is One and alone,
the Maker of all His creatures.
GOD is a Spirit,
deep-hidden from the eye of man and from all things.
GOD is the Spirit of spirits,
of creation the Spirit divine.
GOD is God from the beginning
before all things were He was God.
Lord of existences is He,
Father of all,
God external.
GOD is the One everlasting,
perpetual, eternal, unending.
From endless time hath He been,
and shall be henceforth and for ever.
GOD is hidden,
and no man His form hath perceived nor His likeness.
Unknown of gods and of men,
mysterious, incomprehensible.
GOD is Truth,
and on truth doth He live;
King of truth divine is He.
GOD is life;
and man liveth through Him,
the Primeval Alone.

MILES COVERDALE (*trans*)

The Song of Solomon

The First Chapter
Let him kiss me with the kisses
    of his mouth –
For thy love is better than wine.
Thine ointments have a goodly fragrance,
Thy name is as ointment poured forth;
Therefore do the maidens love thee.

Draw me, we will run after thee.
The king hath brought me into his chambers;
We will be glad and rejoice in thee,
We will find thy love more fragrant than wine.
Sincerely do they love thee.

I am dark, but comely,
O ye daughters of Jerusalem,
As the tents of Kedar,
As the curtains of Solomon.
Look not upon me, because I am swarthy,
Because the sun hath tanned me:
My mother's sons were angry with me;
They made me the keeper of the vineyards;
But mine own vineyard have I not kept.

Tell me, O thou whom my soul loveth,
Where thou feedest, where thou makest
     thy flock to rest at noon;
For why should I be as one that veileth herself
Beside the flocks of thy companions?

If thou know not, O thou fairest among women,
Go thy way forth by the footsteps of the flock
And feed thy kids beside the shepherds' tents.
I have compared thee, O my love,
To a steed in Pharaoh's chariots.
Thy cheeks are comely with rows of jewels,
Thy neck with chains of gold.
We will make thee circlets of gold
With studs of silver.

While the king sat at his table,
My spikenard sent forth its fragrance.
My beloved is unto me as a bag of myrrh,
That lieth betwixt my breasts.
My beloved is unto me as a cluster of henna
In the vineyards of En-gedi.

Behold, thou art fair, my love; behold, thou art fair;
Thou eyes are as doves.

Behold, thou art fair, my beloved, yea, pleasant;
Also our couch is leafy.

The beams of our houses are cedar,
And our rafters of cypresses.

The Second Chapter

I am a rose of Sharon,
A lily of the valleys.

As a lily among thorns,
So is my love among the daughters.

As an apple tree among the trees
    of the wood,
So is my beloved among the youths.

I delight to sit in his shadow
And his fruit is sweet to my taste.
He brought me to the banqueting house,
And his banner of love was over me.

Stay me with flagons, comfort me with apples;
For I am lovesick.
His left hand is under my head,
And his right hand doth embrace me.

I adjure you, O daughters of Jerusalem,
By the gazelles, and by the hinds of the field,
That ye stir not up, nor awake my love,
Till he please.

The voice of my beloved!
Behold, he cometh
Leaping upon the mountains,
Skipping upon the hills.
My beloved is like a gazelle or a young hart:
Behold, he standeth behind our wall,
He looketh in through the windows,
He peereth through the lattice.
My beloved spoke, and said unto me:

'Rise up, my love, my fair one, and come away.
For, lo, the winter is past,
The rain is over and gone;
The flowers appear on the earth;
The time of singing is come,
And the voice of the turtle is heard in our land;
The fig tree putteth forth her green figs,
And the vines in blossom give forth
    their fragrance.
Arise, my love, my fair one, and come away.

O my dove, that art in the clefts of the rock,
In the covert of the cliff.
Let me see thy countenance, let me hear thy voice;
For sweet is thy voice,
And thy countenance is comely.

Take from us the foxes,
The little foxes, that spoil the vineyards;
For our vineyards are in blossom.'

My beloved is mine, and I am his,
That feedeth among the lilies.

Until the day break, and the shadows flee away,
Turn, my beloved,
And be thou like a gazelle or a young hart
Upon the mountains of spices.

The Third Chapter

By night on my bed I sought him whom
    my soul loveth;
I sought him, but I found him not.
I will rise now, and go about the city;
In the streets, and in the broad ways,
I will seek him whom my soul loveth.
I sought him, but I found him not.
The watchmen that go about the city found me:
To whom I said, 'Saw ye him whom my soul loveth?'
Scarce had I passed from them,
But I found him whom my soul loveth:
I held him, and would not let him go,
Until I had brought him into my mother's house,
And into the chamber of her that conceived me.

I adjure you, O daughters of Jerusalem,
By the gazelles, and by the hinds of the field,
That ye awaken not, nor stir up love,
Until it please.

Who is this that cometh up out of the wilderness
Like pillars of smoke,
Perfumed with myrrh and frankincense,
With all powders of the merchant?
Behold, it is the litter of Solomon;
Threescore valiant men are about it,
Of the mighty men of Israel.
They all hold swords, being expert in war:
Every man hath his sword upon his thigh
Because of dread in the night.

King Solomon made himself a palanquin
    of the wood of Lebanon.
He made the pillars thereof of silver,
The bottom thereof of gold,
The seat of it of purple,
The inside thereof being paved with love,
From the daughters of Jerusalem.

Go forth, O ye daughters of Zion,
And gaze upon King Solomon
With the crown wherewith his mother crowned him
On the day of his wedding,
And on the day of the gladness of his heart.

The Fourth Chapter

Behold, thou art fair, my love; behold, thou art fair;
Thine eyes are as doves behind thy veil;
Thy hair is as a flock of goats,
That trail down from Mount Gilead.
Thy teeth are like a flock of ewes all shapes alike
Which came up from the washing;
Whereof all are paired,
And none faileth among them.
Thy lips are like a thread of scarlet,
And thy mouth is comely:
Thy temples are like a pomegranate split open
   behind thy veil.
Thy neck is like the tower of David
Builded with turrets,
Whereon there hang a thousand shields,
All the armor of the mighty men.

Thy two breasts are like two fawns
That are twins of a gazelle,
Which feed among the lilies.

Until the day break,
And the shadows flee away,
I will get me to the mountain of myrrh,
And to the hill of frankincense.

Thou art all fair, my love,
And there is no spot in thee.

Come with me from Lebanon, my bride,
With me from Lebanon:
Look from the top of Amana,
From the top of Shenir and Hermon,
From the lions' dens,
From the mountains of the leopards.

Thou hast ravished my heart, my sister, my bride;
Thou hast ravished my heart with one of thine eyes,
With one bead of thy necklace.

How fair is thy love, my sister, my bride!
How much better is thy love than wine!
And the smell of thine ointments than
   all manner of spices!

Thy lips, O my bride, drop honey –
Honey and milk are under thy tongue;
And the smell of thy garments is like
    the smell of Lebanon.

A garden enclosed is my sister, my bride;
A spring shut up, a fountain sealed.
Thy plants are an orchard of pomegranates,
With precious fruits;
Henna, with spikenard plants,
Spikenard and saffron,
Calamus and cinnamon,
With all trees of frankincense;
Myrrh and aloes, with all the chief spices.
Thou art a fountain of gardens, a well
    of living waters,
And flowing streams from Lebanon.

Awake, O north wind;
And come, thou south;
Blow upon my garden,
That the spices thereof may flow out.
Let my beloved come into his garden,
And eat his pleasant fruits.

The Fifth Chapter

I am come into my garden, my sister, my bride:
I have gathered my myrrh with my spice;
I have eaten my honeycomb with my honey;
I have drunk my wine with my milk:
Eat, O friends;
Drink, yea, drink abundantly, O beloved.

I sleep, but my heart waketh:
Hark: my beloved knocketh, saying,
'Open to me, my sister, my love,
My dove, my undefiled:
For my head is filled with dew,
And my locks with the drops of the night.'

I have put off my coat;
How shall I put it on?
I have washed my feet; how shall I defile them?
My beloved put in his hand by the hole of the door,
And my heart was moved for him.

I rose up to open to my beloved;
And my hands dropped with myrrh,
And my fingers, flowing myrrh,
Upon the handles of the lock.

I opened to my beloved;
But my beloved had turned away,
    and was gone:
My soul failed when he spoke.
I sought him, but I could not find him;

I called him, but he gave me no answer.
The watchmen that went about the city found me,
They smote me, they wounded me;
The keepers of the walls took my mantle from me.

I adjure you, O daughters of Jerusalem,
If ye find my beloved,
That ye tell him, that I am lovesick.

What is thy beloved more than another beloved,
O thou fairest among women?
What is thy beloved more than another beloved,
    that thou dost so adjure us?

My beloved is clear-skinned and ruddy,
Preeminent among ten thousand.
His head is as the finest gold,
His locks are curled, and black as a raven.
His eyes are as the eyes of doves by the rivers of waters,
Washed with milk, and fitly set.
His cheeks are as a bed of spices, as banks of sweet herbs;
His lips are like lilies, dropping with flowing myrrh.
His hands are as rods of gold set with the beryl:
His body is as polished ivory overlaid with sapphires.
His legs are as pillars of marble,
Set upon sockets of fine gold:
He is as majestic as Lebanon,
Stately as the cedars.
His mouth is most sweet:
Yea, he is altogether lovely.
This is my beloved, and this is my friend,
O daughters of Jerusalem.

The Sixth Chapter

Whither is thy beloved gone,
O thou fairest among women?
Whither has thy beloved turned him?
That we may seek him with thee.

My beloved is gone down to his garden,
To the beds of spices,
To feed in the gardens, and to gather lilies.
I am my beloved's, and my beloved is mine:
He feedeth among the lilies.

Thou art beautiful, O my love, as Tirzah,
Comely as Jerusalem,
Terrible as an army with banners.

Turn away thine eyes from me, for they have
    overcome me.
Thy hair is as a flock of goats that trail down from
    Gilead.
Thy teeth are as a flock of ewes which are come up from
    the washing,
Whereof all are paired, and none faileth among them.
Thy temples are like a pomegranate split open
Behind thy veil.

There are threescore queens,
And fourscore concubines,
And maidens without number.
My dove, my undefiled, is but one;
She is the only one of her mother,
She is the choice one of her that bore her.

The daughter saw her, and called her happy;
Yea, the queens and the concubines,
    and they praised her.

Who is she that looketh forth as the dawn,
Fair as the moon, clear as the sun,
And terrible as an army with banners?

I went down into the garden of nuts
To look at the green plants of the valley,
And to see whether the vine budded,
And the pomegranates were in flower.

Before I was aware, my soul set me
Upon the chariots of Ammi-nadib.

The Seventh Chapter

Return, return, O Shulammite;
Return, return, that we may look upon thee.
What will ye see in the Shulammite?
As it were a dance of two companies.

How beautiful are thy steps in sandals,
O prince's daughter!
The roundings of thy thighs are like jewels,
The work of the hands of a skilled workman.
Thy navel is like a round goblet,
Wherein no mingled wine is wanting.
Thy belly is like an heap of wheat
Set about with lilies.
Thy two breasts are like two young fawns
That are twins of a gazelle.
Thy neck is as a tower of ivory;

Thine eyes as the pools in Heshbon,
By the gate of Bath-rabbim:
Thy nose is like the tower of Lebanon
Which looketh toward Damascus.
Thine head upon thee is like Carmel,
And the hair of thy head like purple;
A king is held captive in the tresses.

How fair and how pleasant art thou,
O love, for delights!

This thy stature is like to a palm tree,
And thy breasts to clusters of grapes.
I said, I will go up into the palm tree,
I will take hold of its branches;

And let thy breasts be as clusters of the vine,
And the fragrance of thy breath like apples;
And thy mouth like the best wine
That glideth down sweetly for my beloved,
Moving gently the lips of those that are asleep.

I am my beloved's,
And his desire is toward me.

Come, my beloved, let us go forth into the field;
Let us lodge in the villages.

Let us get up early to the vineyards;
Let us see if the vine has flowered,
Whether the blossoms have opened,
And the pomegranates be in flower;
There will I give thee my love.
The mandrakes give forth fragrance,
And at our doors are all manner of precious fruits,
New and old,
Which I have laid up for thee, O my beloved.

The Eighth Chapter

O that thou wert as my brother,
that sucked the breasts of my mother!
When I should find thee without, I would kiss thee;
Yea, and none would despise me.

I would lead thee, and bring thee
Into my mother's house,
That thou mightest instruct me;
I would cause thee to drink of spiced wine
Of the juice of my pomegranate.

His left hand should be under my head,
And his right hand should embrace me.

I adjure you, O daughters of Jerusalem,
That ye stir not up, nor awake my love, until he please.

Who is this that cometh up from the wilderness,
Leaning upon her beloved?

Under the apple tree I awakened thee;
There thy mother brought thee forth:
There she that bore thee brought thee forth.

Set me as a seal upon thine heart,
As a seal upon thine arm;
For love is strong as death,
Jealousy is cruel as the grave;
The flashes thereof are flashes of fire,
Which hath a most vehement flame.
Many waters cannot quench love,
Neither can the floods drown it;
If a man would give all the substance of his house
    for love,
He would utterly be condemned.

We have a little sister,
And she hath no breasts;
What shall we do for our sister
In the day when she shall be spoken for?
If she be a wall,
We will build upon it a turret of silver:
And if she be a door,
We will enclose her with boards of cedar.

I am a wall,
And my breasts like the towers thereof;
Then was I in his eyes
As one that found peace.

Solomon had a vineyard at Baal-hamon;
He gave over the vineyard unto keepers;
Every one for the fruit thereof
Brought in a thousand pieces of silver.

My vineyard, which is mine, is before me:
Thou, O Solomon, shalt have the thousand,
And those that keep the fruit thereof two hundred.

Thou that dwellest in the gardens,
The companions hearken to thy voice:
'Cause me to hear it.'

Make haste, my beloved,
And be thou like to a gazelle
    or to a young hart
Upon the mountains of spices.

HOMER (*trans* P B Shelley)

From Song to Apollo

I

The sleepless Hours who watch me as I lie,
  Curtained with star-inwoven tapestries
From the broad moonlight of the sky,
  Fanning the busy dreams from my dim eyes, –
Waken me when their Mother, the grey Dawn,
Tells them that dreams and that the moon is gone.

II

Then I arise, and climbing Heaven's blue dome,
  I walk over the mountains and the waves,
Leaving my robe upon the ocean foam;
  My footsteps pave the clouds with fire; the caves
Are filled with my bright presence, and the air
Leaves the green earth to my embraces bare.

III

The sunbeams are my shafts, with which I kill
  Deceit, that loves the night and fears the day;
All men who do or even imagine ill
  Fly me, and from the glory of my ray
Good minds and open actions take new might,
Until diminished by the reign of night.

IV

I feel the clouds, the rainbows and the flowers
  With their ethereal colours; the moon's globe
And the pure stars in their eternal bowers
  Are cinctured with my power as with a robe;
Whatever lamps on Earth or Heaven may shine,
Are portions of one power, which is mine.

V

I stand at noon upon the peak of Heaven,
  Then with unwilling steps I wander down
Into the clouds of the Atlantic even;
  For grief that I depart they weep and frown:
What look is more delightful than the smile
With which I soothe them from the western isle?

VI

I am the eye with which the Universe
   Beholds itself and knows itself divine;
All harmony of instrument or verse,
   All prophecy, all medicine are mine,
All light of art or nature; – to my song,
Victory and praise in its own right belong.

HOMER (*trans* P B Shelley)

Hymn to the Earth: Mother of All

O universal mother, who dost keep
From everlasting thy foundations deep,
Eldest of things, Great Earth, I sing of thee;
All shapes that have their dwelling in the sea,
All things that fly, or on the ground divine
Live, move, and there are nourished – these are thine;
These from thy wealth thou dost sustain; from thee
Fair babes are born, and fruits on every tree
Hang ripe and large, revered Divinity!

The life of mortal men beneath thy sway
Is held; thy power both gives and takes away!
Happy are they whom thy mild favours nourish,
All things unstinted round them grown and flourish.
For them, endures the life-sustaining field
Its load of harvest, and their cattle yield
Large increase, and their house with wealth is filled.
Such honoured dwell in cities fair and free,
The homes of lovely women, prosperously;
Their sons exult in youth's new budding gladness,
And their fresh daughters free from care or sadness,
With bloom-inwoven dance and happy song,
On the soft flowers the meadow-grass among,
Leap round them sporting – such delights by thee
Are given, rich Power, revered Divinity.

Mother of gods, thou wife of starry Heaven,
Farewell! be thou propitious, and be given
A happy life for this brief melody,
Nor thou nor other songs shall unremembered be.

ANONYMOUS (*trans*)
Amergin

I am the wind which breathes upon the sea,
I am the wave of the ocean,
I am the murmur of the billows,
I am the ox of the seven combats,
I am the vulture upon the rocks,
I am a beam of the sun,
I am the fairest of plants,
I am a wild boar in valour,
I am a salmon in the water,
I am a lake in the plain,
I am a word of science,
I am the point of the lance in battle,
I am the God who creates in the head of the fire.
Who is it who throws light into the meeting on the mountain?
Who announces the ages of the moon?
Who teaches the place where couches the sun?

SVETASVATURA (*trans* Juan Mascaro)
From The Svetasvatura Upanishad

Part 3

All this universe is in the glory of God, of Siva the god of love. The heads and faces of men are his own and he is in the hearts of all.

He is indeed the Lord supreme whose grace moves the hearts of men. He leads us unto his own joy and to the glory of his light.

He is the inmost soul of all, which like a little flame the size of a thumb is hidden in the hearts of men. He is the master of wisdom ever reached by thought and love. He is the immortality of those who know him.

He has innumerable heads and eyes and feet, and his vastness enfolds the universe, and even a measure of ten beyond.

God is in truth the whole universe: what was, what is, and what beyond shall ever be. He is the god of life immortal, and of all life that lives by food.

His hands and feet are everywhere, he has heads and mouths everywhere: he sees all, he hears all. He is in all and he is.

The Light of consciousness comes to him through infinite powers of perception, and yet he is above these powers. He is God, the ruler of all, the infinite refuge of all.

The wandering swan of the soul dwells in the castle of nine gates of the body and flies away to enjoy the outer world. He is the master of the universe: of all that moves and of all that moves not.

Without hands he holds all things, without feet he runs everywhere. Without eyes he sees all things, without ears all things he hears. He knows all, but no one knows him, the Spirit before the beginning, the Spirit Supreme everlasting.

Only those who see God in their soul attain the joy eternal.

He is the Eternal among things that pass away, pure Consciousness of conscious beings, the ONE who fulfils the prayers of many. By the vision of Sankhya and the harmony of Yoga a man knows God, and when a man knows God he is free from all fetters.

There the sun shines not, nor the moon, nor the stars; lightnings shine not there and much less earthly fire. From his light all these give light; and his radiance illumines all creation.

He is the wandering swan everlasting, the soul of all in the universe, the Spirit of fire in the ocean of life. To know him is to overcome death, and he is the only Path to life eternal.

He is the never-created Creator of all: he knows all. He is pure consciousness, the creator of time: all-powerful; all-knowing. He is the Lord of the soul and of nature and of the three conditions of nature. From him comes the transmigration of life and liberation: bondage in time and freedom in Eternity.

He is the God of light, immortal in his glory, pure consciousness, omnipresent, the loving protector of all. He is the everlasting ruler of the world: could there be any ruler but he?

Longing therefore for liberation, I go for refuge to God who by his grace reveals his own light; and who in the beginning created the god of creation and gave to him the sacred *Vedas*.

I go for refuge to God who is ONE in the silence of Eternity, pure radiance of beauty and perfection, in whom we find our peace. He is the bridge supreme which leads to immortality, and the Spirit of fire which burns the dross of lower life.

If ever for man it were possible to fold the tent of the sky, in that day he might be able to end his sorrow without the help of God.

By the power of inner harmony and by the grace of God Svetasvatara had the vision of Brahman. He then spoke to his nearest hermit-students about the supreme purification, about Brahman whom the seers adore.

This supreme mystery of the *Vedanta* which was revealed in olden times must only be given to one whose heart is pure and who is a pupil or a son.

If one has supreme love for God and also loves his master as God, then the light of this teaching shines in a great soul: it shines indeed in a great soul.

Concealed in the heart of all beings lies the Atman, the Spirit, the Self; smaller than the smallest atom, greater than the greatest spaces.

When by the grace of God man sees the glory of God, he sees him beyond the world of desire and then sorrows are left behind.

I know that Spirit whose infinity is in all, who is ever one beyond time. I know the Spirit whom the lovers of Brahman call eternal, beyond the birth and rebirth of life.

Part 4

May God, who in the mystery of his vision and power transforms his white radiance into his many-coloured creation, from whom all things come and into whom they all return, grant us the grace of pure vision.

He is the sun, the moon, and the stars. He is the fire, the waters, and the wind. He is Brahma the creator of all, and Prajapati, the Lord of creation.

Thou this boy, and thou this maiden; Thou this man, and thou this woman; Thou art this old man who supports himself on a staff; Thou the God who appears in forms infinite.

Thou the blue bird and thou the green bird; Thou the cloud that conceals the lightning and thou the seasons and the oceans. Beyond beginning, thou art in thy infinity, and all the worlds had their beginning in thee.

There is nature, never-born, who with her three elements – light, fire, and darkness – creates all things in nature. There is the never-born soul of man bound by the pleasures of nature; and there is the Spirit of man, never-born, who has left pleasures behind in the joy of the Beyond.

There are two birds, two sweet friends, who dwell on the self-same tree. The one eats the fruits thereof, and the other looks on in silence.

The first is the human soul who, resting on that tree, though active, feels sad in his unwisdom. But on beholding the power and the glory of the higher Spirit, he becomes free from sorrow.

Of what use is the *Rig Veda* to one who does not know the Spirit from whom the *Rig Veda* comes, and in whom all things abide? For only those who have found him have found peace.

For all the sacred books, all holy sacrifice and ritual and prayers, all the words of the *Vedas*, and the whole past and present and future, come from the Spirit. With Maya, his power of wonder, he made all things, and by Maya the human soul is bound.

Know therefore that nature is Maya, but that God is the ruler of Maya; and that all beings in our universe are parts of his infinite splendour.

He rules over the sources of creation. From him comes the universe and unto him it returns. He is the Lord, the giver of blessings, the one God of our adoration, in whom there is perfect peace.

May Rudra, the seer of Eternity, who gave to the gods their birth and their glory, who keeps all things under his protection, and who in the beginning saw the Golden Seed, grant us the grace of pure vision.

Who is the God to whom we shall offer adoration? The God of gods, in whose glory the worlds are, and who rules this world of man and all living beings.

He is the God of forms infinite in whose glory all things are, smaller than the smallest atom, and yet the Creator of all, everliving in the mystery of his creation. In the vision of this God of love there is everlasting peace.

He is the Lord of all who, hidden in the heart of things, watches over the world of time. The gods and the seers of Brahman are one with him; and when a man knows him he cuts the bonds of death.

When one knows God who is hidden in the heart of all things, even as cream is hidden in milk, and in whose glory all things are, he is free from all bondage.

This is the God whose work is all the worlds, the supreme Soul who dwells for ever in the hearts of men. Those who know him through their hearts and their minds become immortal.

There is a region beyond darkness where there is neither day nor night, nor what is, nor what is not. Only Siva, the god of love, is there. It is the region of the glorious splendour of God from whom came the light of the sun, and from whom the ancient wisdom came in the beginning.

The mind cannot grasp him above, or below, or in the space in between. With whom shall we compare him whose glory is the whole universe?

Far beyond the range of vision, he cannot be seen by mortal eyes; but he can be known by the heart and the mind, and those who know him attain immortality.

A man comes to thee in fearful wonder and says: 'Thou art God who never was born. Let thy face, Rudra, shine upon me, and let thy love be my eternal protection.

'Hurt not my child, nor the child of my child; hurt not my life, my horses, or my cows. Kill not in anger our brave men, for we ever come to thee with adorations.'

Part 5

Two things are hidden in the mystery of infinity of Brahman: knowledge and ignorance. Ignorance passes away and knowledge is immortal; but Brahman is in Eternity above ignorance and knowledge.

He is the ONE in whose power are the many sources of creation, and the root and the flower of all things. The Golden Seed, the Creator, was in his mind in the beginning; and he saw him born when time began.

He is God who spreads the net of transmigration and then withdraws it in the field of life. He is the Lord who created the lords of creation, the supreme Soul who rules over all.

Even as the radiance of the sun shines everywhere in space, so does the glory of God rule over all his creation.

In the unfolding of his own nature he makes all things blossom into flower and fruit. He gives to them all their fragrance and colour. He, the ONE, the only God who rules the universe.

There is a Spirit hidden in the mystery of the *Upanishads* and the *Vedas*; and Brahma, the god of creation, owns him as his own Creator. It is the Spirit of God, seen by gods and seers of olden times who, when one with him, became immortal.

MUNDAKA (*trans* William Butler Yeats and Shree Purohit Swami)

From The Mundaka Upanishad

Book II

1

'This is the truth: the sparks, though of one nature with the fire, leap from it; uncounted beings leap from the Everlasting, but these, my son, merge into It again.

'The Everlasting is shapeless, birthless, breathless, mindless, above everything, outside everything, inside everything.

'From Him are born life, mind, sense, air, wind, water, earth that supports all.

'He is the inmost Self of all. Fire, His head; sun and moon, His eyes; the four quarters, His ears; revelation, His voice; wind, His breath; world, His heart; earth, His feet.

'Fire is from Him, its fuel sun, moon from sun, rain from moon, food from rain, man from food, seed from man; thus all descends from God.

'From Him are hymns, holy chants, ritual, initiation, sacrifice, ceremonial, oblation, time, deeds, everything under sun and moon;

'From Him, gods, angels, men, cattle, birds, living fires, rice, barley, austerity, faith, truth, continence, law;

'From Him seven senses like ritual fires, seven desires like flames, seven objects like oblations, seven pleasures like sacrifices, seven nerves like habitations, seven centres in the heart like hollows in the cavern.

'From Him, seas, rivers, mountains, herbs and their properties: in the middle of the elements the inmost Self.

'My son! There is nothing in this world, that is not God. He is action, purity; everlasting Spirit. Find Him in the cavern; know the knot of ignorance.'

2

'Shining, yet hidden, Spirit lives in the cavern. Everything that sways, breathes, opens, closes, lives in Spirit; beyond learning, beyond everything, better than anything; living, unliving.

'It is the undying blazing Spirit, that seed of all seeds, wherein lay hidden the world and all its creatures. It is life, speech, mind, reality, immortality. It is there to be struck. Strike it, my son!

'Take the bow of our sacred knowledge, lay against it the arrow of devotion, pull the string of concentration, strike the target.

'Ôm is the bow, the personal-self the arrow, impersonal Self the target. Aim accurately, sink therein.

'Into His cloak are woven earth, mind, life, the canopy, the Kingdom of Heaven. He is alone and sole; man's bridge to immortality.

'Come out of all the schools. Meditate upon Ôm as the Self. Remember He takes many shapes, lives in the hub where the arteries meet; and may His blessing bring you out of the darkness.

'He knows all, knows every particular. His glory prevails on earth, in heaven, in His own seat, the holy city of the heart.

'He becomes mind and guides body and life. He lives in man's heart and eats man's food. He that knows Him, in finding joy, finds immortality.

'He that knows Him as the shaped and the shapeless, cuts through the knot of his heart, solves every doubt, exhausts every action.

'In a beautiful golden scabbard hides the stainless, indivisible, luminous Spirit.

'Neither sun, moon, star, neither fire nor lightning, lights Him. When He shines, everything begins to shine. Everything in the world reflects His light.

'Spirit is everywhere, upon the right, upon the left, above, below, behind, in front. What is the world but Spirit?'

Book III

1

'Two birds, bound one to another in friendship, have made their homes on the same tree. One stares about him, one pecks at the sweet fruit.

'The personal self, weary of pecking here and there, sinks into dejection; but when he understands through meditation that the other – the impersonal Self – is indeed Spirit, dejection disappears.

'When the sage meets Spirit, phallus and what it enters, good and evil disappear, they are one.

'The sage who knows Him as life and the giver of life, does not assert himself; playing with Self, enjoying Self, doing his duty, he takes his rank.

'The Self is found by veracity, purity, intelligence, continence. The ascetic, so purged, discovers His burning light in the heart.

'Falsehood turns from the way; truth goes all the way; the end of the way is truth; the way is paved with truth. The sage travels there without desire.

'Truth lies beyond imagination, beyond paradise; great, smaller than the smallest; near, further than the furthest; hiding from the traveller in the cavern.

'Nor can penance discover Him, nor ritual reveal, nor eye see, nor tongue speak; only in meditation can mind, grown pure and still, discover formless truth.

'The Self shines out of the pure heart, when life enters with its five fires and fills the mind.

'A pure man gets all he wants. A man with mind fixed upon some man who knows the Self, gets all he wants.'

SIR EDWIN ARNOLD (*trans*)

From In an Indian Temple

From The Mandukya Upanishad

Now, Sir! we know that A, and U, and M,
In this great Word, are threefold states of life,
Vaiśvânara the first, the waking state;
Next Taijasa, which is the sleep with dreams;
And thirdly Prajna, where man slumbers deep
Seeing no dreams, but floating, quit of flesh,
On that still border-flood whose waters lave
Life on one bank, and on the other Death.
Now would we hear, ap ki mihrbáni se –
Of your kind favour – how the three combine.
P. I read on from Mandukya: – the Fourth
Is that which holdeth all the three; being Life
Past living, sleeping, dreaming, dying – OM!
He who is there is Brahman, knowing all –
Not as we know, peeping inside and out, –
Not as we understand. 'Wise' or 'unwise'
Are words without a meaning for the Soul
Lifted so high! It seeth, all unseen;
Perceiveth, unperceived; not understood,
It comprehendeth; never to be named,
Never made palpable; not limited;
The testimony of it being Itself,
Itself made one with ONE SOUL, wherein
Those states are each transcended and absorbed,
Changeless, rejoicing, passionless, pervading!

And this Eternal Soul of Life, the Self,
is named in naming OM, and OM is named
From those three matras, A and U and M.
A is Vaiśvânara, the Waking-State;
And U is Taijasa, the State of Dreams;
And M is Prajna, sleep deeper than dream,
Where the soul wakes, and moves in larger light,
Knowing a farther knowledge; growing one
With HIM WHO IS!

SIR EDWIN ARNOLD (*trans*)

From The Bhagavad Gita

From Book X

Yes! Thou art Parabrahm! The High Abode!
The Great Purification! Thou art God
Eternal, All-creating, Holy, First,
Without beginning! Lord of Lords and Gods!
Declared by all the Saints – by Narada,
Vyâsa, Asita, and Devalas;
And here Thyself declaring unto me!
What Thou hast said now know I to be truth,
O Keśava! that neither gods nor men
Nor demons comprehend Thy mystery
Made manifest, Divinest! Thou Thyself
Thyself alone dost know, Maker Supreme!
Master of all the living! Lord of Gods!
King of the Universe! To Thee alone
Belongs to tell the heavenly excellence
Of those perfections wherewith Thou dost fill
These worlds of Thine; Pervading, Immanent!
How shall I learn, Supremest Mystery!
To know Thee, though I muse continually?
Under what form of Thine unnumbered forms
Mayst Thou be grasped? Ah! yet again recount,
Clear and complete, Thy great appearances,
The secrets of Thy Majesty and Might,
Thou High Delight of Men! Never enough
Can mine ears drink the Amrit[1] of such words!

---

[1] The nectar of immortality

From Book XVIII

Learn from me, Son of Kunti! also this,
How one, attaining perfect peace, attains
BRAHM, the supreme, the highest height of all!
Devoted – with a heart grown pure, restrained
In lordly self-control, foregoing wiles
Of song and senses, freed from love and hate,
Dwelling 'mid solitudes, in diet spare,
With body, speech, and will tamed to obey,
Ever to holy meditation vowed,
From passions liberate, quit of the Self,
Of arrogance, impatience, anger, pride;
Freed from surroundings, quiet, lacking nought –
Such an one grows to oneness with the BRAHM;
Such an one, growing one with BRAHM, serene,
Sorrows no more, desires no more; his soul,
Equally loving all that lives, loves well
Me, Who have made them, and attains to Me.
By this same love and worship doth he know
Me as I am, how high and wonderful,
And knowing, straightway enters into Me.
And whatsoever deeds he doeth – fixed
In Me, as in his refuge – he hath won
For ever and for ever by My grace
Th' Eternal Rest! So win thou! In thy thoughts
Do all thou dost for Me! Renounce for Me!
Sacrifice heart and mind and will to Me!
Live in the faith of Me! In faith of Me
All dangers thou shalt vanquish, by My grace;
But, trusting to thyself and heeding not,
Thou can'st but perish! If this day thou say'st,
Relying on thyself, 'I will not fight!'
Vain will the purpose prove! thy qualities
Would spur thee to the war. What thou dost shun,
Misled by fair illusions, thou wouldst seek
Against thy will, when the task comes to thee
Waking the promptings in thy nature set.
There lives a Master in the hearts of men
Maketh their deeds, by subtle pulling-strings,
Dance to what tune HE will. With all thy soul
Trust Him, and take Him for thy succour, Prince!
So – only so, Arjuna! – shalt thou gain –
By grace of Him – the uttermost repose.
The Eternal Place!

Thus hath been opened thee
This Truth of Truths, the Mystery more hid
Than any secret mystery. Meditate!
And – as thou wilt – then act!
　　Nay! but once more
Take My last word, My utmost meaning have!
Precious thou art to Me; right well-beloved!
Listen! I tell thee for thy comfort this.
Give Me thy heart! adore Me! serve Me! cling
In faith and love and reverence to Me!
So shalt thou come to Me! I promise true,
For thou art sweet to Me!
　　And let go those –
Rites and writ duties! Fly to Me alone!
Make Me thy single refuge! I will free
Thy soul from all its sins! Be of good cheer!

SIR EDWIN ARNOLD (*trans*)

From The Gita Govinda

Krishna to Radha

Or only speak once more, for though thou slay me,
　　Thy heavenly mouth must move, and I shall hear
Dulcet delights of perfect music sway me
　　Again – again that voice so blest and dear;
Sweet Judge! the prisoner prayeth for his doom
That he may hear his fate divinely come.

Speak once more! then thou canst not choose but show
　　Thy mouth's unparalleled and honeyed wonder
Where, like pearls hid in red-lipped shells, the row
　　Of pearly teeth thy rose-red lips lie under;
Ah me! I am that bird that woos the moon,
And pipes – poor fool! to make it glitter soon.

Yet hear me on – because I cannot stay
　　The passion of my soul, because my gladness
Will pour forth from my heart; – since that far day
　　When through the mist of all my sin and sadness
Thou didst vouchsafe – Surpassing One! – to break,
All else I slighted for thy noblest sake.

Thou, thou hast been my blood, my breath, my being;
    The pearl to plunge for in the sea of life;
The sight to strain for, past the bounds of seeing;
    The victory to win through longest strife;
My Queen! my crownèd Mistress! my sphered bride!
Take this for truth, that what I say beside

Of bold love – grown full-orbed at sight of thee –
    May be forgiven with a quick remission;
For, thou divine fulfilment of all hope!
    Thou all-undreamed completion of the vision!
I gaze upon thy beauty, and my fear
Passes as clouds do, when the moon shines clear.

So if thou'rt angry still, this shall avail,
    Look straight at me, and let thy bright glance wound me;
Fetter me! gyve me! lock me in the gaol
    Of thy delicious arms; make fast around me
The silk-soft manacles of wrists and hands,
Then kill me! I shall never break those bands.

The starlight jewels flashing on thy breast
    Have not my right to hear thy beating heart;
The happy jasmine-buds that clasp thy waist
    Are soft usurpers of my place and part;
If that fair girdle only there must shine,
Give me the girdle's life – the girdle mine!

Thy brow like smooth Bandhûka-leaves; thy cheek
    Which the dark-tinted Madhuk's velvet shows;
Thy long-lashed Lotus eyes, lustrous and meek;
    Thy nose a Tila-bud; thy teeth like rows
Of Kunda-petals! he who pierceth hearts
Points with thy lovelinesses all five darts.

But Radiant, Perfect, Sweet, Supreme, forgive!
    My heart is wise – my tongue is foolish still:
I know where I am come – I know I live –
    I know that thou art Radha – that this will
Last and be heaven: that I have leave to rise
Up from thy feet, and look into thine eyes!

And, nearer coming, I ask for grace
    Now that the blest eyes turn to mine;
Faithful I stand in this sacred place
    Since first I saw them shine:
Dearest glory that stills my voice,
    Beauty unseen, unknown, unthought!
Splendour of love, in whose sweet light
    Darkness is past and nought;
Ah, beyond words that sound on earth,
    Golden bloom of the garden of heaven!
Radha, enchantress! Radha, the queen!
    Be this trespass forgiven –
In that I dare, with courage too much
    And a heart afraid, – so bold it is grown –
To hold thy hand with a bridegroom's touch,
    And take thee for mine, mine own.
        So they met and so they ended
        Pain and parting, being blended
        Life with life – made one for ever
        In high love; and Jayadeva
        Hasteneth on to close the story
        Of their bridal grace and glory.

WILLIAM TYNDALE (*trans*)

From The Gospel According to St John

In the beginning was the Word, and the Word was with God, and the Word was God.

The same was in the beginning with God.

All things were made by him; and without him was not any thing made that was made.

In him was life; and the life was the light of men.

And the light shineth in darkness; and the darkness comprehended it not.

WILLIAM TYNDALE (*trans*)

From Epistle 1 of St John

Beloved, let us love one another: for love is of God.
    He that loveth not knoweth not God; for God is love.
    God is love; and he that dwelleth in love dwelleth in God, and God in him.
    Perfect love casteth out fear.

DRS GRENFELL AND HUNT (*trans*)

From New Sayings of Jesus and the Logia (Fragments of a Lost Gospel)

The key of knowledge ye hid: ye yourselves entered not in, and to them that would enter in ye opened not.
    Let him that seeketh cease not till he find. When he finds he shall be astonished: astonished he shall reach the kingdom: and having reached the kingdom he shall rest.
    The kingdom of heaven is within you: and whosoever knoweth himself shall find it.
    Raise the stone and thou shalt find me. Cleave the wood and I am there.

CHRISTIAN TRADITION (*trans* anon)

From A Hymn of Jesus

I am a Lamp to thee who beholdest Me,
I am a Mirror to thee who perceivest Me,
I am a Door to thee who knockest at Me,
I am a Way to thee a wayfarer.

NAHUATE POEM (*trans* J M Cohen)

The Good Painter

The good painter:
the artist of the black and red ink of wisdom,
the creator of things with the black water . . .

this good painter, understanding,
with god in his heart,
who divines things with his heart,
holds a dialogue with his own heart.

He knows the colours, he applies them, he shades them.
He draws feet and faces,
traces the shadows, brings his work to perfection.
Like an artist
he paints the colours of all the flowers.

LAO TZU (*trans* D C Lau)

From The Tao Te Ching

I

The way that can be spoken of
Is not the constant way;
The name that can be named
Is not the constant name.
The nameless was the beginning of heaven and earth;
The named was the mother of the myriad creatures.
Hence always rid yourself of desires in order to observe its secrets;
But always allow yourself to have desires in order to observe its
    manifestations.
These two are the same
But diverge in name as they issue forth.
Being the same they are called mysteries,
Mystery upon mystery –
The gateway of the manifold secrets.

X

When carrying on your head your perplexed bodily soul
   can you embrace in your arms the One
And not let go?
In concentrating your breath can you become as supple
As a babe?
Can you polish your mysterious mirror
And leave no blemish?
Can you love the people and govern the state
Without resorting to action?
When the gates of heaven open and shut
Are you capable of keeping to the role of the female?
When your discernment penetrates the four quarters
Are you capable of not knowing anything?
It gives them life and rears them.
It gives them life yet claims no possession;
It benefits them yet exacts no gratitude;
It is the steward yet exercises no authority.
Such is called the mysterious virtue.

XVI

I do my utmost to attain emptiness;
I hold firmly to stillness.
The myriad creatures all rise together
And I watch their return.
The teaming creatures
All return to their separate roots.
Returning to one's roots is known as stillness.
This is what is meant by returning to one's destiny.
Returning to one's destiny is known as the constant.
Knowledge of the constant is known as discernment.
Woe to him who wilfully innovates
While ignorant of the constant,
But should one act from knowledge of the constant
One's action will lead to impartiality,
Impartiality to kingliness,
Kingliness to heaven,
Heaven to the way,
The way to perpetuity,
And to the end of one's days one will meet with no danger.

XLI

When the best student hears about the way
He practises it assiduously;
When the average student hears about the way
It seems to him one moment there and gone the next;
When the worst student hears about the way
He laughs out loud.
If he did not laugh
It would be unworthy of being the way.
Hence the *Chien yen* has it:
The way that is bright seems dull;
The way that leads forward seems to lead backward;
The way that is even seems rough.
The highest virtue is like the valley;
The sheerest whiteness seems sullied;
Ample virtue seems defective;
Vigorous virtue seems indolent;
Plain virtue seems soiled;
The great square has no corners.
The great vessel takes long to complete;
The great note is rarefied in sound;
The great image has no shape.
The way conceals itself in being nameless.
It is the way alone that excels in bestowing and in accomplishing.

LXX

My words are very easy to understand and very easy
to put into practice, yet no one in the world can
understand them or put them into practice.
Words have an ancestor and affairs have a sovereign.
It is because people are ignorant that they fail to understand me.
    Those who understand me are few;
    Those who imitate me are honoured.
Therefore the sage, while clad in homespun, conceals on his
    person a priceless piece of jade.
Go up to it and you will not see its head;
Follow behind it and you will not see its rear.
Hold fast to the way of antiquity
In order to keep in control the realm of today.
The ability to know the beginning of antiquity
Is called the thread running through the way.

LXXI

To know yet to think that one does not know is best;
Not to know yet to think that one knows will lead to difficulty.
It is by being alive to difficulty that one can avoid it.
The sage meets with no difficulty. It is because he is
   alive to it that he meets with no difficulty.

CH'EN TZU-ANG (*trans* Arthur Waley)

Business Men

Business men boast of their skill and cunning
But in philosophy they are like little children.
Bragging to each other of successful depredations
They neglect to consider the ultimate fate of the body.
What should they know of the Master of Dark Truth
Who saw the wide world in a jade cup,
By illumined conception got clear of Heaven and Earth:
On the chariot of Mutation entered the Gate of Immutability?

LU YUN (*trans* Arthur Waley)

The Valley Wind

Living in retirement beyond the World,
Silently enjoying isolation,
I pull the rope of my door tighter
And stuff my window with roots and ferns.
My spirit is tuned to the Spring-season:
At the fall of the year there is autumn in my heart.
Thus imitating cosmic changes
My cottage becomes a Universe.

CHI K'ANG (*trans* Arthur Waley)

Taoist Song

I will cast out Wisdom and reject Learning.
My thoughts shall wander in the Great Void
Always repenting of wrongs done
Will never bring my heart to rest.
I cast my hook in a single stream;
But my joy is as though I possessed a Kingdom.
I loose my hair and go singing;
To the four frontiers men join in my refrain.
This is the purport of my song:
'My thoughts shall wander in the Great Void.'

FU HSUAN (*trans* Arthur Waley)

A Gentle Wind

A gentle wind fans the calm night:
A bright moon shines on the high tower.
A voice whispers, but no one answers when I call:
A shadow stirs, but no one comes when I beckon.
The kitchen-man brings in a dish of lentils:
Wine is there, but I do not fill my cup.
Contentment with poverty is Fortune's best gift:
Riches and Honour are the handmaids of Disaster.
Though gold and gems by the world are sought and prized,
To me they seem no more than weeds or chaff.

TAKAKUSU (*trans* Arthur Waley)

On Trust in his Heart

The Perfect Way is only difficult for those who pick and choose;
Do not like, do not dislike; all will then be clear.
Make a hairbreadth difference, and Heaven and Earth are set apart;
If you want the truth to stand clear before you, never be for or
     against.
The struggle between 'for' and 'against' is the mind's worst
     disease;
While the deep meaning is misunderstood, it is useless to meditate
     on Rest.
It is blank and featureless as space; it has no 'too little' or 'too much';
Only because we take and reject does it seem to us not to be so.
Do not chase after Entanglements as though they were real things,
Do not try to drive pain away by pretending that it is not real;
Pain, if you seek serenity in Oneness, will vanish of its own accord.
Stop all movement in order to get rest, and rest will itself be restless;
Linger over either extreme, and Oneness is for ever lost.
Those who cannot attain to Oneness in either case will fail:
To banish Reality is to sink deeper into the Real;
Allegiance to the Void implies denial of its voidness.
The more you talk about It, the more you think about It, the further
     from It you go;
Stop talking, stop thinking, and there is nothing you will not
     understand.
Return to the Root and you will find the Meaning;
Pursue the Light, and you will lose its source,
Look inward, and in a flash you will conquer the Apparent and the
     Void.
For the whirligigs of Apparent and Void all come from mistaken
     views;
There is no need to seek Truth; only stop having views.

Tso Ssu (*trans* Arthur Waley)

The Scholar in the Narrow Street

Flap, flap, the captive bird in the cage
Beating its wings against the four corners.
Depressed, depressed the scholar in the narrow street:
Clasping a shadow, he dwells in an empty house.
When he goes out, there is nowhere for him to go:
Bushes and brambles block up his path.
He composes a memorial, but it is rejected and unread,
He is left stranded, like a fish in a dry pond.
Without it – he has not a single farthing of salary:
Within – there is not a peck of grain in his larder.
His relations upbraid him for his lack of success:
His friends and callers daily decrease in number.
Su Ch'in used to go preaching in the North
And Li Ssu sent a memorandum to the West.
I once hoped to pluck the fruits of life:
But now alas, they are all withered and dry.
Though one drinks at a river, one cannot drink more
    than a bellyful;
Enough is good, but there is no use in satiety.
The bird in a forest can perch but on one bough,
And this should be the wise man's pattern.

MARCUS AURELIUS (*trans* Robert Bridges)

Dear City of God

I am at one with everything, O Universe,
    which is well-fitting in thee.
Nothing to me is early or late which is timely with thee.
All is fruit to me that thy seasons bring.
O Nature, from thee are all things,
    in thee are all things,
    to thee all things return.
The poet saith, Dear city of Cecrops;
    shall not I say, Dear City of God.

PORPHYRY (*trans* Thomas Taylor)

From On the Soul of Plotinus

To strains immortal full of heav'nly fire,
My harp I tune well strung with vocal wire;
Dear to divinity a friend I praise,
Who claims those notes a God alone can raise.
For him a God in verse mellifluous sings,
And beats with golden rod the warbling strings.
Be present Muses, and with general voice
And all the powers of harmony rejoice;
Let all the measures of your art be try'd
In rapt'rous sounds, as when Achilles dy'd.
When Homer's melody the band inspir'd,
And god-like furies every bosom fir'd.
And lo! the sacred choir of Muses join,
And in one general hymn their notes combine.
I Phœbus in the midst, to whom belong
The sacred pow'rs of verse, begin the song.
Genius sublime! once bound in mortal ties,
A dæmon now and more than mortals wise.
Freed from those members that with deadly weight
And stormy whirl enchain'd thy soul of late;
O'er Life's rough ocean thou hast gain'd that shore,
Where storms molest and change impairs no more;
And struggling thro' its deeps with vig'rous mind,
Pass'd the dark stream, and left base souls behind.
Plac'd where no darkness ever can obscure,
Where nothing enters sensual and impure;
Where shines eternal God's unclouded ray,
And gilds the realms of intellectual day.
Oft merg'd in matter, by strong leaps you try'd
To bound aloft, and cast its folds aside;
To shun the bitter stream of sanguine life,
Its whirls of sorrow, and its storm of strife.
While in the middle of its boist'rous waves
Thy soul robust, the deep's deaf tumult braves;
Oft beaming from the Gods thy piercing sight
Beheld in paths oblique a sacred light:
Whence rapt from sense with energy divine,
Before thine eyes immortal splendours shine;
Whose plenteous rays in darkness most profound,
Thy steps directed and illumin'd round.
Nor was the vision like the dreams of sleep,

But seen while vigilant you brave the deep;
While from your eyes you shake the gloom of night,
The glorious prospects burst upon your sight;
Prospects beheld but rarely by the wise,
Tho' men divine and fav'rites of the skies.
But now set free from the lethargic folds,
By which th' indignant soul dark matter holds;
The natal bonds deserted, now you soar,
And rank with dæmon forms a man no more.
In that blest realm where love and friendship reign,
And pleasures ever dwell unmixt with pain;
Where streams ambrosial in immortal course
Irriguous flow, from deity their source.
No dark'ning clouds those happy skies assail,
And the calm æther knows no stormy gale.
Supremely blest thy lofty soul abides,
Where Minos and his brother judge presides;
Just Æacus and Plato the divine,
And fair Pythag'ras there exalted shine;
With other souls who form the general choir
Of love immortal, and of pure desire;
And who one common station are assign'd,
With genii of the most exalted kind.
Thrice happy thou! who, life's long labours past,
With holy dæmons dost reside at last;
From body loosen'd and from cares at rest,
Thy life most stable, and divine thy feast.
Now ev'ry Muse who for Plotinus sings,
Here cease with me to tune the vocal strings;
For thus my golden harp, with art divine,
Has told – Plotinus! endless bliss is thine.

PART 2:
Fourth Century to Thirteenth Century

ST DENIS (*trans* anon)

Prayer

You are wisdom, uncreated and eternal,
    the supreme first cause, above all being,
    sovereign Godhead, sovereign goodness,
    watching unseen the God-inspired wisdom of
        Christian people.
Raise us, we pray, that we may totally respond
    to the supreme, unknown, ultimate, and splendid
        height
    of your words, mysterious and inspired.
There all God's secret matters lie covered and hidden
    under darkness both profound and brilliant, silent
        and wise.

You make what is ultimate and beyond brightness
    secretly to shine in all that is most dark.
In your way, ever unseen and intangible,
    you fill to the full with most beautiful splendour
    those souls who close their eyes that they may see.
And I, please, with love that goes on beyond mind
    to all that is beyond mind,
    seek to gain such for myself through this prayer.

ELEAZAR BEN KALLER (*trans* T Carmi)

The Celestial Fire

Now an angel of the Lord appeared to
Moses in a blazing fire –

    a fire that devours fire;
    a fire that burns in things dry and moist;
    a fire that glows amid snow and ice;
    a fire that is like a crouching lion;
    a fire that reveals itself in many forms;
    a fire that is, and never expires;
    a fire that shines and roars;
    a fire that blazes and sparkles;
    a fire that flies in a storm wind;
    a fire that burns without wood;
    a fire that renews itself every day;

a fire that is not fanned by fire;
a fire that billows like palm branches;
a fire whose sparks are flashes of lightning;
a fire black as a raven;
a fire, curled, like the colours of the rainbow!

RABI'A (*trans* anon)

With My Beloved Alone

With my Beloved I alone have been,
When secrets tenderer than evening airs
Passed, and the Vision blest
Was granted to my prayers,
That crowned me, else obscure, with endless fame;
The while amazed between
His Beauty and His Majesty
I stood in silent ecstasy
Revealing that which o'er my spirit went and came.
Lo, in His face commingled
Is every charm and grace;
The whole of Beauty singled
Into a perfect face
Beholding Him would cry,
'There is no God but He, and He is the most High.'

RABI'A (*trans* anon)

Love

I have loved Thee with two loves –
    a selfish love and a love that is worthy of Thee.
As for the love which is selfish,
    Therein I occupy myself with Thee,
        to the exclusion of all others.
But in the love which is worthy of Thee,
    Thou dost raise the veil that I may see Thee.
Yet is the praise not mine in this or that,
But the praise is to Thee in both that and this.

JUDAH HALEVI (*trans* T Carmi)
From Lord, Where Shall I Find You?

Lord, where shall I find You? Your
place is lofty and secret. And where
shall I not find you? The whole earth is
full of Your glory!

You are found in man's innermost
heart, yet You fixed earth's boundaries.
You are a strong tower for those who
are near, and the trust of those who are
far. You are enthroned on the cherubim,
yet You dwell in the heights of heaven.
You are praised by Your hosts,
but even their praise is not worthy of
You. The sphere of heaven cannot
contain You; how much less the
chambers of the Temple!

Even when You rise above Your hosts
on a throne, high and exalted, You are
nearer to them than their own bodies
and souls. Their mouths attest that they
have no Maker except You. Who shall
not fear You? All bear the yoke of Your
kingdom. And who shall not call to You?
It is You who give them their food.

I have sought to come near You, I have
called to You with all my heart; and
when I went out towards You, I found
You coming towards me. I look upon
Your wondrous power with awe. Who
can say that he has not seen You? The
heavens and their legions proclaim
Your dread – without a sound.

SOLOMON IBN-GABIROL (*trans* anon)

The Royal Crown

Thou existest, but hearing of ear cannot reach Thee,
  nor vision of eye,
Nor shall the How have sway over Thee, nor the
Wherefore and Whence.
Thou existest, but for Thyself and for none other
  with Thee.
Thou existest, and before Time began Thou wast,
And without place Thou didst abide.
Thou existest, and Thy secret is hidden, and who
  shall attain to it?
'So deep, so deep, who can discover it?'

Thou livest, but not from any restricted season nor
  from any known period.
Thou livest, but not through breath and soul, for
Thou art soul of the soul.
Thou livest, but not with the life of man, which is
like unto vanity and its end the moth and the worm.
Thou livest, and he who layeth hold of Thy secret
'He shall eat and live for ever.'

Thou art God, and all things formed are Thy
  servants and worshippers.
Yet is not Thy glory diminished by reason of those
  that worship aught beside Thee,
For the yearning of them all is to draw nigh Thee,
But they are like the blind,
Setting their faces foward on the King's highway,
Yet still wandering from the path.
One sinketh into the well of a pit,
And another falleth into a snare,
But all imagine they have reached their desire,
Albeit they have suffered in vain.
But Thy servants are those walking clear-eyed in the
  straight path,
Turning neither to the right nor the left,
Till they come to the court of the King's palace.
Thou art God, by Thy Godhead sustaining all that
  hath been formed,

SOLOMON IBN-GABIROL (*trans* T Carmi)

The Soul and its Maker

Bow down before God, my precious thinking soul,
and make haste to worship Him with reverence.
Night and day think only of your everlasting world.
Why should you chase after vanity and emptiness?
As long as you live, you are akin to the living God:
just as He is invisible, so are you. Since your
Creator is pure and flawless, know that you too are
pure and perfect. The Mighty One upholds the heavens
on His arm, as you uphold the mute body. My soul,
let your songs come before your Rock, who does not
lay your form in the dust. My innermost heart,
bless your Rock always, whose name is praised by
everything that has breath.

SOLOMON IBN-GABIROL (*trans* T Carmi)

The Face of God

Lovely face, majestic face, face of beauty, face of
flame, the face of the Lord God of Israel when He sits
upon His throne of glory, robed in praise upon His seat
of splendour. His beauty surpasses the beauty of the
aged, His splendour outshines the splendour of newly-weds
in their bridal chamber

Whoever looks at Him is instantly torn; whoever glimpses
His beauty immediately melts away. Those who serve Him
today no longer serve Him tomorrow; those who serve Him
tomorrow no longer serve Him afterwards; for their
strength fails and their faces are charred, their hearts
reel and their eyes grow dim at the splendour and
radiance of their king's beauty.

Beloved servants, lovely servants, swift servants, light-
footed servants, who stand before the stone of the throne
of glory, who wait upon the wheel of the chariot. When
the sapphire of the throne of glory whirls at them, when
the wheel of the chariot hurls past them, those on the
right now stand again to the left, those on the left now
stand again to the right, those in front now stand again
in back, those in back now stand again in front.

He who sees the one says, 'That is the other.' And he who
sees the other says, 'That is the one.' For the visage of
the one is like the visage of the other; and the visage
of the other is like the visage of the one.

Happy the King who has such servants, and happy the servants
who have such a King. Happy the eye that sees and feeds
upon this wondrous light – a wondrous vision and most strange!

And upholding in Thy Unity all creatures.
Thou art God, and there is no distinction betwixt
Thy Godhead and Thy Unity, Thy pre-existence
and Thy existence,
For 'tis all one mystery;
And although the name of each be different,
'Yet they are all proceeding to one place.'
by radiance divine, He is the light
of heaven and earth, His everlasting ray
The Holy Spirit. Whosoe'er has light
within his soul, the ground thereof is light:
within the lantern's glass the niche of night
to radiant morn is turned, and when the soul
sits thus with light, thereafter the heart's steel
contacting it is quickened into flame.
So made the Friend similitude twixt light
and fire, and from that day our lot was cast.
When the Beloved His Face doth show, my sight
augments to vision. Never human eye
hath won pre-excellence above the glance
irradiated by the light of God:
if thou wilt only thine own sight regard,
thine eyes see not, save by the light of God.
If thou wouldst serve the Friend and win His grace,
he is thine eye, thine ear, thy tongue, thy brain;
and since through Him thou speakest, and through
Him hearest, before His Being thou art naught;
for so, when shines the sun's own radiance,
the light of stars is darkened. Never man
of own purpose unto Him hath won,
yet by His power thou canst behold His face!
Though earth may not attain the pure world, soul
shall yet by Soul perceive. The shaft of thought
that silences the shout of alleluia
is honey to the heart, and I am dumb;
I cannot count His praises infinite.

SOLOMON IBN-GABIROL (*trans* Israel Zangwill)

Lord of the World

Lord of the world, He reigned alone
  While yet the universe was naught.
  When by His will all things were wrought,
Then first His sovran Name was known.

And when the All shall cease to be,
  In dread lone splendour He shall reign,
  He was, He is, He shall remain
In glorious eternity.

For He is one, no second shares
  His nature or His loneliness;
  Unending and beginningless,
All strength is His, all sway He bears.

He is the living God to save,
  My Rock while sorrow's toils endure,
  My banner and my stronghold sure,
The cup of life whene'er I crave.

I place my soul within His palm
  Before I sleep as when I wake,
  And though my body I forsake,
Rest in the Lord in fearless calm.

ST ISAAC OF STELLA (*trans* anon)

Love

Incited by something external
Is like a small lamp
Whose flame is fed with oil,
Or like a stream fed by rains,
Where flows stop when the rains cease.
But love whose object is God is like
A fountain gushing forth
From the earth.
Its flow never ceases,
For He Himself is the source of this love
And also its food,
Which never grows scarce.

ANSARI (*trans* anon)

The Path of Devotion

In this path the eye must cease to see,
And the ear to hear.
Save unto Him, and about Him.
Be as dust on His path.
Even the kings of this earth
Make the dust of His feet
The balm of their eyes.

ANSARI (*trans* anon)

O Lord, Give Me Eyes

O Lord, give me eyes
Which see nothing by Thy glory.
Give me a mind
That finds delight in Thy service.
Give me a soul
Drunk in the wine of Thy wisdom.

ANSARI (*trans* anon)

Devotion for Thee

Life in my body pulsates only for Thee,
My heart beats in resignation to Thy will.
If on my dust a tuft of grass were to grow
Every blade would tremble with my devotion for Thee!

ST FRANCIS OF ASSISI (*trans* anon)

A Prayer

Lord, make me an instrument of Thy Peace.
Where there is hatred, let me sow love;
Where there is injury, pardon;
Where there is doubt, faith;
Where there is despair, hope;
Where there is darkness, light;
Where there is sadness, joy.

O Divine Master, grant that I may not so much seek to
    be consoled as to console;
to be understood, as to understand;
to be loved, as to love.
For it is in giving that we receive;
It is in pardoning that we are pardoned;
It is in dying that we are born to eternal life.

LUIS DE LEON (*trans* anon)

A New Light Doth Shine

At whose blest sound divine
My soul that in forgetfulness hath lain
    With a new light doth shine
And unto memory plain
    Of its first splendid origin attain.

Up through the fields of air
It wings, till in the highest sphere it dwells
And a new music there
It hears, music that wells
Undying, and all other kinds excels.

MECHTHILD OF MAGDEBURG (*trans* anon)

Love Flows From God

Love flows from God to man without effort
As a bird glides through the air
Without moving its wings –
Thus they go whithersoever they will
United in body and soul

Yet in their form separate –
As the Godhead strikes the note
Humanity sings,
The Holy Spirit is the harpist
And all the strings must sound
Which are strung in love.

MECHTHILD OF MAGDEBURG (*trans* anon)

Light of Splendor

With the dull hearing of my misery –
A light of utmost splendor
Glows on the eyes of my soul.
Therein have I seen the inexpressible ordering
Of all things, and recognized God's unspeakable glory –
That incomprehensible wonder –
The tender caress between God and the soul,
The sufficiency in the Highest,
Discipline in understanding,
Realization with withdrawal,
According to the power of the senses,
The unmingled joy of union,
The living love of Eternity
As it now is and evermore shall be.

MECHTHILD OF MAGDEBURG (*trans* anon)

Prayer

X

Lord, God, I am now a naked soul
And Thou art arrayed all gloriously!
We are Two in One, we have reached the goal,
Immortal rapture that cannot die.
Now, a blessed silence doth o'er us flow,
Both wills together would have it so.
He is given to her, she is given to Him –
What now shall befall her, the soul doth know –
And therefore am I consoled.

ANONYMOUS (*trans*)

For I am Faint With Love

In a valley of this restless mind
I sought in mountain and in mead,
Trusting a true love for to find.
Upon a hill then took I heed;
A voice I heard, and near I yede,
In great dolor complaining tho:
See, dear soul, how my sides bleed:
    Quia amore langueo.

. . .

I am true love that false was never;
My sister, man's soul, I loved her thus.
Because we would in no wise dissever
I left my Kingdom glorious.
I purveyed her a palace full precious;
She fled, I followed, I loved her so
That I suffered this pain piteous,
    Quia amore langueo.

Jacopone da Todi (*trans* anon)

From Love That Is Silent

Love, silent as the night,
  Who not one word wilt say,
That none may know thee right!

O Love that lies concealed,
  Through heat and storm and cold,
That none may guess nor read
  Thy secrets manifold;
Lest thieves should soon grow bold
  To steal away thy treasure,
    Snatch it and take to flight!

Deep-hid, thy secret fires
  More ardently shall glow;
And he who screens thee close,
  Thy fiercest heat shall know.

Jacopone da Todi (*trans* anon)

Sing for Very Love

Thou, Jubilus,[1] the heart dost move;
And makest us sing for very love.

The Jubilus in fire awakes,
  And straight the man must sing and pray;
His tongue in childish stammering shakes,
  Nor knows he what his lips may say;
  He cannot quench nor hide away
  That Sweetness pure and infinite.

The Jubilus in flame is lit,
  And straight the man must shout and sing;
So close to Love his heart is knit,
  He scarce can bear the honeyed sting;
  His clamor and his cries must ring,
  And shame forever take to flight.

The Jubilus enslaves man's heart
  – A love-bewildered prisoner –
And see! his neighbors stand apart,
    And mock the senseless chatterer:
They deem his speech a foolish blur,
    A shadow of his spirit's light.

Yea, when thou enterest the mind,
    O Jubilus, thou rapture fair,
The heart of man new skill doth find
    Love's own disguise to grasp and wear,
    The suffering of Love to bear,
    With song and clamor of delight!

And thus the uninitiate
    Will deam that thou art crazed indeed;
They see thy strange and fevered state,
    But have not wit thy heart to read;
    Within, deep-pierced, that heart may bleed,
    Hidden from curious mortal sight.

[1] Name of God in His Personal aspect.

JACOPONE DA TODI (*trans* anon)

Of Man's Perfection in Love

O minstrel, raise thy plaintive melody,
and let thy song be tender to my soul:
upon the subtle ninefold modes of love
display the secrets of a lover's heart.
One moment parted from the Friend, I die:
revive my heart with thy life-giving stream
that I may come into the lovers' ring
and grace the lovers' circle. Let me pass
one moment from the world, and for an hour
I will not heed my selfhood: being lost
to this false being, let me swiftly move
to realms of drunkenness where, like the drunk,
I will commence the dance, and raise the cry
of yearning love – for truly I do yearn
for my Beloved – standing in the field
of high ambition. I will shake my wings

like sacrificial bird, and fly at last
from empty word to true reality.
Then will I tell in order, each by each,
the beauty of the Friend, the lover's love.

JACOPONE DA TODI (*trans* anon)
Lord, Thou Hast Shown Me

Lord, Thou hast shown me now,
  In Thy fair holiness,
  Mine utter nothingness;
    Yea, less than nothing I!
And from this gazing springs
  An eager humbleness;
  Prisoned in wretchedness,
    My will but lives to die.
  My mind's humility
Is not made vile by ill,
But, loving virtue still,
    Through vileness, gains Thy height.

I cannot be re-born
  Till mine own self be dead;
  My life out-poured, out-shed,
    Sheer essence to renew:
On glorious Nothingness
    He only can be fed,
    Whom God Himself hath led;
    Here man hath naught to do.
    O glorious state and true!
In Nothingness to cease,
Desire and mind at peace
    In calmness infinite.

Ah! how my earth-bound thoughts
   Are hideous and mean,
    Beside those heights serene,
      Where virtue's treasures be.
That Deep whereon I gaze,
    I cannot swim therein,
    I must be swallowed clean,
    Like men who drown at sea.
    Shoreless Infinity!
I sink in Thee, the Whole:
Thy fulness storms my soul,
    Thou Sweetness and Thou Light!

JACOPONE DA TODI (*trans* anon)

Rapture Divine

When the mind's very being is gone,
   Sunk in a conscious sleep,
In a rapture divine and deep,
   Itself in the Godhead lost:
It is conquered, ravished, and won!
   Set in Eternity's sweep,
   Gazing back on the steep,
Knowing not how it was crossed –
To a new world now it is tossed,
   Drawn from its former state,
   To another, measureless, great,
   Where Love is drowned in the Sea.

HUSSEIN IBN MANSUR AL-HALLAJ (*trans* J M Cohen)

Release into Reality

True to the pledge He made me, our treaty of alliance,
God raised me into Reality.
All that attests to it now is below my consciousness
and outside my created personality.
Here it is my subconsciousness; down there it was the Way.

Make me one with the One, thou unique One,
in a true act of confession that God is one,
to which no path serves as Way! As I am potential Truth,
and actual Truth is my own potential, may our separateness cease
to be!
So with the thunderbolt all is illumined
and bathed in the radiance of the storm.

I have two watchers (my ears) which observe that I love him; and two
others (my eyes) which observe that You see me.
No thought but of You crosses my secret heart; my tongue utters
nothing that is not the love of You.
Should I look to the East, You are the risen sun; to the West,
You are straight before me.
If I look upwards, You are what lies above, if downwards, You are
everywhere.
It is You that give everything its place, yet You have no place.
You are the whole of everything, yet are not perishable.
You are my heart, my spirit, my inspiration, the rhythm
of my breath and the kernel of my organic being.

ATTAR (*trans* Edward Fitzgerald)

From The Parliament of the Birds

All who, reflecting as reflected see
Themselves in Me, and Me in them; not *Me*,
But all of Me that a contracted Eye
Is comprehensive of Infinity;
Nor yet *Themselves*: no Selves, but of The All
Fractions, from which they split and wither fall.
As Water lifted from the Deep, again
Falls back in individual Drops of Rain,
Then melts into the Universal Main.
All you have been, and seen, and done, and thought,
Not *You* but *I*, have seen and been and wrought:
I was the Sin that from Myself rebell'd;
I the Remorse that tow'rd Myself compell'd;
I was the Tajidar who led the Track;
I was the little Briar that pull'd you back:
Sin and Contrition – Retribution owed,
And cancell'd – Pilgrim, Pilgrimage, and Road,
Was but Myself toward Myself; and Your
Arrival but *Myself* at my own Door;

Who in your Fraction of Myself behold
Myself within the Mirror Myself hold
To see Myself in, and each part of Me
That sees himself, though drown'd, shall ever see.
Come you lost Atoms to your Centre draw,
And *be* the Eternal Mirror that you saw:
Rays that have wander'd into Darkness wide
Return, and back into your Sun subside.'

ATTAR (*trans* Edward Fitzgerald)

The Birds Find Their King

Once more they ventured from the Dust to raise
Their Eyes – up to the Throne – into the Blaze,
And in the Centre of the Glory there
Beheld the Figure of – *Themselves* – as 'twere
Transfigured – looking to Themselves, beheld
The Figure on the Throne en-miracled,
Until their Eyes themselves and *That* between
Did hesitate which *Seer* was, which *Seen*;
They That, That They: Another, yet the Same;
Dividual, yet One: from whom there came
A Voice of awful Answer, scarce discern'd,
From *which* to Aspiration *whose* return'd
They scarcely knew; as when some Man apart
Answers aloud the Question in his Heart:
'The Sun of my Perfection is a Glass
Wherein from *Seeing* into *Being* pass.

ATTAR (*trans* Margaret Smith)

The Triumph of the Soul

From Jawhar Al-Dhat

Joy! joy! I triumph! now no more I know
Myself as simply me, I burn with love
Unto myself, and bury me in love.
The Centre is within me and its wonder
Lies as a circle everywhere about me.
Joy! joy! no mortal thought can fathom me.
I am the merchant and the pearl at once.
Lo, Time and Space lie crouching at my feet.
Joy! joy! when I would revel in a rapture,
I plunge into myself and all things know.

ATTAR (*trans* Margaret Smith)

From The Jawhar Al-Dhat

Intoxicated by the Wine of Love.
From each a mystic silence Love demands.
What do all seek so earnestly? 'Tis Love.
What do they whisper to each other? Love.
Love is the subject of their inmost thoughts.
In Love no longer 'thou' and 'I' exist,
For Self has passed away in the Beloved.
Now will I draw aside the veil from Love,
And in the temple of mine inmost soul,
Behold the Friend; Incomparable Love.
He who would know the secret of both worlds,
Will find the secret of them both, is Love.

ATTAR (*trans* anon)

All-Pervading Consciousness

And as His Essence all the world pervades
Naught in Creation is, save this alone.
Upon the waters has He fixed His Throne,
This earth suspended in the starry space,
Yet what are seas and what is air? For all
Is God, and but a talisman are heaven and earth
To veil Divinity. For heaven and earth,
Did He not permeate them, were but names;
Know then, that both this visible world and that
Which unseen is, alike are God Himself,
Naught is, save God: and all that is, is God.
And yet, alas! by how few is He seen,
Blind are men's eyes, though all resplendent shines
The world by Deity's own light illumined,
O Thou whom man perceiveth not, although
To him Thou deignest to make known Thyself;
Thou all Creation art, all we behold, but Thou,
The soul within the body lies concealed,
And Thou dost hide Thyself within the soul,
O soul in soul! Myst'ry in myst'ry hid!
Before all wert Thou, and are more than all!

ATTAR (*trans* anon)

Immerse Yourself for Evermore

Meditate, O my mind, on the Lord,
The Stainless One, Pure Spirit through and through.
How peerless is the light that in Him shines!
How soul-bewitching is His wondrous form!
How dear is He to all His devotees!

Ever more beauteous in fresh-blossoming love
That shames the splendor of a million moons,
Like lightning gleams the glory of His form,
Raising erect the hair for very joy.

Worship His feet in the lotus of your heart;
With mind serene and eyes made radiant
With heavenly love, behold that matchless sight.
Caught in the spell of His love's ecstasy,
Immerse yourself for evermore, O mind,
In Him who is Pure Knowledge and Pure Bliss.

'IRAQI (*trans* anon)

That Single Essence

No atom doth exist apart from It,
    that Essence single:
'Tis when Itself doth reveal that first
    those 'others' mingle.
O Thou whose outward seeming Lover is,
    Beloved thine Essence,
Who hitherto e'er saw the Object Sought
    seek its own presence?

'IRAQI (*trans* anon)

All Is He

He perfect is alone, and glorious
for evermore, His Unity supreme
above imagining, His wondrous work
beyond analysis. I do not say,

He is the soul's soul: whatsoe'er I say,
that He transcends, for He is free of space,
and may not be attained by swiftest thought
or further sense. Before His essence true
denial, affirmation, both are vain;
Whatever thing is borne by sense to mind
or shaped in fantasy, be all the fruit
or all the mind, all has its life in Him,
nay, all is He. Whatever else but Him
in either world appears is but the double
descried in image by the twisted eye.
His word is first and last: He of creation
outward and inward is. The body's house
is lighted through the spirit's open door

'IRAQI (*trans* anon)

We Yield Our Hearts

Lodgers we who on Thy threshold dwell,
and nightingales that in Thy garden sing,
whether we leave Thy door, or waiting stand,
of only Thee we speak, of Thee we hear.
Since we are captives caught within Thy nets,
where shall we trust our passion of our heads?
And since in Thy affection we draw breath,
how shall we yearn for strangers? Lo, we lay
our heads upon the threshold of Thy door,
waiting to come to Thee. Since we have quaffed
the beaker of Thy love, we yield our hearts
and make our Lives Thy ransom; since we come
again into Thy street, we turn our backs
on all that is, save Thee. Our souls are bound
to serve Thee, though in grief, and we have died
to selfhood! We are captives of Thy love
and have not strength to flee. Thy beauty's fever
hath lit a flame: shall not our hearts be burned?

'IRAQI (*trans* anon)

When in Love's Snare

When in love's snare the soul doth lie
   it is no sin for eye to see:
though far Thy face from outward eye,
   with inward sight I gaze on Thee.

My soul is drunken with the wine
   quaffed on that first primeval day
when Thou wast mine, and I was Thine,
   and promised so to be for aye.

I cannot let my Lover go,
   though I am doomed to banishment:
the spark betrays the ember's glow,
   this blush, my soul's bewilderment.

Thy languorous eye is lover's bane,
   the earth Thou treadest, China's throne:
whate'er Thou willest, Thou dost reign,
   and humbly I obedience own.

RÚMÍ (*trans* F Hadland Davis)

This is Love

This is Love: to fly heavenward,
To rend, every instant, a hundred veils.
The first moment, to renounce Life:
The last step, to feel without feet.
To regard this world as invisible,
Not to see what appears to one's self.
'O heart,' I said, 'may it bless thee
To have entered the circle of lovers,
To look beyond the range of the eye,
To penetrate the windings of the bosom!
Whence did this breath come to thee, O my soul,
Whence this throbbing, O my heart?'

RÚMÍ (*trans* F Hadland Davis)

The Journey to the Beloved

O lovers, O lovers, it is time to abandon the
    world:
The drum of departure reaches my spiritual ear
    from heaven.
Behold, the driver has risen and made ready his
    files of camels,
And begged us to acquit him of blame: why,
    O travellers, are you asleep?
These sounds before and behind are the din of
    departure and of the camel-bells;
With each moment a soul and spirit is setting
    off into the Void.
From these inverted candles, from these blue
    awnings
There has come forth a wondrous people, that
    the mysteries may be revealed.
A heavy slumber fell upon thee from the circling
    spheres:
Alas, for this life so light, beware of this slumber
    so heavy!
O soul, seek the Beloved, O friend, seek the
    Friend,
O watchman, be wakeful: it behoves not a
    watchman to sleep.

RÚMÍ (*trans* F Hadland Davis)

The Religion of Love

The sect of lovers is distinct from all others,
Lovers have a religion and a faith of their own.
Though the ruby has no stamp, what matters it?
Love is fearless in the midst of the sea of fear.

Rúmí (*trans* F Hadland Davis)

Pain is a Treasure

Pain is a treasure, for it contains mercies;
The kernel is soft when the rind is scraped off.
O brother, the place of darkness and cold
Is the fountain of Life and the cup of ecstasy.
So also is endurance of pain and sickness and
　　disease.
For from abasement proceeds exaltation.
The spring seasons are hidden in the autumns,
And the autumns are charged with springs.

Rúmí (*trans* F Hadland Davis)

Spirit Greater than Form

If spiritual manifestations had been sufficient,
The creation of the world had been needless and
　　vain.
If spiritual thought were equivalent of love of
　　God,
Outward forms of temples and prayers would
　　not exist.

Rúmí (*trans* F Hadland Davis)

To a Sweet Garden

'We bow down our heads before His edict
　　and ordinance,
We stake precious life to gain His favour.
While the thought of the Beloved fills our hearts,
All our work is to do Him service and spend life
　　for Him.
Wherever He kindles His destructive torch,
Myriads of lovers' souls are burnt therewith.
The lovers who dwell within the sanctuary
Are moths burnt with the torch of the Beloved's
　　face.'
O heart, haste thither, for God will shine upon
　　you,

And seem to you a sweet garden instead of a
terror.
He will infuse into your soul a new Soul,
So as to fill you, like a goblet, with wine.
Take up your abode in His Soul!
Take up your abode in heaven, O bright full moon!
Like the heavenly Scribe, He will open your
heart's book
That He may reveal mysteries unto you.

RÚMÍ (*trans* F Hadland Davis)

The Day of Resurrection

On every side is clamour and tumult, in every
street are candles and torches,
For to-night the teeming world gives birth to the
World Everlasting.
Thou wert dust and art spirit, thou wert ignorant
and art wise.
He who has led thee thus far will lead thee
further also.
How pleasant are the pains He makes thee suffer
while He gently draws thee to Himself!

RÚMÍ (*trans* F Hadland Davis)

The Return of the Beloved

Always at night returns the Beloved: do not
eat opium to-night;
Close your mouth against food, that you may
taste the sweetness of the mouth.
Lo, the cup-bearer is no tyrant, and in his
assembly there is a circle:
Come into the circle, be seated; how long will
you regard the revolution (of Time)?

. . .

Why, when God's earth is so wide, have you
fallen asleep in a prison?

RÚMÍ (*trans* F Hadland Davis)

The Divine Union

Avoid entangled thoughts, that you may see
  the explanation of Paradise.
Refrain from speaking, that you may win speech
  hereafter.
Abandon life and the world, that you may
  behold the Life of the world.

RÚMÍ (*trans* F Hadland Davis)

The Call of the Beloved

Every morning a voice comes to thee from
  heaven:
'When thou lay'st the dust of the way, thou
  win'st thy way to the goal.'
On the road to the Ka'ba of Union, lo, in every
  thorn-bush
Are thousands slain of desire who manfully
  yielded up their lives.
Thousands sank wounded on this path, to whom
  there came not
A breath of the fragrance of Union, a token from
  the neighbourhood of the Friend.

RÚMÍ (*trans* F Hadland Davis)

The Banquet of Union

In memory of the banquet of Union, in yearning
  for His beauty
They are fallen bewildered by the wine Thou
  knowest.

How sweet, in the hope of Him, on the threshold
  of His Abode,
For the sake of seeing His face, to bring night
  round to day!
Illumine thy bodily senses by the Light of the
  soul:

. . .

Look not in the world for bliss and fortune,
   since thou wilt not find them;
Seek bliss in both worlds by serving Him,
Put away the tale of Love that travellers tell;
Do thou serve God with all thy might.

RÚMÍ (*trans* Reynold Nicholson)

The Spirit Helpeth our Infirmity

The good thou art set upon, whate'er it be,
Its imperfection hath been hid from thee;
For were the vice laid bare, thy loathing soul
Would turn and fly from pole to farthest pole.
So, when an act of sin thou leav'st undone,
'Tis because God hath shown thee what to shun.

O gracious Lord, with whom disguise is vain,
Mask not our evil, let us see it plain!
But veil the weakness of our good desire,
Lest we lose heart and falter and expire.

RÚMÍ (*trans* Reynold Nicholson)

The Uses of Tribulation

Look at a chickpea in the pot, how it leaps up when it is
   subjected to the fire.
Whilst it is boiling, it always comes up to the top, crying
   ceaselessly,
'Why are you setting the fire on me? You bought me:
   why are you tormenting me like this?'
The housewife goes on hitting it with the ladle. 'Now,'
   says she, 'boil nicely and don't jump away from her who
   makes the fire.
I boil thee, but not because thou art hateful to me; nay,
   'tis that thou mayst get savour
And become nutriment and mingle with the vital spirit:
   such affliction is no abasement.
When thou wert green and fresh, thou drankest water
   in the garden: that water-drinking was for the sake of
   this fire.

God's mercy is prior to His wrath, to the end that by His
    mercy thou mayst suffer tribulation.
His mercy preceded His wrath in order that the stock-in-
    trade, which is existence, should be produced;
For without pleasure flesh and skin do not grow, and unless
    they grow, what shall Divine Love consume?
If, because of that requirement, acts of wrath come to pass
    to the end that thou shouldst give up thy stock-in-trade,
Yet afterwards the Grace of God will justify them, saying
    "Now thou art washed clean and hast jumped out of the
    river."
Continue, O chickpea, to boil in tribulation until neither
    existence nor self remains to thee.
If thou hast been severed from the garden of earth, yet
    thou wilt be food in the mouth and enter into the living.
Be nutriment, energy, thought! Thou wert milky sap:
    now be a lion of the jungle!
Thou grewest from God's Attributes in the beginning:
    pass again into His Attributes!
Thou wert a part of the cloud and the sun and the stars:
    thou wilt become soul and action and speech and
    thought.
The life of the animal arose from the death of the plant:
    hence the injunction, "Slay me, O trusty friends," is right.
Since such a victory awaits us after death, the words, "Lo,
    in being slain I live," are true.'

RÚMÍ (*trans* Reynold Nicholson)

Faith and Works

God hath placed a ladder before us: we must climb it,
    step by step.
You have feet: why pretend to be lame? You have hands:
    why conceal the fingers that grip?
Freewill is the endeavour to thank God for His Beneficence;
    your necessitarianism denies that Beneficence.
Thanksgiving for the power of acting freely gives you more
    power to thank Him; necessitarianism takes away what
    God hath given.
The brigands are on the road: do not sleep until you see
    the gate and the threshold!
If you put trust in God, trust Him with your work! Sow
    the seed, then rely upon the Almighty!

RÚMÍ (*trans* Reynold Nicholson)

The Divine Factory

The Worker is hidden in the workshop: enter the workshop
and behold Him!
Inasmuch as the work has woven a veil over the Worker,
you cannot see Him outside of His work.
The Worker dwells in the workshop: none who stays outside
is aware of Him.
Come, then, into the workshop of Not-being, that you may
contemplate the work and the Worker together.
Pharaoh set his face towards material existence; therefore
he was blind to God's workshop
And wished to alter and avert that which was eternally
ordained.

RÚMÍ (*trans* Reynold Nicholson)

The World of Time

Every instant thou art dying and returning. 'This world
is but a moment,' said the Prophet.
Our thought is an arrow shot by Him: how should it stay
in the air? It flies back to God.
Every instant the world is being renewed, and we unaware
of its perpetual change.
Life is ever pouring in afresh, though in the body it has the
semblance of continuity.
From its swiftness it appears continuous, like the spark
thou whirlest with thy hand.
Time and duration are phenomena produced by the
rapidity of Divine Action,
As a firebrand dexterously whirled presents the appearance
of a long line of fire.

RÚMÍ (*trans* Reynold Nicholson)

Omnes Eodem Cogimur

Every blind wayfarer, be he righteous or wicked, God is dragging,
bound in chains, into His Presence.
All are dragged along this Way reluctantly, save those who are
acquainted with the mysteries of Divine action.

The command *Come against your will* is addressed to the blind follower;
   Come willingly is for the man moulded of truth.
While the former, like an infant, loves the Nurse for the sake of milk,
   the other has given his heart away to this Veiled One.
The 'infant' hath no knowledge of Her beauty: he wants nothing of
   Her except milk;
The real lover of the Nurse is disinterested, single-minded in pure
   devotion.
Whether God's seeker love Him for something other than He, that he
   may continually partake of His good,
Or whether he love God for His Very Self, for naught beside Him, lest
   he be separated from Him,
In either case the quest and aspiration proceed from that Source: the
   heart is made captive by that Heart-ravisher.

RÚMÍ (*trans* Hasan Shahid Suhrawardy, revised by Robert Bridges)

The Pursuit of God

Grasp the Skirt of his Grace, for on a sudden He will flee away:
But draw Him not impatiently to thee, lest He fly as an arrow from
   the bow.
What shape will He not assume? What shifts He employeth!
If He be apprehended in Form, He will flee by way of the Spirit:
If thou seek Him in the sky, He will gleam in the water like the moon:
If thou go into the water, He fleeth to the sky:
If thou seek him in the spaceless, He beckoneth to Space:
When thou seekest Him in Space, He fleeth to the spaceless . . .
His Name will flee, the while thou mouldest thy lips for speech:
Thou may'st not even say, Such an one will flee:
He will flee from thee, so that if thou paint his picture,
The picture will flee from the tablet, and his features from thy soul.

RÚMÍ (*trans* Coleman Barks and John Moyne)

From Quatrains of Rúmí

Keep walking, though there's no place to get to.
Don't try to see through the distances.
That's not for human beings. Move within,
but don't move the way fear makes you move.

Walk to the well.
Turn as the earth and the moon turn,
circling what they love.
Whatever circles comes from the center.

Two hands, two feet, two eyes, good,
as it should be, but no separation
of the Friend and your loving.

Any dividing there
makes other untrue distinctions like 'Jew,'
and 'Christian,' and 'Muslim.'

The wine we really drink is our own blood.
Our bodies ferment in these barrels.
We give everything for a glass of this.
We give our minds for a sip.

Wine to intensify love,
fire to consume, we bring these,
not like images from a dream reality,
but as an actual night to live through until dawn.

RÚMÍ (*trans* Coleman Barks and John Moyne)

From Moses and the Shepherd

                              Inside the Kaaba
it doesn't matter which direction you point
your prayer rug!
                    The ocean diver doesn't need snowshoes!
The Love-Religion has no code or doctrine.
                                        Only God.
So the ruby has nothing engraved on it!
It doesn't need markings.
                              God began speaking
deeper mysteries to Moses. Vision and words,
which cannot be recorded here, poured into
and through him. He left himself and came back.
He went to Eternity and came back here.
Many times this happened.
                                        It's foolish of me
to try and say this. If I did say it,
it would uproot our human intelligences.
It would shatter all writing pens.

Moses ran after the shepherd.
He followed the bewildered footprints,
in one place moving straight like a castle
across a chessboard. In another, sideways,
like a bishop.
                    Now surging like a wave cresting,
now sliding down like a fish,
                              with always his feet
making geomancy symbols in the sand,
                                    recording
his wandering state.
                    Moses finally caught up
with him.
              'I was wrong. God has revealed to me
that there are no rules for worship.
                              Say whatever
and however your loving tells you to.'

EDWARD FITZGERALD (*trans*)

From The Rubaiyat of Omar Khayyam

XLIV

The mighty Mahmúd, the victorious Lord
That all the misbelieving and black Horde
    Of Fears and Sorrows that infest the Soul
Scatters and slays with his enchanted Sword.

XLV

But leave the Wise to wrangle, and with me
The Quarrel of the Universe let be:
    And, in some corner of the Hubbub coucht,
Make Game of that which makes as much of Thee.

XLVI

For in and out, above, about, below,
'Tis nothing but a Magic Shadow-show,
    Play'd in a Box whose Candle is the Sun,
Round which we Phantom Figures come and go.

XLVII

And the Wine you drink, the Lip you press,
End in the Nothing all Things end in – Yes –
    Then fancy while Thou art, Thou art but what
Thou shalt be – Nothing – Thou shalt not be less.

XLVIII

While the Rose blows along the River Brink,
With old Khayyam the Ruby Vintage drink:
   And when the Angel with his darker Draught
Draws up to Thee – take that, and do not shrink.

XLIX

'Tis all a Chequer-board of Nights and Days
Where Destiny with Men for Pieces plays:
   Hither and thither moves, and mates, and slays,
And one by one back in the Closet lays.

L

The Ball no Question makes of Ayes and Noes,
But Right or Left as strikes the Player goes;
   And He that toss'd Thee down into the Field,
He knows about it all – He knows – HE knows!

LI

The Moving Finger writes: and, having writ,
Moves on: nor all thy Piety nor Wit
   Shall lure it back to cancel half a Line,
Nor all thy Tears wash out a Word of it.

DANTE (*trans* H F Carey)

From The Divine Comedy: Paradiso

Canto XXX

             Mine eyes did look
On beauty, such, as I believe in sooth,
Not merely to exceed our human; but,
That save its Maker, none can to the full
Enjoy it. At this point o'erpowered I fail;
Unequal to my theme;

     . . .

'Forth from the last corporeal are we come
Into the heaven, that is unbodied light;
Light intellectual, replete with love;
Love of true happiness, replete with joy;
Joy, that transcends all sweetness of delight.
Here shalt thou look on either mighty host

Of Paradise; and one in that array,
Which in the final judgement thou shalt see.'
   As when the lightning, in a sudden spleen
Unfolded, dashes from the blinding eyes
The visive spirits, dazzled and bedimmed;
So, round about me, fulminating streams
Of living radiance played, and left me swathed
And veiled in dense impenetrable blaze.

Such weal is in the love, that stills this heaven:
For its own flame the torch thus fitting ever.
   No sooner to my listening ear had come
The brief assurance, than I understood
New virtue into me infused, and sight
Kindled afresh, with vigour to sustain
Excess of light however pure. I looked;
And, in the likeness of a river, saw
Light flowing, from whose amber-seeming waves
Flashed up effulgence, as they glided on
'Twixt banks, on either side, painted with spring.
Incredible how fair: and, from the tide,
There ever and anon, outstarting, flew
Sparkles instinct with life; and in the flowers
Did set them, like to rubies chased in gold:
Then, as if drunk with odours, plunged again
Into the wondrous flood;

. . .

            All is one beam.
Reflected from the summit of the first,
That moves, which being hence and vigour takes.
And as some cliff, that from the bottom eyes
His image mirrored in the crystal flood,
As if to admire his brave apparelling
Of verdure and of flowers; so, round about,
Eyeing the light, on more than million thrones,
Stood, eminent, whatever from our earth
Has to the skies returned. How wide the leaves,
Extended to their utmost, of this rose,
Whose lowest step embosoms such a space
Of ample radiance! Yet, nor amplitude
Nor height impeded, but my view with ease
Took in the full dimensions of that joy.
Near or remote, what there avails, where God
Immediate rules, and Nature, awed, suspends

Her sway? Into the yellow of the rose
Perennial, which, in bright expansiveness,
Lays forth its gradual blooming, redolent
Of praises to the never-wintering sun,
As one, who fain would speak yet holds his peace,
Beatrice led me; and, 'Behold,' she said,
'This fair assemblage; stoles of snowy white,
How numberless. The city, where we dwell,
Behold how vast; and these our seats so thronged,
Few now are wanting here. In that proud stall,
On which, the crown, already o'er its state
Suspended, holds thine eyes – or e'er thyself
Mayst at the wedding sup, – shall rest the soul'

. . .

Canto XXXI

In fashion, as a snow-white rose, lay then
Before my view the saintly multitude,
Which in his own blood Christ espoused. Meanwhile,
That other host, that soar aloft to gaze
And celebrate his glory, whom they love,
Hovered around; and, like a troop of bees,
Amid the vernal sweets alighting now,
Now, clustering, where their fragrant labour glows,
Flew downward to the mighty flower, or rose
From the redundant petals, streaming back
Unto the steadfast dwelling of their joy.
Faces had they of flame, and wings of gold:
The rest was whiter than the driven snow;
And, as they flitted down into the flower,
From range to range, fanning their plumy loins,
Whispered the peace and ardour, which they won
From that soft winnowing. Shadow none, the vast
Interposition of such numerous flight
Cast, from above, upon the flower, or view
Obstructed aught. For, through the universe,
Wherever merited, celestial light
Glides freely, and no obstacle prevents.
    All there, who reign in safety and in bliss,
Ages long past or new, on one sole mark
Their love and vision fixed. O trinal beam
Of individual star, that charm'st them thus!
Vouchsafe one glance to gild our storm below.

. . .

Re-entered, still another rose. 'The thirst
Of knowledge high, whereby thou art inflamed,
To search the meaning of what here thou seest,
The more it warms thee, pleases me the more.
But first behoves thee of this water drink.
Or e'er that longing be allayed.' So spake
The day-star of mine eyes: then thus subjoined:
'This stream; and these, forth issuing from its gulf.
And diving back, a living topaz each;
With all this laughter on its bloomy shores;
Are but a preface, shadowy of the truth
They emblem.'

DANTE (*trans* L Binyon)

O Light Eternal

From The Divine Comedy: Paradiso

O Light Eternal, who in thyself alone
   Dwell'st and thyself know'st, and self-understood,
   Self-understanding, smilest on thine own!
That circle which, as I conceived it, glowed
   Within thee like reflection of a flame,
   Being by mine eyes a little longer wooed,
Deep in itself, with colour still the same,
   Seemed with our human effigy to fill,
   Wherefore absorbed in it my sight became.
As the geometer who bends all his will
   To measure the circle, and howso'er he try
   Fails, for the principle escapes him still,
Such as this mystery new-disclosed was I,
   Fain to understand how the image doth alight
   Upon the circle, and with its form comply.
But these my wings were fledged not for that flight,
   Save that my mind a sudden glory assailed
   And its wish came revealed to it in that light.
To the high imagination force now failed;
   But like to a wheel whose circling nothing jars
   Already on my desire and will prevailed
The Love that moves the sun and the other stars.

DANTE (*trans* L Binyon)

The Ladder of Paradise

From The Divine Comedy: Paradiso

Within the crystal's ever-circling sphere –
   Named after its bright regent, him whose reign
   Made wickedness to die and disappear, –
Coloured like gold which flashes back again
   The sun, I saw a ladder stand, that seemed
   So high that the eye followed it in vain.
Moreover on the rungs descending gleamed
   So many splendours that each several star
   From heaven, methought, collected thither, streamed.
As rooks, after their natural habit, fare
   Forth all together at beginning day
   To warm their feathers chilled by the night air;
Then some, without returning, wing away,
   Some to the boughs they have their nests among
   Return, and others circling make a stay;
Such a behaviour had that sparkling throng,
   It seemed to me, coming in bands abreast,
   Soon as they lighted on a certain rung.
And that one which most near to us came to rest
   Became so bright that I said in my thought:
   'I see the love to me thou signallest.'

DANTE (*trans* D G Rossetti)

From The Vita Nova

38

A gentle thought there is will often start,
   Within my secret self, to speech of thee:
   Also of Love it speaks so tenderly
That much of me consents and takes its part.
'And what is this,' the soul saith to the heart,
   'That cometh thus to comfort thee and me,
   And thence where it would dwell, thus potently
Can drive all other thoughts by its strange art?'
And the heart answers: 'Be no more at strife
   'Twixt doubt and doubt: this is Love's messenger
   And speaketh but his words, from him received;

And all the strength it owns and all the life
    It draweth from the gentle eyes of her
    Who, looking on our grief, hath often grieved.'

40

Ye pilgrim-folk, advancing pensively
    As if in thought of distant things, I pray,
    Is your own land indeed so far away –
As by your aspect it would seem to be –
That this our heavy sorrow leaves you free
    Though passing through the mournful town mid-way;
    Like unto men that understand to-day
Nothing at all of her great misery?
Yet if ye will but stay, whom I accost,
    And listen to my words a little space,
    At going ye shall mourn with a loud voice.
It is her Beatrice that she hath lost;
    Of whom the least word spoken holds such grace
    That men weep hearing it, and have no choice.

PART 3:
Fourteenth Century to Fifteenth Century

Ni'mat-Allah (*trans* anon)

The Sea Is Our Essence

We are of the sea, and the sea is our essence;
why then is there this duality between us?
The world is an imaginary line before the sight;
read well that line, for it was inscribed by us.
Whatsoever we possess in both the worlds
in reality, my friend, belongs to God.

His love I keep secretly in my heart;
the less of the pain of His love is our cure.
Companions are we of the cup, comrades of the saki,
lest thou suppose that he is apart from us:
it is the assembly of love, and we are drunk –
who ever enjoyed so royal a party?
So long as Ni'mat Allah is the slave of the Lord,
the king of the world is as a beggar at his door.

Jami (*trans* anon)

Truth Is One

In long devotion to forms that cheat
Thou hast suffered the days of thy life to fleet:
But outward forms are still passing away,
Changing their fashion from day to day.
Tread not ever on stones that are rough to thy feet;
Nor shift from one branch to another thy seat.
Seek high o'er the sphere of the world thy rest;
In the world of reality make thee a nest.
If Truth be thine object, form-worshippers shun;
For form is manifold, Truth is one.
In number trouble and error lie.
To Unity then for sure refuge fly.
If the might of the foeman oppress thee sore,
Fly to the fortress and fear no more.

APPAR (*trans* Indira Petersen)

From The Lord is All Things

The Lord of Āppāṭi
is both inside and outside,
form and no-form.
He is both the flood and the bank,
he is the broad-rayed sun.
Himself the highest mystery,
he is in all hidden thoughts.
He is thought and meaning, and embraces
all who embrace him.

. . .

The gorgeous gem, delicious honey, milk,
the sweet taste of sugar cane, clear sugar syrup,
precious gem, the sound
of flute, drum, cymbals, and lute,
great gem, coral, pure gold and pearl,
the crest jewel of Paruppatam hill,
rare gem who destroys our sin,
our Lord in Ārūr –
I was a dog, who once failed
to know and remember him.

. . .

My treasure and good fortune, Lord sweet as honey,
golden flame of heaven, O form of blazing light,
my friend, my flesh,
heart within my flesh, soul within my heart,
wish-fulfilling tree,
my eye, dark pupil in the eye, image that dances within!
Save me from the hidden disease of karma,
bull among the gods, you who live in cool Āvaṭutuṟai!

APPAR (*trans* Indira Petersen)

From The Cosmic Person

The god who has
a thousand feet like a thousand red lotuses,
a thousand shoulders like a thousand golden hills,
a thousand long strands of hair like a thousand suns,
and has taken for himself a thousand names,
is our Lord who lives in Ārūr.

. . .

1

He is my bright diamond,
good days, and auspicious stars,
and evil planets, too.
He is ambrosia untasted,
butter in milk, juice in the fruit,
melody in song.
With Umā as half his self, he is

2

He is the seed, he the sprout and root;
True friend to his devotees, he takes the forms we desire.
Milk-white god, the refuge we seek,
he is the supreme Light.
He conceals himself from
all the gods in heaven who praise him,
yet dwells within my heart.
My Father in Karukāvūr
is the eye that reveals all things
to me, his devotee.

3

My Lord is the flower and its color,
the King who dwells as fragrance within the flower.
The Lord who shares his form
with the lady of the beautiful bracelets
is the god of all the true faiths,
and brings endless pain
to those who do not praise him.
Dwelling in my heart, he saved me from Death.
My father in Karukāvūr
is my eye.

. . .

5

None can fully grasp
the greatness of his manifestations
as the creator of the universe,
as the god who dug into the earth.
he smashed the enemy's three citadels,
burning them with terrible fire.
He bears the trident, axe, and snake,
and rides the bull.
Absent from evil hearts,
My Father in Karukāvūr
is my eye.

. . .

7

A snake encircles his waist,
he sits under the banyan tree,
the Ātirai is his festival day.
The cosmic gods themselves honor the sacred crown
on which he bears the moon.
Destroyer of karma, he dwells in my thoughts,
and in every human heart on this wide-famed earth.
He who shares his form with Umā
drank the poison that arose from the surging sea.
My Father in Karukāvūr
is my eye.

8

He is drum and drumbeat,
the measure of all speech.
The ash-smeared god, the supreme Light,
destroyer of our sin, is our one path to release.
The Lord who kicked at terrible Death
firmly eludes evil men –
they can't see him.
My Father in Karukāvūr,
is my eye.

. . .

11

He burned the enemy's three cities
with terrible fire;
pressing down on the arrogant demon,
in an instant he crushed his ten heads,
then graciously listened to his sweet songs.
he quelled the five senses,
he felled Death with his foot,
he is the mantra that gives us release.
My Father in Karukāvūr
is my eye.

Anonymous (*trans*)

Fibres of Light

I do not know why, but when I say 'Hail, Master!'
the sun and stars seem to run in my breath,
my muscles are as if fibres of light,
my being flies to strange lands and waters,
my lips touch gardens of flowers, my hands I
    exchange with some other hands,
a stranger moves my tongue.
The Universe runs into me, and I into the Universe.
I seem a strange misty form. Like vapor I pass into
    the being of others, and they passing within me
    become my guests.
It seems fair forms of rolling beauty roll as waves on
    the sea – Hail, Lord! All are each other's!
Our shape and limbs run into each other.
I find my bones at times strike within me against the
    bones of someone else.
Our deeds and thoughts jostle and run into each
    other.
I see a hundred souls blend in me, and I interchange
    my blood and brain thus with a hundred more
    in a single breath; and, calm in solitude, I find
    a society.

ANONYMOUS

Tears of Joy

When I behold Thy peerless face, beaming with love, O Lord,
What fear have I of earthly woe or of the frown of sorrow?
As the first ray of the dawning sun dispels the dark,
So too, Lord, when Thy blessed light bursts forth within the heart,
It scatters all our grief and pain with sweetest balm.
When on Thy love and grace I ponder, in my heart's deepest depths,
Tears of joy stream down my cheeks beyond restraining.
Hail, Gracious Lord! Hail, Gracious One! I shall proclaim Thy love.
May my life-breath depart from me as I perform Thy works!

ANONYMOUS

Blissful Awareness

Upon the Sea of Blissful Awareness waves of ecstatic
love arise:
Rapture divine! Play of God's Bliss!
Ah, how enthralling!
Wondrous waves of the sweetness of God, ever new
and ever enchanting,
Rise on the surface, ever assuming
Forms ever fresh.
Then once more in the Great Communion all are
merged, as the barrier walls
of time and space dissolve and vanish:
Dance then, O mind!
Dance in delight, with hands upraised, chanting
Lord Hari's holy name.

SHANKARA (*trans* S Nikhilananda)

Hymn to Annapūrṇā

1

O benign Mother, who pourest out upon us Everlasting Bliss!
Thou, the Ocean of Beauty! Bestower of boons and of fearlessness!
O Supreme Purifier, who washest away all sins!
Thou, the visible Ruler of the world, the sanctifier of King
    Himālaya's line!
O Thou, the Queen Empress of holy Kāśī! Divine Annapūrṇā!
Be gracious unto me and grant me alms.

2

Thou whose apparel sparkles, sewn with innumerable gems;
Who wearest a golden sāri to heighten Thine unsurpassable loveliness!
Thou on whose comely bosom reposes a necklace of many pearls;
Who dost breathe forth a fragrance, being anointed with saffron and
    sandal-paste!
O benign Mother! Thou whose form is soothing to the eyes!
O Thou, the Queen Empress of holy Kāśī! Divine Annapūrṇā!
Be gracious unto me and grant me alms.

3

Bestower of yoga's bliss! Destroyer of the foe!
Fulfiller of wealth and of righteousness!
Thou who appearest like waves of light, or the radiance of sun and
    moon and fire!
Protectress of the three worlds! Giver of wealth and of all things
    wished for!
O Thou, the Queen Empress of holi Kāśī! Divine Annapūrṇā!
Be gracious unto me and grant me alms.

4

O Gauri! O Umā! O S'ankarī! O Kaumārī
Thou who hast Thy dwelling in the cave of sacred Mount Kailās!
Thou who dost reveal the meaning of the holy Vedas;
Who art the very Embodiment of the mystic syllable *Om*;
Who openest the gates of Liberation!
O Thou, the Queen Empress of holy Kāśī! Divine Annapūrṇā!
Be gracious unto me and grant me alms.

5

Thou who bearest the manifold world of the visible and the invisible;
Who holdest the universe in Thy womb!
Thou who severest the thread of the play we play upon this earth!
Who lighest the lamp of wisdom; who bringest joy to the heart of S'iva,
    Thy Lord!
O Thou, the Queen Empress of holy Kāśī! Divine Annapūrṇā!
Be gracious unto me and grant me alms.

6

O Bhagavatī! Thou who art the Sovereign of the world!
O Mother Annapūrṇā! O Supreme Deity! Ocean of mercy!
Thou whose long tresses, falling to Thy knees,
Ripple restlessly like a river's current and sparkle like a blue gem!
Mother, ever eager to give us food and bliss and all good fortune!
O Thou, the Queen Empress of holy Kāśī! Divine Annapūrṇā!
Be gracious unto me and grant me alms.

7

Thou who revealest all the letters, from the first to the last!
Mother of the cosmos, gross and subtle, and of its Lord as well!
Ruler of earth and heaven and the nether world,
Who dost embody in Thyself the waves of creation, sustenance,
    and dissolution!
Eternal, uncaused Cause, who art the thick darkness of the
    cosmic dissolution!
Thou who bringest desire to the heart of man; who dost bestow on
    him well-being in this world!

8

Thou who holdest in Thy right hand a ladle of gold studded
    with jewels,
And in Thy left hand holdest a cup of delicious food!
Thou Giver of good fortune, who dost fulfil the wishes of
    Thy worshippers.
And bringest about their welfare with a mere wink of Thine eye!
O Thou, the Queen Empress of holy Kāśī! Divine Annapūrṇā!
Be gracious unto me and grant me alms.

9

Thou whose radiance burns a million times more bright than sun and
    moon and fire:
For whom the light of the moon is but the shadow of Thy lips;
Whose ear-rings sparkle like the sun and moon and fire; who shinest
    like the sun and moon!

Thou, the Supreme Empress, who in Thy four hands holdest rosary
    and book and goad and dice!
O Thou, the Queen Empress of holy Kāśī! Divine Annapūrṇā
Be gracious unto me and grant me alms.

10

Protectress of the ksatriya line! Giver of utter fearlessness!
Benign Mother of all! Ocean of infinite mercy!
Thou, the Bestower of instantaneous Liberation, the Giver of Eternal
    Good!
Provider of S'iva's welfare! Destroyer of every bodily ill!
O Thou, the Queen Empress of holy Kāśī! Divine Annapūrṇā!
Be gracious unto me and grant me alms.

11

O Annapūrṇā! Thou who never lackest for anything, who holdest
    S'ankara's heart in thrall!
O Pārvati! Grant me alms: I supplicate Thee for the boon of wisdom
    and renunciation above all.

12

My Mother is the Goddess Pārvati; my Father is S'iva, the Lord whose
    power none can withstand.
Their worshippers I own as my kith and kin; and the three worlds are
    my native land.

From Zen Poets

LAYMAN SOTOBA (*trans* Lucien Stryk)

The mountain – Buddha's body.
The torrent – his preaching.
Last night, eighty-four thousand poems.
How, how make them understand?

HOGE (*trans* Lucien Stryk)

How long the tree's been barren.
At its tip long ropes of cloud.
Since I smashed the mud-bull's horns,
The stream's flowed backwards.

EIAN (*trans* Lucien Stryk)

Joshu's 'Oak in the courtyard' –
Nobody's grasped its roots.
Turned from sweet plum trees,
They pick sour pears on the hill.

HOIN (*trans* Lucien Stryk)

On the rocky slope, blossoming
Plums – from where?
Once he saw them, Reiun
Danced all the way to Sandai.

MONJU-SHINDO (*trans* Lucien Stryk)

Joshu's 'Oak in the courtyard'
Handed down, yet lost in leafy branch
They miss the root. Disciple Kaku shouts –
'Joshu never said a thing!'

SHOFU (*trans* Lucien Stryk)

No dust speck anywhere.
What's old? new?
At home on my blue mountain,
I want for nothing.

HAKUYO (*trans* Lucien Stryk)

Over the peak spreading clouds,
At its source the river's cold.
If you would see,
Climb the mountain top.

LAYMAN MAKUSHO (*trans* Lucien Stryk)

Loving old priceless things,
I've scorned those seeking
Truth outside themselves:
Here, on the tip of the nose.

SUIAN (*trans* Lucien Stryk)

Traceless, no more need to hide.
Now the old mirror
Reflects everything – autumn light
Moistened by faint mist.

CHIFU (*trans* Lucien Stryk)

No mind, no Buddhas, no live beings,
Blue peaks ring Five Phoenix Tower.
In late spring light I throw this body
Off – fox leaps into the lion's den.

SOAN (*trans* Lucien Stryk)

Sailing on Men River, I heard
A call: how deep, how ordinary.
Seeking what I'd lost,
I found a host of saints.

JINZU (*trans* Lucien Stryk)

In serving, serve,
In fighting, kill.
Tokusan, Ganto –
A million-mile bar!

ANBUN (*trans* Lucien Stryk)

Years keeping *that* in mind,
Vainly questioning masters.
A herald cries, 'He's coming!'
Liver, gall burst wide.

GOJUSAN (*trans* Lucien Stryk)

Seamless –
Touched, it glitters.
Why spread *such* nets
For sparrows?

MOAN (*trans* Lucien Stryk)

Clear, clear – clearest!
I ran barefoot east and west.
Now more lucid than the moon,
The eighty-four thousand
Dharma gates!

GEKKUTSU-SEI (*trans* Lucien Stryk)

I set down the emerald lamp,
Take it up – exhaustless.
Once lit,
A sister is a sister.

SEIGEN-YUIIN (*trans* Lucien Stryk)

How vast karma,
Yet what's there
To cling to? Last night,
Turning, I was blinded
By a ray of light.

NAN-O-MYO (*trans* Lucien Stryk)

Not falling, not ignoring –
A pair of mandarin ducks
Alighting, bobbing, anywhere.

LAYMAN YAKUSAI (*trans* Lucien Stryk)

A deafening peal,
A thief escaped
My body. What
Have I learnt?
The Lord of Nothingness
Has a dark face.

MUMON-EKAI (*trans* Lucien Stryk)

A thunderbolt – eyes wide,
All living things bend low.
Mount Sumeru dances
All the way to Sandai.

KANZAN-SHIGYO (*trans* Lucien Stryk)

Where is the dragon's cave?
Dozing this morn in Lord Sunyata's
Palace, I heard the warbler.
Spring breeze shakes loose
The blossoms of the peach.

TEKKAN (*trans* Lucien Stryk)

No mind, no Buddha, no being.
Bones of the Void are scattered.
Why should the golden lion
Seek out the fox's lair?

DANGAI (*trans* Lucien Stryk)

Earth, river, mountain:
Snowflakes melt in air.
How could I have doubted?
Where's north? south? east? west?

KEPPO (*trans* Lucien Stryk)

Searching Him took
My strength.
One night I bent
My pointing finger –
Never such a moon!

JENTI (*trans* anon)

The Pure Mind

The Seven Factors of the awakened mind –
Seven ways whereby we may Nibbana win –
All, all have I developed and made ripe,
Even according to the Buddha's word.

For I therein have seen as with mine eyes
The Bless'd, the Exalted One. Last of all lives
Is this that makes up Me. The round of births
Is vanquished – Ne'er shall I be again!

PATACARA (*trans* anon)

My Heart Is Free

With ploughshares ploughing up the fields, with seed
Sown in the breast of earth, men with their crops,
Enjoy their gains and nourish wife and child
Why cannot I, whose life is pure, who seek
To do the Master's will, no sluggard am
Nor puffed up, win to Nibbana's bliss?

One day, bathing my feet, I sit and watch
The water as it trickles down the slope.
Thereby I set my heart in steadfastness,
As one doth train a horse of noble breed.
Then going to my call, I take my lamp,
And seated on my couch I watch the flame.
Grasping the pin, I pull the wick right down
Into the oil . . .
Lo! the Nibbana of the little lamp!
Emancipation dawns! My heart is free!

YUNUS EMRES (*trans* Suha Faiz)

From The City of the Heart

7

I came one morning on a burial round – and there I saw the dead:
Solitary, each one having lost life's road, now lying there.

Nearer I drew, more close to them, and then I saw death's awefulness;
Valiant youths, hopes unfulfilled, unsatisfied, now lying there.

Food for worm and carrion, bodies ravaged by all creeping things,
The young who died before their prime, frost-struck roses, lying there.

Flesh now fast held in death's trap, their souls attain at last to Truth;
O you, whose turn is nigh upon you, see you not these now
    lying there?

Fallen the teeth which once were pearl, gone the gleaming,
    golden hair;
But ended the torture of the brain for those in dark damp lying there.

Fled is the shining of their eyes for naught abides that they hold dear;
A single-sheeted shroud alone surrounds these bones now lying there.

Yunus, if you true lover are, be drawn not to possessions' charms:
Who once those charms had known are now become but dark earth
lying there.

27

This city of real Being, how I long each day to enter in
And, being there, to see the glory of my Sultan's Face within.

For though His voice comes ever to me I have here no sight of Him;
My life I willingly would give if I could only glimpse that Face.

Within that Sultan's private rooms are seven places of retreat;
Would that I might at each of these, in turn, find for my soul a place.

Before each gate a sentinel; a hundred thousand at command;
Girded, I long to seize the sword of Love and put them all to flight.

The Leylā of Mejnün am I; and lover of the Merciful;
I would the Face of my Beloved see – so would that I were mad.

The Friend has come to us as guest, time without number, year
on year;
I would that I might be for Him, like Ismaīl, a sacrifice.

Earth into jewels is transformed when saints their gaze bestow on it;
Could I be but the dust in which the footsteps of the saints have trod.

Poor Yunus is, as all, by nature's fourfold elements sustained;
I yearn to be within the mystery of Love and life contained.

123

Engulfed by fire of Love I walk, blood-hued, for all the world to see;
No more is mind, nor mindlessness: come, see what Love has
made of me.

One moment I am dust upon the Road – the next, as breezes free;
And now, a flowing brook become: come, see what Love has
made of me.

I am a foaming mountain stream; my Being writhes in agony;
Weeping, as I recall my Sheykh: come, see what Love has made of me.

My eyes with tears of blood are filled; a stone is set where heart
     should be;
You sufferers, you know my state; come, see what Love has
     made of me.

O raise me by the hand – O bring me to You, where I long to be;
You made me weep – let me now smile: come, see what Love has
     made of me.

From every tongue I seek to find a Sheykh in every land I flee;
But who, in exile, knows my state? Come, see what Love has
     made of me.

As Mejnūn once, so now I roam; in dreams alone my Love I see;
And, waking, am brought low again: come, see what Love has
     made of me.

Poor Yunus I, now wholly spent; from head to foot my body rent;
Far, far from Friendship's lands now sent: come, see what Love has
     made of me.

146

I am he who weeps before that Lover's face,
Who willingly surrenders soul to his Beloved.

In rapturous awe throughout each night till dawn am I
Waiting, before the Lover's Face, expectantly.

And when the light of morning comes still am I sad;
As though I were a nightingale among Love's blooms.

Since when my soul was taken hold by Love Divine,
I am become a wanderer, like to Mejnūn.

A moth made mad by radiance from that Beauty's light,
My wings, my body, wholly by Its fire consumed.

Since when I drank a draught of His sweet wine of Love
He penetrates my depth, the wound that is my heart.

Today upon Love's Road with Mansūr – I am one;
There may I walk till to his scaffold I, too, come.

I am the love-lorn nightingale among Love's flowers
Who would to every heart bring tidings of that Love.

Yunus the lover now in lands afar must dwell,
An exile, that to strangers he his Love might tell.

ABU MENBA CARAWASH, SULTAN OF MOUSEL (*trans* J D Carlyle)

To Adversity

Hail, chastening friend, Adversity! 'tis thine
The mental ore to temper and refine;
To cast in Virtue's mould the yielding heart,
And Honour's polish to the mind impart.

Without thy wakening touch, thy plastic aid,
I'd lain the shapeless mass that Nature made;
But formed, great artist, by thy magic hand,
I gleam a sword, to conquer and command.

LALLA (*trans* Coleman Barks)

From Naked Song: Poems of Lalla

Dance, Lalla, with nothing on
but air. Sing, Lalla,
wearing the sky.

Look at this glowing day! What clothes
could be so beautiful, or
more sacred?

I began as a bloom of cotton,
outdoors. Then they brought me to a room
where they washed me. Then the hard strokes
of the carder's wife. Then another woman
spun thin threads, twisting me
around her wheel. Then the kicks
of the weaver's loom made cloth,
and on the washing stone, washermen
wet and slung me about
to their satisfaction, whitened me
with earth and bone,
and cleaned me to my own
amazement. Then the scissors
of the tailor, piece by piece,
and his careful finishing work.

Now, at last, as clothes,
I find You and freedom.
This living is so difficult
before one takes your hand.

That one is blessed and at peace
who doesn't hope, to whom
desire makes no more loans.

Nothing coming, nothing owed.

Just for a moment, flowers appear
on the empty, nearly-spring tree.

Just for a second, wind
through the wild thicket thorns.

Self inside self, You are nothing but me.
Self inside self, I am only You.

What we are together
will never die.

The why and how of this?
What does it matter?

You are the sky and the ground.
You alone the day, the night air.
You are all things born into being.

Also, these flower offerings
that someone brought.

Sir, have you forgotten the promise
you made in your mother's womb,
to die before you die?

When will you remember
what you intended?

Don't let your donkey wander loose!
It will stray into your neighbor's
saffron garden. Think of the damage
it might do, and the punishment!

Who then will carry you naked
to your own death?

Forgetful one, get up!
It's dawn, time to start searching.

Open your wings and lift.
Give like the blacksmith
even breath to the bellows.

Tend the fire that changes
the shape of metal.

Alchemical work begins at dawn,
as you walk out to meet the Friend.

There is a lake so tiny
that a mustard seed would cover it
easily, yet everyone drinks from this lake.

Deer, jackals, rhinoceroses, and sea elephants
keep falling into it, falling and dissolving
almost before they have time to be born.

I wearied myself searching for the Friend
with efforts beyond my strength.

I came to the door and saw how
powerfully the locks were bolted.

And the longing in me became that strong,
and then I saw that I was gazing
from within the presence.

With that waiting, and in giving up all trying,
only then did Lalla flow out
from where I knelt.

Your way of knowing is a private herb garden.
Enclose it with a hedge of meditation,
and self-discipline, and helpfulness to others.

Then everything you've done before
will be brought as a sacrifice
to the mother goddess.

And each day, as you eat the herbs,
the garden grows more bare and empty.

Beautifully full of juice they come from the mother,
causing many birth-pains.

Again and again, they wait at her door to enter.
Shiva is not often among them!
Meditate on that.

The pedestal rock can also serve as pavement,
or as a handsome millstone turning perfectly.

Each is just a hardened piece of the ground.
Shiva is so rarely found.

Sunlight shines everywhere equally.
Water flows into every house.

It's also true that Shiva
can scarcely be located.

The woman who nurses her child with milk
acts with a different love as your wife,

and talking secretly to other men,
she may be dangerous to you, the same woman.

Meditate on how seldom
Shiva appears.

If I could control the channels of my breath,
if I could perform precise surgery on myself,
I could create the substance that awareness is.

There's nothing more valuable than that!
God does not often come as a person.

Wear just enough clothes to keep warm.
Eat only enough to stop the hunger-pang.

And as for your mind, let it work
to recognize who you are,
and the Absolute, and that
this body will become food
for the forest crows.

Meditation and self-discipline
are not all that's needed, nor even
a deep longing to go through
the door of freedom.

You may dissolve in contemplation,
as salt does in water,
but there's something more.

Enlighten your desires.
Meditate on who you are.
Quit imagining.

What you want is profoundly expensive,
and difficult to find,
yet closeby.

Don't search for it. It is nothing,
and a nothing within nothing.

Awareness is the ocean of existence.
Let it loose and your words will rage
and cause wounds like fishing spears.

But if you tend it like a fire
to discover the truth,
you'll find how much of that
there is in what you say. None.

                    . . .

I locked the doors and windows.
I grabbed the onion-thief
and yelled for help.

I tied him up in an inside closet
and threatened him with *Om. Om.*

I shut the body openings
and found out what steals

the even-breath, the truth
of Who we are.

If you want a kingdom and get it,
you'll have no peace.

If you give it away,
still you won't be content.

Only a soul free of desire
can taste eternity.

Be living, yet dead!
Then knowing comes
to live in you.

Let them throw their curses.
If inside, I am connected
to what's true, my soul
stays quiet and clear.

Do you think Shiva worries
what people say!

If a few ashes fall on a mirror,
use them to polish it.

I, Lalla, entered the jasmine garden,
where Shiva and Shakti were making love.

I dissolved into them,
and what is this
to me, now?

I seem to be here,
but really I'm walking
in the jasmine garden.

Fearful, always-moving mind,
the One who has no beginning
is thinking of how hunger
may fall away from you.

No ritual,
no religion,
is needed.

Just cry out one
unobstructed cry.

The royal fan, sunshade, and chariot,
the throne itself, the happy feasting,
the theatre nights, your soft, down bed,
which of these can help your fear of death?

You've demolished the highbanked marsh road.
How is it now out in the swamp?
Death will come at one specific moment.
How does that make you feel?

There are two results and three causes.
Practice the breath. Rise
through the disc of the sun.
Your death panic will fade.

Let your body wear your knowing.
Let your heart sing songs.

Lalla has become a syllable
of soul-light. There is no death.

Shiva is the horse.
Vishnu puts the saddle on.
Brahma adjusts the stirrup.

And there is that in you
that will recognize the rider
those are waiting on: the unobstructed
sound, the nothing without name,
or lineage, or form,

which is continually changing
into the Sound and the Dot
within a human being who is
That meditating inside That,

the Sound and the Dot,
which are one thing, alone,
and the rider who mounts to ride.

Three times I have seen the lake
of the universe overflowing.

Once, I remember seeing
the only existent place
as a whirling without form,

and once, as a bridge over this
that is now Kashmir,

and seven times, I saw the whole
as emptiness.

Men and women now, even the best,
can barely remember their past lives,

and as for the children, whose lives
are getting harder and harder,
what will they do?

A time is coming so deformed
and unnatural that pears and apples
will ripen with the apricots,

and a daughter and a mother
will leave the house every day
hand in hand to find new strangers
to lie down with.

For a moment I saw a beautiful moving river.
Then a vast water with no means of crossing it.

For a moment, I saw a bush full of opening buds.
Then no roses, no thorns, nothing.

For a moment I saw a busy cooking fire.
Then no hearth, no smoke, no flame.

I saw the great mother of kings, Kunti.
Then, the next moment, sitting here, is
the helpless old aunt of the potter's wife.

Whatever I do, the responsibility is mine,
but like one who plants an orchard,
what comes of what I do, the fruit,
will be for others.

I offer the actions of this life
to the God within,
and wherever I go, the way is blessed.

Some people abandon their homes.
Others abandon hermitages.

All this renunciation does nothing,
if you're not deeply conscious.

Day and night, be aware
with each breath,
and live there.

My teacher, you are God to me!
Tell me the inner meaning
of my two breathings,
the one warm, the other cool.

'In your pelvis near the navel is the source
of many motions called the sun,
the city of the bulb.

As your vitality rises from that sun,
it warms, and in your mouth it meets
the downward flow through the fontanelle
of your higher self, which is cool
and called the moon, or Shiva.

This rivering mixture feels,
by turns, warm and cool.'

My body caught fire like an ember,
as I brought the syllable *OM*,
the one that says *You are That*,
into me. I moved through
the six chakra centers
that urge human beings to action
and out into the lightedness
where Lalla lives now.

Lalla, there's no birth or death.
You are one, but not with happiness
or difficulty, not with
desire or anger.

You do not walk with people
who only *talk about* truth.

The experience of God
is continuous amazement.

Dying and giving birth go on
inside the one consciousness,
but most people misunderstand
the pure play of creative energy,
how inside that, those
are one event.

Lalla, you've wandered so many places
trying to find your husband!

Now at last, inside the walls
of this body-house, in the heart-shrine,
you discover where he lives.

KABIR (*trans* H P Shastri)

From Poems of Kabir

All things are created by the Om;
The love-form is His body.
He is without form, without quality,
    without decay:
Seek thou union with Him!

By surrendering my mind to my Guru
I had it polished,
And now it is transparent.

The disciple is a used garment
And the Guru is the washerman;
When he washed my personality
On the rock of meditation;
It became free of all the dirt of nescience.

The love and devotion I gave my Guru
Brought me knowledge in return,
As well as affectionate association and delight,
Compassion, devotion and faith.

He who regards his Guru as a man,
He is blind; he will remain unhappy in this life
And he will fall into darkness after his death.

O Kabir! How blind are those small-minded disciples
Who think that the Guru is other than God;
If God is angry your Guru can reconcile Him,
But if the Guru is displeased
There is none who can make intercession.

Your Guru is the ladder to Godhead;
Time has no power over him
Who has sacrificed body, mind and all
On the Guru.

He is a true yogi, says Kabir,
Who unites his mind with the light within;
He who is indifferent to the world,
Whose faith in, and devotion to, his Guru,
Are unshakable.

Produce the divine light in your intellect,
And sitting quiet therein, worship Atman;
Thus the natural samadhi will shine
In your being.

Give up pride and vanity;
In this market place of the world
Purchase the commodity of wisdom.

The pleasures and achievements of the world are empty;
It is mere talk;
The barren woman rocks the cradle,
Is there any joy therein?

Holding the staff in his hand,
Kabir is standing in the highway;
His cry is: 'Let him who is willing to burn up his home
Come and follow me.'

The sun drives away darkness;
The heedless treacherous intellect
Destroys the fruit of the Guru's teachings;
Avarice kills all good name.
Pride is an enemy of devotion to God.

It is easy to have devotion
When the Guru is sweet.

KABIR (*trans* Rabindranath Tagore)

From Songs of Kabir

VI

The moon shines in my body, but my blind eyes cannot see it;
The moon is within me, and so is the sun.
The unstruck drum of Eternity is sounded within me; but my deaf ears
    cannot hear it.

So long as man clamours for the *I* and the *Mine*, his works are
    as naught:
When all love of the *I* and the *Mine* is dead, then the work of the Lord
    is done.
For work has no other aim than the getting of knowledge:
When that comes, then work is put away.

The flower blooms for the fruit: when the fruit comes, the
    flower withers.

VIII

Within this earthen vessel are bowers and groves, and within it is
    the Creator:
Within this vessel are the seven oceans and the unnumbered stars.
The touchstone and the jewel-appraiser are within;
And within this vessel the Eternal soundeth, and the spring wells up.
Kabir says: 'Listen to me, my Friend! My beloved Lord is within.'

IX

O how may I ever express that secret word?
O how can I say He is not like this, and He is like that?
If I say that He is within me, the universe is ashamed:
If I say that He is without me, it is falsehood.
He makes the inner and the outer worlds to be indivisibly one;
The conscious and the unconscious, both are His footstools.
He is neither manifest nor hidden, He is neither revealed
    nor unrevealed:
There are no words to tell that which
He is.

XV

Where Spring, the lord of the seasons, reigneth, there the Unstruck
    Music sounds of itself,
There the streams of light flow in all directions;
Few are the men who can cross to that shore!
There, where millions of Krishnas stand with hands folded,
Where millions of Vishnus bow their heads,
Where millions of Brahmas are reading the Vedas,
Where millions of Shivas are lost in contemplation,
Where millions of Indras dwell in the sky,
Where the demi-gods and the munis are unnumbered,
Where millions of Saraswatis, Goddess of Music, play on the vina –
There is my Lord self-revealed: and the scent of sandal and flowers
    dwells in those deeps.

XVI

Between the poles of the conscious and the unconscious, there has the
    mind made a swing:
Thereon hang all beings and all worlds, and that swing never ceases
    its sway.
Millions of beings are there: the sun and the moon in their courses
    are there:
Millions of ages pass, and the swing goes on
All swing! the sky and the earth and the air and the water; and the
Lord Himself taking form:
And the sight of this has made Kabir a servant.

L

The flute of the Infinite is played without ceasing, and its sound is love:
When love renounces all limits, it reaches truth.
How widely the fragrance spreads! It has no end, nothing stands in
    its way.
The form of this melody is bright like a million suns: incomparably
    sound the vina, the vina of the notes of truth.

LI

Dear friend, I am eager to meet my Beloved! My youth has flowered,
    and the pain of separation from Him troubles my breast.
I am wandering yet in the alleys of knowledge without purpose, but I
    have received His news in these alleys of knowledge.
I have a letter from my Beloved: in this letter is an unutterable
    message, and now my fear of death is done away.
Kabir says: 'O my loving friend! I have got for my gift the
    Deathless One'.

DHAN GOPAL MUKERJI (*trans* anon)
Thou Art the Path

Thou art the Path,
And the Goal that paths never reach;
Thou art the Lawful Lord
In Whom laws are lost
Like rivers in the sea.

This, I say, is the stillness:
A retreat to one's roots:
Or better yet, return
To the will of God,
Which is, I say, to constancy;
I call enlightenment, and say
That not to know it
Is blindness that works evil.

But when you know
What eternally is so,
You have stature,
And stature means righteousness,
And righteousness is kingly,
And kingliness divine,
And divinity is the Way
Which is final.

Then, though you die,
You shall not perish.
Thou feedest and sustainest
All that one sees, or seems;
Yet Thou art ever hungry for love,
And there is no end to Thy thirst for peace.

Though all Time is as mail on Thy nakedness;
Though all space sandal thy feet,
Yet they are torn by the thorns of my prayers,
And Thy Body is pierced with bliss.

All-healer, yet all-wounds,
All-life, yet ever-dying,
All-praised, yet praiseless,
All-ending, yet no end for Thee!

Thou art the agony of men,
Thou art the cry of the wounded beast,
Thou art the haughty mountain,
And the eagle swooping down its side.

The unborn that sings under its mother's heart,
The battle-cry of the new-born child;
The song in the throat of the lover,
And the pang of joy that brims in the eye of a bride.

Thou art the curve-pattern that bird-wings
Make in the sky,
Thou art the trembling grass,
And the tiger that creeps under it.

TAYUMANAVAR (*trans* anon)

Fulfillment

Marvelous indeed was the expedient,
by which you took me to be your own
and said 'Be still,' so that I sank within
and became That, that floodtide of Bliss.

NANAK (*trans* anon)

Naked Wilt Thou Depart

Relish not, O thou, the taste of poison,
O thou foolish and crazy one, thou art involved with the world,
As is the stray cattle let loose upon a farm.
The things thou thinkest are of avail to thee,
Go not with thee; no, not even a trite.
Thou camest naked, naked wilt thou depart.
Thou wert destined to go the Round, and death clasped thee in
    her grip.
Thou see-est the bloom of the safflower, and thou art lured by its
    passing fragrance.
And thy string of life wears off each day,
And yet thou doest not a thing to save thy soul.
Thus becometh thou old, thy speech falters and thy body fails thee:
And as thou wert lured by Maya in youth, so verily thou hast
    remained in age.

When I saw thus the world, through the Guru's grace,
I lost my ego and sought the Lord's refuge.
Yea, Nanak knew then the Path of the Lord through the Saints.

SANKARA DEVI (*trans* anon)

Prostrate at Thy Feet

Oh, my Lord, prostrate at Thy feet, I lay myself down and beseech Thee
    with a contrite heart to save my soul.
My soul is on the point of perishing through the poison of the
    venomous serpent of worldly things.
On this earth all is transitory and uncertain: wealth, kinsmen, life,
    youth, and even the world itself.
Children, family, all are uncertain. On what shall I place reliance?
Like a drop of water on the lotus leaf, the mind is unsteady. There is no
    firmness in it.
There is nothing uncertain in Thy grace and no cause for fear under
    the shadow of Thy feet.
I, Sankara, pray to thee, O Hrishikesh, the dweller in my heart, to pilot
    me across this world of trouble.
Turn my heart to Thee and lead me to Thyself, Oh Lord of all blessing
    and all grace.
Vouchsafe unto me the truth, the right path, and Thy kindly guidance.
Thou art my mind. Thou art my destiny, Thou art my spiritual guide.
    Saith Sankara, steer me across the vale of sorrows.

MICHELANGELO (*trans* V S de Pinto)

Sonnet XXIII

Lord, make me see thy glory in every place:
    If mortal beauty sets my heart aglow,
    Shall not that earthly fire by thine burn low,
Extinguisht by the great light of thy grace?
Dear Lord, I cry to thee for help, O raise
    Me from the misery of this blind woe,
    Thy spirit alone can save me, let it flow
Through will and sense redeeming what is base.

Thou hast given me on earth this god-like soul,
   And a poor prisoner of it thou hast made
      Behind weak flesh walls, from that wretched state
How can I rescue it, how my true life find?
   All goodness, Lord, must fail without thy aid:
      Thy power alone has strength to alter fate.

MICHELANGELO (*trans* William Wordsworth)

A Sonnet

The prayers I make will then be sweet indeed,
If Thou the spirit give by which I pray;
My unassisted heart is barren clay,
That of its native self can nothing feed;
Of good and pious works Thou art the seed
That quickens only where Thou say'st it may.
Unless Thou show to us Thy own true way,
No man can find it: Father! Thou must lead;
Do Thou then breathe those thoughts into my mind
By which such virtue may in me be bred
That in Thy holy footsteps I may tread;
The fetters of my tongue do Thou unbind,
That I may have the power to sing to Thee,
And sound Thy praises everlastingly!

ST TERESA OF AVILA (*trans* anon)

I Am Thine, and Born for Thee

I am Thine, and born for Thee:
What wilt Thou have done with me?

Sov'reign Lord upon Thy throne,
Endless Wisdom, One and Whole,
Goodness that dost feed my soul,
Good and great, One God alone:
Vile Thou seest me, yet Thine own,
As I sing my love for Thee.
What wilt Thou have done with me?

Thine I am, for Thou didst make me;
Thine, for Thou alone didst save me;
Thine – Thou couldst endure to have me;
For Thine own didst deign to take me.

ST TERESA OF AVILA (*trans* anon)

My Beloved One is Mine

I gave myself to Love Divine,
And lo! my lot so changed is
That my Beloved One is mine
And I at last am surely His.

When that sweet Huntsman from above
First wounded me and left me prone,
Into the very arms of Love
My stricken soul forthwith was thrown.
Since then my life's no more my own
And all my lot so changed is
That my Beloved One is mine
And I at last am surely His.

ST TERESA OF AVILA (*trans* anon)

Prayer

The dart wherewith He wounded me
Was all embarbed round with love,
And thus my spirit came to be
One with its Maker, God above.
No love but this I need to prove:
My life to God surrender'd is
And my Beloved One is mine
And I at last am surely His.

ST JOHN OF THE CROSS (*trans* Roy Campbell)

From Without God I Cannot Live

I live without inhabiting
Myself – in such a wise that I
Am dying that I do not die.

ST JOHN OF THE CROSS (*trans* Roy Campbell)

The Soul Aflame

Within myself I do not dwell
Since without God I cannot live.
Reft of myself, and God as well,
What serves this life (I cannot tell)
Except a thousand deaths to give?
Since waiting here for life I lie –
And die because I do not die.

This life I live in vital strength
Is loss of life unless I win You:
And thus to die I shall continue
Until in You I live at length.
Listen (my God!) my life is in You.
This life I do not want, for I
Am dying that I do not die.

Thus in your absence and your lack
How can I in myself abide
Nor suffer here a death more black
Than ever was by mortal died.
For pity of myself I've cried
Because in such a plight I lie
Dying because I do not die.

The fish that from the stream is lost
Derives some sort of consolation
That in his death he pays the cost
At least of death's annihilation.
To this dread life with which I'm crossed
What fell death can compare, since I,
The more I live, the more must die.

ST JOHN OF THE CROSS (*trans* Roy Campbell)

Verses Written after an Ecstasy of High Exaltation

I entered in, I know not where,
And I remained, though knowing naught,
Transcending knowledge with my thought.

Of when I entered I know naught,
But when I saw that I was there
(Though where it was I did not care)
Strange things I learned, with greatness fraught.
Yet what I heard I'll not declare.
But there I stayed, though knowing naught,
Transcending knowledge with my thought.

Of peace and piety interwound
This perfect science had been wrought,
Within the solitude profound
A straight and narrow path it taught,
Such secret wisdom there I found
That there I stammered, saying naught,
But topped all knowledge with my thought.

So borne aloft, so drunken-reeling,
So rapt was I, so swept away,
Within the scope of sense or feeling
My sense or feeling could not stay.
And in my soul I felt, revealing,
A sense that, though its sense was naught,
Transcended knowledge with my thought.

The man who truly there has come
Of his own self must shed the guise;
Of all he knew before the sum.

ST JOHN OF THE CROSS (*trans* Roy Campbell)

Song of the Soul in Intimate Communication and Union with the Love of God

Oh flame of love so living,
How tenderly you force
To my soul's inmost core your fiery probe!
Since now you've no misgiving,
End it, pursue your course
And for our sweet encounter tear the robe!

Oh cautery most tender!
Oh gash that is my guerdon!
Oh gentle hand! Oh touch how softly thrilling!
Eternal life you render,
Raise of all debts the burden
And change my death to life, even while killing!

Oh lamps of fiery blaze
To whose refulgent fuel
The deepest caverns of my soul grow bright,
Late blind with gloom and haze,
But in this strange renewal
Giving to the belov'd both heat and light.

What peace, with love enwreathing,
You conjure to my breast
Which only you your dwelling place may call:
While with delicious breathings
In glory, grace, and rest,
So daintily in love you make me fall!

ST JOHN OF THE CROSS (*trans* Roy Campbell)

Other Verses with a Divine Meaning

Not without hope did I ascend
Upon an amorous quest to fly
And up I soared so high, so high,
I seized my quarry in the end.

As on this falcon quest I flew
To chase a quarry so divine,
I had to soar so high and fine
That soon I lost myself from view.
With loss of strength my plight was sorry
From straining on so steep a course.
But love sustained me with such force
That in the end I seized my quarry.

The more I rose into the height
More dazzled, blind, and lost I spun.
The greatest conquest ever won
I won in blindness, like the night.
Because love urged me on my way
I gave that mad, blind, reckless leap
That soared me up so high and steep
That in the end I seized my prey.

The steeper upward that I flew
On so vertiginous a quest
The humbler and more lowly grew
My spirit, fainting in my breast.
I said 'None yet can find the way'
But as my spirit bowed more low,
Higher and higher did I go
Till in the end I seized my prey.

JACOB REVIUS (*trans* anon)

The Knowledge of God

When starlight shines on the surface of the sea,
The fishes underneath do all agree.

JACOB REVIUS (*trans* anon)

The Intellectual Fire

And think that there the stars of Heaven show,
Although reflection scant is all they know;
But we who here above the water live
Can see the bright hosts of the night arrive.
So Man: all that he sees on earth this while,
Of God and of his glory, is not real:
'Tis image mere; who naked truth can bear,
They only see God's shining visage clear.

ANGELUS SILESIUS (*trans* anon)

God's Lute

A heart that to God's will
Submits in patience mute
Loves to be touched by Him:
It serves God as His lute.

ANGELUS SILESIUS (*trans* J M Cohen)
From The Cherubic Wanderer

Let go and you snare God. But letting God go too
Is more than any but the rarest man can do.

Sin is no more than this: that a man turns his head
away from God, and looks towards death instead.

ANGELUS SILESIUS (*trans* anon)
The Known Must Be the Knower

In God nought e'er is known.
Forever one is He.
What we in Him e'er know
Ourselves must grow and be.

ANGELUS SILESIUS (*trans* J M Cohen)
From The Cherubic Wanderer

Friend, you have read enough. If you desire still more,
Then be the poem yourself, and all that it stands for.

PART 4:
Sixteenth Century

MĪRĀBĀĪ (*trans* A J Alston)
From Devotional Poems of Mīrābāī

190

Strange are the decrees of fate.
Behold the large eyes of the deer!
Yet he is forced to roam the forests.
The harsh crane has brilliant plumage.
While the sweet-voiced cuckoo is black.
The rivers flow in pure streams,
But the sea makes them salt.
Fools sit on thrones as kings.
While the wise beg their bread.
Mīrā's Lord is the courtly Giridhara:
The King persecutes the Bhaktas.

191

Do not mention the name of love,
O my simple-minded companion.
Strange is the path
When you offer your love.
Your body is crushed at the first step.
If you want to offer love
Be prepared to cut off your head
And sit on it.
Be like the moth,
Which circles the lamp and offers its body.
Be like the deer, which, on hearing the horn.
Offers its head to the hunter.
Be like the partridge,
Which swallows burning coals
In love of the moon.
Be like the fish,
Which yields up its life
When separated from the sea.
Be like the bee,
Entrapped in the closing petals of the lotus.
Mīrā's Lord is the courtly Giridhara
She says: Offer your mind
To those lotus feet.

192

Only he knows the bitterness of love
Who has deeply felt its pangs.
When you are in trouble
No one comes near you:
When fortune smiles.
All come to share the joy.
Love shows no external wound,
But the pain pervades every pore
Devotee Mīrā offers her body
As a sacrifice to Giridhara for ever.

193

Go to that impenetrable realm
That Death himself trembles to look upon.
There plays the fountain of love
With swans sporting on its waters.
There the company of holy men is available,
And one may talk of spiritual knowledge.
There one can meditate on Shyām
And purify one's mind.
There one may bind on
The anklets of good-conduct,
And dance the dance of inner contentment.
There one may adopt a headpiece of gold
And the sixteen kinds of adornment.
Let there be love for Shyām
And indifference to all else.

194

That dark Dweller in Braj
Is my only refuge.
O my companion,
Worldly comfort is an illusion,
As soon you get it, it goes.
I have chosen the Indestructible for my refuge.
Him whom the snake of death
Will not devour.
My Beloved dwells in my heart,
I have actually seen that Abode of Joy.
Mīrā's Lord is Hari, the Indestructible.
My Lord, I have taken refuge with Thee,
Thy slave.

195

O my mind,
Worship the lotus feet of the Indestructible One!
Whatever thou seest twixt earth and sky
Will perish.
Why undertake fasts and pilgrimages?
Why engage in philosophical discussions?
Why commit suicide in Banāras?
Take no pride in the body,
It will soon be mingling with the dust.
This life is like the sporting of sparrows.
It will end with the onset of night.
Why don the ochre robe
And leave home as a sannyāsī?
Those who adopt the external garb of a Jogī,
But do not penetrate to the secret,
Are caught again in the net of rebirth.
Mīrā's Lord is the courtly Giridhara.
Deign to sever, O Master,
All the knots in her heart.

196

We do not get a human life
Just for the asking.
Birth in a human body
Is the reward for good deeds
In former births.
Life waxes and wanes imperceptibly,
It does not stay long.
The leaf that has once fallen
Does not return to the branch.
Behold the Ocean of Transmigration,
With its swift, irresistible tide.
O Lāl Giridhara, O pilot of my soul,
Swiftly conduct my barque to the further shore.
Mīrā is the slave of Lāl Giridhara.
She says: Life lasts but a few days only.

197

Life in the world is short,
Why shoulder an unnecessary load
Of Worldly relationships?
Thy parents gave thee birth in the world,
But the Lord ordained thy fate.
Life passes in getting and spending,
No merit is earned by virtuous deeds.
I will sing the praises of Hari
In the company of holy men,
Nothing else concerns me.
Mīrā's Lord is the courtly Giridhara,
She says: Only by Thy power
Have I crossed to the further shore.

198

Do not forget thy duty to serve,
O servant.
The joys are of short duration.

SIR THOMAS WYATT

Rondeau

Help me to seek, for I lost it there,
And if that ye have found it, ye that be here,
And seek to convey it secretly,
Handle it soft and treat it tenderly,
Or else it will plain and then appear:

But rather restore it mannerly,
Since that I do ask it thus honestly:
For to lose it, it sitteth me too near.
   Help me to seek.

Alas, and is there no remedy?
But have I thus lost it wilfully?
I wish it was a thing all too dear
To be bestowed and wist not where:
It was my heart, I pray you heartily
   Help me to seek.

EDMUND SPENSER

From An Hymn of Heavenly Love

Before this world's great frame, in which all things
Are now contained, found any being place
Ere flitting Time could wag his eyas wings
About that mighty bound, which doth embrace
The rolling spheres, and parts their hours by space,
That high eternal power, which now doth move
In all these things, moved in itself by love.

It loved itself, because itself was fair
(For fair is loved); and of itself begot
Like to itself his eldest son and heir,
Eternal, pure, and void of sinful blot,
The firstling of his joy, in whom no jot
Of love's dislike, or pride was to be found,
Whom he therefore with equal honour crowned.

EDMUND SPENSER

Guardian Angels

From The Faerie Queene II, VIII

And is there care in heaven? and is there love
  In heavenly spirits to these creatures base,
That may compassion of their evils move?
  There is: else much more wretched were the case
  Of men, than beasts. But, O! th' exceeding grace
Of highest God, that loves his creatures so,
  And all his works with mercy doth embrace,
That blessed angels he sends to and fro,
To serve to wicked man, to serve his wicked foe.

How oft do they their silver bowers leave,
  To come to succour us, that succour want?
How oft do they with golden pinions cleave
  The flitting skies, like flying pursuivant,
  Against foul fiends to aid us militant?
They for us fight, they watch and duly ward,
  And their bright squadrons round about us plant,
And all for love, and nothing for reward:
O! why should heavenly God to men have such regard?

SIR PHILIP SIDNEY

The Bargain

My true loue hath my hart, and I haue his,
By iust exchange, one for another giu'ne.
I hold his deare, and myne he cannot misse:
There neuer was a better bargaine driu'ne.

His hart in me, keepes me and him in one,
My hart in him, his thoughts and senses guides:
He loues my hart, for once it was his owne:
I cherish his because in me it bides.

His hart his wound receiued from my sight:
My hart was wounded, with his wounded hart,
For as from me, on him his hurt did light,
So still me thought in me his hurt did smart:
    Both equall hurt, in this change sought our blisse:
    My true loue hath my hart and I haue his.

SIR PHILIP SIDNEY

My Sheep Are Thoughts

My sheep are thoughts, which I both guide and serve:
Their pasture is fair hills of fruitless love.
On barren sweets they feed, and feeding sterve.
I wail their lot but will not other prove;
My sheephook is wanhope, which all upholds;
My weeds desire, cut out in endless folds;
What wool my sheep shall bear, whiles thus they live,
In you it is, you must the judgment give.

SIR PHILIP SIDNEY

Splendidis Longum Valedico Nugis

Leave me, O Love, which reaches but to dust;
    And thou, my mind, aspire to higher things;
Grow rich in that which never taketh rust;
    Whatever fades but fading pleasure brings.

Draw in thy beams, and humble all thy might
    To that sweet yoke where lasting freedoms be;
Which breaks the clouds and opens forth the light,
    That doth both shine and give us sight to see.
O take fast hold; let that light be thy guide
    In this small course which birth draws out to death,
And think how evil becometh him to slide,
    Who seeketh heaven, and comes of heavenly breath.
        Then farewell, world; thy uttermost I see;
        Eternal Love, maintain thy life in me.

SIR PHILIP SIDNEY

Why Fear to Die?

Since Nature's works be good, and death doth serve
As Nature's work, why should we fear to die?
Since fear is vain but when it may preserve,
Why should we fear that which we cannot fly?
Fear is more pain than is the pain it fears,
Disarming human minds of native might;
While each conceit an ougly figure bears,
Which were not evil, well view'd in reason's light
Our only eyes, which dimm'd with passions be,
And scarce discern the dawn of coming day,
Let them be clear'd, and now begin to see
Our life is but a step in dusty way:
Then let us hold the bliss of peaceful mind,
Since this we feel, great loss we cannot find.

SIR PHILIP SIDNEY

From Astrophel and Stella

XLVIII

Soul's joy, bend not those morning stars from me
Where Virtue is made strong by Beauty's might:
Where Love is chasteness Pain doth learn delight,
And Humbleness grows one with Majesty.
Whatever may ensue, O let me be
Co-partner of the riches of that sight.
Let not mine eyes be hell-driv'n from that light:
O look, O shine, O let me die, and see.
For though I oft myself of them bemoan
That through my heart their beamy darts be gone

Whose cureless wounds even now most freshly bleed,
Yet since my death-wound is already got,
Dear killer, spare not thy sweet-cruel shot:
A kind of grace it is to slay with speed.

SIR WALTER RALEIGH

What Is Our Life?

What is our life? A play of passion.
And what our mirth but music of division?
Our mother's wombs the tiring-houses be
Where we are drest for this short comedy.
Heaven the judicious sharp spectator is
Who sits and marks what here we do amiss.
The graves that hide us from the searching sun
Are like drawn curtains when the play is done.
Thus playing post we to our latest rest,
And then we die, in earnest, not in jest.

SIR WALTER RALEIGH

The Pilgrimage

Give me my scallop-shell of quiet,
My staff of faith to walk upon,
My scrip of joy, immortal diet,
My bottle of salvation,
My gown of glory, hope's true gage;
And thus I'll take my pilgrimage.

Blood must be my body's balmer;
No other balm will there be given;
Whilst my soul, like a white palmer,
Travels to the land of heaven;
Over the silver mountains,
Where spring the nectar fountains:
　　There will I kiss
　　The bowl of bliss;
And drink mine everlasting fill
On every milken hill.
My soul will be a-dry before;
But, after, it will thirst no more.

Then by that happy blissful day,
More peaceful pilgrims I shall see,
That have cast off their rags of clay,
And walk apparelled fresh like me.
   I'll take them first
   To quench their thirst
And taste of nectar suckets,
   At those clear wells
   Where sweetness dwells,
Drawn up by saints in crystal buckets.

And when our bottles and all we
Are filled with immortality,
Then the blessed paths we'll travel,
Strowed with rubies thick as gravel;
Ceilings of diamonds, sapphire floors,
High walls of coral and pearly bowers.
From thence to heaven's bribeless hall,
Where no corrupted voices brawl;
No conscience molten into gold,
No forged accuser bought or sold,
No cause deferred, no vain-spent journey,
For there Christ is the King's Attorney,
Who pleads for all without degrees,
And He hath angles, but no fees.
And when the grand twelve-million jury
Of our sins, with direful fury,
Against our souls black verdicts give,
Christ pleads His death, and then we live.

Be Thou my speaker, taintless pleader,
Unblotted lawyer, true proceeder!
Thou givest salvation even for alms;
Not with a bribèd lawyer's palms.

HENRY CONSTABLE

To God the Father

Great God, within whose simple essence we
Nothing but that which is thyself can find;
When on thyself thou didst reflect thy mind,
Thy thought was God, and took the form of thee:
And when this God, thus born, thou lov'st, and he

Loved thee again, with passion of like kind
(As lovers' sighs which meet become one wind),
Both breathed one sprite of equal deity.
Eternal Father, whence these two do come
And wilt the title of my father have,
And heavenly knowledge in my mind engrave,
That it thy son's true Image may become:
    And cleanse my heart with sighs of holy love,
    That it the temple of the Sprite may prove.

WILLIAM SHAKESPEARE

Sonnet 146

Poor soul, the centre of my sinful earth,
Fooled by these rebel powers that thee array,
Why dost thou pine within and suffer dearth,
Painting thy outward walls so costly gay?
Why so large cost, having so short a lease,
Dost thou upon thy fading mansion spend?
Shall worms, inheritors of this excess,
Eat up thy charge? Is this thy body's end?
Then, soul, live thou upon thy servant's loss,
And let that pine to aggravate thy store;
Buy terms divine in selling hours of dross;
Within be fed, without be rich no more:
    So shalt thou feed on Death, that feeds on men,
    And Death once dead, there's no more dying then.

WILLIAM SHAKESPEARE

From The Tempest

Act V

PROSPERO: Ye elves of hills, brooks, standing lakes,
    and groves;
  And ye that on the sands with printless foot
  Do chase the ebbing Neptune, and do fly him
  When he comes back; you demi-puppets that
  By moonshine do the green sour ringlets make,
  Whereof the ewe not bites; and you whose pastime
  Is to make midnight mushrooms, that rejoice
  To hear the solemn curfew; by whose aid –
  Weak masters though ye be – I have bedimm'd
  The noontide sun, call'd forth the mutinous winds,

And 'twixt the green sea and the azured vault
Set roaring war: to the dread rattling thunder
Have I given fire, and rifted Jove's stout oak
With his own bolt: the strong-based promontory
Have I made shake: and by the spurs pluck'd up
The pine and cedar: graves, at my command,
Have waked their sleepers, oped, and let them forth
By my so potent art. But this rough magic
I here abjure: and, when I have required
Some heavenly music – which even now I do –
To work mine end upon their senses, that
This airy charm is for, I'll break my staff,
Bury it certain fathoms in the earth,
And deeper than did ever plummet sound
I'll drown my book.

WILLIAM SHAKESPEARE

From Hamlet

Act IV, Scene 1

POLONIUS: And these few precepts in thy memory
  See thou character. Give thy thoughts no tongue,
  Nor any unproportion'd thought his act.
  Be thou familiar, but by no means vulgar.
  The friends thou hast, and their adoption tried,
  Grapple them to thy soul with hoops of steel;
  But do not dull thy palm with entertainment
  Of each new-hatch'd, unfledg'd comrade. Beware
  Of entrance to a quarrel; but, being in,
  Bear't that the opposed may beware of thee.
  Give every man thine ear, but few thy voice:
  Take each man's censure, but reserve thy judgment.
  Costly thy habit as thy purse can buy,
  But not express'd in fancy; rich, not gaudy:
  For the apparel oft proclaims the man;
  And they in France of the best rank and station
  Are most select and generous chief in that.
  Neither a borrower nor a lender be:
  For a loan oft loses both itself and friend;
  And borrowing dulls the edge of husbandry.
  This above all – to thine own self be true;
  And it must follow, as the night the day,
  Thou canst not then be false to any man.
  Farewell: my blessing season this in thee!

WILLIAM SHAKESPEARE

From The Merchant of Venice

Act IV, Scene 1

PORTIA: The quality of mercy is not strain'd, –
It droppeth as the gentle rain from heaven
Upon the place beneath: it is twice blest, –
It blesseth him that gives, and him that takes:
'Tis mightiest in the mightiest: it becomes
The throned monarch better than his crown;
His sceptre shows the force of temporal power,
The attribute to awe and majesty,
Wherein doth sit the dread and fear of kings;
But mercy is above this sceptred sway, –
It is enthroned in the hearts of kings,
It is an attribute to God himself;
And earthly power doth then show likest God's
When mercy seasons justice.

Act V, Scene 1

LORENZO: How sweet the moonlight sleeps upon this bank!
Here will we sit, and let the sounds of music
Creep in our ears. Soft stillness and the night
Become the touches of sweet harmony.
Sit, Jessica. Look how the floor of heaven
Is thick inlaid with patens of bright gold.
There's not the smallest orb which thou behold'st
But in his motion like an angel sings,
Still quiring to the young-eyed cherubins:
Such harmony is in immortal souls;
But whilst this muddy vesture of decay
Doth grossly close it in, we cannot hear it.

WILLIAM ALABASTER

To Be Born is God's Greatest Gift

Like as the fountain of all light created
    Doth pour out streams of brightness undefined
    Through all the conduits of transparent kind,
That heaven and air are both illuminated,
And yet his light is not thereby abated;
    So God's eternal bounty ever shined
    The beams of being, moving, life, sense, mind,

And to all things himself communicated
But for the violent diffusive pleasure
   Of goodness, that left not till God had spent
Himself, by giving us himself his treasure
   In making man a God omnipotent.
How might this goodness draw ourselves above
Which drew down God with such attractive love!

SIR JOHN DAVIES

Why the Soul is United to the Body

From *Nosce Teipsum*

This substance, and this spirit of God's own making,
Is in the body placed, and planted here:
'That both of God, and of the world partaking,
Of all that is, Man might the image bear.'

God first made angels bodiless pure minds,
Then other things, which mindless bodies be;
Last, He made Man, the horizon 'twixt both kinds,
In whom we do the World's abridgement see.

Besides, this World below did need one wight
Which might thereof distinguish every part,
Make use thereof, and take therein delight,
And order things with industry and art:

Which also God might in His works admire,
And here, beneath, yield Him both prayer and praise,
As there, above, the holy angels' quire
Doth spread His glory with spiritual lays.

Lastly, the brute unreasonable wights
Did want a visible king on them to reign:
And God Himself thus to the World unites,
That so the World might endless bliss obtain.

SIR JOHN DAVIES

In What Manner the Soul is United to the Body

From *Nosce Teipsum*

But how shall we this union well express?
Naught ties the Soul: her subtilty is such,
She moves the Body, which she doth possess,
Yet no part toucheth but by Virtue's touch.

Then dwells she not therein as in a tent,
Nor as a pilot in his ship doth sit,
Nor as the spider in her web is pent,
Nor as the wax retains the print in it,

Nor as a vessel water doth contain,
Nor as one liquor in another shed,
Nor as the heat doth in the fire remain,
Nor as a voice throughout the air is spread:

But as the fair and cheerful morning light
Doth here and there her silver beams impart,
And in an instant doth herself unite
To the transparent air, in all and part:

Still resting whole when blows the air divide,
Abiding pure when the air is most corrupted,
Throughout the air, her beams dispersing wide,
And when the air is tost, not interrupted:

So doth the piercing Soul the body fill,
Being all in all, and all in part diffused;
Indivisible, incorruptible still,
Not forced, encountered, troubled, or confused.

And as the sun above the light doth bring,
Though we behold it in the air below,
So from the Eternal Light the Soul doth spring,
Though in the body she her powers do show.

SIR JOHN DAVIES

The Power of Sense

From *Nosce Teipsum*

This power is Sense, which from abroad doth bring
The colour, taste, and touch, and scent, and sound,
The quantity and shape of every thing
Within the Earth's centre or Heaven's circle found.

This power, in parts made fit, fit objects takes,
Yet not the things but forms of things receives;
As when a seal in wax impression makes,
The print therein, but not itself, it leaves.

And, though things sensible be numberless,
But only five the Sense's organs be,
And in those five all things their forms express
Which we can touch, taste, feel, or hear, or see.

These are the windows through the which she views
The light of knowledge, which is life's loadstar:
'And yet while she these spectacles doth use,
Oft worldly things seem greater than they are.'

JOHN DONNE

Good Friday, 1613: Riding Westward

Let mans' Soule be a Spheare, and then, in this,
The intelligence that moves, devotion is,
And as the other Spheares, by being growne
Subject to forraigne motions, lose their owne,
And being by others hurried every day,
Scarce in a yeare their naturall forme obey:
Pleasure or businesse, so, our Soules admit
For their first mover, and are whirld by it.
Hence is't, that I am carryed towards the West
This day, when my Soules forme bends toward the East.
There I should see a Sunne, by rising set,
And by that setting endlesse day beget;
But that Christ on this Crosse, did rise and fall,
Sinne had eternally benighted all.
Yet dare I'almost be glad, I do not see
That spectacle of too much weight for mee.
Who sees God's face, that is selfe life, must dye;

What a death were it then to see God dye?
It made his owne Lieutenant Nature shrinke,
It made his footstoole crack, and the Sunne winke.
Could I behold those hands which span the Poles,
And turne all spheares at once, peirc'd with those holes?
Could I behold that endlesse height which is
Zenith to us, and our Antipodes,
Humbled below us? or that blood which is
The seat of all our Soules, if not of his,
Made durt of dust, or that flesh which was worne
By God, for his apparell, rag'd, and torne?
If on these things I durst not looke, durst I
Upon his miserable mother cast mine eye,
Who was God's partner here, and furnish'd thus
Halfe of that Sacrifice, which ransom'd us?
Though these things, as I ride, be from mine eye,
They're present yet unto my memory,
For that looks towards them; and thou look'st towards mee,
O Saviour, as thou hang'st upon the tree;
I turne my backe to thee, but to receive
Corrections, till thy mercies bid thee leave.
O thinke mee worth thine anger, punish mee,
Burne off my rusts, and my deformity,
Restore thine Image, so much, by thy grace,
That thou may'st know mee, and I'll turne my face.

JOHN DONNE

From Holy Sonnets: Divine Meditations

II

As due by many titles I resigne
My selfe to thee, O God, first I was made
By thee, and for thee, and when I was decay'd
Thy blood bought that, the which before was thine,
I am thy sonne, made with thy selfe to shine,
Thy servant, whose paines thou hast still repaid,
Thy sheepe, thine Image, and till I betray'd
My selfe, a temple of thy Spirit divine;
Why doth the devill then usurpe in mee?
Why doth he steale, nay ravish that's thy right?
Except thou rise and for thine owne worke fight,
Oh I shall soone despaire, when I doe see
That thou lov'st mankind well, yet wilt not chuse me.
And Satan hates mee, yet is loth to lose mee.

JOHN DONNE

Resurrection, imperfect

Sleep sleep old Sun, thou canst not have repast
As yet, the wound thou took'st on friday last;
Sleepe then, and rest; The world may beare thy stay,
A better Sun rose before thee to day,
Who, not content to enlighten all that dwell
On the earth's face, as thou, enlightened hell,
And made the darke fires languish in that vale,
As, at thy presence here, our fires grow pale.
Whose body having walk'd on earth, and now
Hasting to Heaven, would, that he might allow
Himselfe unto all stations, and fill all,
For these three daies become a minerall;
Hee was all gold when he lay downe, but rose
All tincture, and doth not alone dispose
Leaden and iron wills to good, but is
Of power to make even sinfull flesh like his.
Had one of those, whose credulous pietie
Thought, that a Soule one might discerne and see
Goe from a body, at this sepulcher been,
And, issuing from the sheet, this body seen,
He would have justly thought this body a soule,
If not of any man, yet of the whole.

JOHN DONNE

Aire and Angels

Twice or thrice had I loved thee,
Before I knew thy face or name;
So in a voice, so in a shapelesse flame,
Angells affect us oft, and worship'd bee;
    Still when, to where thou wert, I came,
Some lovely glorious nothing I did see.
    But since my soule, whose child love is,
Takes limmes of flesh, and else could nothing doe,
    More subtile than the parent is,
Love must not be, but take a body too,
    And therefore what thou wert, and who,
    I bid Love aske, and now
That it assume thy body, I allow,

And fixe it selfe in thy lip, eye, and brow.
Whilst thus to ballast love, I thought,
And so more steddily to have gone,
With wares which would sinke admiration,
I saw, I had loves pinnace overfraught,
   Ev'ry thy haire for love to worke upon
Is much too much, some fitter must be sought;
   For, nor in nothing, nor in things
Extreme, and scatt'ring bright, can love inhere.

JOHN DONNE

Loves Growth

I scarce beleeve my love to be so pure
   As I had thought it was,
   Because it doth endure
Vicissitude, and season, as the grasse;
Me thinkes I lyed all winter, when I swore,
My love was infinite, if spring make it more.
But if this medicine, love, which cures all sorrow
With more, not onely bee no quintessence,
But mixt of all stuffes, paining soule, or sense,
And of the Sunne his working vigour borrow,
Love's not so pure, and abstract, as they use
To say, which have no Mistresse but their Muse,
But as all else, being elemented too,
Love sometimes would contemplate, sometimes do.

And yet no greater, but more eminent,
   Love by the spring is growne;
   As, in the firmament,
Starres by the Sunne are not inlarg'd, but showne.
Gentle love deeds, as blossomes on a bough,
From loves awakened root do bud out now.
If, as in water stir'd more circles bee
Produc'd by one, love such additions take,
Those like so many spheares, but one heaven make,
For, they are all concentrique unto thee.
And though each spring doe adde to love new heate,
As princes doe in times of action get
New taxes, and remit them not in peace,
No winter shall abate the springs encrease.

PHINEAS FLETCHER

The Divine Lover

I

Me Lord? can'st thou mispend
One word, misplace one look on me?
Call'st me thy Love, thy Friend?
Can this poor soul the object be
Of these love-glances, those life-kindling eyes?
What? I the Centre of thy arms embraces?
Of all thy labour I the prize?
Love never mocks, Truth never lies.
Oh how I quake: Hope fear, fear hope displaces:
I would, but cannot hope: such wondrous love amazes.

II

See, I am black as night,
See I am darkness: dark as hell.
Lord thou more fair than light;
Heav'ns Sun thy Shadow; can Sunns dwell
With Shades? 'twixt light, and darkness what commerce?
True: thou art darkness, I thy Light: my ray
Thy mists, and hellish foggs shall pierce.
With me, black soul, with me converse.
I make the foul *December* flowry *May*,
Turn thou thy night to me: I'le turn thy night to day.

III

See Lord, see I am dead:
Tomb'd in my self: my self my grave
A drudge: so born, so bred:
My self even to my self a slave.
Thou Freedome, Life: can Life, and Liberty
Love bondage, death? Thy Freedom I: I tyed
To loose thy bonds; be bound to me:
My Yoke shall ease, my bonds shall free.
Dead soul, thy Spring of life, my dying side:
There dye with me to live: to live in thee I dyed.

PHINEAS FLETCHER

An Hymn

Wake, O my soul; awake, and raise
Up every part to sing his praise,
Who from his sphere of glory fell
To raise thee up from death and hell:
See how his soul, vexed for thy sin,
Weeps blood without, feels hell within:
    See where he hangs;
        Hark how he cries:
    Oh bitter pangs!
        Now, now he dies.

Wake, O mine eyes; awake, and view
Those two twin-lights, whence heavens drew
Their glorious beams, whose gracious sight
Fills you with joy, with life, and light:
See how with clouds of sorrow drowned
They wash with tears thy sinful wound;
    See how with streams
        Of spit they're drenched;
    See how their beams
        With death are quenched.

Wake, O mine ear; awake, and hear
That powerful voice, which stills thy fear,
And brings from heaven those joyful news,
Which heaven commands, which hell subdues;

Hark how his ears (heaven's mercy-seat)
Foul slanders with reproaches beat:
    Hark how the knocks
        Our ears resound;
    Hark how their mocks
        His hearing wound.

Wake O my heart, tune every string;
Wake O my tongue, awake, and sing:
Think not a thought in all thy lays,
Speak not a word but of his praise.
Tell how his sweetest tongue they drowned

With gall; think how his heart they wound:
    That bloody spout
      Gagged for thy sin,
    His life lets out,
      Thy death lets in.

PHINEAS FLETCHER

Ocean of Light

Vast ocean of light, whose rays surround
The universe, who knowst nor ebb nor shore,
Who lendst the sun his sparkling drop, to store
With overflowing beams heaven, air, ground;
Whose depths beneath the centre none can sound,
Whose heights 'bove heav'n, and thoughts so lofty soar,

Whose breadth no feet, no lines, no chains, no eyes survey,
    Whose length no thoughts can reach, no worlds can bound,
    What cloud can mask thy face? Where can thy ray
Find an eclipse? What night can hide eternal day?

    Our seas (a drop of thine) with arms dispread
    Through all the Earth make drunk the thirsty plains;
    Our sun (a spark of thine) dark shadows drains,
    Gilds all the world, paints Earth, revives the dead;
    Seas (through earth pipes distilled) in cisterns shed,
    And power their liver springs in river veins.
The sun peeps through jet clouds, and when his face and gleams
    Are masked, his eyes their light through airs spread,
    Shall dullard Earth bury life-giving streams?
Earth's fogs impound heaven's light? Hell quench
    heaven-kindling beams?

    How miss I then? In bed I sought by night,
    But found not him in rest, nor rest without him.
    I sought in towns, in broadest streets I sought him,
    But found not him where all are lost. Dull sight,
    Thou canst not see him in himself: his light
    Is masked in light; brightness his cloud about him.
Where, when, how he'll be found, there, then, thus seek thy love:
    Thy lamb in flocks, thy food with appetite,
    Thy rest on resting days, thy turtle dove
Seek on his cross: there, then, thus love stands nailed with love.

PHINEAS FLETCHER

From The Purple Island

And at the foot of this celestial frame
Two radiant stars, than stars yet better being,
Endued with living fire and seeing flame,
Yet with heaven's stars in this too near agreeing:
    They timely warmth, themselves not warm, inspire;
    These kindle thousand hearts with hot desire,
And burning all they see, feel in themselves no fire.

Yet matchless stars (yet each the other's match),
Heav'n's richest diamonds set on amel white,
From whose bright spheres all grace the Graces catch,
And will not move but by your lodestars bright,
    How have you stolen and stored your armoury
    With love's and death's strong shafts, and from your sky
Pour down thick showers of darts to force whole armies fly?

Above those suns two rainbows high aspire,
Not in light shows but sadder liveries dressed:
Fair Iris seemed to mourn in sable tire.
Yet thus more sweet the greedy eye they feast,
    And but that wondrous face it well allowed,
    Wondrous it seemed that two fair rainbows showed
Above their sparkling suns, without or rain or cloud.

A bed of lilies flower upon her cheek,
And in the midst was set a circling rose,
Whose sweet aspect would force Narcissus seek
New liveries, and fresher colours choose
    To deck his beauteous head in snowy tire;
    But all in vain: for who can hope to aspire
To such a fair, which none attain but all admire?

Her ruby lips lock up from gazing sight
A troop of pearls which march in goodly row,
But when she deigns those precious bones undight,
Soon heavenly notes from those divisions flow,
    And with rare music charm the ravished ears;
    Daunting bold thoughts, but cheering modest fears:
The spheres so only sing, so only charm the spheres.

Her dainty breasts, like to an April rose
From green silk fillets yet not all unbound,
Began their little rising heads disclose,
And fairly spread their silver circlets round;
   From those two bulwarks love doth safely fight,
   Which swelling easily, may seem to sight
To be enwombèd both of pleasure and delight.

Yet all these stars which deck this beauteous sky,
By force of the inward sun both shine and move:
Thronged in her heart sits love's high majesty;
In highest majesty the highest love.
   As when a taper shines in glassy frame,
   The sparkling crystal burns in glittering flame:
So does that brightest love brighten this lovely dame.

FRANCIS QUARLES

Emblem III, vii: Wherefore Hidest Thou Thy Face, and Holdest Me for Thine Enemy?

Why dost thou shade thy lovely face? Oh why
Does that eclipsing hand so long deny
The sunshine of thy soul-enlivening eye?

Without that light, what light remains in me?
Thou art my life, my way, my light; in thee
I live, I move, and by thy beams I see.

Thou art my life: if thou but turn away,
My life's a thousand deaths; thou art my way:
Without thee, Lord, I travel not, but stray.

My light thou art: without thy glorious sight,
My eyes are darkened with perpetual night.
My God, thou art my way, my life, my light.

Thou art my way: I wander, if thou fly;
Thou art my light: if hid, how blind am I!
Thou art my life: if thou withdraw, I die.

My eyes are blind and dark, I cannot see;
To whom, or whither, should my darkness flee,
But to the light? and who's that light but thee?

My path is lost, my wandering steps do stray;
I cannot safely go, nor safely stay;
Whom should I seek but thee, my path, my way?

Oh, I am dead: to whom shall I, poor I,
Repair? To whom shall my sad ashes fly,
But life? And where is life but in thine eye?

And yet thou turnst away thy face, and fly'st me;
And yet I sue for grace, and thou deny'st me;
Speak, art thou angry, Lord, or only try'st me?

Unscreen those heavenly lamps, or tell me why
Thou shad'st thy face. Perhaps thou thinkst no eye
Can view those flames, and not drop down and die.

If that be all, shine forth, and draw thee nigher;
Let me behold and die; for my desire
Is, phoenix-like, to perish in that fire.

Death-conquered Laz'rus was redeemed by thee;
If I am dead, Lord, set death's prisoner free;
Am I more spent, or stink I worse than he?

If my puffed life be out, give leave to tine
My shameless snuff at that bright lamp of thine;
Oh, what's thy light the less for lighting mine?

If I have lost my path, great shepherd, say,
Shall I still wander in a doubtful way?
Lord, shall a lamb of Israel's sheepfold stray?

Thou art the pilgrim's path, the blind man's eye,
The dead man's life: on thee my hopes rely;
If thou remove, I err, I grope, I die.

Disclose thy sunbeams; close thy wings and stay;
See, see how I am blind and dead, and stray,
O thou that art my light, my life, my way.

Epigram

If heaven's all-quickening eyes vouchsafe to shine
Upon our souls, we slight; if not, we whine:
Our equinoctial hearts can never lie
Secure beneath the tropics of that eye.

FRANCIS QUARLES

Emblem IV: I Am My Beloved's, and His Desire Is Towards Me

Like to the arctic needle, that doth guide
   The wandering shade by his magnetic power,
And leaves his silken gnomon to decide
   The question of the controverted hour,
First frantics up and down from side to side,
    And restless beats his crystall'd ivory case
    With vain impatience; jets from place to place,
And seeks the bosom of his frozen bride;
    At length he slacks his motion, and doth rest
His trembling point at his bright pole's beloved breast.

Even so my soul, being hurried here and there,
   By every object that presents delight,
Fain would be settled, but she knows not where;
   She likes at morning what she loathes at night:
She bows to honour, then she lends an ear
    To that sweet swan-like voice of dying pleasure,
    Then tumbles in the scatter'd heaps of treasure;
Now flatter'd with false hope, now foil'd with fear:
    Thus finding all the world's delight to be
But empty toys, good God, she points alone to thee.

But hath the virtued steel a power to move?
   Or can the untouch'd needle point aright?
Or can my wandering thoughts forbear to rove,
   Unguided by the virtue of thy sprite?
Oh hath my laden soul the art to improve
    Her wasted talent, and, unrais'd, aspire
    In this sad moulting time of her desire?
Not first belov'd, have I the power to love?
    I cannot stir but as thou please to move me,
Nor can my heart return thee love until thou love me.

The still commandress of the silent night
   Borrows her beams from her bright brother's eye;
His fair aspect fills her sharp horns with light,
   If he withdraw, her flames are quench'd and die:
Even so the beams of thy enlightening sprite,
    Infus'd and shot into my dark desire,
    Inflame my thoughts, and fill my soul with fire,

That I am ravish'd with a new delight;
    But if thou shroud thy face, my glory fades,
And I remain a nothing, all compos'd of shades.

Eternal God! O thou that only art,
    The sacred fountain of eternal light,
And blessed loadstone of my better part,
    O thou, my heart's desire, my soul's delight!
Reflect upon my soul, and touch my heart,
    And then my heart shall prize no good above thee;
    And then my soul shall know thee; knowing, love thee;
And then my trembling thoughts shall never start
    From thy commands, or swerve the least degree,
Or once presume to move, but as they move in thee.

GEORGE HERBERT

Clasping of Hands

Lord, Thou art mine, and I am Thine,
If mine I am; and Thine much more
Then I or ought or can be mine.
Yet to be Thine doth me restore,
So that again I now am mine,
And with advantage mine the more,
Since this being mine brings with it Thine,
And Thou with me dost Thee restore:
    If I without Thee would be mine,
    I neither should be mine nor Thine.

Lord, I am Thine, and Thou art mine;
So mine Thou art, that something more
I may presume Thee mine then Thine,
For Thou didst suffer to restore
Not Thee, but me, and to be mine:
And with advantage mine the more,
Since Thou in death wast none of Thine,
Yet then as mine didst me restore:
    O, be mine still; still make me Thine;
    Or rather make no Thine and Mine.

GEORGE HERBERT

Man

My God, I heard this day,
That none doth build a stately habitation,
  But he that means to dwell therein.
  What house more stately hath there been,
Or can be, then is Man? to whose creation
    All things are in decay.

    For Man is ev'ry thing,
And more: He is a tree, yet bears no fruit;
  A beast, yet is, or should be more:
  Reason and speech we onely bring.
Parrats may thank us, if they are not mute,
    They go upon the score.

    Man is all symmetrie,
Full of proportions, one limbe to another,
  And all to all the world besides:
  Each part may call the farthest, brother:
For head with foot hath private amitie,
    And both with moons and tides.

    Nothing hath got so farre,
But Man hath caught and kept it, as his prey.
  His eyes dismount the highest starre:
  He is in little all the sphere.
Herbs gladly cure our flesh; because that they
    Finde their acquaintance there.

    For us the windes do blow,
The earth doth rest, heav'n move, and fountains flow.
  Nothing we see, but means our good,
  As our *delight*, or as our *treasure*:
The whole is, either our cupboard of *food*,
    Or cabinet of *pleasure*.

    The starres have us to bed;
Night draws the curtain, which the sunne withdraws;
  Musick and light attend our head.
  All things unto our *flesh* are kinde
In their *descent* and *being*; to our *minde*
    In their *ascent* and *cause*.

Each thing is full of dutie:
Waters united are our navigation;
  Distinguished, our habitation;
  Below, our drink; above, our meat;
Both are our cleanlinesse. Hath one such beautie?
    Then how are all things neat?

    More servants wait on Man,
Then he'l take notice of: in ev'ry path
  He treads down that which doth befriend him,
  When sicknesse makes him pale and wan.
Oh mightie love! Man is one world, and hath
    Another to attend him.

    Since then, my God, thou hast
So brave a Palace built; O dwell in it,
  That it may dwell with thee at last!
  Till then, afford us so much wit;
That, as the world serves us, we may serve thee,
    And both thy servants be.

GEORGE HERBERT

The Altar

A broken ALTAR, Lord, thy servant reares,
Made of a heart, and cemented with teares:
  Whose parts are as thy hand did frame;
  No workmans tool hath touch'd the same.
            A   HEART   alone
            Is   such   a   stone,
            As   nothing   but
            Thy pow'r doth cut.
            Wherefore each part
            Of my hard heart
            Meets in this frame,
            To praise thy name.
  That if I chance to hold my peace,
  These stones to praise thee may not cease.
O   let   thy   blessed   SACRIFICE   be   mine,
And   sanctifie   this   ALTAR   to   be   thine.

GEORGE HERBERT

Avarice

Money, thou bane of blisse, and source of woe,
    Whence com'st thou, that thou art so fresh and fine?
    I know thy parentage is base and low:
Man found thee poore and dirtie in a mine.

Surely thou didst so little contribute
    To this great kingdome, which thou now hast got,
    That he was fain, when thou wert destitute,
To digge thee out of thy dark cave and grot:

Then forcing thee, by fire he made thee bright:
    Nay, thou hast got the face of man; for we
    Have with our stamp and seal transferr'd our right:
Thou art the man, and man but drosse to thee.

    Man calleth thee his wealth, who made thee rich;
    And while he digs out thee, falls in the ditch.

GEORGE HERBERT

Coloss 3:3 – Our Life is Hid with Christ in God

    My words and thoughts do both expresse this notion,
    That *Life* hath with the sun a double motion.
    The first *Is* straight, and our diurnall friend,
    The other *Hid* and doth obliquely bend.
    One life is wrapt *In* flesh, and tends to earth.
    The other winds towards *Him*, whose happie birth
    Taught me to live here so, *That* still one eye
    Should aim and shoot at that which *Is* on high:
    Quitting with daily labour all *My* pleasure,
    To gain at harvest an eternall *Treasure*.

GEORGE HERBERT

Vanitie (I)

The fleet Astronomer can bore,
And thred the spheres with his quick-piercing minde:
He views their stations, walks from doore to doore,
  Surveys, as if he had design'd
To make a purchase there: he sees their dances,
  And knoweth long before,
Both their full-ey'd aspects, and secret glances.

The Church

The nimble Diver with his side
Cuts through the working waves, that he may fetch
His dearely-earned pearl, which God did hide
  On purpose from the ventrous wretch;
That he might save his life, and also hers,
  Who with excessive pride
Her own destruction and his danger wears.

The subtil Chymick can devest
And strip the creature naked, till he finde
The callow principles within their nest:
  There he imparts to them his minde,
Admitted to their bed-chamber, before
  They appear trim and drest
To ordinarie suitours at the doore.

What hath not man sought out and found,
But his deare God? who yet his glorious law
Embosomes in us, mellowing the ground
  With showres and frosts, with love and aw,
So that we need not say, Where's this command?
  Poore man, thou searchest round
To finde out *death*, but missest *life* at hand.

CHRISTOPHER HARVEY

The Nativity

Unfold thy face, unmaske thy ray,
Shine forth, bright Sunne, double the day.
Let no malignant misty fume,
Nor foggy vapour, once presume
To interpose thy perfect sight
This day, which makes us love thy light
For ever better, that we could
That blessèd object once behold,
Which is both the circumference,
And center of all excellence:
Or rather neither, but a treasure
Unconfinèd without measure,
Whose center and circumference,
Including all preheminence,
Excluding nothing but defect,
And infinite in each respect,
Is equally both here and there,
And now and then and every where,
And alwaies, one, himselfe, the same.
A beeing farre above a name.
Draw neer then, and freely poure
Forth all thy light into that houre,
Which was crownèd with his birth,
And made heaven envy earth.
    Let not his birth-day clouded be,
    By whom thou shinest, and we see.

PART 5:
Seventeenth Century

TUKARAMA (*trans* Nelson Fraser and K B Marathe)

From Poems of Tukarama

28

I live in the world so far as I am required to, but let my faith dwell at your feet. O generous master, what can I do? You have bound me fast; I am trudging along with the load that is set upon me. The body performs its appointed duty; O mind of mine, let not the secret lapse from you. The forces of the world drag me from place to place, but let me never be slothful in contemplation. Let the senses perform their own part; do thou give their fond passion a resting place at your feet. Tukā says, Do not, I entreat thee, hand me over to destruction.

29

I cannot sing or speak with clear utterance; but I have brought body, speech and mind to seek thy protection. O accept me, reject me not, O Hari! O Saviour of the sinful, vindicate thy name! I know nothing of faith or devotion; I call myself thy servant; if you abandon me, who will be disgraced? Tukā's brother says, I have embraced thy feet; now whom else have we but thee?

203

As sweetness pervades sugar, so God pervades my frame; now I will worship him as best I may; God is within and without the soul at once. A ripple is not different from the water it belongs to; gold is still gold, though it be known as an ornament. Tukā says, So are we in him.

204

How can a child's longing fail to be gratified? We who are God's babes trust not to knowledge of Brahma or union with the supreme soul. We will master by experience those words which have been published. Tukā says, This shall be the effort I make in my simplicity, when the last end comes I will show this fond desire.

205

Faith was designed to spread the glory of God; otherwise whence in the nature of things arises a second to speak of? To display his glory the test of worship was designed. Tukā says, The worshipper of God is an ornament to mankind.

206

Without a worshipper, how can God assume a form or accept service? The one makes the other beautiful, as a gold setting shows off a jewel. Who but God can make the worshipper free from desires? Tukā says, They feel to each other like mother and child.

207

What does the lotus flower know of its own perfumes? The bee enjoys it all. Thus thou knowest not thy own name, but we know the happiness of love that proceeds from it. The mother cow eats grass, but the calf enjoys the sweet milk; he enjoys who produces not. Tukā says, The pearl lies in the shell, but the shell cannot see or enjoy it.

208

Liberation belongs to you, O God; keep to yourself that hard acquisition. What I prefer is worship; I will not renounce that delight. According to your powers, take care of that generous master. Tukā says, It is enough if you meet me once in the last end.

209

To repeat your name is to string pearls together; this pleasure in your embodied form is ever new. I have ceased to desire the unembodied God; your worshippers do not seek liberation. With you it is still left possible to give and to receive. What avails the spot where a dish stood, when it is taken away? Tukā says, Give me the gift of freedom from fear; say, O thou that pervadest the world, I have given it thee!

219

Narayana gives and himself enjoys the gift; now what is left to say? Few words remain to speak. Whatever object our eyes behold is our own form dancing before us. Tukā says, Every sound is Govinda.

229

I have renounced all vehicles of sense: I shall not allow any trouble to come near me hereafter. Why should we have to clean our hands? Why should we put obstacles in a practised path? What has God not created for you? Every thing is in its proper place. Tukā says, When our pride disappears, with it goes the relation of I and you.

230

You cannot make cakes without pounding wheat; if you are idle, you will spoil them. Do not be angry if I tell you the secret! The thread-bound pole dances when the conjuror beats the ground with his rod. Tukā says, The secret is in the rod; it puts its skill in every thing.

887

I have no work; see I have nothing more to do! I will go through such movements as present themselves, sitting still like a spectator. Through their needless appetites, mankind of their own will undergo trouble. Tukā has set himself apart; he lives in the world, yet he lives apart from it.

940

One is safe when he calls himself a servant of the saints; a ready and comfortable alms awaits him. It takes toil to form a deep impression; a slight error of principle brings destruction. To cook a meal, there must be materials ready; when these are well arranged, the dinner is pleasant. Tukā says, It is easy to make up tales, as long as the battle-field of impressions presents itself before the eyes.

RALPH KNEVET

The Habitation

Man is no microcosm, and they detract
   From his dimensions who apply
This narrow term to his immensity.
   Heaven, Earth, and hell in him are packed:
He's a miscellany of goods and evils,
A temper mixed with angels, beasts, and devils.

Yea, the immortal Deity doth deign
   To inhabit in a carnal cell:
So precious gems in the dark centre dwell,
   So gloomy mines fine gold retain;
But by vicissitudes these essences
The various heart of man wont to possess.

For God no inn-mate will with Satan be:
   Angels will not consort with beasts.
If man would pursue his best interests,
   What blessed seasons might he see?
But he invites the devil and the beast,
Nor God nor angels will he lodge or feast.

JOHN MILTON

From Samson Agonistes

A little onward lend thy guiding hand
To these dark steps, a little further on;
For yonder bank hath choice of Sun or shade;
There I am wont to sit, when any chance
Relieves me from my task of servile toyl,
Daily in the common Prison else enjoyn'd me,

Where I, a Prisoner chain'd, scarce freely draw
The air imprison'd also, close and damp,
Unwholsom draught: but here I feel amends,
The breath of Heav'n fresh-blowing, pure and sweet,
With day-spring born; here leave me to respire . . .

JOHN MILTON

At a Solemn Music

Blest pair of Sirens, pledges of heaven's joy,
Sphere-born harmonious sisters, Voice and Verse,
Wed your divine sounds, and mixed power employ
Dead things with inbreathed sense able to pierce,
And to our high-raised phantasy present
That undisturbed song of pure concent,
Aye sung before the sapphire-coloured throne
To him that sits thereon,
With saintly shout and solemn jubilee,
Where the bright Seraphim in burning row
Their loud uplifted angel-trumpets blow,
And the Cherubic host in thousand quires
Touch their immortal harps of golden wires,
With those just spirits that wear victorious palms,
Hymns devout and holy psalms
Singing everlastingly;
That we on earth with undiscording voice
May rightly answer that melodious noise;
As once we did, till disproportioned sin
Jarred against Nature's chime, and with harsh din
Broke the fair music that all creatures made
To their great Lord, whose love their motion swayed
In perfect diapason, whilst they stood
In first obedience and their state of good.
O may we soon again renew that song,
And keep in tune with heaven, till God ere long
To his celestial consort us unite,
To live with him, and sing in endless morn of light.

JOHN MILTON

Hymn to Light

From Paradise Lost

Hail holy Light, ofspring of Heav'n first-born,
Or of th'Eternal Coeternal beam
May I express thee unblam'd? since God is Light,
And never but in unapproached Light
Dwelt from Eternitie, dwelt then in thee,
Bright effluence of bright essence increate.
Or hear'st thou rather pure Ethereal stream,
Whose Fountain who shall tell? before the Sun,
Before the Heav'ns thou wert, and at the voice
Of God, as with a Mantle didst invest
The rising world of waters dark and deep,
Won from the void and formless infinite.
Thee I re-visit now with bolder wing,
Escap't the *Stygian* Pool, though long detained
In that obscure sojourn, while in my flight
Through utter and through middle darkness borne
With other notes than to th'*Orphean* Lyre
I sung of *Chaos* and *Eternal Night*.

JOHN MILTON

The Inner Light

From Paradise Lost

He that has light within his own clear breast
May sit i' the centre, and enjoy bright day:
But he that hides a dark soul and foul thoughts
Benighted walks under the midday sun;
Himself is his own dungeon.

SIR WILLIAM DAVENANT

A Present, Upon a New-Year's Day

Go! Hunt the whiter ermine, and present
His wealthy skin, as this day's tribute sent
To my Endymion's love; though she be far
More gently smooth, more soft than ermines are.

Go! Climb that rock; and when thou there hast found
A star, contracted in a diamond,
Give it Endymion's love; whose glorious eyes
Darken the starry jewels of the skies.
Go! Dive into the southern sea; and when
Thou hast found (to trouble the nice sight of men)
A swelling pearl, and such whose single worth
Boasts all the wonders which the seas bring forth,
Give it Endymion's love; whose every tear
Would more enrich the skillful jeweller.

ANNE BRADSTREET

The Flesh and the Spirit

In secret place where once I stood
Close by the Banks of *Lacrim* flood
I heard two sisters reason on
Things that are past, and things to come;
One flesh was call'd, who had her eye
On Worldly wealth and vanity;
The other Spirit, who did rear
Her thoughts unto a higher sphere:
Sister, quoth Flesh, what liv'st thou on
Nothing but Meditation?
Doth Contemplation feed thee so
Regardlessly to let earth goe?
Can Speculation satisfy
Notion without Reality?
Dost dream of things beyond the Moon
And dost thou hope to dwell there soon?
Hast treasures there laid up in store
That all in th' world thou count'st but poor?
Art fancy sick, or turn'd a Sot
To catch at shadowes which are not?
Come, come, Ile shew unto thy sence,
Industry hath its recompence.
What canst desire, but thou maist see
True substance in variety?
Dost honour like? Acquire the same,
As some to their immortal fame:
And trophyes to thy name erect
Which wearing time shall ne'er deject.
For riches dost thou long full sore?
Behold enough of precious store.

Earth hath more silver, pearls and gold,
Than eyes can see, or hands can hold.
Affect's thou pleasure? take thy fill,
Earth hath enough of what you will.
Then let not goe, what thou maist find,
For things unknown, only in mind.
    SPIR: Be still thou unregenerate part,
Disturb no more my setled heart,
For I have vow'd (and so will doe)
Thee as a foe, still to pursue.
And combate with thee will and must,
Untill I see thee laid in th' dust.
Sisters we are, ye[a] twins we be,
Yet deadly feud 'twixt thee and me;
For from one father are we not,
Thou by old Adam wast begot,
But my arise is from above,
Whence my dear Father I do love.
Thou speakst me fair, but hatst me sore,
Thy flatt'ring shews Ile trust no more.
How oft thy slave, hast thou me made,
When I believ'd, what thou hast said,
And never had more cause of woe
Then when I did what thou bad'st doe.
Ile stop mine ears at these thy charms,
And count them for my deadly harms.
Thy sinfull pleasures I doe hate,
Thy riches are to me no bait,
Thine honours doe, nor will I love;
For my ambition lyes above.
My greatest honour it shall be
When I am victor over thee,
And triumph shall, with laurel head,
When thou my Captive shalt be led,
How I do live, thou need'st not scoff,
For I have meat thou know'st not off;
The hidden Manna I doe eat,
The word of life it is my meat.
My thoughts do yield me more content
Then can thy hours in pleasure spent.
Nor are they shadows which I catch,
Nor fancies vain at which I snatch,
But reach at things that are so high,
Beyond thy dull Capacity;
Eternal substance I do see,
With which inriched I would be:

Mine Eye doth pierce the heavens, and see
What is Invisible to thee.
My garments are not silk nor gold,
Nor such like trash which Earth doth hold,
But Royal Robes I shall have on,
More glorious then the glistring Sun;
My Crown not Diamonds, Pearls, and gold,
But such as Angels heads infold.
The City where I hope to dwell,
There's none on Earth can parallel;
The stately Walls both high and strong,
Are made of pretious *Jasper* stone,
The Gates of Pearl, both rich and clear,
And Angels are for Porters there;
The Streets thereof transparent gold,
Such as no Eye did e're behold,
A Chrystal River there doth run,
Which doth proceed from the Lambs Throne.
Of Life, there are the waters sure,
Which shall remain for ever pure,
Nor Sun, nor Moon, they have no need,
For glory doth from God proceed:
No Candle there, nor yet Torch light,
For there shall be no darksome night.
From sickness and infirmity,
For evermore they shall be free,
Nor withering age shall e'er come there,
But beauty shall be bright and clear;
This City pure is not for thee,
For things unclean there shall not be:
If I of Heaven may have my fill,
Take thou the world, and all that will.

ANNE BRADSTREET

From Contemplations

18

When I behold the heavens as in their prime,
And then the earth (though old) stil clad in green,
The stones and trees, insensible of time,
Nor age nor wrinkle on their front are seen;
If winter come, and greeness then do fade,
A Spring returns, and they more youthfull made;
But Man grows old, lies down, remains where once he's laid.

20 [19]

By birth more noble then those creatures all,
Yet seems by nature and by custome curs'd,
No sooner born, but grief and care makes fall
That state obliterate he had at first:
Nor youth, nor strength, nor wisdom spring again
Nor habitations long their names retain,
But in oblivion to the final day remain.

20

Shall I then praise the heavens, the trees, the earth
Because their beauty and their strength last longer
Shall I wish there, or never to had birth,
Because they're bigger, and their bodyes stronger?
Nay, they shall darken, perish, fade and dye,
And when unmade, so ever shall they lye,
But man was made for endless immortality.

RICHARD CRASHAW

A Song

Lord, when the sense of thy sweet grace
Send up my soul to seek thy face.
Thy blessed eyes breed such desire,
I dy in love's delicious Fire.
   O love, I am thy Sacrifice.
Be still triumphant, blessed eyes.
Still shine on me, fair suns! that I
Still may behold, though still I dy.

   Though still I dy, I live again;
Still longing so to be still slain,
So gainfull is such losse of breath.
I dy even in desire of death.
   Still live in me this loving strife
Of living Death and dying Life.
For while thou sweetly slayest me
Dead to my selfe, I live in Thee.

RICHARD CRASHAW

A Hymn

From To the Name Above Every Name

I sing the Name which None can say
But touch't with An interiour Ray:
The Name of our New Peace; our Good:
Our Blisse: and Supernaturall Blood:
The Name of All our Lives and Loves.
Hearken, And Help, ye holy Doves!
The high-born Brood of Day; you bright
Candidates of blissefull Light,
The Heirs Elect of Love; whose Names belong
Unto The everlasting life of Song;
All ye wise Soules, who in the wealthy Brest
Of This unbounded Name build your warm Nest.
Awake, My glory. Soul, (if such thou be,
And That fair Word at all referr to Thee)
    Awake and sing
    And be All Wing;
Bring hither thy whole Self; and let me see
What of thy Parent Heavn yet speakes in thee,
    O thou art Poore
    Of noble Powres, I see,
And full of nothing else but empty Me,
Narrow, and low, and infinitely lesse
Then this Great mornings mighty Busynes.
    One little World or two
    (Alas) will never doe.
    We must have store.
Goe, Soul, out of thy Self, and seek for More.
    Goe and request
Great Nature for the Key of her huge Chest

. . .

Come, lovely Name! Appeare from forth the Bright
    Regions of peacefull Light,
Look from thine own Illustrious Home,
Fair King of Names, and come.
Leave All thy native Glories in their Georgeous Nest,
And give thy Self a while The gracious Guest
Of humble Soules, that seek to find
    The hidden Sweets
    Which man's heart meets

When Thou art Master of the Mind.
Come, lovely Name; life of our hope!
Lo we hold our Hearts wide ope!
Unlock thy Cabinet of Day
Dearest Sweet, and come away.
   Lo how the thirsty Lands
Gasp for thy Golden Showres! with longstretch'd Hands.
   Lo how the laboring Earth
   That hopes to be
   All Heaven by Thee,
   Leapes at thy Birth.
The' attending World, to wait thy Rise,
   First turn'd to eyes;
And then, not knowing what to doe;
Turn'd Them to Teares, and spent Them too.
Come Royall Name, and pay the expence
Of All this Pretious Patience.

                    . . .

   With Curtains drawn,
To catch The Day-break of Thy Dawn.
O dawn, at last, long look't for Day!
Take thine own wings, and come away.
Lo, where Aloft it comes! It comes, Among
The Conduct of Adoring Spirits, that throng
Like diligent Bees, And swarm about it.
   O they are wise;
And know what Sweetes are suck't from out of it.
   It is the Hive,
   By which they thrive,
Where All their Hoard of Hony lyes.
Lo where it comes, upon The snowy Dove's
Soft Back; And brings a Bosom big with Loves.
Welcome to our dark world, Thou
   Womb of Day!
Unfold thy fair Conceptions; And display
The Birth of our Bright Ioyes.

                    . . .

But such alone whose sacred Pedigree
Can prove it Self some kin (sweet name) to Thee.
Sweet Name, in Thy each Syllable
A Thousand Blest Arabias dwell;
A Thousand Hills of Frankincense;

Mountains of myrrh, and Beds of species,
And ten Thousand Paradises,
The soul that tasts thee takes from thence.
How many unknown Worlds there are
Of Comforts, which Thou hast in keeping!
How many Thousand Mercyes there
In Pitty's soft lap ly a sleeping!
Happy he who has the art
   To awake them,
   And to take them
Home, and lodge them in his Heart.

               . . .

Wellcome dear, All-Adored Name!
   For sure there is no Knee
   That knowes not Thee.
Or if there be such sonns of shame,
   Alas what will they doe
   When stubborn Rocks shall bow
And Hills hang down their Heavn-saluting Heads
   To seek for humble Beds
Of Dust, where in the Bashfull shades of night
Next to their own low Nothing they may ly,
And couch before the dazeling light of thy dread majesty.
They that by Love's mild Dictate now
   Will not adore thee,
Shall Then with Just Confusion, bow
   And break before thee.

ANDREW MARVELL

From A Dialogue Between the Resolved Soul and Created Pleasure

Courage my Soul, now learn to wield
The weight of thine immortal Shield.
Close on thy Head thy Helmet bright.
Ballance thy Sword against the Fight.
See where an Army, strong as fair,
With silken Banners spreads the air.
Now, if thou bee'st that thing Divine,
In this day's Combat let it shine:
And shew that Nature wants an Art
To conquer one resolved Heart.

ANDREW MARVELL
On a Drop of Dew

See how the Orient Dew,
Shed from the Bosom of the Morn
   Into the blowing Roses,
Yet careless of its Mansion new,
For the clear Region where 'twas born,
   Round in its self incloses,
   And in its little Globes Extent,
Frames as it can its native Element.
How it the purple flow'r does slight,
   Scarce touching where it lyes,
But gazing back upon the Skies,
   Shines with a mournful Light;
     Like its own Tear,
Because so long divided from the Sphear.
   Restless it roules and unsecure,
     Trembling lest it grow impure:
   Till the warm Sun pitty it's Pain,
And to the Skies exhale it back again.
   So the Soul, that Drop, that Ray
Of the clear Fountain of Eternal Day,
Could it within the humane flow'r be seen,
   Remembring still its former height,
   Shuns the sweet leaves and blossoms green;
   And, recollecting its own Light,
Does, in its pure and circling thoughts, express
The greater Heaven in an Heaven less.
   In how coy a Figure wound,
   Every way it turns away:
   So the World excluding round,
   Yet receiving in the Day.
   Dark beneath, but bright above:
   Here disdaining, there in Love,
   How loose and easie hence to go:
   How girt and ready to ascend.
   Moving but on a point below,
   It all about does upwards bend.
Such did the Manna's sacred Dew destil;
White, and intire, though congeal'd and chill.
Congeal'd on Earth: but does, dissolving, run
Into the Glories of th' Almighty Sun.

HENRY VAUGHAN

The Pursuit

From Silex Scintillans: Silex I (674–682)

Lord! what a busy, restless thing
    Hast thou made man!
Each day and hour he is on wing,
    Rests not a span;
Then having lost the sun and light,
    By clouds surprised
He keeps a commerce in the night
    With air disguised.
Hadst thou given to this active dust
    A state untired,
The lost son had not left the husk
    Nor home desired:
That was thy secret, and it is
    Thy mercy too;
For when all fails to bring to bliss,
    Then, this must do.
Ah! Lord! and what a purchase will that be
To take us sick, that sound would not take thee?

HENRY VAUGHAN

Vanity of Spirit

Quite spent with thoughts I left my cell, and lay
Where a shrill spring tuned to the early day.
    I begged here long, and groaned to know
    Who gave the clouds so brave a bow,
    Who bent the spheres, and circled in
    Corruption with this glorious ring,
    What is his name, and how I might
    Descry some part of his great light.

I summoned nature: pierced through all her store,
Broke up some seals, which none had touched before;
    Her womb, her bosom and her head
    Where all her secrets lay a bed
    I rifled quite; and, having passed
    Through all the creatures, came at last
    To search my self, where I did find
    Traces, and sounds of a strange kind.

Here of this mighty spring, I found some drills,
With echoes beaten from the eternal hills;
  Weak beams and fires flashed to my sight,
  Like a young east, or moon-shine night,
  Which showed me in a nook cast by
  A piece of much antiquity,
  With hieroglyphics quite dismembered,
  And broken letters scarce remembered.

I took them up, and (much joyed) went about
T' unite those pieces, hoping to find out
  The mystery; but this near done,
  That little light I had was gone:
  It grieved me much. 'At last,' said I,
  'Since in these veils my eclipsèd eye
  May not approach thee (for at night
  Who can have commerce with the light?)
  I'll disapparel, and to buy
  But one half glance, most gladly die.'

HENRY VAUGHAN

The Retreat

  Happy those early days! when I
  Shined in my angel-infancy.
  Before I understood this place
  Appointed for my second race,
  Or taught my soul to fancy aught
  But a white, celestial thought;
  When yet I had not walked above
  A mile or two from my first love,
  And looking back (at that short space)
  Could see a glimpse of his bright face;
  When on some gilded cloud or flower
  My gazing soul would dwell an hour,
  And in those weaker glories spy
  Some shadows of eternity;
  Before I taught my tongue to wound
  My conscience with a sinful sound,
  Or had the black art to dispense
  A several sin to every sense,
  But felt through all this fleshly dress
  Bright shoots of everlastingness.
    Oh how I long to travel back

And tread again that ancient track!
That I might once more reach that plain
Where first I left my glorious train,
From whence the enlightened spirit sees
That shady city of palm trees;
But (ah!) my soul with too much stay
Is drunk, and staggers in the way.
Some men a forward motion love,
But I by backward steps would move,
And when this dust falls to the urn
In that state I came return.

HENRY VAUGHAN

The Morning Watch

Oh joys! Infinite sweetness! with what flowers,
And shoots of glory, my soul breaks and buds!
    All the long hours
    Of night and rest,
    Through the still shrouds
    Of sleep and clouds,
  This dew fell on my breast;
    Oh how it bloods
And spirits all my Earth! Hark! in what rings
And hymning circulations the quick world
    Awakes and sings;
    The rising winds
    And falling springs,
    Birds, beasts, all things
  Adore him in their kinds.
    Thus all is hurled

Afforded visits, and still paradise lay
  In some green shade or fountain.
Angels lay ledger here; each bush and cell,
  Each oak and highway knew them:
Walk but the fields, or sit down at some well,
  And he was sure to view them.
Almighty love! where art thou now? Mad man
  Sits down, and freezeth on,
He raves, and swears to stir nor fire nor fan,
  But bids the thread be spun.
I see, thy curtains are close-drawn; thy bow
  Looks dim too in the cloud;

Sin triumphs still, and man is sunk below
   The centre and his shroud;
All's in deep sleep and night; thick darkness lies
   And hatcheth o'er thy people;
But hark! what trumpet's that! what angel cries
   'Arise! Thrust in thy sickle.'

HENRY VAUGHAN

Unprofitableness

How rich, O Lord! how fresh thy visits are!
'Twas but just now my bleak leaves hopeless hung
   Sullied with dust and mud;
Each snarling blast shot through me, and did share
Their youth and beauty, cold showers nipped and wrung
   Their spiciness and blood;
But since thou didst in one sweet glance survey
Their sad decays, I flourish, and once more
   Breathe all perfumes and spice;
I smell a dew like myrrh, and all the day
Wear in my bosom a full sun; such store
   Hath one beam from thy eyes.
But ah, my God! what fruit hast thou of this?
What one poor leaf did ever I yet fall
   To wait upon thy wreath?
Thus thou all day a thankless weed dost dress,
And when th' hast done, a stench or fog is all
   The odour I bequeath.

The fuller whose pure blood did flow
To make stained man more white than snow.
   He alone
  And none else can
  Bring bone to bone
  And rebuild man,
And by his all-subduing might
Make clay ascend more quick than light.

HENRY VAUGHAN

World of Light

They are all gone into the world of light!
   And I alone sit ling'ring here;
Their very memory is fair and bright,
    And my sad thoughts doth clear.

It glows and glitters in my cloudy breast
   Like stars upon some gloomy grove,
Or those faint beams in which this hill is dressed,
    After the sun's remove.

I see them walking in an air of glory,
   Whose light doth trample on my days:
My days, which are at best but dull and hoary,
    Mere glimmering and decays.

O holy hope! and high humility,
   High as the heavens above!
These are your walks, and you have showed them me
    To kindle my cold love.

Dear, beauteous death! the jewel of the just,
   Shining nowhere but in the dark;
What mysteries do lie beyond thy dust,
    Could man outlook that mark?

He that hath found some fledged bird's nest may know
   At first sight, if the bird be flown;
But what fair well or grove he sings in now,
    That is to him unknown.

HENRY VAUGHAN

From Ascension Day

I soar and rise
Up to the skies,
   Leaving the world their day,
And in my flight,
For the true light
   Go seeking all the way.

HENRY VAUGHAN
Preface (1655 edition)
From Silex Scintillans

Vain wits and eyes
Leave, and be wise
Abuse not, shun not holy fire,
But with true tears wash off your mire. Tears and these flames
   will soon grow kind,
And mix an eye-salve for the blind.
Tears cleanse and supple without fail,
And fire will purge your callous veil,
Then comes the light! which when you spy,
And see your nakedness thereby,
Praise Him, Who dealt His gifts so free
In tears to you, in fire to me.

HENRY VAUGHAN
The Star

Whatever 'tis, whose beauty here below
Attracts thee thus and makes thee stream and flow,
   And wind and curl, and wink and smile,
     Shifting thy gait and guile:

Though thy close commerce nought at all imbars
My present search, for eagles eye not stars,
   And still the lesser by the best
     And highest good is blest.

Yet, seeing all things that subsist and be,
Have their commissions from Divinity,
   And teach us duty, I will see
     What man may learn from thee.

First, I am sure, the subject so respected
Is well disposed, for bodies once infected,
   Depraved or dead, can have with thee
     No hold, nor sympathy.

Next, there's in it a restless, pure desire
And longing for thy bright and vital fire,
   Desire that never will be quenched,
      Nor can be writhed, nor wrenched.

These are the magnets, which so strongly move
And work all night upon thy light and love;
   As beauteous shapes, we know not why,
      Command and guide the eye.

For where desire, celestial, pure desire,
Hath taken root, and grows, and doth not tire,
   There God a commerce states, and sheds
      His secret on their heads.

This is the heart he craves; and whoso will
But give it Him, and grudge not, he shall feel
   That God is true; as herbs unseen
      Put on their youth and green.

HENRY VAUGHAN

Peace

My soul, there is a country
   Far beyond the stars,
Where stands a wingèd sentry
   All skilful in the wars,
There above noise and danger
   Sweet peace sits crowned with smiles,
And one born in a manger
   Commands the beauteous files,
He is thy gracious friend,
   And (O my soul awake!)
Did in pure love descend
   To die here for thy sake,
If thou canst get but thither,
   There grows the flower of peace,
The Rose that cannot wither,
   Thy fortress and thy ease;
Leave then thy foolish ranges;
   For none can thee secure,
But one, who never changes,
   Thy God, thy life, thy cure.

HENRY VAUGHAN

From Disorder and Frailty

4

O, yes! but give wings to my fire,
And hatch my soul, until it fly
Up where thou art, amongst thy tire
Of stars, above infirmity;
    Let not perverse
And foolish thoughts add to my bill
  Of forward sins, and kill
    That seed, which thou
    In me didst sow,
But dress and water with thy grace,
Together with the seed, the place;
    And for his sake
    Who died to stake
His life for mine, tune to thy will
    My heart, my verse.

HENRY VAUGHAN

Cheerfulness

Lord, with what courage, and delight
  I do each thing,
When Thy least breath sustains my wing!
  I shine, and move
  Like those above,
  And, with much gladness
  Quitting sadness,
Make me fair days of every night.

JOHN BUNYAN

The Pilgrim Song

Who would true Valour see,
Let him come hither;
One here will Constant be,
Come Wind, come Weather.
There's no Discouragement
Shall make him once Relent
His first avow'd Intent
To be a Pilgrim.

Whoso beset him round
With dismal Stories,
Do but themselves Confound;
His strength the more is.
No Lyon can him fright,
He'll with a Giant fight,
But he will have a right
To be a Pilgrim.

Hobgoblin nor foul fiend
Can daunt his spirit;
He knows he at the end
Shall life inherit.
Then fancies fly away,
He'll fear not what men say,
He'll labour night and day
To be a pilgrim.

THOMAS TRAHERNE

The Rapture

Sweet Infancy!
O Fire of heaven! O sacred Light
How fair and bright,
How great am I,
Whom all the world doth magnify!

O Heavenly Joy!
O great and sacred blessedness
   Which I possess!
   So great a joy
Who did into my arms convey?

   From God above
Being sent, the Heavens me enflame:
   To praise his Name
   The stars do move!
The burning sun doth shew His love.

   O how divine
Am I! To all this sacred wealth,
   This life and health,
   Who raised? Who mine
Did make the same? What hand divine?

THOMAS TRAHERNE

Amendment

That all things should be mine,
This makes His bounty most divine.
But that they all more rich should be,
   And far more brightly shine,
     As used by me;
It ravishes my soul to see the end,
To which this work so wonderful doth tend.

That we should make the skies
  More glorious far before Thine eyes
Than Thou didst make them, and even Thee
   Far more Thy works to prize,
     As used they be
Than as they're made, is a stupendous work,
Wherein Thy wisdom mightily doth lurk.

Thy greatness, and Thy love,
  Thy power, in this, my joy doth move;
Thy goodness, and felicity
   In this exprest above
     All praise I see:
While Thy great Godhead over all doth reign,
And such an end in such a sort attain.

What bound may we assign,
O God, to any work of Thine!
Their endlessness discovers Thee
　　In all to be divine;
　　　　A Deity,
That will for evermore exceed the end
Of all that creature's wit can comprehend.

　　Am I a glorious spring
Of joys and riches to my King?
Are men made Gods? And may they see
　　So wonderful a thing
　　　　As God in me?
And is my soul a mirror that must shine
Even like the sun and be far more divine?

　　Thy Soul, O God, doth prize
The seas, the earth, our souls, the skies;
As we return the same to Thee
　　They more delight Thine eyes,
　　　　And sweeter be
As unto Thee we offer up the same,
Than as to us from Thee at first they came.

　　O how doth Sacred Love
His gifts refine, exalt, improve!
Our love to creatures makes them be
　　In Thine esteem above
　　　　Themselves to Thee!
O here His Goodness evermore admire!
He made our souls to make His creatures higher.

THOMAS TRAHERNE

The Anticipation

My contemplation dazzles in the End
　　Of all I comprehend,
　　And soars above all heights,
Diving into the depths of all delights.
　　Can He become the End,
　　To whom all creatures tend,
Who is the Father of all Infinites?
Then may He benefit receive from things,
And be not Parent only of all springs.

The End doth want the means, and is the cause,
   Whose sake, by Nature's laws,
   Is that for which they are.
Such sands, such dangerous rocks we must beware:
   From all Eternity
   A perfect Deity
Most great and blessed He doth still appear;
His essence perfect was in all its features,
He ever blessed in His joys and creatures.

From everlasting He those joys did need,
   And all those joys proceed
   From Him eternally.
From everlasting His felicity
   Complete and perfect was,
   Whose bosom is the glass,
Wherein we all things everlasting see.
His name is Now, His Nature is For-ever:
None can His creatures from their Maker sever.

The End in Him from everlasting is
   The fountain of all bliss:
   From everlasting it
Efficient was, and influence did emit,
   That caused all. Before
   The world, we do adore
This glorious End. Because all benefit
From it proceeds: both are the very same,
The End and Fountain differ but in Name.

That so the End should be the very Spring
   Of every glorious thing;
   And that which seemeth last,
The fountain and the cause; attained so fast
   That it was first; and mov'd
   The Efficient, who so lov'd
All worlds and made them for the sake of this;
It shews the End complete before, and is
A perfect token of His perfect bliss.

The End complete, the means must needs be so,
   By which we plainly know,
   From all Eternity
The means whereby God is, must perfect be.
   God is Himself the means
   Whereby He doth exist:
And as the Sun by shining's cloth'd with beams,
So from Himself to all His glory streams,
Who is a Sun, yet what Himself doth list.

His endless wants and His enjoyments be
   From all Eternity
   Immutable in Him:
They are His joys before the Cherubim.
   His wants appreciate all,
   And being infinite,
Permit no being to be mean or small
That He enjoys, or is before His sight.
His satisfactions do His wants delight.

Wants are the fountains of Felicity;
   No joy could ever be
   Were there no want. No bliss,
No sweetness perfect, were it not for this.
   Want is the greatest pleasure
   Because it makes all treasure.
O what a wonderful profound abyss
Is God! In whom eternal wants and treasures
Are more delightful since they both are pleasures.

He infinitely wanteth all His joys;
   (No want the soul e'er cloys.)
   And all those wanted pleasures
He infinitely hath. What endless measures,
   What heights and depths may we
   In His felicity
Conceive! Whose very wants are endless pleasures.
His life in wants and joys is infinite,
And both are felt as His Supreme Delight.

He's not like us; possession doth not cloy,
   Nor sense of want destroy;
   Both always are together;
No force can either from the other sever.
   Yet there's a space between
   That's endless. Both are seen
Distinctly still, and both are seen for ever.
As soon as e'er He wanteth all His bliss,
His bliss, tho' everlasting, in Him is.

His Essence is all Act: He did that He
   All Act might always be.
   His nature burns like fire;
His goodness infinitely does desire
   To be by all possesst;
   His love makes others blest.
It is the glory of His high estate,
And that which I for evermore admire,
He is an Act that doth communicate.

From all to all Eternity He is
   That Act: an Act of bliss:
   Wherein all bliss to all
That will receive the same, or on Him call,
   Is freely given: from whence
   'Tis easy even to sense
To apprehend that all receivers are
In Him, all gifts, all joys, all eyes, even all
At once, that ever will or shall appear.

He is the means of them, they not of Him.
   The Holy Cherubim,
   Souls, Angels from Him came
Who is a glorious bright and living Flame,
   That on all things doth shine,
   And makes their face divine.
And Holy, Holy, Holy is His Name:
He is the means both of Himself and all,
Whom we the Fountain, Means, and End do call.

In Whom as in the fountain all things are,
   In whom all things appear
   As in the means, and end
From whom they all proceed, to whom they tend.
   By whom they are made ours
   Whose souls are spacious bowers
Of all like His. Who ought to have a sense
Of all our wants, of all His excellence,
That while we all, we Him might comprehend.

THOMAS TRAHERNE

Love

   O nectar! O delicious stream!
O ravishing and only pleasure! Where
   Shall such another theme
Inspire my tongue with joys or please mine ear!
   Abridgement of delights!
   And Queen of sights!
O mine of rarities! O Kingdom wide!
O more! O cause of all! O glorious Bride!
   O God! O Bride of God! O King!
   O soul and crown of everything!

   Did not I covet to behold
Some endless monarch, that did always live
   In palaces of gold,
Willing all kingdoms, realms, and crowns to give
   Unto my soul! Whose love
   A spring might prove
Of endless glories, honours, friendships, pleasures,
Joys, praises, beauties and celestial treasures!
   Lo, now I see there's such a King,
   The fountain-head of everything!
   This made me present evermore
     With whatso'er I saw.
   An object, if it were before
   My eye, was by Dame Nature's law,
     Within my soul. Her store
Was all at once within me; all Her treasures
Were my immediate and internal pleasures,
Substantial joys, which did inform my mind.
     With all she wrought
     My soul was fraught,

And every object in my heart a thought
    Begot, or was; I could not tell,
      Whether the things did there
      Themselves appear,
Which in my Spirit truly seem'd to dwell;
    Or whether my conforming mind
    Were not even all that therein shin'd.

    But yet of this I was most sure,
      That at the utmost length,
    (So worthy was it to endure)
    My soul could best express its strength.
      It was so quick and pure,
That all my mind was wholly everywhere,
What'er it saw, 'twas ever wholly there;
The sun ten thousand legions off, was nigh:
      The utmost star,
      Though seen from far,
Was present in the apple of my eye.
    There was my sight, my life, my sense,
      My substance, and my mind;
      My spirit shin'd
Even there, not by a transient influence:
    The act was immanent, yet there:
    The thing remote, yet felt even here.

    O Joy! O Wonder and delight!
      O sacred mystery!
    My Soul a Spirit infinite!
    An image of the Deity!
      A pure substantial light!
That Being greatest which doth nothing seem!
Why, 'twas my all, I nothing did esteem
But that alone. A strange mysterious sphere!
      A deep abyss
      That sees and is
The only proper place of Heavenly Bliss.
    To its Creator 'tis so near
      In love and excellence,
      In life and sense,
In greatness, worth, and nature; and so dear,
    In it, without hyperbole,
      The son and friend of God we see.

A strange extended orb of Joy,
　　Proceeding from within,
　　Which did on every side, convey
　　Itself, and being nigh of kin
　　　To God did every way
Dilate itself even in an instant, and
Like an indivisible centre stand,
At once surrounding all eternity.
　　　'Twas not a sphere,
　　　Yet did appear,
One infinite. 'Twas somewhat every where,
　　And though it had a power to see
　　　Far more, yet still it shin'd
　　　And was a mind
Exerted, for it saw Infinity.
　　'Twas not a sphere, but 'twas a might
　　Invisible, and yet gave light.

　　Did my ambition ever dream
Of such a Lord, of such a love! Did I
　　Expect so sweet a stream
As this at any time! Could any eye
　　Believe it? Why all power
　　Is used here;
Joys down from Heaven on my head do shower,
And Jove beyond the fiction doth appear
　　Once more in golden rain to come
　　To Danae's pleasing fruitful womb.

　　His Ganymede! His life! His joy!
Or He comes down to me, or takes me up
　　That I might be His boy,
And fill, and taste, and give, and drink the cup.
　　But those (tho' great) are all
　　Too short and small,
Too weak and feeble pictures to express
The true mysterious depths of Blessedness.
　　I am His image, and His friend,
　　His son, bride, glory, temple, end.

THOMAS TRAHERNE

My Spirit

My naked simple Life was I;
  That Act so strongly shin'd
Upon the earth, the sea, the sky,
It was the substance of my mind;
  The sense itself was I.
I felt no dross nor matter in my soul,
No brims nor borders, such as in a bowl
We see. My essence was capacity,
  That felt all things;
  The thought that springs
Therefrom's itself. It hath no other wings
  To spread abroad, nor eyes to see,
    Nor hands distinct to feel,
    Nor knees to kneel;
But being simple like the Deity
  In its own centre is a sphere
  Not shut up here, but everywhere.

It acts not from a centre to
  Its object as remote,
But present is when it doth view,
Being with the Being it doth note
  Whatever it doth do.
It doth not by another engine work,
But by itself; which in the act doth lurk.
Its essence is transformed into a true
    And perfect act.
    And so exact
Hath God appeared in this mysterious fact,
  That 'tis all eye, all act, all sight,
    And what it please can be,
    Not only see,
Or do; for 'tis more voluble than light,
  Which can put on ten thousand forms,
  Being cloth'd with what itself adorns.

O wondrous Self! O sphere of light,
  O sphere of joy most fair
O act, O power infinite;
  O subtile and unbounded air!
    O living orb of sight!

Thou which within me art, yet me! Thou eye,
And temple of His whole infinity!
   O what a world art Thou! A world within!
     All things appear,
     All objects are
Alive in Thee! Supersubstantial, rare,
   Above themselves, and nigh of kin
     To those pure things we find
     In His great mind
Who made the world! Tho' now eclipsed by sin
   There they are useful and divine,
   Exalted there they ought to shine.

THOMAS TRAHERNE

An Hymn upon St Bartholomew's Day

What powerful Spirit lives within!
What active Angel doth inhabit here!
   What heavenly light inspires my skin,
Which doth so like a Deity appear!
A living Temple of all ages, I
    Within me see
   A Temple of Eternity!
    All Kingdoms I descry
     In me.

An inward Omnipresence here
Mysteriously like His within me stands,
   Whose knowledge is a Sacred Sphere
That in itself at once includes all lands.
There is some Angel that within me can
    Both talk and move,
   And walk and fly and see and love,
    A man on earth, a man
     Above.

Dull walls of clay my Spirit leaves,
And in a foreign Kingdom doth appear,
   This great Apostle it receives,
Admires His works and sees them, standing here.
Within myself from East to West I move
    As if I were
   At once a Cherubim and Sphere,
    Or was at once above
     And here.

The Soul's a messenger whereby
Within our inward Temple we may be
Even like the very Deity
In all the parts of His Eternity.
O live within and leave unwieldy dross!
Flesh is but clay!
O fly my Soul and haste away
To Jesus' Throne or Cross!
Obey!

Thomas Traherne

Wonder

How like an angel came I down!
How bright are all things here!
When first among his works I did appear,
Oh, how their Glory me did crown!
The world resembled his Eternity,
In which my soul did walk;
And every thing that I did see
Did with me talk.

The skies in their magnificence,
The lively, lovely air;
Oh, how divine, how soft, how sweet, how fair!
The stars did entertain my sense,
And all the works of God so bright and pure,
So rich and great did seem
As if they ever must endure
In my esteem.

A native health and innocence
Within my bones did grow,
And while my God did all his glories show,
I felt a vigour in my sense
That was all spirit. I within did flow
With seas of life, like wine;
I nothing in the world did know,
But 'twas divine.

Harsh, ragged objects were concealed,
    Oppressions, tears, and cries,
Sins, griefs, complaints, dissentions, weeping eyes,
    Were hid: and only things revealed
Which heavenly spirits and the angels prize.
    The State of Innocence
And Bliss, not trades and poverties,
    Did fill my sense.

The streets were paved with golden stones,
    The boys and girls were mine;
Oh, how did all their lovely faces shine!
    The Sons of Men were Holy Ones,
Joy, Beauty, Welfare did appear to me,
    And every thing which here I found,
    While like an angel I did see,
    Adorned the ground.

Rich diamond, and pearl, and gold
    In every place was seen;
Rare splendours, yellow, blue, red, white, and green,
    Mine eyes did everywhere behold;
Great Wonders clothed with Glory did appear,
    Amazement was my Bliss.
    That and my wealth was everywhere:
    No Joy to this . . .

THOMAS TRAHERNE

The Bible

1

That! That! There I was told
That I the son of God was made,
His image. O divine! And that fine gold,
    With all the joys that here do fade,
Are but a toy, compared to the bliss
Which heavenly, God-like, and eternal is.

2

That we on earth are kings;
    And, tho we're cloth'd with mortal skin,
Are inward cherubins, have angels' wings;
    Affections, thoughts, and minds within,
Can soar through all the coasts of Heaven and earth;
And shall be sated with celestial mirth.

THOMAS TRAHERNE
Rise, Noble Soul

1

Rise, noble soul, and come away;
Let us no longer waste the day.
Come, let us haste to yonder hill,
Where pleasures fresh are growing still.
  The way at first is rough and steep,
  And something hard for to ascend;
  But on the top do pleasures keep,
  And ease and joys do still attend.

2

Come, let us go; and do not fear
The hardest way, while I am near.
My heart with thine shall mingl'd be;
Thy sorrows mine, my joys with thee.
  And all our labours as we go
  True love shall sweeten still,
  And strew our way with flowers too,
  Whilst we ascend the hill.

3

The hill of rest, where angels live:
Where Bliss her palace hath to give;
Where thousands shall thee welcome make,
And joy that thou their joys dost take.
  O come, let's haste to this sweet place,
  I pray thee quickly heal thy mind!
  Sweet, let us go with joyful pace
  And leave the baser world behind.

4

Come, let's unite; and we'll aspire
Like brighter flames of heavenly fire,
That with sweet incense do ascend,
Still purer to their journey's end.
  Two rising flames in one we'll be,
  And with each other twining play,
  And how, 'twill be a joy to see,
  We'll fold and mingle all the way.

THOMAS TRAHERNE

Dumbness

Sure man was born to meditate on things,
And to contemplate the eternal springs
Of God and nature, glory, bliss, and pleasure;
That life and love might be his heavenly treasure:
And therefore speechless made at first, that he
Might in himself profoundly busied be:
And not vent out, before he hath ta'en in
Those antidotes that guard his soul from sin.
     Wise nature made him deaf too, that he might
Not be disturb'd, while he doth take delight
In inward things, nor be deprav'd with tongues,
Nor injur'd by the errors and the wrongs
That mortal words convey. For sin and death
Are most infused by accursed breath,
That flowing from corrupted entrails, bear
Those hidden plagues that souls alone may fear.
     This, my dear friends, this was my blessed case;
For nothing spoke to me but the fair face
Of Heaven and earth, before myself could speak.
I then my bliss did, when my silence, break.
My non-intelligence of human words
Ten thousand pleasures unto me affords;
For while I knew not what they to me said,
Before their souls were into mine convey'd,
Before that living vehicle of wind
Could breathe into me their infected mind,
Before my thoughts were leaven'd with theirs, before
There any mixture was; the holy door,
Or gate of souls was clos'd, and mine being one
Within itself to me alone was known.
Then did I dwell within a world of light,
Distinct and separate from all men's sight,
Where I did feel strange thoughts, and such things see
That were, or seem'd, only reveal'd to me.
There I saw all the world enjoy'd by one;
There I was in the world myself alone;
These therefore were occasion'd all by sin.
The first and only work he had to do,
Was in himself to feel his bliss, to view
His sacred treasures, to admire, rejoice,
Sing praises with a sweet and heavenly voice,

See, prize, give thanks within, and love,
Which is the high and only work, above
Them all. And this at first was mine; these were
My exercises of the highest sphere.
To see, approve, take pleasure, and rejoice
Within, is better than an empty voice:
No melody in words can equal that;
The sweetest organ, lute, or harp is flat
And dull, compar'd thereto. And O that still
I might admire my Father's love and skill!
This is to honour, worship, and adore,
This is to love Him: nay it is far more.
It is to enjoy Him, and to imitate
The life and glory of His high estate.
'Tis to receive with holy reverence,
To understand His gifts, and with a sense
Of pure devotion, and humility,
To prize His works, His love to magnify.
O happy ignorance of other things,
Which made me present with the King of Kings!
And like Him too! All spirit, life, and power,
All love and joy, in His eternal bower.
A world of innocence as then was mine,
In which the joys of Paradise did shine,
And while I was not here I was in Heaven,
Not resting one, but every day in seven.
Forever minding with a lively sense
The universe in all its excellence.
No other thoughts did intervene, to cloy,
Divert, extinguish, or eclipse my joy.
No other customs, new-found wants, or dreams
Invented here polluted my pure streams.
No aloes or dregs, no Wormwood star
Was seen to fall into the sea from far.
No rotten soul did, like an apple, near
My soul approach. There's no contagion here.
An unperceived donor gave all pleasures,
There nothing was but I, and all my treasures.
In that fair world one only was the friend,
One golden stream, one spring, one only end.
There only one did sacrifice and sing
To only one eternal heavenly King.
The union was so strait between them two,
That all was either's which my soul could view.
His gifts, and my possessions, both our treasures;
He mine, and I the ocean of His pleasures.

He was an ocean of delights from whom
The living springs and golden streams did come:
My bosom was an ocean into which
They all did run. And me they did enrich.
A vast and infinite capacity
Did make my bosom like the Deity,
In whose mysterious and celestial mind
All ages and all worlds together shin'd.
Who tho He nothing said did always reign,
And in Himself eternity contain.
The world was more in me than I in it.
The King of Glory in my soul did sit.
And to Himself in me He always gave
All that He takes delight to see me have.
For so my spirit was an endless sphere,
Like God Himself, and Heaven and earth was there.

THOMAS TRAHERNE

Insatiableness

I

1

No walls confine! Can nothing hold my mind?
Can I no rest nor satisfaction find?
   Must I behold eternity
       And see
   What things above the heavens be?
     Will nothing serve the turn?
    Nor earth, nor seas, nor skies?
      Till I what lies
   In time's beginning find:
  Must I till then forever burn?

2

Not all the crowns; not all the heaps of gold
On earth; not all the tales that can be told,
   Will satisfaction yield to me:
      Nor tree,
  Nor shade, nor sun, nor Eden, be
    A joy: nor gems in gold
    (Be't pearl or precious stone),
     Nor spring, nor flowers,

3

Till I what was before all time descry,
The world's beginning seems but vanity.
　　My soul doth there long thoughts extend;
　　　　No end
　　Doth find, or being comprehend:
　　　　Yet somewhat sees that is
　　　　The obscure shady face
　　　　　Of endless space,
　　　　All room within; where I
Expect to meet eternal bliss.

II

1

This busy, vast, inquiring soul
　　　Brooks no control,
　　No limits will endure,
　Nor any rest: it will all see,
Not time alone, but even eternity.
　　　What is it? Endless sure.

2

'Tis mean ambition to desire
　　　A single world:
　　　To many I aspire,
　Tho one upon another hurl'd;
Nor will they all, if they be all confin'd,
　　　Delight my mind.

3

This busy, vast, inquiring soul
　　　Brooks no control:
　　'Tis hugely curious too.
Each one of all those worlds must be
Enrich'd with infinite variety
　　And worth; or 'twill not do.

4

'Tis nor delight nor perfect pleasure
　　　To have a purse
　　That hath a bottom of its treasure,
Since I must thence endless expense disburse.
Sure there's a GOD (for else there's no delight),
　　　One infinite.

EDWARD TAYLOR

Huswifery

Make me, O Lord, thy Spining Wheele compleate.
   Thy Holy Worde my Distaff make for mee.
Make mine Affections thy Swift Flyers neate
   And make my Soule thy holy Spoole to bee.
   My Conversation make to be thy Reele
   And reele the yarn thereon spun of thy Wheele.

Make me thy Loome then, knit therein this Twine:
   And make thy Holy Spirit, Lord, winde quills:
Then weave the Web thyselfe. The yarn is fine.
   Thine Ordinances make my Fulling Mills.
   Then dry the same in Heavenly Colours Choice,
   All pinkt with Varnisht Flowers of Paradise.

Then cloath therewith mine Understanding, Will,
   Affections, Judgment, Conscience, Memory
My Words, and Actions, that their shine may fill
   My wayes with glory and thee glorify.
   Then mine apparell shall display before yee
   That I am Cloathd in Holy robes for glory.

EDWARD TAYLOR

Meditation, Canticles 6, 11: I Went Down into the Garden of Nuts, to See the Fruits

Oh that I was the Bird of Paradise!
   Then in the nutmeg garden, Lord, thy bower,
Celestial music blossom should my voice,
   Enchanted with thy garden's air and flower.
   This aromatic air would so inspire
   My ravish'd soul to sing with angels' choir.

What is thy church, my Lord, thy garden which
   Doth gain the best of soils? Such spots indeed
Are choicest plots empal'd with palings rich
   And set with slips, herbs best, and best of seed,
   As th' Hanging Gardens rare of Babylon
   And palace garden of King Solomon.

But that which doth excel all gardens here
    Was Eden's garden, Adam's palace bright.
The Tree of Life, and Knowledge too, were there,
    Sweet herbs and sweetest flowers, all sweet delight,
    A Paradise indeed of all perfume
    That to the nose, the eyes and ears doth tune.

But all these artificial gardens bright
    Enamelèd with bravest knots of pinks
And flowers enspangled with black, red and white,
    Compar'd with this are truly stinking sinks.
    As dunghills reek with stinking scents that dish
    Us out, so these, when balancèd with this.

For Zion's Paradise, Christ's garden dear,
    His church, enwalled with heavenly crystal fine,
Hath every bed beset with pearl all clear
    And alleys opal'd with gold, and silver shrine.
    The shining angels are its sentinels
    With flaming sword chanting out madrigals.

The sparkling plants, sweet spices, herbs and trees,
    The glorious shows of aromatic flowers,
The pleasing beauties soak'd in sweet breath lees
    Of Christ's rich garden ever upward towers.
    For Christ sweet showers of Grace makes on it fall.
    It therefore bears the bell away from all.

The nut of ev'ry kind is found to grow big
    With food, and physic, lodg'd within a tower,
A wooden wall with husky coverlid
    Or shell flesh'd o'er, or in an arching bower:
    Beech, hazel, walnut, cocho, almond brave,
    Pistick or chestnut in its prickly cave.

These all as meat and med'cine, emblems choice
    Of spiritual food and physic are, which sport
Up in Christ's garden. Yet the nutmeg's spice
    A leathern coat wears, and a macy shirt,
    Doth far excel them all. Aromatize
    My soul therewith, my Lord, and spiritual-wise.

Oh sweet, sweet Paradise, whose spicèd spring
   Will make the lips of him asleep to tune
Heart-ravishing tunes, sweet music for our king
   In aromatic air of blest perfume,
   Open thy garden door. Me entrance give,
   And in thy nut-tree garden make me live.

If, Lord, thou ope'st, and in thy garden bring
   Me, then thy linnet sweetly will
Upon thy nut-tree sit and sweetly sing,
   Will crack a nut and eat the kernel still.
   Thou wilt mine eyes, my nose and palate greet
   With curious flowers, sweet odours, viands sweet.

Thy garden's odoriferous air me make
   Suck in and out, to aromatize my lungs,
That I thy garden and its spicy state
   May breathe upon with such ensweetened songs,
   My lungs and breath ensweetened thus shall raise
   The glory of thy garden in its praise.

ISAAC WATTS

The Incomprehensible

Far in the Heavens my God retires:
My God, the mark of my desires,
   And hides his lovely face;
When he descends within my view,
He charms my reason to pursue,
But leaves it tir'd and fainting in th' unequal chase.

Or if I reach unusual height
   Till near his presence brought,
There floods of glory check my flight,
Cramp the bold pinions of my wit,
   And all untune my thought;
Plunged in a sea of light I roll,
Where wisdom, justice, mercy, shines;
   Infinite rays in crossing lines
Beat thick confusion on my sight, and overwhelm my soul . . .

Great God! behold my reason lies
Adoring: yet my love would rise
   On pinions not her own:
Faith shall direct her humble flight,
Through all the trackless seas of light,
To Thee, th' Eternal Fair, the infinite Unknown.

ALEXANDER POPE

From An Essay on Man

All are but parts of one stupendous whole,
Whose body Nature is, and God the soul;
That, changed through all, and yet in all the same,
Great in the earth, as in th' ethereal frame,
Warms in the sun, refreshes in the breeze,
Glows in the stars, and blossoms in the trees,
Lives through all life, extends through all extent,
Spreads undivided, operates unspent:
Breathes in our soul, informs our mortal part;
As full, as perfect, in a hair as heart;
As full, as perfect, in vile man that mourns
As the rapt Seraphim, that sings and burns:
To him no high, no low, no great, no small –
He fills, he bounds, connects, and equals all . . .
All nature is but art, unknown to thee;
All chance, direction, which thou canst not see;
All discord, harmony not understood;
All partial evil, universal good.

. . .

Learn from the birds what food the thickets yield;
Learn from the beasts the physic of the field;
Thy arts of building from the bee receive;
Learn of the mole to plow, the worm to weave;
Learn of the little Nautilus to fail,
Spread the thin oar, and catch the driving gale.
Here too all forms of social union find,
And hence let Reason, late, instruct Mankind:
Here subterranean works and cities see;
There towns aerial on the waving tree.
Learn each small People's genius, policies,
The Ant's republic, and the realm of Bees;

How those in common all their wealth bestow,
And Anarchy without confusion know;
And these for ever, tho' a Monarch reign.
Their sep'rate cells and properties maintain.
Mark what unvary'd laws preserve each state,
Laws wife as Nature, and as fix'd as Fate.
In vain thy Reason finer webs shall draw,
Entangle Justice in her net of Law,
And right, too rigid, harden into wrong;
Still for the strong too weak, the weak too strong.
Yet go! and thus o'er all the creatures sway,
Thus let the wiser make the rest obey;
And for those Arts mere Instinct could afford,
Be crown'd as Monarchs or as Gods adored.

. . .

See the sole bliss Heav'n could on all bestow!
Which who but feels can taste, but thinks can know;
Yet poor with fortune, and with learning blind,
The bad must miss, the good, untaught, will find;
Slave to no sect, who takes no private road,
But looks through Nature, up to Nature's God:
Pursues that Chain which links th' immense design,
Joins heav'n and earth, and mortal and divine;
Sees, that no Being any bliss can know,
But touches some above, and some below;
Learns, from this union of the rising Whole,
The first, last purpose of the human soul;
And knows where Faith, Law, Morals, all began,
All end, in Love of God, and Love of Man.
For him alone, Hope leads from goal to goal,
And opens still, and opens on his soul.

Alexander Pope

Ode on Solitude

Happy the man, whose wish and care
A few paternal acres bound,
Content to breathe his native air,
        In his own ground

Whose herds with milk, whose fields with bread,
   Whose flocks supply him with attire,
Whose trees in summer yield him shade,
        In winter fire.

Blest, who can unconcern'dly find
   Hours, days, and years slide soft away,
In health of body, peace of mind,
        Quiet by day,

Sound sleep by night; study and ease,
   Together mixt; sweet recreation,
And innocence, which most does please
        With meditation.

Thus let me live, unseen, unknown;
   Thus unlamented let me die;
Steal from the world, and not a stone
        Tell where I lie.

ALEXANDER POPE

The Dying Christian to his Soul: Ode

Vital spark of heav'nly flame!
Quit, oh quit this mortal frame:
Trembling, hoping, ling'ring, flying,
Oh the pain, the bliss of dying!
Cease, fond Nature, cease thy strife,
And let me languish into life.

Hark! they whisper; Angels say,
Sister spirit, come away.
What is this absorbs me quite?
Steals my senses, shuts my sight,
Drowns my spirits, draws my breath?
Tell me, my Soul, can this be Death?

The world recedes; it disappears!
Heav'n opens on my eyes! my ears
With sounds seraphic ring:
Lend, lend your wings! I mount! I fly!
O Grave! where is thy Victory?
O Death! where is thy Sting?

PART 6:
Eighteenth Century

JOHN BYROM

From A Poetical Version of a Letter from Jacob Behmen

'Tis Man's own Nature, which in its own Life,
Or Centre, stands in Enmity and Strife,
And anxious, selfish, doing what it lists,
(Without God's Love) that tempts him, and resists;
The Devil also shoots his fiery Dart,
From Grace and Love to turn away the Heart.

JOSEPH ADDISON

The Confirmation of Faith

The spacious firmament on high,
With all the blue ethereal sky,
And spangled heavens, a shining frame,
Their great Original proclaim.
The unwearied sun, from day to day,
Does his Creator's power display;
And publishes to every land
The work of an Almighty hand.

Soon as the evening shades prevail,
The moon takes up the wondrous tale;
And nightly to the listening earth,
Repeats the story of her birth;
Whilst all the stars that round her burn,
And all the planets in their turn,
Confirm the tidings as they roll,
And spread the truth from pole to pole.

What though in solemn silence all
Move round the dark terrestrial ball;
What though nor real voice nor sound
Amid their radiant orbs be found?
In reason's ear they all rejoice,
And utter forth a glorious voice;
For every singing, as they shine,
'The hand that made us is divine.'

PHILIP DODDRIDGE

Self-Dedication Reviewed

O happy day that fix'd my choice
    On Thee, my Saviour and my God!
Well may this glowing heart rejoice,
    And tell its raptures all abroad.

'Tis done, the great transaction's done!
    I am my Lord's, and He is mine;
He drew me, and I follow'd on,
    Charm'd to confess the voice divine.

Now rest my long-divided heart,
    Fix'd on this blissful centre, rest:
Nor ever from thy Lord depart,
    With Him of every good possess'd.

High Heav'n, that heard the solemn vow,
    That vow renew'd shall daily hear;
Till in life's latest hour I bow,
    And bless in death a bond so dear.

MARK AKENSIDE

God's Excellence

From heaven my strains begin; from heaven descends
The flame of genius to the human breast,
And love, and beauty, and poetic joy,
And inspiration. Ere the radiant sun
Sprang from the east, or 'mid the vault of night
The moon suspended her serener lamp;
Ere mountains, woods, or streams, adorned the globe,
Or Wisdom taught the sons of men her lore,
Then lived the Almighty One; then deep retired
In his unfathomed essence, viewed the forms,
The forms eternal, of created things:
The radiant sun, the moon's nocturnal lamp,
The mountains, woods, and streams, the rolling globe,
And Wisdom's mien celestial. From the first
Of days on them his love divine he fixed,
It is admiration, till, in time complete,
What he admired and loved his vital smile

Unfolded into being. Hence the breath
Of life informing each organic frame,
Hence the green earth, and wild resounding waves,
Hence light and shade alternate, warmth and cold,
And clear autumnal skies and vernal showers,
And all the fair variety of things.

CHRISTOPHER SMART

From *Jubilate Agno*

For I will consider my Cat Jeoffry.
For he is the servant of the Living God duly and daily serving him.
For at the first glance of the glory of God in the East he worships in his way.
For is this done by wreathing his body seven times round with elegant quickness.
For then he leaps up to catch the musk, which is the blessing of God upon his prayer.
For he rolls upon prank to work it in.
For having done duty and received blessing he begins to consider himself.
For this he performs in ten degrees.
For first he looks upon his fore-paws to see if they are clean.
For secondly he kicks up behind to clear away there.
For thirdly he works it upon stretch with the fore paws extended.
For fourthly he sharpens his paws by wood.
For fifthly he washes himself.
For sixthly he rolls upon wash.
For seventhly he fleas himself, that he may not be interrupted upon the beat.
For eighthly he rubs himself against a post.
For ninthly he rubs himself against a post.
For tenthly he goes in quest of food.
For having consider'd God and himself he will consider his neighbour.
For if he meets another cat he will kiss her in kindness.
For when he takes his prey he plays with it to give it a chance.
For one mouse in seven escapes by his dallying.
For when his day's work is done his business more properly begins.
For he keeps the Lord's watch in the night against the adversary.
For he counteracts the powers of darkness by his electrical skin & glaring eyes.
For he counteracts the Devil, who is death, by brisking about the life.
For in his morning orisons he loves the sun and the sun loves him.

For he is of the tribe of Tiger.

For the Cherub Cat is a term of the Angel Tiger.

For he has the subtlety and hissing of a serpent, which in goodness
he suppresses.

For he will not do destruction if he is well-fed, neither will he spit
without provocation.

For he purrs in thankfulness, when God tells him he's a good Cat.

For he is an instrument for the children to learn benevolence upon.

For every house is incompleat without him & a blessing is lacking in
the spirit.

For the Lord commanded Moses concerning the cats at the departure
of the Children of Israel from Egypt.

For every family had one cat at least in the bag.

For the English Cats are the best in Europe.

For he is the cleanest in the use of his fore-paws of any quadrupede.

For the dexterity of his defence is an instance of the love of God to him
exceedingly.

For he is the quickest to his mark of any creature.

For he is tenacious of his point.

For he is a mixture of gravity and waggery.

For he knows that God is his Saviour.

For there is nothing sweeter than his peace when at rest.

For there is nothing brisker than his life when in motion.

For he is of the Lord's poor and so indeed is he called by benevolence
perpetually – Poor Jeoffry! poor Jeoffry! the rat has bit thy throat.

For I bless the name of the Lord Jesus that Jeoffrey is better.

For the divine spirit comes about his body to sustain it in compleat cat.

For his tongue is exceeding pure so that it has in purity what it wants
in musick.

For he is docile and can learn certain things.

For he can set up with gravity which is patience upon approbation.

For he can fetch and carry, which is patience in employment.

For he can jump over a stick which is patience upon proof positive.

For he can spraggle upon waggle at the word of command.

For he can jump from an eminence into his master's bosom.

For he can catch the cork and toss it again.

For he is hated by the hypocrite and miser.

For the former is afraid of detection.

For the latter refuses the charge.

For he camels his back to bear the first notion of business.

For he is good to think on, if a man would express himself neatly.

For he made a great figure in Egypt for his signal services.

For he killed the Icneumon-rat very pernicious by land.

For his ears are so acute that they sting again.

For from this proceeds the passing quickness of his attention.

For by stroaking of him I have found out electricity.

For I have perceived God's light about him both wax and fire.
For the Electrical fire is the spiritual substance, which God sends from
 heaven to sustain the bodies both of man and beast.
For God has blessed him in the variety of his movements.
For, tho he cannot fly, he is an excellent clamberer.
For his motions upon the face of the earth are more than any other
 quadrupede.
For he can tread to all the measures upon the musick.
For he can swim for life.
For he can creep.

CHRISTOPHER SMART

From The Song to David

O thou, that sit'st upon a throne,
With harp of high majestic tone,
 To praise the King of Kings;
And voice of heaven-ascending swell,
Which, while its deeper notes excel,
 Clear, as a clarion, rings:

To bless each valley, grove, and coast,
And charm the cherubs to the post
 Of gratitude in throngs;
To keep the days on Zion's mount,
And send the year to his account,
 With dances and with songs:

O Servant of God's holiest charge,
The minister of praise at large,
 Which thou may'st now receive;
From thy blest mansion hail and hear,
From topmost eminence appear
 To this the wreath I weave.

He sang of God – the mighty source
Of all things – the stupendous force
 On which all strength depends;
From whose right arm, beneath whose eyes,
All period, power, and enterprise
 Commences, reigns, and ends.

Angels – their ministry and meed,
Which to and fro with blessings speed,
　　Or with their citterns wait;
Where Michael with his millions bows,
Where dwells the seraph and his spouse,
　　The cherub and her mate.

Of man – the semblance and effect
Of God and Love – the Saint elect
　　For infinite applause –
To rule the land, and briny broad,
To be laborious in his laud,
　　And heroes in his cause.

The world, the clustering spheres, He made;
The glorious light, the soothing shade,
　　Dale, champaign, grove, and hill;
The multitudinous abyss,
Where Secrecy remains in bliss,
　　And Wisdom hides her skill.

Trees, plants, and flowers – of virtuous root;
Gem yielding blossom, yielding fruit,
　　Choice gums and precious balm;
Bless ye the nosegay in the vale,
And with the sweetness of the gale
　　Enrich the thankful psalm.

Of fowl – e'en every beak and wing
Which cheer the winter, hail the spring,
　　That live in peace or prey;
They that make music, or that mock,
The quail, the brave domestic cock,
　　The raven, swan, and jay.

Of fishes – every size and shape,
Which nature frames of light escape,
　　Devouring man to shun:
The shells are in the wealthy deep,
The shoals upon the surface leap,
　　And love the glancing sun.

Of beasts – the beaver plods his task;
While the sleek tigers roll and bask,
   Nor yet the shades arouse:
Her cave the mining coney scoops;
Where o'er the mead the mountain stoops,
   The kids exult and browse.

Of gems – their virtue and their price,
Which hid in earth from man's device,
   Their darts of lustre sheathe;
The jasper of the master's stamp,
The topaz blazing like a lamp
   Among the mines beneath.

Blest was the tenderness he felt
When to his graceful harp he knelt,
   And did for audience call;
When Satan with his hand he quelled,
And in serene suspense he held
   The frantic throes of Saul.

His furious foes no more maligned
As he such melody divined,
   And sense and soul detained;
Now striking strong, now soothing soft,
He sent the godly sounds aloft,
   Or in delight refrained.

When up to heaven his thoughts he piled,
From fervent lips fair Michal smiled,
   As blush to blush she stood;
And chose herself the queen, and gave
Her utmost from her heart, 'so brave,
   And plays his hymns so good.'

The pillars of the Lord are seven,
Which stand for earth to topmost heaven;
   His wisdom drew the plan;
His Word accomplished the design,
From brightest gem to deepest mine,
   From Christ enthroned to man.

Thou art – to give and to confirm,
For each his talent and his term;
   All flesh thy bounties share:
Thou shalt not call thy brother fool;
The porches of the Christian school
   Are meekness, peace, and prayer.

Open, and naked of offence,
Man's made of mercy, soul, and sense;
   God armed the snail and wilk;
Be good to him who pulls thy plough;
Due food and care, due rest, allow
   For her that yields thee milk.

Rise up before the hoary head,
And God's benign commandment dread,
   Which says thou shalt not die:
'Not as I will, but as thou wilt,'
Prayed He whose conscience knew no guilt;
   With whose blessed pattern vie.

Use all thy passions! – love is thine,
And joy, and jealousy divine;
   Thine hope's eternal fort,
And care thy leisure to disturb,
With fear concupiscence to curb,
   And rapture to transport.

Act simply, as occasion asks;
Put mellow wine in seasoned casks;
   Till not with ass and bull:
Remember thy baptismal bond;
Keep from commixtures foul and fond,
   Nor work thy flax with wool.

Distribute: pay the Lord his tithe,
And make the widow's heart-strings blithe;
   Resort with those that weep:
As you from all and each expect,
For all and each thy love direct,
   And render as you reap.

The slander and its bearer spurn,
And propagating praise sojourn
   To make thy welcome last;
Turn from old Adam to the New;
By hope futurity pursue;
   Look upwards to the past.

Control thine eye, salute success,
Honour the wiser, happier bless,
   And for thy neighbour feel;
Grudge not of mammon and his leaven,
Work emulation up to heaven
   By knowledge and by zeal.

O David, highest in the list
Of worthies, on God's ways insist,
   The genuine word repeat:
Vain are the documents of men,
And vain the flourish of the pen
   That keeps the fool's conceit.

For Adoration all the ranks
Of Angels yield eternal thanks,
   And David in the midst;
With God's good poor, which, last and least
In man's esteem, Thou to Thy feast,
   O blessèd Bridgegroom, bidd'st!

For Adoration seasons change,
And order, truth, and beauty range,
   Adjust, attract, and fill:
The grass the polyanthus checks;
And polished porphyry reflects,
   By the descending rill.

Rich almonds colour to the prime
For Adoration; tendrils climb,
   And fruit-trees pledge their gems;
And Ivis with her gorgeous vest
Builds for her eggs her cunning nest,
   And bell-flowers bow their stems.

With vinous syrup cedars spout;
From rocks pure honey gushing out,
    For Adoration springs:
All scenes of painting crowd the map
Of nature; to the mermaid's pap
    The scalèd infant clings.

The spotted ounce and playsome cubs
Run rustling 'mongst the flowering shrubs,
    And lizards feed the moss;
For Adoration beasts embark,
While waves upholding halcyon's ark
    No longer roar and toss.

While Israel sits beneath his fig,
With coral root and amber sprig
    The weaned adventurer sports;
Where to the palm the jasmin cleaves,
For Adoration 'mongst the leaves
    The gale his peace reports.

Increasing days their reign exalt,
Nor in the pink and mottled vault
    Th' opposing spirits tilt,
And, by the coasting reader spied,
The silverlings and crusions glide
    For Adoration gilt.

For Adoration ripening canes
And cocoa's purest milk detains
    The western pilgrim's staff;
Where rain in clasping boughs inclosed,
And vines with oranges disposed,
    Embower the social laugh.

Now labour his reward receives,
For Adoration counts his sheaves
    To peace, his bounteous prince;
The nectarine his strong tint imbibes,
And apples of ten thousand tribes,
    And quick peculiar quince.

The wealthy crops of whitening rice,
'Mongst thyine woods and groves of spice,
   For Adoration grow;
And, marshalled in the fencèd land,
The peaches and pomegranates stand,
   Where wild carnations blow.

The laurels with the winter strive;
The crocus burnishes alive
   Upon the snow-clad earth:
For Adoration myrtles stay
To keep the garden from dismay,
   And bless the sight from dearth.

The pheasant shows his pompous neck;
And ermine, jealous of a speck,
   With fear eludes offence:
The sable, with his glossy pride,
For Adoration is descried,
   Where frosts the wave condense.

The cheerful holly, pensive yew,
And holy thorn, their trim renew;
   The squirrel hoards his nuts:
All creatures batten o'er their stores,
And careful nature all her doors
   For Adoration shuts.

For Adoration, David's psalms
Lift up the heart to deeds of alms;
   And he, who kneels and chants,
Prevails his passions to control,
Finds meat and medicine to the soul,
   Which for translation pants.

Sweet is the dew that falls betimes,
And drops upon the leafy limes;
   Sweet Hermon's fragrant air:
Sweet is the lily's silver bell,
And sweet the wakeful tapers smell
   That watch for early prayer.

Sweet the young nurse with love intense,
Which smiles o'er sleeping innocence;
    Sweet when the lost arrive:
Sweet the musician's ardour beats,
While his vague mind's in quest of sweets,
    The choicest flowers to hive.

Sweeter in all the strains of love,
The language of thy turtle dove,
    Paired to thy swelling chord;
Sweeter with every grace endued,
The glory of thy gratitude,
    Respired unto the Lord.

Strong is the horse upon his speed;
Strong in pursuit the rapid glede,
    Which makes at once his game:
Strong the tall ostrich on the ground;
Strong through the turbulent profound
    Shoots Xiphias to his aim.

Strong is the lion – like a coal
His eyeball – like a bastion's mole
    His chest against the foes:
Strong the gier-eagle on his sail;
Strong against tide and enormous whale
    Emerges as he goes.

But stronger still, in earth and air,
And in the sea, the man of prayer,
    And far beneath the tide,
And in the seat to faith assigned,
Where ask is have, where seek is find,
    Where knock is open wide.

Beauteous the fleet before the gale;
Beauteous the multitudes in mail,
    Ranked arms, and crested heads:
Beauteous the garden's umbrage mild,
Walk, water, meditated wild,
    And all the bloomy beds.

Beauteous the moon full on the lawn;
And beauteous, when the veil's withdrawn,
    The virgin to her spouse:
Beauteous the temple, decked and filled,
When to the heaven of heavens they build
    Their heart-directed vows.

Beauteous, yea beauteous more than these,
The shepherd king upon his knees,
    For his momentous trust;
With wish of infinite conceit,
For man, beast, mute, the small and great,
    And prostrate dust to dust.

Previous the bounteous widow's mite;
And precious, for extreme delight,
    The largess from the churl:
Precious the ruby's blushing blaze,
And alba's blest imperial rays,
    And pure cerulean pearl.

Precious the penitential tear;
And precious is the sigh sincere,
    Acceptable to God:
And precious are the winning flowers,
In gladsome Israel's feast of bowers,
    Bound on the hallowed sod.

More precious that diviner part
Of David, even the Lord's own heart,
    Great, beautiful, and new:
In all things where it was intent,
In all extremes, in each event,
    Proof – answering true to true.

Glorious the sun in mid career;
Glorious the assembled fires appear;
    Glorious the comet's train:
Glorious the trumpet and alarm;
Glorious the Almighty's stretched-out arm;
    Glorious the enraptured main;

Glorious the northern lights astream;
Glorious the song, when God's the theme;
   Glorious the thunder's roar:
Glorious Hosanna from the den;
Glorious the catholic Amen;
   Glorious the martyr's gore:

Glorious – more glorious – is the crown
Of Him that brought salvation down
   By meekness, called Thy Son:
Thou that stupendous truth believed; –
And now the matchless deed's achieved,
   DETERMINED, DARED, and DONE.

WILLIAM COWPER

From The Winter Morning Walk

Acquaint thyself with God, if thou wouldst taste
His works. Admitted once to his embrace,
Thou shalt perceive that thou wast blind before:
Thine eye shall be instructed; and thine heart
Made pure shall relish, with divine delight,
Till then unfelt, what hands divine have wrought.
Brutes graze the mountain-top, with faces prone,
And eyes intent upon the scanty herb
It yields them; or, recumbent on its brow,
Ruminate heedless of the scene outspread
Beneath, beyond, and stretching far away
From inland regions to the distant main.
Man views it, and admires; but rests content
With what he views. The landscape has his praise,
But not its Author. Unconcerned who formed
The paradise he sees, he finds it such,
And, such well pleased to find it, asks no more.
Not so the mind that has been touched from Heaven,
And in the school of sacred wisdom taught
To read his wonders, in whose thought the world,
Fair as it is, existed ere it was.
Not for its own sake merely, but for His
Much more who fashioned it, he gives it praise,
Praise that, from earth resulting, as it ought,
To earth's acknowledged Sovereign, finds at once
Its only just proprietor in Him.

The soul that sees him or receives sublimed
New faculties, or learns at least to employ
More worthily the powers she owned before;
Discerns in all things what, with stupid gaze
Of ignorance, till then she overlooked,
A ray of heavenly light, gilding all forms
Terrestrial in the vast and the minute –
The unambiguous footsteps of the God
Who gives its lustre to an insect's wing,
And wheels his throne upon the rolling worlds.

WILLIAM COWPER

From The Task

The Lord of all, himself through all diffus'd,
Sustains, and is the life of all that lives.
Nature is but a name for an effect,
Whose cause is God. He feeds the secret fire
By which the mighty process is maintain'd,
Who sleeps not, is not weary; in whose sight
Slow circling ages are as transient days;
Whose work is without labour; whose designs
No flaw deforms, no difficulty thwarts;
And whose beneficence no charge exhausts.

. . .

Not a flow'r
But shows some touch, in freckle, streak, or stain,
Of his unrivall'd pencil. He inspires
Their balmy odours, and imparts their hues,
And bathes their eyes with nectar, and includes,
In grains as countless as the sea-side sands,
The forms with which he sprinkles all the earth.
Happy who walks with him! whom what he finds
Of flavour or of scent in fruit or flow'r,
Or what he views of beautiful or grand
In nature, from the broad majestic oak
To the green blade that twinkles in the sun,
Prompts with remembrance of a present God!

WILLIAM COWPER

From Retirement

Mark the matchless workings of the power,
That shuts within its seed the future flower;
Bids these in elegance of form excel,
Incolour these, and those delight the smell;
Sends Nature forth, the daughter of the skies,
To dance on earth, and charm all human eyes.

SIR WILLIAM JONES

A Hymn to Narayena

Spirit of Spirits, who, through ev'ry part
    Of space expanded and of endless time,
    Beyond the stretch of lab'ring thought sublime,
    Badst uproar into beauteous order start.
        Before Heav'n was. Thou art;
Ere spheres beneath us roll'd or spheres above,
    Ere earth in firmamental ether hung,
    Thou satst alone; till, through thy mystick Love,
    Things unexisting to existence sprung,
        And grateful descant sung.
What first impell'd thee to exert thy might?
    Goodness unlimited. What glorious light
    Thy pow'r directed? Wisdom without bound.
    What prov'd it first? Oh! guide my fancy right,
        Oh! raise from cumbrous ground
        My soul in rapture drown'd,
    That fearless it may soar on wings of fire;
For Thou, who only knowst, Thou only canst inspire.

Wrapt in eternal solitary shade,
    Th' impenetrable gloom of light intense,
    Impervious, inaccessible, immense,
    Ere spirits were infus'd or forms display'd,
        BREHM his own Mind survey'd,
As mortal eyes (thus finite we compare
  . With infinite) in smoothest mirrors gaze:
    Swift, at his look, a shape supremely fair
    Leap'd into being with a boundless blaze,
        That fifty suns might daze.

Primeval MAYA was the Goddess nam'd,
    Who to her sire, with Love divine inflam'd,
    A casket gave with rich *Ideas* till'd,
    From which this gorgeous Universe he fram'd;
        For, when th' Almighty will'd,
        Unnumber'd worlds to build,
    From Unity diversified he sprang,
While gay Creation laugh'd, and procreant Nature rang.

First an all-potent all-pervading sound
    Bade flow the waters – and the waters flow'd,
    Exulting in their measureless abode,
    Diffusive, multitudinous, profound,
        Above, beneath, around;
Then o'er the vast expanse primordial wind
    Breath'd gently, till a lucid bubble rose,
    Which grew in perfect shape an Egg refin'd:
    Created substance no such lustre shows,
        Earth no such beauty knows.
Above the warring waves it danc'd elate,
    Till from its bursting shell with lovely state
    A form cerulean flutter'd o'er the deep,
    Brightest of beings, greatest of the great:
        Who, not as mortals steep,
        Their eyes in dewy sleep,
    But heav'nly-pensive on the Lotos lay,
That blossom'd at his touch and shed a golden ray.

Hail, primal blossom! hail empyreal gem!
    KEMEL, or PEDMA, or whate'er high name
    Delight thee, say, what four-form'd Godhead came,
    With graceful stole and beamy diadem,
        Forth from thy verdant stem?
Full-gifted BREHMA! Rapt in solemn thought
    He stood, and round his eyes fire-darting threw;
    But, whilst his viewless origin he sought,
    One plain he saw of living waters blue,
        Their spring nor saw nor knew.
Then, in his parent stalk again retir'd,
    With restless pain for ages he inquir'd
    What were his pow'rs, by whom, and why conferr'd:
    With doubts perplex'd, with keen impatience fir'd
        He rose, and rising heard
        Th' unknown all-knowing Word.
'Brahma! no more in vain research persist:
    My veil thou canst not move – Go; bid all worlds exist!'

Hail, self-existent, in celestial speech
   NARAYEN, from thy watry cradle, nam'd;
   Or VENAMALY may I sing unblam'd,
   With flow'ry braids, that to thy sandals reach,
     Whose beauties, who can teach?
Or high PEITAMBER clad in yellow robes
   Than sunbeams brighter in meridian glow,
   That weave their heav'n-spun light o'er circling globes?
   Unwearied, lotos-eyed, with dreadful bow,
     Dire Evil's constant foe!
Great PEDMANABHA, o'er thy cherish'd world
   The pointed *Checra*, by thy fingers whirl'd,
   Fierce KYTABH shall destroy and MEDHU grim
   To black despair and deep destruction hurl'd.
     Such views my senses dim,
     My eyes in darkness swim:
   What eye can bear thy blaze, what utt'rance tell
Thy deeds with silver trump or many-wreathed shell?

Omniscient Spirit, whose all-ruling pow'r
   Bids from each sense bright emanations beam;
   Glows in the rainbow, sparkles in the stream,
   Smiles in the bud, and glistens in the flow'r
     That crowns each vernal bow'r;
Sighs in the gale, and warbles in the throat
   Of ev'ry bird, that hails the bloomy spring,
   Or tells his love in many a liquid note,
   Whilst envious artists touch the rival string,
     Till rocks and forests ring;
Breathes in rich fragrance from the sandal grove,
   Or where the precious musk-deer playful rove;
   In dulcet juice from clust'ring fruit distills,
   And burns salubrious in the tasteful clove:
     Soft banks and verd'rous hills
     Thy present influence fills;
   In air, in floods, in caverns, woods, and plains;
Thy will inspirits all, thy sov'reign MAYA reigns.

Blue crystal vault, and elemental fires,
   That in th' ethereal fluid blaze and breathe;
   Thou, tossing main, whose snaky branches wreathe
   This pensile orb with intertwisted gyres;
     Mountains, whose radiant spires
Presumptious rear their summits to the skies,
   And blend their em'rald hue with sapphire light;

Smooth meads and lawns, that glow with varying dyes
   Of dew-bespangled leaves and blossoms bright,
     Hence! vanish from my sight:
Delusive Pictures! unsubstantial shows!
    My soul absorb'd One only Being knows,
    Of all perceptions One abundant source,
    Whence ev'ry object ev'ry moment flows:
     Suns hence derive their force,
     Hence planets learn their course;
   But suns and fading worlds I view no more:
GOD only I perceive; GOD only I adore.

SIR WILLIAM JONES

Hymn to Súyra

Fountain of living light,
That o'er all nature streams,
Of this vast microcosm both nerve and soul;
Whose swift and subtil beams,
Eluding mortal sight,
Pervade, attract, sustain th' effulgent whole,
Unite, impel, dilate, calcine,
Give to gold its weight and blaze,
Dart from the diamond many-tinted rays,
Condense, protrude, transform, concoct, refine
The sparkling daughters of the mine;
Lord of the lotos, father, friend, and king,
O Sun, thy pow'rs I sing:
Thy substance *Indra* with his heav'nly bands
Nor sings nor understands;
Nor e'en the *Védas* three to man explain
Thy mystick orb triform, though *Brahmà* tun'd the strain.

Thou, nectar-beaming Moon,
Regent of dewy night,
From yon black roe, that in thy bosom sleeps,
Fawn-spotted *Sasin* hight;
Wilt thou desert so soon
Thy night-flow'rs pale, whom liquid odour steeps,
And *Oshadhi*'s transcendent beam
Burning in the darkest glade?
Will no lov'd name thy gentle mind persuade
Yet one short hour to shed thy cooling stream?

But ah! we court a passing dream:
  Our pray'r nor *Indu* nor *Himánsu* hears;
  He fades; he disappears –
E'en *Casyapa*'s gay daughters twinkling die,
  And silence lulls the sky,
Till *Chátacs* twitter from the moving brake,
And sandal-breathing gales on beds of ether wake.

   Burst into song, ye spheres;
A greater light proclaim,
And hymn, concentrick orbs, with sev'nfold chime
  The God with many a name;
  Nor let unhallow'd ears
Drink life and rapture from your charm sublime:
  'Our bosoms, *Aryama*, inspire,
  Gem of heav'n, and flow'r of day,
  Vivaswat, lancer of the golden ray,
  Divácara, pure source of holy fire,
  Victorious *Ráma*'s fervid sire,
  Dread child of *Aditi*, *Martunda* bless'd,
  Or *Súra* be address'd,
  Ravi, or *Mihira*, or *Bhánu* bold,
  Or *Arca*, title old,
  Or *Heridaswa* drawn by green-hair'd steeds,
  Or *Carmasacshi* keen, attesting secret deeds.

   'What fiend, what monster fierce
E'er durst thy throne invade?
Malignant *Ráhu*. Him thy wakeful sight,
  That could the deepest shade
  Of snaky *Narac* pierce,
Mark'd quaffing nectar; when by magick sleight
  A *Sura*'s lovely form he wore,
  Rob'd in light, with lotos crown'd,
What time th' immortals peerless treasures found
On the churn'd Ocean's gem-bespangled shore,
  And *Mandar*'s load the tortoise bore:
Thy voice reveal'd the daring sacrilege;
  Then, by the deathful edge
  Of bright *Sudersan* cleft, his dragon head
  Dismay and horror spread
Kicking the skies, and struggling to impair
The radiance of thy robes, and stain thy golden hair.

'With smiles of stern disdain
Thou, sov'reign victor, seest
His impious rage: soon from the mad assault
Thy coursers fly releas'd;
Then toss each verdant mane,
And gallop o'er the smooth aerial vault;
Whilst in charm'd *Gócul*'s od'rous vale
Blue-ey'd *Yamunà* descends
Exulting, and her tripping tide suspends,
The triumph of her mighty sire to hail:
So must they fall, who Gods assail!
For now the demon rues his rash emprise,
Yet, bellowing blasphemies
With pois'nous throat, for horrid vengeance thirsts,
And oft with tempest bursts,
As oft repell'd he groans in fiery chains,
And o'er the reams of day unvanquish'd *Súrya* reigns.'

Ye clouds, in wavy wreathes
Your dusky van unfold;
O'er dimpled sands, ye surges, gently flow,
With sapphires edg'd and gold!
Loose-tressed morning breathes,
And spreads her blushes with expansive glow;
But chiefly where heav'n's op'ning eye
Sparkles at her saffron gate,
How rich, how regal in his orient state!
Erelong he shall emblaze th' unbounded sky:
The fiends of darkness yelling fly;
While birds of liveliest note and lightest wing
The rising daystar sing,
Who skirts th' horizon with a blazing line
Of topazes divine;
E'en, in their prelude, brighter and more bright,
Flames the red east, and pours insufferable light.

First o'er blue hills appear,
With many an agate hoof
And pasterns fring'd with pearl, sev'n coursers green;
Nor boasts yon arched woof,
That girds the show'ry sphere,
Such heav'n-spun threads of colour'd light serene,
As tinge the reins, which *Arun* guides,
Glowing with immortal grace,
Young *Arun*, loveliest of *Vinatian* race,
Though younger He, whom *Mádhava* bestrides,

When high on eagle-plumes he rides:
But oh! what pencil of a living star
Could paint that gorgeous car,
In which, as in an ark supremely bright,
The lord of boundless light
Ascending calm o'er th' empyrean sails,
And with ten thousand beams his awful beauty veils.

   Behind the glowing wheels
Six jocund seasons dance,
A radiant month in each quick-shifting hand;
Alternate they advance,
While buxom nature feels
The grateful changes of the frolick band:
Each month a constellation fair
Knit in youthful wedlock holds,
And o'er each bed a varied sun unfolds,
Lest one vast blaze our visual force impair,
A canopy of woven air.
Vasanta blythe with many a laughing flow'r
Decks his *Candarpa*'s bow'r;
The drooping pastures thirsty *Grishma* dries,
Till *Vershà* bids them rise;
Then *Sarat* with full sheaves the champaign fills,
Which *Sisira* bedews, and stern *Hémanta* chills.

   Mark, how the all-kindling orb
Meridian glory gains!
Round *Méru*'s breathing zone he winds oblique
O'er pure cerulean plains:
His jealous flames absorb
All meaner lights, and unresisted strike
The world with rapt'rous joy and dread.
Ocean, smit with melting pain,
Shrinks, and the fiercest monster of the main
Mantles in caves profound his tusky head
With sea-weeds dank and coral spread:
Less can mild earth and her green daughters bear
The noon's wide-wasting glare;
To rocks the panther creeps; to woody night
The vulture steals his flight;
E'en cold cameleons pant in thickets dun,
And o'er the burning grit th' unwinged locusts run!

But when thy foaming steeds
Descend with rapid pace
Thy fervent axle hast'ning to allay,
What majesty, what grace
Dart o'er the western meads
From thy relenting eye their blended ray!
Soon may th' undazzled sense behold
Rich as *Vishnu*'s diadem,
Or *Amrit* sparkling in an azure gem,
Thy horizontal globe of molten gold,
Which pearl'd and rubied clouds infold.
It sinks; and myriads of diffusive dyes
Stream o'er the tissued skies,
Till *Sóma* smiles, attracted by the song
Of many a plumed throng
In groves, meads, vales; and, whilst he glides above,
Each bush and dancing bough quaffs harmony and love.

Then roves thy poet free,
Who with no borrow'd art
Dares hymn thy pow'r, and durst provoke thy blaze,
But felt thy thrilling dart;
And now, on lowly knee,
From him, who gave the wound, the balsam prays.
Herbs, that assuage the fever's pain,
Scatter from thy rolling car,
Cull'd by sage *Aswin* and divine *Cumàr*;
And, if they ask, 'What mortal pours the strain?'
Say (for thou seest earth, air, and main)
Say: 'From the bosom of yon silver isle,
Where skies more softly smile,
He came; and, lisping our celestial tongue
Though not from *Brahmà* sprung,
Draws orient knowledge from its fountains pure,
Through caves obstructed long, and paths too long obscure.'

Yes; though the *Sanscrit* song
Be strown with fancy's wreathes,
And emblems rich, beyond low thoughts refin'd,
Yet heav'nly truth it breathes
With attestation strong,
That, loftier than thy sphere, th' Eternal Mind,
Unmov'd, unrival'd, undefil'd,
Reigns with providence benign:
He still'd the rude abyss, and bade it shine
(Whilst Sapience with approving aspect mild

Saw the stupendous work, and smil'd);
Next thee, his flaming minister, bade rise
O'er young and wondering skies.
Since thou, great orb, with all-enlight'ning ray
Rulest the golden day,
How far more glorious He, who said serene,
BE, and *thou wast* – Himself unform'd, unchang'd, unseen!

NAZIR (*trans* H P Shastri)

Poems of Nazir

I am a lump of gold – melt me in the fire whenever Thou wishest.
At Thy pleasure I will dance to any tune Thou playest.
Test me, reveal my hidden purposes,
  My only happiness lies in the performance of Thy will;
  Whether it lead to pleasure or pain, I am content.

Cover me, if it please Thee, with love and tenderness,
Or draw Thy sowrd and cut me limb from limb;
Defend and sustain me, or take my life – it is all one to me;
I am a fakir, a lover, and this is my refrain:
  My only happiness lies in the performance of Thy will;
  Whether it lead to happiness or pain, I am content.

Keep me at Thy door or dismiss me – I shall be satisfied:
I am a Zalandor, a lover, what care I where I sit?
Lift me to heaven or make the dust my bed,
  My only happiness lies in the performance of Thy will;
  Whether it lead to pleasure or pain, I am content.

. . .

'What is thy name, O wandering yogi?
Where dost thou live? Who is thy preceptor?'
'Vagrant lovers have no dwelling place,
They are here by day and there by night;
No name have I, and my dwelling place
Is the contemplation of the face of my Love!
No God do I worship save Her charming looks;
Her waving locks my willing chains;
I eat sorrow and drink anxiety,
My life's span is separation from Her.'

. . .

Each blossom, leaf, branch and fruit in the world
Has its own place and function to perform.
Reins and spurs are used by the invisible Lord.
So, quietly and patiently bear the grief which visits thee.
Being a fakir, do not seek relationship with any here,
Alone and in tranquillity suffer whatever comes, unmoved.

Do not awaken the sleeping beauties;
Leave thy silken robe and ornaments, discard thy turban;
Do not expect to be remembered after death; do not seek love
    while living.
Being a fakir, do not seek relationship with any here,
Alone and in tranquillity suffer whatever comes, unmoved.

The earth and sky are not thine; thou hast no home;
The body and mind do not belong to thee;
Except the One for whose sake thou hast become a fakir,
Thou hast no friend, no companion, no trusted fellow traveller.
Being a fakir, do not seek relationship with any here,
Alone and in tranquiillity suffer whatever comes; unmoved.

Here it shines in the blue sapphire,
There it enriches the lapiz and the emerald.
Since it unveiled itself it has come to the origin of being.

It is the fragrance permeating every petal of the blossom,
It is the water in the pearl and the light in the twinkling stars,
It is in every form – close as the jugular vein –
It is nearest to all, and in it has the world its being.

When our inner eye is opened we recognize Him.

The dove with the ring, the complaining nightingale,
The blossoming garden and the waving grass,
They all proclaim, and so does the cosmos:
'He is the rose. He is the hanging wisteria,
He is the narcissus and He the water-lily.'

To see Himself He has come into the garden.

All-pervading space, the houris, the angels,
The nymphs and the ferocious genii,
Beast and bird, they all subsist in Him.
Day and night this is our only refrain:
'He is the beginning and the end, the interior and the exterior.'

The words of the Koran proclaim the same truth.

Here He is the clay in the figure of clay, elsewhere He is the soul.
He is the dust and He pervades all,
He is the Creator and He the created.
With all humility the angels salute the august One.

When He comes in the form of man.

Sometimes with His beauty He sets the heart on fire,
Sometimes He induces ecstasy.
Those who know Him cry with one voice:
'He is the singer, He the song and He the music.'

He speaks through every tune, He is manifest in every melody.

. . .

Take up thy mirror and look again therein,
See, in thine image, the handiwork of the Creator.
Consider the dark mole and delicate lines of thy face;
Gaze on the curling locks, redolent with the fragrance of ambergris.
O rose, dwell ever on the radiance of thine eyes,
Be not indifferent to the springs of thine own beauty!

The mirror is thy purified and tranquil heart;
The mole is the mark of anguish left by love;
The flowing hair is thine apprehension of the supreme secret.
O rose, dwell ever on the radiance of thine eyes,
Be not indifferent to the springs of thine own beauty!

If it be thy desire to divine the mystery of the wide-eyed daisy,
Brood on thine own form, and on that sun which is hidden in thee;
The fragrant rose-water and the leaf of the rose are thine,
Are not thy cheeks also the petals bedewed by that essence?

O rose, dwell ever on the radiance of thine eyes,
Be not indifferent to the springs of thine own beauty!

Do not desire to be the narcissus, or become enamoured of the cypress;
They are thyself, meditate on thine own nature, the Self,
Everything in the world of beauty and attraction has its roots in thee;
O rose, dwell ever on the radiance of thine eyes,
Be not indifferent to the springs of thine own beauty!

Look into thy heart! Listen to the music of nightingale
    and dove;
Thy lips are the doves, thy tongue the nightingale,
Thou art the garden and the gardener,
The secret of all gardens is in thee!
O rose, dwell ever on the radiance of thine eyes,
Be not indifferent to the springs of thine own beauty!

Be not imprisoned in bud, blossom or garden,
Be not attracted to the cooing of the dove,
Or the song of the nightingale.
Know thyself, O Nazir!
In the alphabet of knowledge is hidden wisdom's meaning:
It is thy Self!
O rose, dwell ever on the radiance of thine eyes,
Be not indifferent to the springs of thine own beauty!

. . .

In this world some have acquired much knowledge,
And are deemed intellectual and wise;
They carry their libraries on camels
And know the meaning of every word;
They have read logic and philosophy
And are skilled in debate;
They have crossed all the rivers of learning.
These are the concerns and complexities of life,
You may call on truth when death comes and beats the
    drum of farewell,
But the tale will have been told; the dream will have fled.

They become famous doctors
And acquire proficiency in the science of healing,
Their rooms are stocked with books,
Their private records are filled with prescriptions;
But when the disease of death threatens them,
They forget how to feel the pulse and administer relief;
Though they know a thousand remedies, not even one avails.
These are the concerns and complexities of life,
You may call on truth when death comes and beats the
    drum of farewell,
But the tale will have been told; the dream will have fled.

Some become drunkards and are always inebriated,
Others are men of prayer, fasting and meditating;
Some drink the juice of the grape of youthful love;
But when the cup of lover and beloved is full
And death comes,
Then neither rosary nor flask, neither cup nor kisses
Are of any avail.
These are the affairs and complexities of life,
If you call on truth when death comes and beats the drum of farewell.

One was proud of his robe, another of his long beard.
Finding no comfort there, I departed in tears and confusion.
Then my heart said: 'Perchance He is in a school.
Go there and you will find Him.'
When I entered, it was worse than the mosque.
I saw the open books and the scholars
Parading their knowledge in debate;
Everything was being discussed from the point of view of self-interest!
I visited the holy places to see if perchance my Beloved were there;
I found Him not, and retired to the woods.

In the lonely glades I wept and cried:
'What shall I do now? How long must I live, starving and neglected?
On whom can I depend?
It were better to end this life by drowning or poison,
Then, out of compassion, my Beloved will visit me.'
I passed my days in deep forests, a poor and lonely stranger;
Unconscious of thirst and hunger I searched for Him;
Often dashing my head against rocks and stones,
Still I pursued my quest,
Under the scorching sun on the burning sands,
Death staring at me.
Yet I meditated on Him, and had no other thought –
I was helpless, nor could I compel Him to visit me.

While in this wretched state,
That indifferent One came and stood by my side;
Gently lifting my head and placing it on His thigh, He said:
'Lo, gaze on Me now – then I will unfold a great secret.
Know that first we try our lover;
Torment him, wound him, make him weep,
Then, when we have proved him constant under trial,
We call him and come to embrace him forever;
Such a yogi is a true contemplative.'

Hearing the words of the Beloved,
My sufferings ended and I was revived.
I opened my eyes and gazed on the face
Of the One I had sought;
The veils rolled away from earth and sky,
And the fourteen planes of existence stood revealed!
In an instant sorrow was past forever.
Non-duality became my friend,
Duality took wings, like quicksilver in fire,
Doubts and imaginings vanished.

Says Nazir: Since that day I have visited every place,
And found Him everywhere!
He is the object of understanding and knowledge.
Oh, I see He has always been with me!
Now the Hindu, the Moslem and the Jew
Are the same in my eyes.

. . .

When the eye of wisdom opened in me, all duality and
   unity disappeared;
A great wonder possessed my soul, neither subject nor
   object remained.
When the music of Reality fell on mine ear, all other sounds ceased;
Love withdrew all name and form from my being; sorrow and joy
   vanished forever.

J W von Goethe (*trans* Louis MacNeice)

Faust's Confession

I, image of the Godhead, who deemed myself but now
On the brink of the mirror of eternal truth and seeing
My rapturous fill of the blaze of clearest Heaven,
Having stripped off my earthly being;
I, more than an angel, I whose boundless urge
To flow through Nature's veins and in the act of creation
To revel it like the gods – what a divination,
What an act of daring – and what an expiation!
One thundering word has swept me over the verge.

To boast myself thine equal I do not dare.
Granted I owned the power to draw thee down,
I lacked the power to hold thee there.
In that blest moment I felt myself,
Felt myself so small, so great;
Cruelly thou didst thrust me back
Into man's uncertain fate.
Who will teach me? What must I shun?
Or must I go where that impulse drives?
Alas, our very actions like our sufferings
Put a brake upon our lives.

WILLIAM BLAKE

Song

Love and harmony combine,
And around our souls intwine,
While thy branches mix with mine,
And our roots together join.

Joys upon our branches sit,
Chirping loud, and singing sweet;
Like gentle streams beneath our feet
Innocence and virtue meet.

Thou the golden fruit dost bear,
I am clad in flowers fair;
Thy sweet boughs perfume the air,
And the turtle buildeth there.

There she sits and feeds her young,
Sweet I hear her mournful song;
And thy lovely leaves among,
There is love: I hear his tongue.

There his charming nest doth lay,
There he sleeps the night away;
There he sports along the day,
And doth among our branches play.

WILLIAM BLAKE

The Divine Image

To Mercy, Pity, Peace, and Love
All pray in their distress;
And to these virtues of delight
Return their thankfulness.

For Mercy, Pity, Peace, and Love
Is God, our father dear,
And Mercy, Pity, Peace, and Love
Is Man, his child and care.

For Mercy has a human heart,
Pity a human face,
And Love, the human form divine,
And Peace, the human dress.

Then every man, of every clime,
That prays in his distress,
Prays to the human form divine,
Love, Mercy, Pity, Peace.

And all must love the human form,
In heathen, turk, or jew;
Where Mercy, Love, & Pity dwell
There God is dwelling too.

WILLIAM BLAKE

From Auguries of Innocence

To see a World in a grain of sand,
And a Heaven in a wild flower,
Hold Infinity in the palm of your hand,
And Eternity in an hour . . .

The bat that flits at close of eve
Has left the brain that won't believe.
The owl that calls upon the night
Speaks the unbeliever's fright . . .

Joy and woe are woven fine,
A clothing for the soul divine;
Under every grief and pine
Runs a joy with silken twine . . .

Every tear from every eye
Becomes a babe in Eternity . . .
The bleat, the bark, bellow, and roar
Are waves that beat on Heaven's shore . . .

He who doubts from what he sees
Will ne'er believe, do what you please.
If the Sun and Moon should doubt,
They'd immediately go out . . .

God appears, and God is Light,
To those poor souls who dwell in Night;
But does a Human Form display
To those who dwell in realms of Day.

WILLIAM BLAKE

To Thomas Butts

To my friend Butts I write
My first vision of light,
On the yellow sands sitting.
The sun was emitting
His glorious beams
From Heaven's high streams.
Over sea, over land,
My eyes did expand
Into regions of air,
Away from all care;
Into regions of fire,
Remote from desire;
The light of the morning
Heaven's mountains adorning:
In particles bright,
The jewels of light
Distinct shone and clear.
Amaz'd and in fear
I each particle gazèd,
Astonish'd, amazèd;

For each was a Man
Human-form'd. Swift I ran,
For they beckon'd to me,
Remote by the sea,
Saying: 'Each grain of sand,
Every stone on the land,
Each rock and each hill,
Each fountain and rill,
Each herb and each tree,
Mountain, hill, earth, and sea,
Cloud, meteor, and star,
Are men seen afar.'
I stood in the streams
Of heaven's bright beams,
And saw Felpham sweet
Beneath my bright feet,
In soft Female charms;
And in her fair arms
My Shadow I knew,
And my wife's Shadow too,
And my sister, and friend.
We like infants descend
In our Shadows on earth,
Like a weak mortal birth.
My eyes, more and more,
Like a sea without shore,
Continue expanding,
The Heavens commanding;
Till the jewels of light,
Heavenly men beaming bright,
Appear'd as One Man,
Who complacent began
My limbs to enfold
In His beams of bright gold;
Like dross purg'd away
All my mire and my clay.
Soft consum'd in delight,
In His bosom sun-bright
I remain'd. Soft He smil'd,
And I heard His voice mild,
Saying: 'This is My fold,
O thou ram horn'd with gold,
Who awakest from sleep
On the sides of the deep.
On the mountains around
The roarings resound

Of the lion and wolf,
The loud sea, and deep gulf.
These are guards of My fold,
O thou ram horn'd with gold!'
And the voice faded mild;
I remain'd as a child;
All I ever had known
Before me bright shone:
I saw you and your wife
By the fountains of life.
Such the vision to me
Appear'd on the sea.

WILLIAM BLAKE

From Jerusalem

I give you the end of a golden string;
    Only wind it into a ball,
It will lead you in at Heaven's gate,
    Built in Jerusalem's wall . . .

England! awake! awake! awake!
    Jerusalem thy sister calls!
Why wilt thou sleep the sleep of death,
    And close her from thy ancient walls?

Thy hills and valleys felt her feet
    Gently upon their bosoms move:
Thy gates beheld sweet Zion's ways;
    Then was a time of joy and love.

And now the time returns again:
    Our souls exult, and London's towers
Receive the Lamb of God to dwell
    In England's green and pleasant bowers.

WILLIAM BLAKE

Night

The sun descending in the west,
The evening star does shine;
The birds are silent in their nest,
And I must seek for mine.
The moon, like a flower,
In heaven's high bower,
With silent delight
Sits and smiles on the night.

Farewell, green fields and happy groves,
Where flocks have took delight.
Where lambs have nibbled, silent moves
The feet of angels bright;
Unseen they pour blessing,
And joy without ceasing,
On each bud and blossom,
And each sleeping bosom.

They look in every thoughtless nest,
Where birds are cover'd warm;
They visit caves of every beast,
To keep them all from harm.
If they see any weeping
That should have been sleeping,
They pour sleep on their head,
And sit down by their bed.

When wolves and tigers howl for prey,
They pitying stand and weep;
Seeking to drive their thirst away,
And keep them from the sheep.
But if they rush dreadful,
The angels, most heedful,
Receive each mild spirit,
New worlds to inherit.

And there the lion's ruddy eyes
Shall flow with tears of gold,
And pitying the tender cries,
And walking round the fold,
Saying: 'Wrath, by His meekness,
And, by His health, sickness
Is driven away
From our immortal day.

'And now beside thee, bleating lamb,
I can lie down and sleep;
Or think on Him who bore thy name,
Graze after thee and weep.
For, wash'd in life's river,
My bright mane for ever
Shall shine like the gold
As I guard o'er the fold.'

WILLIAM WORDSWORTH

From The Excursion

I

Such was the Boy – but for the growing Youth
What soul was his, when, from the naked top
Of some bold headland, he beheld the sun
Rise up, and bathe the world in light! He looked –
Ocean and earth, the solid frame of earth
And ocean's liquid mass, in gladness lay
Beneath him: – Far and wide the clouds were touched,
And in their silent faces could he read
Unutterable love. Sound needed none,
Nor any voice of joy; his spirit drank
The spectacle: sensation, soul, and form,
All melted into him; they swallowed up
His animal being; in them did he live,
And by them did he live; they were his life.
In such access of mind, in such high hour
Of visitation from the living God,
Thought was not; in enjoyment it expired.
No thanks he breathed, he proffered no request;
Rapt into still communion that transcends
The imperfect offices of prayer and praise,
His mind was a thanksgiving to the power
That made him; it was blessedness and love!

II

Thou, who didst wrap the cloud
Of infancy around us, that thyself,
Therein, with our simplicity awhile
Might'st hold, on earth, communion undisturbed;
Who from the anarchy of dreaming sleep,
Or from its death-like void, with punctual care,
And touch as gentle as the morning light,
Restor'st us, daily, to the powers of sense
And reason's steadfast rule – thou, thou alone
Art everlasting, and the blessed Spirits,
Which thou includest, as the sea her waves:
For adoration thou endur'st; endure
For consciousness the motions of thy will;
For apprehension those transcendent truths
Of the pure intellect, that stands as laws
(Submission constituting strength and power)

Even to thy Being's infinite majesty!
This universe shall pass away – a work
Glorious! because the shadow of thy might,
A step, or link, for intercourse with thee.
Ah! if the time must come, in which my feet
No more shall stray where meditation leads,
By flowing stream, through wood, or craggy wild,
Loved haunts like these; the unimprisoned Mind
May yet have scope to range among her own,
Her thoughts, her images, her high desires.
If the dear faculty of sight should fail,
Still, it may be allowed me to remember
What visionary powers of eye and soul
In youth were mine; when, stationed on the top
Of some huge hill, expectant, I beheld
The sun rise up, from distant climes returned
Darkness to chase, and sleep; and bring the day
His bounteous gift! or saw him toward the deep
Sink, with a retinue of flaming clouds
Attended; then, my spirit was entranced
With joy exalted to beatitude;
The measure of my soul was filled with bliss,
And holiest love; as earth, sea, air, with light,
With pomp, with glory, with magnificence!

III

I have seen
A curious child, who dwelt upon a tract
Of inland ground, applying to his ear
The convolutions of a smooth-lipped shell;
To which, in silence hushed, his very soul
Listened intensely; and his countenance soon
Brightened with joy; for from within were heard
Murmurings, whereby the monitor expressed
Mysterious union with its native sea.
Even such a shell the universe itself
Is to the ear of Faith; and there are times,
I doubt not, when to you it doth impart
Authentic tidings of invisible things;
Of ebb and flow, and ever-during power;
And central peace, subsisting at the heart
Of endless agitation.

IV

To every Form of being is assigned
An *active* Principle: – howe'er removed
From sense and observation, it subsists
In all things, in all natures; in the stars
Of azure heaven, the unenduring clouds,
In flower and tree, in every pebbly stone
That paves the brooks, the stationary rocks,
The moving waters, and the invisible air.
Whate'er exists hath properties that spread
Beyond itself, communicating good,
A simple blessing, or with evil mixed;
Spirit that knows no insulated spot,
No chasm, no solitude; from link to link
It circulates, the Soul of all the worlds.
This is the freedom of the universe;
Unfolded still the more, more visible,
The more we know; and yet is reverenced least,
And least respected in the human Mind,
Its most apparent home.

. . .

How beautiful this dome of sky;
And the vast hills, in fluctuation fixed
At Thy command, how awful! Shall the Soul,
Human and rational, report if Thee
Even less than these? – Be mute who will, who can,

Yet I will praise Thee with impassioned voice:
My lips, that may forget Thee in the crowd,
Cannot forget Thee here; where Thou hast built,
For Thy own glory, in the wilderness!
– Come, labour, when the worn-out frame requires
Perpetual sabbath; come, disease and want,
And sad exclusion through decay of sense;
But leave me unabated trust in Thee,
And let Thy favour, to the end of life,
Inspire me with ability to seek
Repose and hope among eternal things –
Father of heaven and earth! and I am rich,
And will possess my portion in content!

WILLIAM WORDSWORTH

From On the Power of Sound

By one pervading spirit
Of tones and numbers all things are controlled,
As sages taught, where faith was found to merit
Initiation in that mystery old.
The heavens, whose aspect makes our minds as still
As they themselves appear to be,
Innumerable voices fill
With everlasting harmony;
The towering headlands, crowned with mist,
Their feet among the billows, know
That Ocean is a mighty harmonist;
Thy pinions, universal Air,
Ever waving to and fro,
Are delegates of harmony, and bear
Strains that support the Seasons in their round;
Stern Winter loves a dirge-like sound.

Break forth into thanksgiving,
Ye banded instruments of wind and chords;
Unite, to magnify the Ever-living,
Your inarticulate notes with the voice of words!
Nor hushed be service from the lowing mead,
Nor mute the forest hum of noon;
Thou too be heard, lone eagle! freed
From snowy peak and cloud, attune
Thy hungry barkings to the hymn

Of joy, that from her utmost walls
The six-days' Work by flaming Seraphim
Transmits to Heaven! As Deep to Deep
Shouting through one valley calls,
All worlds, all natures, mood and measure keep
For praise and ceaseless gratulation, poured
Into the ear of God, their Lord!

A Voice to Light gave Being;
To Time, and Man his earth-born chronicler;
A Voice shall finish doubt and dim foreseeing,
And sweep away life's visionary stir;
The trumpet (we, intoxicate with pride,
Arm at its blast for deadly wars)
To archangelic lips applied,
The grave shall open, quench the stars.
O Silence! are Man's noisy years
No more than moments of thy life?
Is Harmony, blest queen of smiles and tears,
With her smooth tones and discords just,
Tempered into rapturous strife,
Thy destined bond-slave? No! though earth be dust
And vanish, though the heavens dissolve, her stay
Is in the WORD, that shall not pass away.

WILLIAM WORDSWORTH

From Ode: Intimations of Immortality from Recollections of Early Childhood

There was a time when meadow, grove, and stream,
    The earth, and every common sight
        To me did seem
        Apparelled in celestial light,
The glory and the freshness of a dream.
It is not now as it hath been of yore; –
        Turn wheresoe'er I may,
        By night or day,
The things which I have seen I now can see no more.

The Rainbow comes and goes,
And lovely is the Rose,
The Moon doth with delight
Look round her when the heavens are bare,
Waters on a starry night
Are beautiful and fair;
The sunshine is a glorious birth;
But yet I know, where'er I go,
That there hath past away a glory from the earth.

Now, while the birds thus sing a joyous song,
And while the young lambs bound
As to the tabor's sound,
To me alone there came a thought of grief:
A timely utterance gave that thought relief,
And I again am strong:
The cataracts blow their trumpets from the steep;
No more shall grief of mine the season wrong;
I hear the Echoes through the mountains throng,
The Winds come to me from the fields of sleep.

O joy! that in our embers
Is something that doth live,
That nature yet remembers
What was so fugitive!
The thought of our past years in me doth breed
Perpetual benediction: not indeed
For that which is most worthy to be blest;
Delight and liberty, the simple creed
Of Childhood, whether busy or at rest,
With new-fledged hope still fluttering in his breast: –
Not for these I raise
The song of thanks and praise;
But for those obstinate questionings
Of sense and outward things,

. . .

Be now for ever taken from my sight,
Though nothing can bring back the hour
Of splendour in the grass, of glory in the flower;
We will grieve not, rather find
Strength in what remains behind;
In the primal sympathy
Which having been must ever be;

In the soothing thoughts that spring
Out of human suffering;
In the faith that looks through death,
In years that bring the philosophic mind.

And O, ye Fountains, Meadows, Hills, and Groves,
Forebode not any severing of our loves!
Yet in my heart of hearts I feel your might;
I only have relinquished one delight
To live beneath your more habitual sway.
I love the Brooks which down their channels fret,
Even more than when I tripped lightly as they;
The innocent brightness of a new-born Day
      Is lovely yet;
The Clouds that gather round the setting sun
Do take a sober colouring from an eye
That hath kept watch o'er man's mortality;
Another race hath been, and other palms are won.
Thanks to the human heart by which we live,
Thanks to its tenderness, its joys, and fears,
To me the meanest flower that blows can give
Thoughts that do often lie too deep for tears.

WILLIAM WORDSWORTH

From Lines Composed a Few Miles Above Tintern Abbey

For I have learned
To look on nature, not as in the hour
Of thoughtless youth; but hearing oftentimes
The still, sad music of humanity,
Nor harsh nor grating, though of ample power
To chasten and subdue. And I have felt
A presence that disturbs me with the joy
Of elevated thoughts; a sense sublime
Of something far more deeply interfused,
Whose dwelling is the light of setting suns,
And the round ocean and the living air,
And the blue sky, and in the mind of man:
A motion and a spirit, that impels
All thinking things, all objects of all thought,
And rolls through all things. Therefore am I still
A lover of the meadows and the woods,

And mountains; and of all that we behold
From this green earth; of all the mighty world
Of eye, and ear, – both what they half create,
And what perceive; well pleased to recognize
In nature and the language of the sense,
The anchor of my purest thoughts, the nurse,
The guide, the guardian of my heart, and soul
Of all my moral being.

WILLIAM WORDSWORTH

From The Prelude

I

Thus while the days flew by, and years passed on,
From Nature and her overflowing soul
I had received so much, that all my thoughts
Were steeped in feeling; I was only then
Contented, when with bliss ineffable
I felt the sentiment of Being spread
O'er all that moves and all that seemeth still;
O'er all that, lost beyond the reach of thought
And human knowledge, to the human eye
Invisible, yet liveth to the heart;
O'er all that leaps and runs, and shouts and sings,
Or beats the gladsome air; o'er all that glides
Beneath the wave, yea, in the wave itself,
And mighty depth of waters. Wonder not
If high the transport, great the joy I felt
Communing in this sort through earth and heaven
With every form of creature, as it looked
Towards the Uncreated with a countenance
Of adoration, with an eye of love.
One song they sang, and it was audible,
Most audible, then, when the fleshly ear,
O'ercome by humblest prelude of that strain,
Forgot her functions, and slept undisturbed.
– Of that external scene which round me lay,
Little, in this abstraction, did I see;
Remembered less; but I had inward hopes
And swellings of the spirit, was rapt and soothed,
Conversed with promises, had glimmering views
How life pervades the undecaying mind;
How the immortal soul with God-like power

Informs, creates, and thaws the deepest sleep
That time can lay upon her; how on earth,
Man, if he do but live within the light
Of high endeavours, daily spreads abroad
His being armed with strength that cannot fail.

        Visionary power
Attends the motions of the viewless winds,
Embodied in the mystery of words:
There, darkness makes abode, and all the host
Of shadowy things work endless changes, – there,
As in a mansion like their proper home,
Even forms and substances are circumfused
By that transparent veil with light divine,
And, through the turnings intricate of verse,
Present themselves as objects recognized,
In flashes, and with glory not their own.

                IV
Imagination – here the Power so called
Through sad incompetence of human speech,
That awful Power rose from the mind's abyss
Like an unfathered vapour that enwraps,
At once, some lonely traveller. I was lost;
Halted without an effort to break through;
But to my conscious soul I now can say –
'I recognize thy glory': in such strength
Of usurpation, when the light of sense
Goes out, but with a flash that has revealed
The invisible world, doth greatness make abode,
There harbours; whether we be young or old,
Our destiny, our being's heart and home,
Is with infinitude, and only there;
With hope it is, hope that can never die,
Effort, and expectation, and desire,
And something evermore about to be.
Under such banners militant, the soul
Seeks for no trophies, struggles for no spoils
That may attest her prowess, blest in thoughts
That are their own perfection and reward,
Strong in herself and in beatitude
That hides her, like the mighty flood of Nile
Poured from his fount of Abyssinian clouds
To fertilize the whole Egyptian plain.

V

                    The brook and road
Were fellow-travellers in this gloomy strait,
And with them did we journey several hours
At a slow pace. The immeasurable height
Of woods decaying, never to be decayed,
The stationary blasts of waterfalls,
And in the narrow rent at every turn
Winds thwarting winds, bewildered and forlorn,
The torrents shooting from the clear blue sky,
The rocks that muttered close upon our ears,
Black drizzling crags that spake by the way-side
As if a voice were in them, the sick sight
And giddy prospect of the raving stream,
The unfettered clouds and region of the Heavens,
Tumult and peace, the darkness and the light –
Were all like workings of one mind, the features
Of the same face, blossoms upon one tree;
Characters of the great Apocalypse,
The types and symbols of Eternity,
Of first, and last, and midst, and without end,

VI

                    In some green bower
Rest, and be not alone, but have thou there
The One who is thy choice of all the world:
There linger, listening, gazing, with delight
Impassioned, but delight how pitiable!
Unless this love by a still higher love
Be hallowed, love that breathes not without awe;
Love that adores, but on the knees of prayer,
By heaven inspired; that frees from chains the soul,
Lifted, in union with the purest, best,
Of earth-born passions, on the wings of praise
Bearing a tribute to the Almighty's Throne.

VII

This spiritual Love acts not nor can exist
Without Imagination, which, in truth,
Is but another name for absolute power
And clearest insight, amplitude of mind,
And Reason in her most exalted mood.
This faculty hath been the feeding source
Of our long labour: we have traced the stream
From the blind cavern whence is faintly heard

Its natal murmur; followed it to light
And open day; accompanied its course
Among the ways of Nature, for a time
Lost sight of it bewildered and engulphed;
Then given it greeting as it rose once more
In strength, reflecting from its placid breast
The works of man and face of human life;
And lastly, from its progress have we drawn
Faith in life endless, the sustaining thought
Of human Being, Eternity, and God.

Dust as we are, the immortal spirit grows
Like harmony in music; there is a dark
Inscrutable workmanship that reconciles
Discordant elements, makes them cling together
In one society. How strange, that all
The terrors, pains, and early miseries,
Regrets, vexations, lassitudes interfused
Within my mind, should e'er have borne a part,
And that a needful part, in making up
The calm existence that is mine when I
Am worthy of myself. Praise to the end!

SAMUEL TAYLOR COLERIDGE

From Religious Musings

This is the time, when most divine to hear,
The voice of Adoration rouses me,
As with a Cherub's trump: and high upborne,
Yea, mingling with the Choir, I seem to view
The vision of the heavenly multitude,

. . .

For the Great
Invisible (by symbols only seen)
With a peculiar and surpassing light
Shines from the visage of the oppressed good man,

. . .

Fair the vernal mead,
Fair the high grove, the sea, the sun, the stars;
True impress each of their creating Sire!
Yet nor high grove, nor many-colour'd mead,
Nor the green ocean with his thousand isles,
Nor the starred azure, nor the sovran sun,
E'er with such majesty of portraiture
Imagined the supreme beauty uncreate.

. . .

Harped by Archangels, when they sing of mercy!
Which when the Almighty heard from forth his throne
Diviner light filled Heaven with ecstasy!
Heaven's hymnings paused: and Hell her yawning mouth
Closed a brief moment.

Lovely was the death
Of Him whose life was Love? Holy with power
He on the thought-benighted Sceptic beamed
Manifest Godhead, melting into day
What floating mists of dark idolatry
Broke and misshaped the omnipresent Sire:
And first by Fear uncharmed the drowsèd Soul.
Till of its nobler nature it 'gan feel
Dim recollections; and thence soared to Hope.
Strong to believe whate'er of mystic good
The Eternal dooms for His immortal sons.
From Hope and firmer Faith to perfect Love
Attracted and absorbed: and centered there
God only to behold, and know, and feel,
Till by exclusive consciousness of God
All self-annihilated it shall make
God its Identity: God all in all!
We and our Father one!

And blest are they,
Who in this fleshly World, the elect of Heaven,
Their strong eye darting through the deeds of men,
Adore with steadfast unpresuming gaze
Him Nature's essence, mind, and energy!
And gazing, trembling, patiently ascend
Treading beneath their feet all visible things
As steps, that upward to their Father's throne
Lead gradual – else nor glorified nor loved.
They nor contempt embosom nor revenge:

For they dare know of what may seem deform
The Supreme Fair sole operant: in whose sight
All things are pure, his strong controlling love
Alike from all educing perfect good.
Their's too celestial courage, inly armed –
Dwarfing Earth's giant brood, what time they muse
On their great Father, great beyond compare!
And marching onwards view high o'er their heads
His waving banners of Omnipotence.

. . .

                    Soon refresh'd from Heaven
He calms the throb and tempest of his heart.
His countenance settles; a soft solemn bliss
Swims in his eye – his swimming eye uprais'd:
And Faith's whole armour glitters on his limbs!
And thus transfigured with a dreadless awe,
A solemn hush of soul, meek he beholds
All things of terrible seeming: yea, unmoved
Views e'en the immitigable ministers
That shower down vengeance on these latter days.
For kindling with intenser Deity
From the celestial Mercy-seat they come.
And at the renovating wells of Love
Have fill'd their vials with salutary wrath,
To sickly Nature more medicinal
Than what soft balm the weeping good man pours
Into the lone despoiled traveller's wounds!

Thus from the Elect, regenerate through faith,
Pass the dark Passions and what thirsty cares
Drink up the spirit, and the dim regards
Self-centre. Lo they vanish! or acquire
New names, new features – by supernal grace
Enrobed with Light, and naturalised in Heaven.
As when a shepherd on a vernal morn
Through some thick fog creeps timorous with slow foot,
Darkling he fixes on the immediate road
His downward eye all else of fairest kind
Hid or deformed. But lo! the bursting Sun!
Touched by the enchantment of that sudden beam
Straight the black vapour melteth, and in globes
Of dewy glitter gems each plant and tree;
On every leaf, on every blade it hangs!
Dance glad the new-born intermingling rays,
And wide around the landscape streams with glory!

There is one Mind, one omnipresent Mind,
Omnific. His most holy name is Love.
Truth of subliming import! with the which
Who feeds and saturates his constant soul,
He from his small particular orbit flies
With blest outstarting! From himself he flies,
Stands in the sun, and with no partial gaze
Views all creation; and he loves it all,
And blesses it, and calls it very good!
This is indeed to dwell with the Most High!
Cherubs and rapture-trembling Seraphim
Can press no nearer to the Almighty's throne.
But that we roam unconscious, or with hearts
Unfeeling of our universal Sire,
And that in His vast family no Cain
Injures uninjured (in her best-aimed blow
Victorious Murder a blind Suicide)
Haply for this some younger Angel now
Looks down on Human Nature: and, behold!
A sea of blood bestrewed with wrecks, where mad
Embattling Interests on each other rush
With unhelmed rage!

                    Tis the sublime of man,
Our noontide Majesty, to know ourselves
Parts and proportions of one wondrous whole!
This fraternises man, this constitutes
Our charities and bearings. But 'tis God
Diffused through all, that doth make all one whole;
This the worse superstition, him except
Aught to desire, Supreme Reality!
The plenitude and permanence of bliss!
I will raise up a mourning. O ye friends.
And curse your spells, that film the eye of Faith,
Hiding the present God; whose presence lost,
The moral world's cohesion, we become
An Anarchy of Spirits! Toy-bewitched,
Made blind by lusts, disherited of soul,
No common centre Man, no common sire
Knoweth! A sordid solitary thing,
Mid countless brethren with a lonely heart
Through courts and cities the smooth savage roams
Feeling himself, his own low self the whole;
When he by sacred sympathy might make
The whole one Self! Self, that no alien knows!
Self, far diffused as Fancy's wing can travel!

Self, spreading still! Oblivious of its own,
Yet all of all possessing! This is Faith!
This the Messiah's destined victory!

. . .

                     Lord of unsleeping Love,
From everlasting Thou! We shall not die.
These, even these, in mercy didst thou form,
Teachers of Good through Evil, by brief wrong
Making Truth lovely, and her future might
Magnetic o'er the fixed untrembling heart.

In the primeval age a dateless while
The vacant Shepherd wander'd with his flock,
Pitching his tent where'er the green grass waved.
But soon Imagination conjured up
An host of new desires: with busy aim,
Each for himself, Earth's eager children toiled.
So Property began, twy-streaming fount,
Whence Vice and Virtue flow, honey and gall.
Hence the soft couch, and many-coloured robe,
The timbrel, and arched dome and costly feast,
With all the inventive arts, that nursed the soul
To forms of beauty, and by sensual wants
Unsensualised the mind, which in the means
Learnt to forget the grossness of the end,
Best pleasured with its own activity.
And hence Disease that withers manhood's arm,
The daggered Envy, spirit-quenching Want,
Warriors, and Lords, and Priests – all the sore ills
That vex and desolate our mortal life.
Wide-wasting ills! yet each the immediate source
Of mightier good. Their keen necessities
To ceaseless action goading human thought
Have made Earth's reasoning animal her Lord;
And the pale-featured Sage's trembling hand
Strong as an host of armèd Deities,
Such as the blind Ionian fabled erst.

From Avarice thus, from Luxury and War
Sprang heavenly Science; and from Science Freedom.
O'er waken'd realms Philosophers and Bards
Spread in concentric circles: they whose souls,
Conscious of their high dignities from God,
Brook not Wealth's rivalry! and they, who long

Enamoured with the charms of order, hate
The unseemly disproportion: and whoe'er
Turn with mild sorrow from the Victor's car
And the low puppetry of thrones, to muse
On that blest triumph, when the Patriot Sage
Called the red lightnings from the o'er-rushing cloud
And dashed the beauteous terrors on the earth
Smiling majestic. Such a phalanx ne'er
Measured firm paces to the calming sound
Of Spartan flute! These on the fated day,
When, stung to rage by Pity, eloquent men
Have roused with pealing voice the unnumbered tribes
That toil and groan and bleed, hungry and blind –
These, hush'd awhile with patient eye serene,
Shall watch the mad careering of the storm;
Then o'er the wild and wavy chaos rush
And tame the outrageous mass, with plastic might
Moulding Confusion to such perfect forms,
As erst were wont – bright visions of the day! –
To float before them, when, the summer noon,
Beneath some arched romantic rock reclined
They felt the sea-breeze lift their youthful locks;
Or in the month of blossoms, at mild eve,
Wandering with desultory feet inhaled
The wafted perfumes, and the flocks and woods
And many-tinted streams and setting sun
With all his gorgeous company of clouds
Ecstatic gazed! then homeward as they strayed
Cast the sad eye to earth, and inly mused
Why there was misery in a world so fair.

. . .

The kingdoms of the world are your's: each heart
Self-governed, the vast family of Love
Raised from the common earth by common toil
Enjoy the equal produce. Such delights
As float to earth, permitted visitants!
When in some hour of solemn jubilee
The massy gates of Paradise are thrown
Wide open, and forth come in fragments wild
Sweet echoes of unearthly melodies,
And odours snatched from beds of Amaranth,
And they, that from the crystal river of life
Spring up on freshened wing, ambrosial gales!
The favoured good man in his lonely walk

Perceives them, and his silent spirit drinks
Strange bliss which he shall recognise in heaven.
And such delights, such strange beatitudes
Seize on my young anticipating heart

. . .

When that blest future rushes on my view!
For in his own and in his Father's might
The Saviour comes! While as the Thousand Years
Lead up their mystic dance, the Desert shouts!
Old Ocean claps his hands! The mighty Dead
Rise to new life, whoe'er from earliest time
With conscious zeal had urged Love's wondrous plan,
Coadjutors of God.

. . .

                    Believe thou, O my soul,
Life is a vision shadowy of Truth;
And vice, and anguish, and the wormy grave,
Shapes of a dream! The veiling clouds retire,
And lo! the Throne of the redeeming God
Forth flashing unimaginable day
Wraps in one blaze earth, heaven, and deepest hell.

Contemplant Spirits! ye that hover o'er
With untired gaze the immeasurable fount
Ebullient with creative Deity!
And ye of plastic power, that interfused
Roll through the grosser and material mass
In organizing surge! Holies of God!
(And what if Monads of the infinite mind?)
I haply journeying my immortal course
Shall sometime join your mystic choir! Till then
I discipline my young and novice thought
In ministeries of heart-stirring song,
And aye on Meditation's heaven-ward wing
Soaring aloft I breathe the empyreal air
Of Love, omnific, omnipresent Love,
Whose day-spring rises glorious in my soul
As the great Sun, when he his influence
Sheds on the frost-bound waters – The glad stream
Flows to the ray and warbles as it flows.

SAMUEL TAYLOR COLERIDGE

Self-Knowledge

Know yourself – and is this the prime
And heaven-sprung adage of the olden time! –
Say, canst thou make thyself? – Learn first that trade; –
Haply thou mayst know what thyself had made.
What hast thou, Man, that thou dar'st call thine own? –
What is there in thee, Man, that can be known? –
Dark fluxion, all unfixable by thought,
A phantom dim of past and future wrought,
Vain sister of the worm, – life, death, soul, clod –
Ignore thyself, and strive to know thy God!

SAMUEL TAYLOR COLERIDGE

From The Pains of Sleep

Here on my bed my limbs I lay,
It hath not been my use to pray
With moving lips or bended knees;
But silently, by slow degrees,
My spirit I to Love compose,
In humble trust mine eye-lids close,
With reverential resignation,
No wish conceived, no thought exprest,
Only a sense of supplication;
A sense o'er all my soul imprest
That I am weak, yet not unblest,
Since in me, round me, every where
Eternal Strength and Wisdom are.

JOHN KEATS

From Before Reading Lear

. . . Chief Poet! and ye clouds of Albion,
    Begetters of our deep eternal theme,
When I am through the old oak forest gone,
    Let me not wander in a barren dream;
But when I am consuméd with the Fire,
Give me new Phœnix-wings to fly at my desire.

JOHN KEATS

From Endymion: Book I

Feel we these things? – that moment have we stept
Into a sort of oneness, and our state
Is like a floating spirit's. But there are
Richer entanglements, enthralments far
More self-destroying, leading, by degrees,
To the chief intensity: the crown of these
Is made of love and friendship, and sits high
Upon the forehead of humanity.
All its more ponderous and bulky worth
Is friendship, whence there ever issues forth
A steady splendour; but at the tip-top,
There hangs by unseen film, an orbed drop
Of light, and that is love: its influence,
Thrown in our eyes, genders a novel sense,
At which we start and fret; till in the end,
Melting into its radiance, we blend,
Mingle, and so become a part of it, –
Nor with aught else can our souls interknit
So wingedly: when we combine therewith,
Life's self is nourish'd by its proper pith.
And we are nurtured like a pelican brood.
Aye, so delicious is the unsating food,
That men, who might have tower'd in the van
Of all the congregated world, to fan
And winnow from the coming step of time
All chaff of custom, wipe away all slime
Left by men-slugs and human serpentry,
Have been content to let occasion die,
Whilst they did sleep in love's elysium.
And, truly, I would rather be struck dumb,
Then speak against this ardent listlessness:
For I have ever thought that it might bless
The world with benefits unknowingly;
As does the nightingale, upperched high,
And cloister'd among cool and bunched leaves –
She sings but to her love, nor e'er conceives
How tiptoe Night holds back her dark-grey hood.
Just so may love, although 'tis understood
The mere commingling of passionate breath,
Produce more than our searching witnesseth.

JOHN KEATS

From Endymion: Book II

How long must I remain in jeopardy
Of blank amazements that amaze no more?
Now I have tasted her sweet soul to the core
All other depths are shallow: essences,
Once spiritual, are like muddy lees,
Meant but to fertilize my earthly root.
And make my branches lift a golden fruit
Into the bloom of heaven: other light.

JOHN KEATS

From Endymion: Book III

One million times ocean must ebb and flow.
And he oppressed. Yet he shall not die,
These things accomplish'd: – If he utterly
Scans all the depths of magic, and expounds
The meanings of all motions, shapes and sounds;
If he explores all forms and substances
Straight homeward to their symbol-essences;
He shall not die. Moreover, and in chief,
He must pursue this task of joy and grief
Most piously; – all lovers tempest-tost,
And in the sarage overwhelming lost,
He shall deposit side by side, until
Time's creeping shall the dreary space fulfil:
Which done, and all these labours ripened,
A youth, by heavenly power lov'd and led,
Shall stand before him; whom he shall direct
How to consumate all. The youth elect
Must do the thing, or both will be destroy'd.

JAMES MONTGOMERY

From The Brahmin

Canto I

Once on the mountain's balmy lap reclined,
The Sage unlocked the treasures of his mind;
Pure from his lips, sublime instruction came,
As the blest altar breathes celestial flame:
A band of youths and virgins round him pressed,
Whom thus the prophet and the sage addressed.

'Thro' the wide universe's boundless range,
All that exist decay, revive and change:

No atom torpid or inactive lies;
A being, once created, never dies.
The waning moon, when quenched in shades of night,
Renews her youth with all the charms of light;
The flowery beauties of the blooming year
Shrink from the shivering blast, and disappear;
Yet, warmed with quickening showers of genial rain.
Spring from their graves, and purple all the plain.
As day the night, and night succeeds the day,
So death reanimates, so lives decay:
Like billows on the undulating main,
The swelling fall, the falling swell again;
Thus on the tide of time, inconstant, roll
The dying body and the living soul.
In every animal, inspired with breath,
The flowers of life produce the seeds of death; –
The seeds of death, though scattered in the tomb,
Spring with new vigour, vegetate and bloom.

'When wasted down to dust the creature dies,
Quick, from its cell, the enfranchised spirit flies;
Fills, with fresh energy, another form,
And towers an elephant, or glides a worm;
The awful lion's royal shape assumes;
The fox's subtlety, or peacock's plumes;
Swims, like an eagle, in the eye of noon,
Or wails, a screech owl, to the deaf, cold moon;
Haunts the dread brakes, where serpents hiss and glare,
Or hums, a glittering insect, in the air.
The illustrious souls of great and virtuous men.

In noble animals revive again:
But base and vicious spirits wind their way,
In scorpions, vultures, sharks and beasts of prey.
The fair, the gay, the witty, and the brave,
The fool, the coward, courtier, tyrant, slave;
Each, in congenial animals, shall find
An home and kindred for his wandering mind.

   'Even the cold body, when enshrined in earth,
Rises again in vegetable birth:
From the vile ashes of the bad proceeds
A baneful harvest of pernicious weeds;
The relics of the good, awaked by showers,
Peep from the lap of death, and live in flowers;
Sweet modest flowers, that blush along the vale,
Whose fragrant lips embalm the passing gale.'

LORD BYRON

If that High World

I

If that high world, which lies beyond
   Our own, surviving Love endears;
If there the cherish'd heart be fond,
   The eye the same, except in tears –
Flow welcome those untrodden spheres!
   How sweet this very hour to die!
To soar from earth, and find all fears
   Lost in thy light – Eternity!

II

It must be so: 'f is not for self
   That we so tremble on the brink;
And striving to o'erleap the gulf
   Yet cling to Being's severing link.
Oh! in that future let us think
   To hold each heart the heart that shares,
With them the immortal waters drink,
   And soul in soul grow deathless theirs!

LORD BYRON

From Manfred

Mysterious Agency!
Ye spirits of the unbounded Universe!
Whom I have sought in darkness and in light –
Ye, who do compass earth about, and dwell
In subtler essence – ye, to whom the tops
Of mountains inaccessible are haunts,
And earth's and ocean's caves familiar things –
I call upon ye by the written charm
Which gives me power upon you – Rise! appear!

They come not yet. – Now by the voice of him
Who is the first among you – by this sign,
Which makes you tremble – by the claims of him
Who is undying, – Rise! appear! – Appear!

If it be so. – Spirits of earth and air,
Ye shall not thus elude me: by a power,
Deeper than all yet urged, a tyrant-spell,
Which had its birthplace in a star condemn'd,
The burning wreck of a demolish'd world,
A wandering hell in the eternal space;
By the strong curse which is upon my soul,
The thought which is within me and around me,
I do compel ye to my will – Appear!

LORD BYRON

From The Dream

I

Our life is twofold: Sleep hath its own world,
A boundary between the things misnamed
Death and existence: Sleep hath its own world,
And a wide realm of wild reality,
And dreams in their development have breath,
And tears, and tortures, and the touch of joy;
They leave a weight upon our waking thoughts,
They take a weight from off our waking toils,
They do divide our being; they become
A portion of ourselves as of our time,

And look like heralds of eternity;
They pass like spirits of the past, – they speak
Like sybils of the future; they have power –
The tyranny of pleasure and of pain;
They make us what we were not – what they will,
And shake us with the vision that's gone by,
The dread of vanish'd shadows – Are they so?
Is not the past all shadow? What are they?
Creations of the mind? – The mind can make
Substance, and people planets of its own
With beings brighter than have been, and give
A breath to forms which can outlive all flesh.
I would recall a vision which I dream'd
Perchance in sleep – for in itself a thought,
A slumbering thought, is capable of years,
And curdles a long life into one hour.

II

I saw two beings in the hues of youth
Standing upon a hill, a gentle hill,
Green and of mild declivity, the last
As't were the cape of a long ridge of such,
Save that there was no sea to lave its base,
But a most living landscape, and the wave
Of woods and cornfields, and the abodes of men
Scatter'd at intervals, and wreathing smoke
Arising from such rustic roofs: – the hill
Was crown'd with a peculiar diadem
Of trees, in circular array, so fix'd,
Not by the sport of nature, but of man:
These two, a maiden and a youth, were there
Gazing – the one on all there was beneath
Fair as herself – but the boy gazed on her;
And both were young – yet not alike in youth.
As the sweet moon on the horizon's verge,
The maid was on the eve of womanhood;
The boy had fewer summers, but his heart
Had far outgrown his years, and to his eye
There was but one beloved face on earth,
And that was shining on him: he had look'd
Upon it till it could not pass away;
He had no breath, no being, but in hers;
She was his voice: he did not speak to her,
But trembled on her words; she was his sight,
For his eye follow'd hers, and saw with hers,

Which colour'd all his objects: – he had ceased
To live within himself; she was his life,
The ocean to the river of his thoughts,
Which terminated all.

LORD BYRON

From Don Juan

Between two worlds life hovers like a star
'Twixt night and morn upon the horizon's verge.
How little do we know that which we are!
How less what we may be. The eternal surge
Of time and tide rolls on and bears afar
Our bubbles. As the old burst new emerge,
Lashed from the foam of ages while the graves
Of empires heave but like some passing waves.

PERCY BYSSHE SHELLY

From Prometheus Unbound

This is the day, which down the void abysm
At the Earth-born's spell yawns for Heaven's despotism.
    And Conquest is dragged captive through the deep:
Love, from its awful throne of patient power
In the wise heart, from the last giddy hour
    Of dread endurance, from the slippery, steep,
And narrow verge of crag-like agony, springs
And folds over the world its healing wings.

Gentleness, Virtue, Wisdom, and Endurance,
These are the seals of that most firm assurance
    Which bars the pit over Destruction's strength;
And if, with infirm hand, Eternity,
Mother of many acts and hours, should free
    The serpent that would clasp her with his length;
These are the spells by which to reassume
An empire o'er the disentangled doom.

To suffer woes which Hope thinks infinite;
To forgive wrongs darker than death or night;
    To defy Power, which seems omnipotent;
To love, and bear; to hope till Hope creates
From its own wreck the thing it contemplates;
    Neither to change, nor falter, nor repent;
This, like thy glory, Titan, is to be
Good, great and joyous, beautiful and free;
This is alone Life, Joy, Empire, and Victory.

PERCY BYSSHE SHELLEY

From Adonais

The splendours of the firmament of time
May be eclipsed, but are extinguished not;
Like stars to their appointed height they climb
And death is a low mist which cannot blot
The brightness it may veil. When lofty thought
Lifts a young heart above its mortal lair,
And love and life contend in it, for what
Shall be its earthly doom, the dead live there
And more like winds of light on dark and stormy air.

The One remains, the many change and pass;
Heaven's light forever shines, Earth's shadows fly;
Life, like a dome of many-coloured glass,
Stains the white radiance of Eternity,

. . .

That Light whose smile kindles the Universe,
That Beauty in which all things work and move,
That Benediction which the eclipsing Curse
Of birth can quench not, that sustaining Love
Which through the web of being blindly wove
By man and beast and earth and air and sea,
Burns bright or dim, as each are mirrors of
The fire for which all thirst; now beams on me,
Consuming the last clouds of cold mortality.

PERCY BYSSHE SHELLEY

Cancelled Passage of the Ode to Liberty

Within a cavern of man's trackless spirit
   Is throned an Image, so intensely fair
That the adventurous thoughts that wander near it
   Worship, and as they kneel, tremble and wear
The splendour of its presence, and the light
   Penetrates their dreamlike frame
Till they become charged with the strength of flame.

PERCY BYSSHE SHELLEY

From The Invitation

. . . Radiant Sister of the Day,
Awake! arise! and come away!
To the wild woods and the plains,
And the pools where winter rains
Image all their roof of leaves,
Where the pine its garland weaves
Of sapless green and ivy dun
Round stems that never kiss the sun;
Where the lawns and pastures be
And the sandhills of the sea; –
Where the melting hoar-frost wets
The daisy-star that never sets,
And wind-flowers, and violets,
Which yet join not scent to hue,
Crown the pale year weak and new;
When the night is left behind
In the deep east, dun and blind,
And the blue noon is over us,
And the multitudinous
Billows murmur at our feet,
Where the earth and ocean meet,
And all things seem only one
In the universal sun. . .

PERCY BYSSHE SHELLEY

From On Death

O man! hold thee on in courage of soul
   Through the stormy shades of thy worldly way,
And the billows of cloud that around thee roll
   Shall sleep in the light of a wondrous day,
Where hell and heaven shall leave thee free
To the universe of destiny.

Who telleth a tale of unspeaking death?
   Who lifteth the veil of what is to come?
Who painteth the shadows that are beneath
   The wide-winding caves of the peopled tomb?
Or uniteth the hopes of what shall be
With the fears and the love for that which we see?

PERCY BYSSHE SHELLEY

Hymn to Intellectual Beauty

I

The awful shadow of some unseen Power
   Floats through unseen among us, – visiting
   This various world with as inconstant wing
As summer winds that creep from flower to flower, –
Like moonbeams that behind some piny mountain shower,
   It visits with inconstant glance
   Each human heart and countenance;
Like hues and harmonies of evening, –
   Like clouds in starlight widely spread, –
   Like memory of music fled, –
   Like aught that for its grace may be
Dear, and yet dearer for its mystery.

II

Spirit of BEAUTY, that dost consecrate
   With thine own hues all thou dost shine upon
   Of human thought or form, – where art thou gone?
Why dost thou pass away and leave our state,
This dim vast vale of tears, vacant and desolate?
   Ask why the sunlight not for ever
   Weaves rainbows o'er yon mountain-river,

Why aught should fail and fade that once is shown,
    Why fear and dream and death and birth
    Cast on the daylight of this earth
    Such gloom, – why man has such a scope
For love and hate, despondency and hope?

III

No voice from some sublimer world hath ever
    To sage or poet these responses given –
    Therefore the names of Demon, Ghost, and Heaven
Remain the records of their vain endeavour,
Frail spells – whose uttered charm might not avail to sever,
    From all we hear and all we see,
    Doubt, chance, and mutability.
Thy light alone – like mist o'er mountains driven,
    Or music by the night-wind sent
    Through strings of some still instrument,
    Or moonlight on a midnight stream,
Gives grace and truth to life's unquiet dream.

IV

Love, Hope, and Self-esteem, like clouds depart
    And come, for some uncertain moments lent.
    Man were immortal, and omnipotent,
Didst thou, unknown and awful as thou art,
Keep with thy glorious train firm state within his heart.
    Thou messenger of sympathies,
    That wax and wane in lovers' eyes –
Thou – that to human thought art nourishment,
    Like darkness to a dying flame!
    Depart not as thy shadow came,
    Depart not – lest the grave should be,
Like life and fear, a dark reality.

V

While yet a boy I sought for ghosts, and sped
    Through many a listening chamber, cave and ruin,
    And starlight wood, with fearful steps pursuing
Hopes of high talk with the departed dead.
I called on poisonous names with which our youth is fed:
    I was not heard – I saw them not –
    When musing deeply on the lot
Of life, at that sweet time when winds are wooing
    All vital things that wake to bring
    News of birds and blossoming, –
    Sudden, thy shadow fell on me;
I shrieked, and clasped my hands in ecstasy!

VI

I vowed that I would dedicate my powers
    To thee and thine – have I not kept the vow?
    With beating heart and streaming eyes, even now
I call the phantoms of a thousand hours
Each from his voiceless grave: they have in visioned bowers
    Of studious zeal or love's delight
    Outwatched with me the envious night –
They know that never joy illumed my brow
    Unlinked with hope that thou wouldst free
    This world from its dark slavery,
    That Thou – O awful LOVELINESS,
Wouldst give whate'er these words cannot express.

VII

The day becomes more solemn and serene
    When noon is past – there is a harmony
    In autumn, and a lustre in its sky,
Which through the summer is not heard or seen,
As if it could not be, as if it had not been!
    Thus let thy power, which like the truth
    Of nature on my passive youth
Descended, to my onward life supply
    Its calm – to one who worships thee,
    And every form containing thee,
    Whom, SPIRIT fair, thy spells did bind
To fear himself, and love all human kind.

PART 7:
Nineteenth Century

RALPH WALDO EMERSON
Give All to Love

Give all to love;
Obey thy heart;
Friends, kindred, days,
Estate, good-frame,
Plans, credit, and the Muse, –
Nothing refuse.

'Tis a brave master;
Let it have scope:
Follow it utterly,
Hope beyond hope:
High and more high
It dives into noon,
With wing unspent,
Untold intent;
But it is a god,
Knows its own path,
And the outlets of the sky.

It was not for the mean;
It requireth courage stout,
Souls above doubt,
Valour unbending;
Such 'twill reward, –
They shall return
More than they were,
And ever ascending.

Cling with life to the maid;
But when the surprise,
First vague shadow of surmise
Flits across her bosom young
Of a joy apart from thee,
Free be she, fancy-free;
Nor thou detain her vesture's hem,
Nor the palest rose she flung
From her summer diadem.

Though thou loved her as thyself,
As a self of purer clay,
Though her parting dims the day,
Stealing grace from all alive;
Heartily know,
When half-gods go
The gods arrive.

Leave all for love;
Yet, hear me, yet,
One word more thy heart behoved,
One pulse more of firm endeavour, –
Keep thee to-day,
To-morrow, for ever,
Free as an Arab
Of thy beloved.

RALPH WALDO EMERSON

From Ode to Beauty

Ah, what avails it
To hide or to shun
Whom the Infinite One
Hath granted His throne?
The heaven high over
Is the deep's lover;
The sun and sea,
Informed by thee,
Before me run,
And draw me on,
Yet fly me still,
As Fate refuses
To me the heart Fate for me chooses.
Is it that my opulent soul
Was mingled from the generous whole;
Sea-valleys and the deep of skies
Furnished several supplies;
And the sands whereof I'm made
Draw me to them, self-betrayed?
I turn the proud portfolios
Which hold the grand designs.

RALPH WALDO EMERSON

The Rhodora: On Being Asked, Whence Is the Flower?

In May, when sea-winds pierced our solitudes,
I found the fresh Rhodora in the woods,
Spreading its leafless blooms in a damp nook,
To please the desert and the sluggish brook.
The purple petals, fallen in the pool,
Made the black water with their beauty gay;
Here might the red-bird come his plumes to cool,
And court the flower that cheapens his array.
Rhodora! if the sages ask thee why
This charm is wasted on the earth and sky,
Tell them, dear, that if eyes were made for seeing,
Then Beauty is its own excuse for being:
Why thou wert there, O rival of the rose!
I never thought to ask, I never knew:
But, in my simple ignorance, suppose
The self-same Power that brought me there brought you.

RALPH WALDO EMERSON

From Each and All

I thought the sparrow's note from heaven,
Singing at dawn on the alder bough;
I brought him home, in his nest, at even;
He sings the song, but it cheers not now,
For I did not bring home the river and sky; –
He sang to my ear, – they sang to my eye.
The delicate shells lay on the shore;
The bubbles of the latest wave
Fresh pearls to their enamel gave,
And the bellowing of the savage sea
Greeted their safe escape to me.
I wiped away the weeds and foam,
I fetched my sea-born treasures home;
But the poor, unsightly, noisome things
Had left their beauty on the shore
With the sun and the sand and the wild uproar.
The lover watched his graceful maid,
As 'mid the virgin train she strayed,

Nor knew her beauty's best attire
Was woven still by the snow-white choir.
At last she came to his hermitage,
Like the bird from the woodlands to the cage;
The gay enchantment was undone,
A gentle wife, but fairy none.
Then I said, 'I covet truth;
Beauty is unripe childhood's cheat;
I leave it behind with the games of youth:' –
As I spoke, beneath my feet
The ground-pine curled its pretty wreath,
Running over the club-moss burrs;
I inhaled the violet's breath;
Around me stood the oaks and firs;
Pine-cones and acorns lay on the ground;
Over me soared the eternal sky,
Full of light and of deity;
Again I saw, again I heard,
The rolling river, the morning bird; –
Beauty through my senses stole;
I yielded myself to the perfect whole.

ELIZABETH BARRETT BROWNING

From Sonnets from the Portuguese

X

Yet, love, mere love, is beautiful indeed,
And worthy of acceptation. Fire is bright,
Let temple burn, or flax! An equal light
Leaps in the flame from cedar-plank or weed.
And love is fire: and when I say at need
I love thee . . . mark! . . . *I love thee!* . . . in thy sight
I stand transfigured, glorified aright,
With conscience of the new rays that proceed
Out of my face toward thine. There's nothing low
In love, when love the lowest; meanest creatures
Who love God, God accepts while loving so.
And what I *feel*, across the inferior features
Of what I *am*, doth flash itself, and show
How that great work of Love enhances Nature's.

ELIZABETH BARRETT BROWNING

Human Life's Mystery

We sow the glebe, we reap the corn,
    We build the house where we may rest,
And then, at moments, suddenly,
We look up to the great wide sky,
Inquiring wherefore we were born . . .
    For earnest or for jest?

The senses folding thick and dark
    About the stifled soul within,
We guess diviner things beyond,
And yearn to them with yearning fond;
We strike out blindly to a mark
    Believed in, but not seen.

We vibrate to the pant and thrill
    Wherewith Eternity has curled
In serpent-twine about God's seat;
While, freshening upward to His feet,
In gradual growth His full-leaved will
    Expands from world to world.

And, in the tumult and excess
    Of act and passion under sun,
We sometimes hear – oh, soft and far,
As silver star did touch with star,
The kiss of Peace and Righteousness
    Through all things that are done.

God keeps His holy mysteries
    Just on the outside of man's dream;
In diapason slow, we think
To hear their pinions rise and sink,
While they float pure beneath His eyes,
    Like swans adown a stream.

Abstractions, are they, from the forms
    Of His great beauty? – exaltations
From His great glory? – strong previsions
Of what we shall be? – intuitions
Of what we are – in calms and storms,
    Beyond our peace and passions?

Things nameless! which, in passing so,
    Do stroke us with a subtle grace.
We say, 'Who passes?' – they are dumb.
We cannot see them go or come:
Their touches fall soft, cold, as snow
    Upon a blind man's face.

Yet, touching so, they draw above
    Our common thoughts to Heaven's unknown,
Our daily joy and pain advance
To a divine significance,
Our human love – O mortal love,
    That light is not its own!

And sometimes horror chills our blood
    To be so near such mystic Things,
And we wrap round us for defence
Our purple manners, moods of sense –
As angels from the face of God
    Stand hidden in their wings.

And sometimes through life's heavy swound
    We grope for them! – with strangled breath
We search our hands abroad and try
To reach them in our agony, –
And widen, so, the broad life-wound
    Which soon is large enough for death.

ELIZABETH BARRETT BROWNING

From Aurora Leigh

Truth, so far, in my book; – the truth which draws
Through all things upwards, – that a twofold world
Must go to a perfect cosmos. Natural things
And spiritual, – who separates those two
In art, in morals, or the social drift
Tears up the bond of nature and brings death,
Paints futile pictures, writes unreal verse,
Leads vulgar days, deals ignorantly with men,
Is wrong, in short, at all points. We divide
This apple of life, and cut it through the pips, –
The perfect round which fitted Venus' hand
Has perished as utterly as if we ate

Both halves. Without the spiritual, observe,
The natural's impossible, – no form,
No motion: without sensuous, spiritual
Is inappreciable, – no beauty or power:
And in this twofold sphere the twofold man
(For still the artist is intensely a man)
Holds firmly by the natural, to reach
The spiritual beyond it, – fixes still
The type with mortal vision, to pierce through,
With eyes immortal, to the antetype
Some call the ideal, – better call the real,
And certain to be called so presently
When things shall have their names. Look long enough
On any peasant's face here, coarse and lined,
You'll catch Antinous somewhere in that clay,
As perfect featured as he yearns at Rome
From marble pale with beauty; then persist,
And, if your apprehension's competent,
You'll find some fairer angel at his back,
As much exceeding him as he the boor,
And pushing him with empyreal disdain
For ever out of sight. Aye, Carrington
Is glad of such a creed: an artist must,
Who paints a tree, a leaf, a common stone
With just his hand, and finds it suddenly
A-piece with and conterminous to his soul.
Why else do these things move him, leaf, or stone?
The bird's not moved, that pecks at a spring-shoot;
Nor yet the horse, before a quarry, a-graze:
But man, the twofold creature, apprehends
The twofold manner, in and outwardly,
And nothing in the world comes single to him,
A mere itself, – cup, column, or candlestick,
All patterns of what shall be in the Mount;
The whole temporal show related royally,
And built up to eterne significance
Through the open arms of God. 'There's nothing great
Nor small', has said a poet of our day,
Whose voice will ring beyond the curfew of eve
And not be thrown out by the matin's bell:
And truly, I reiterate, nothing's small!
No lily-muffled hum of a summer-bee,
But finds some coupling with the spinning stars;
No pebble at your foot, but proves a sphere;
No chaffinch, but implies the cherubim;
And (glancing on my own thin, veinèd wrist),

In such a little tremor of the blood
The whole strong clamour of a vehement soul
Doth utter itself distinct. Earth's crammed with heaven,
And every common bush afire with God;
But only he who sees, takes off his shoes,
The rest sit round it and pluck blackberries,
And daub their natural faces unaware
More and more from the first similitude.

ELIZABETH BARRETT BROWNING

The Soul's Expression

With stammering lips and insufficient sound
I strive and struggle to deliver right
That music of my nature, day and night
With dream and thought and feeling interwound,
And inly answering all the senses round
With octaves of a mystic depth and height
Which step out grandly to the infinite
From the dark edges of the sensual ground.
This song of soul I struggle to outbear
Through portals of the sense, sublime and whole,
And utter all myself into the air.
But if I did it as the thunder-roll
Breaks its own cloud my flesh would perish there,
Before that dread apocalypse of soul.

ELIZABETH BARRETT BROWNING

Life

Each creature holds an insular point in space;
Yet what man stirs a finger, breathes a sound,
But all the multitudinous beings round
In all the countless worlds with time and place
For their conditions, down to the central base,
Thrill, haply, in vibration and rebound,
Life answering life across the vast profound,
In full antiphony, by a common grace?

I think this sudden joyaunce which illumes
A child's mouth sleeping, unaware may run
From some soul newly loosened from earth's tombs:
I think this passionate sigh, which half-begun
I stifle back, may reach and stir the plumes
Of God's calm angel standing in the sun.

HENRY WADSWORTH LONGFELLOW

From A Day of Sunshine

I hear the wind among the trees
Playing celestial symphonies;
I see the branches downward bent,
Like keys of some great instrument.

And over me unrolls on high
The splendid scenery of the sky,
Where through a sapphire sea the sun
Sails like a golden galleon.

HENRY WADSWORTH LONGFELLOW

From To a Child

O child! O new-born denizen
Of life's great city! on thy head
The glory of the morn is shed,
Like a celestial benison!
Here at the portal thou dost stand,
And with thy little hand
Thou openest the mysterious gate
Into the future's undiscovered land.

HENRY WADSWORTH LONGFELLOW

From The Divine Tragedy

All these make up the sum of human life;
A dream within a dream, a wind at night
Howling across the desert in despair,
Seeking for something lost it cannot find.
Fate or foreseeing, or whatever name
Men call it, matters not; what is to be
Hath been forewritten in the thought divine
From the beginning. None can hide from it,
But it will find him out; nor run from it,
But it o'ertaketh him! The Lord hath said it.

HARRIET MARTINEAU

Arise, My Soul! and Urge Thy Flight

I

Arise, my soul! and urge thy flight,
    And fix thy view on God alone,
As eagles spring to meet the light,
    And gaze upon the radiant sun.

As planets on and onward roll,
    As streams pour forth their swelling tide,
Press on thy steady course, my soul,
    Nor pause, nor stop, nor turn aside.

Planets and suns shall dim their fire;
    Earth, air, and sea, shall melt away;
But though each star of heaven expire,
    Thou may'st survive that awful day.

In life, in death, thy course hold on:
    Though nature's self in ruins lie,
Pause not till heaven-gate be won;
    Then rest; for there thou canst not die.

II

Beneath this starry arch
    Nought resteth or is still;
But all things hold their march,
    As if by one great will:
        Moves one, move all;
        Hark to the footfall!
            On, on, for ever!

Yon sheaves were once but seed:
Will ripens into deed.
As cave-drops swell the streams,
Day-thoughts feed nightly dreams;
And sorrow tracketh wrong,
As echo follows song.
        On, on, for ever!

By night, like stars on high,
    The hours reveal their train;
They whisper, and go by;
    I never watch in vain:
        Moves one, move all:
        Hark to the footfall!
            On, on, for ever!

They pass the cradle-head,
And there a promise shed;
They pass the moist new grave,
And bid rank verdure wave;
They bear through every clime
The harvests of all time,
        On, on, for ever!

III

All men are equal in their birth,
    Heirs of the earth and skies;
All men are equal when that earth
    Fades from their dying eyes.

All wait alike on Him whose power
    Upholds the life He gave;
The sage within his star-lit tower,
    The savage in his cave.

God meets the throngs that pay their vows
   In courts their hands have made;
And hears the worshipper who bows
   Beneath the plantain shade.

'Tis man alone who difference sees,
   And speaks of high and low,
And worships those and tramples these,
   While the same path they go.

Oh, let man hasten to restore
   To all their rights of love;
In power and wealth exult no more;
   In wisdom lowly move.

Ye great! renounce your earth-born pride;
   Ye low, your shame and fear:
Live as ye worship side by side;
   Your brotherhood revere.

EMILY PFEIFFER

The Winged Soul

My soul is like some cage-born bird, that hath
   A restless prescience – howsoever won –
   Of a broad pathway leading to the sun,
With promptings of an oft-reprovèd faith
In sun-ward yearnings. Stricken though her breast,
   And faint her wing with beating at the bars
   Of sense, she looks beyond outlying stars,
And only in the Infinite sees rest.

Sad soul! If ever thy desire be bent
   Or broken to thy doom, and made to share
The ruminant's beatitude – content –
   Chewing the cud of knowledge, with no care
For germs of life within; *then* will I say,
Thou art not caged, but fitly *stalled* in clay!

ALFRED LORD TENNYSON

From The Ancient Sage

If thou would'st hear the Nameless, and wilt dive
Into the Temple-cave of thine own self,
There, brooding by the central altar, thou
May'st haply learn the Nameless hath a voice,
By which thou wilt abide, if thou be wise,
As if thou knewest, tho' thou canst not know;
For Knowledge is the swallow on the lake
That sees and stirs the surface-shadow there
But never yet hath dipt into the abysm,
The Abysm of all Abysms, beneath, within
The blue of sky and sea, the green of earth,
And in the million-millionth of a grain
Which cleft and cleft again for evermore,
And ever vanishing, never vanishes,
To me, my son, more mystic than myself,
Or even than the Nameless is to me.
    And when thou sendest thy free soul thro' heaven,
Nor understandest bound nor boundlessness,
Thou seest the Nameless of the hundred names.
    And if the Nameless should withdraw from all
Thy frailty counts most real, all thy world
Might vanish like thy shadow in the dark.
'And since – from when this earth began –
    The Nameless never came
Among us, never spake with man,
    And never named the Name' –

                    . . .

I know not and I speak of what has been.
    And more, my son! for more than once when I
Sat all alone, revolving in myself
The word that is the symbol of myself,
The mortal limit of the Self was loosed,
And past into the Nameless, as a cloud
Melts into Heaven. I touch'd my limbs, the limbs
Were strange not mine – and yet no shade of doubt,
But utter clearness, and thro' loss of Self
The gain of such large life as match'd with ours
Were Sun to spark – unshadowable in words,
Themselves but shadows of a shadow-world.

                    . . .

And lay thine uphill shoulder to the wheel,
And climb the Mount of Blessing, whence, if thou
Look higher, then – perchance – thou mayest – beyond
A hundred ever-rising mountain lines,
And past the range of Night and Shadow – see
The high-heaven dawn of more than mortal day
Strike on the Mount of Vision!
So, farewell.

ALFRED LORD TENNYSON

The Making of Man

Where is one that, born of woman, altogether can escape
From the lower world within him, moods of tiger, or of ape?
    Man as yet is being made, and ere the crowning Age of ages,
Shall not æon after æon pass and touch him into shape?

All about him shadow still, but, while the races flower and fade,
Prophet-eyes may catch a glory slowly gaining on the shade,
    Till the peoples all are one, and all their voices blend in choric
Hallelujah to the Maker 'It is finish'd.
    Man is made.'

ALFRED LORD TENNYSON

The Higher Pantheism

The sun, the moon, the stars, the seas, the hills and the plains –
Are not these, O Soul, the Vision of Him who reigns?

Is not the Vision He? tho' He be not that which He seems?
Dreams are true while they last, and do we not live in dreams?

Earth, these solid stars, this weight of body and limb,
Are they not sign and symbol of thy division from Him?

Dark is the world to thee: thyself art the reason why;
For is He not all but that which has power to feel 'I am I'?

Glory about thee, without thee; and thou fulfillest thy doom
Making Him broken gleams, and a stifled splendour and gloom.

Speak to Him thou for He hears, and Spirit with Spirit can meet –
Closer is He than breathing, and nearer than hands and feet.

God is law, say the wise; O Soul, and let us rejoice,
For if He thunder by law the thunder is yet His voice.

Law is God, say some: no God at all, says the fool;
For all we have power to see is a straight staff bent in a pool;

And the ear of man cannot hear, and the eye of man cannot see;
But if we could see and hear, this Vision – were it not He?

ALFRED LORD TENNYSON

From Locksley Hall, Sixty Years After

Might we not in glancing heavenward on a star so silver-fair,
Yearn, and clasp the hands and murmur, 'Would to God that we
    were there'?

Forward, backward, backward, forward, in the immeasurable sea,
Sway'd by vaster ebbs and flows than can be known to you or me.

All the suns – are these but symbols of innumerable man,
Man or Mind that sees a shadow of the planner or the plan?

Is there evil but on earth? or pain in every peopled sphere?
Well be grateful for the sounding watchword 'Evolution' here.

Evolution ever climbing after some ideal good,
And Reversion ever dragging Evolution in the mud.

What are men that He should heed us? cried the king of sacred song;
Insects of an hour, that hourly work their brother insect wrong,

While the silent Heavens roll, and Suns along their fiery way,
All their planets whirling round them, flash a million miles a day.

Many an Æon moulded earth before her highest, man, was born,
Many an Æon too may pass when earth is manless and forlorn,

Earth so huge, and yet so bounded – pools of salt, and plots of land –
Shallow skin of green and azure – chains of mountain, grains of sand!

Only That which made us, meant us to be mightier by and by,
Set the sphere of all the boundless Heavens within the human eye,

Sent the shadow of Himself, the boundless, thro' the human soul;
Boundless inward, in the atom, boundless outward, in the Whole.

Alfred Lord Tennyson

The Mystic

Angels have talked with him, and showed him thrones:
Ye knew him not: he was not one of ye,
Ye scorned him with an undiscerning scorn:
Ye could not read the marvel in his eye,
The still serene abstraction: he hath felt
The vanities of after and before;
Albeit, his spirit and his secret heart
The stern experiences of converse lives,
The linked woes of many a fiery change
Had purified, and chastened, and made free
Always there stood before him, night and day,
Of wayward varycoloured circumstance
The imperishable presences serene
Colossal, without form, or sense, or sound.
Dim shadows but unwaning presences
Fourfacèd to four corners of the sky:
And yet again, three shadows, fronting one,
One forward, one respectant, three but one;
And yet again, again and evermore,
For the two first were not, but only seemed,
One shadow in the midst of a great light,
One reflex from eternity on time,
One mighty countenance of perfect calm,
Awful with most invariable eyes.
For him the silent congregated hours,
Daughters of time, divinely tall, beneath
Severe and youthful brows, with shining eyes
Smiling a godlike smile (the innocent light
Of earliest youth pierced through and through with all
Keen knowledges of low-embowèd eld)
Upheld, and ever hold aloft the cloud
Which droops lowhung on either gate of life,
Both birth and death: he in the centre fixt,
Saw far on each side through the grated gates

Most pale and clear and lovely distances.
He often lying broad awake, and yet
Remaining from the body, and apart
In intellect and power and will, hath heard
Time flowing in the middle of the night,
And all things creeping to a day of doom.
How could ye know him? Ye were yet within
The narrower circle; he had wellnigh reached
The last, which with a region of white flame,
Pure without heat, into a larger air
Upburning, and an ether of black blue,
Investeth and ingirds all other lives.

JOHN STUART BLACKIE

All Things are Full of God

All things are full of God. Thus spoke
    Wise Thales in the days
When subtle Greece to thought awoke
    And soared in lofty ways.
And now what wisdom have we more?
    No sage divining-rod
Hath taught than this a deeper lore,
    ALL THINGS ARE FULL OF GOD.

The Light that gloweth in the sky
    And shimmers in the sea,
That quivers in the painted fly
    And gems the pictured lea,
The million hues of Heaven above
    And Earth below are one,
And every lightful eye doth love
    The primal light, the Sun.

Even so, all vital virtue flows
    From life's first fountain, God;
And he who feels, and he who knows,
    Doth feel and know from God.
As fishes swim in briny sea,
    As fowl do float in air,
From Thy embrace we cannot flee;
    We breathe, and Thou art there.

Go, take thy glass, astronomer,
 And all the girth survey
Of sphere harmonious linked to sphere,
 In endless bright array.
All that far-reaching Science there
 Can measure with her rod,
All powers, all laws, are but the fair
 Embodied thoughts of God.

William Bell Scott
Pebbles in the Stream

Here on this little bridge in this warm day
We rest us from our idle sauntering walk.
 Over our shadows its continuous talk
The stream maintains, while now and then a stray
Dry leaf may fall where the still waters play
 In endless eddies, through whose clear brown deep
 The gorgeous pebbles quiver in their sleep.
The stream still hastes but cannot pass away.

Could I but find the words that would reveal
 The unity in multiplicity,
And the profound strange harmony I feel
 With those dead things, God's garments of to-day,
The listener's soul with mine they would anneal,
 And make us one within eternity.

William Bell Scott
From The Year of the World

Give reverence, O man, to mystery,
Keep your soul patient, and with closed eye hear.
Know that the Good is in all things, the whole
Being by him pervaded and upheld.
He is the will, the thwarting circumstance,
The two opposing forces equal both –
Birth, Death, are one. Think not the Lotus flower
Or tulip is more honoured than the grass,
The bindweed, or the thistle. He who kneels
To Cama, kneeleth unto me; the maid

Who sings to Ganga sings to me; I am
Wisdom unto the wise, and cunning lore
Unto the subtle. He who knows his soul,
And from thence looketh unto mine; who sees
All underneath the moon regardlessly,
Living on silent, as a shaded lamp
Burns with steady flame: – he sure shall find me –
He findeth wisdom, greatness, happiness.
Know, further, the Great One delighteth not
In him who works, and strives, and is against
The nature of the present. Not the less
Am I the gladness of the conqueror –
And the despair of impotence that fails.
I am the ultimate, the tendency
Of all things to *their* nature, which is *mine*.
Put round thee garments of rich softness, hang
Fine gold about thine ankles, hands, and ears,
Set the rich ruby and rare diamond
Upon thy brow. – I made them, I also
Made them be sought by thee; thou lack'st them not?
Then throw them whence they came, and leave with them
The wish to be aught else than nature forms.
Know that the great Good in the age called First,
Beheld a world of mortals, 'mong whom none
Enquired for Truth, because no falsehood was:
Nature was Truth: man held whate'er he wished:
No will was thwarted, and no deed was termed,
Good, Evil. In much wisdom is much grief.
He who increases knowledge sorrow also
Takes with it, till he rises unto me,
Knowing that I am in all, still the same:
Knowing that I am Peace in the contented.
I, Great, revealed unto the Seer, how man
Had wandered, and he gave a name and form
To my communings and he called it Veda.
To him who understands it is great gain –
Who understandeth not, to him the Sign
And ritual is authority and guide,
A living and expiring confidence.

ROBERT BROWNING

Pippa's Song

The year's at the spring
And day's at the morn;
Morning's at seven;
The hillside's dew-pearled;
The lark's on the wing;
The snail's on the thorn;
God's in his heaven –
All's right with the world.

ROBERT BROWNING

From Pauline

O God, where does this tend – these struggling aims?
What would I have? What is this 'sleep', which seems
To bound all? can there be a 'waking' point
Of crowning life? The soul would never rule –
It would be first in all things – it would have
Its utmost pleasure filled, – but that complete
Commanding for commanding sickens it.
The last point I can trace is, rest beneath
Some better essence than itself – in weakness;
This is 'myself' – not what I think should be
And what is that I hunger for but God?

Fool! All that is, at all,
Lasts ever, past recall;
Earth changes, but thy soul and God stand sure:
What entered into thee,
That was, is, and shall be:
Time's wheel runs back or stops: Potter and clay endure.

He fixed thee mid this dance
Of plastic circumstance,
This Present, thou, forsooth, wouldst fain arrest:
Machinery just meant
To give thy soul its bent,
Try thee and turn thee forth, sufficiently impressed.

What though the earlier grooves
Which ran the laughing loves
Around thy base, no longer pause and press?
What though, about thy rim,
Skull-things in order grim
Grow out, in graver mood, obey the sterner stress?

Look not thou down but up!
To uses of a cup,
The festal board, lamp's flash and trumpet's peal,
The new wine's foaming flow,
The Master's lips aglow!
Thou, heaven's consummate cup, what need'st thou with
    earth's wheel?

But I need, now as then,
Thee, God, who mouldest men;
And since, not even while the whirl was worst,
Did I, – to the wheel of life
With shapes and colours rife,
Bound dizzily, – mistake my end, to slake Thy thirst:

So, take and use Thy work!
Amend what flaws may lurk,
What strain o' the stuff, what warpings past the aim!
My times be in Thy hand!
Perfect the cup as planned!
Let age approve of youth, and death complete the same!

ROBERT BROWNING

From Paracelsus, Book I

                        But, friends,
    Truth is within ourselves; it takes no rise
    From outward things, whate'er you may believe.
    There is an inmost centre in us all,
    Where truth abides in fulness; and around
    Wall upon wall, the gross flesh hems it in,
    This perfect, clear perception – which is truth.
    A baffling and perverting carnal mesh
    Blinds it, and makes all error: and TO KNOW
    Rather consists in opening out a way
    Whence the imprisoned splendour may escape,

Than in effecting entry for a light
Supposed to be without. Watch narrowly
The demonstration of a truth, its birth,
And you trace back the effluence to its spring
And source within us; where broods radiance vast,
To be elicited ray by ray, as chance
Shall favour: chance – for hitherto, your sage
Even as he knows not how those beams are born,
As little knows he what unlocks their fount.

ROBERT BROWNING

From Paracelsus, Book V

I knew, I felt, (perception unexpressed,
Uncomprehended by our narrow thought,
But somehow felt and known in every shift
And change in the spirit, – nay, in every pore
Of the body, even,) – what God is, what we are,
What life is – how God tastes an infinite joy
In infinite ways – one everlasting bliss,
From whom all being emanates, all power
Proceeds; in whom is life for evermore,
Yet whom existence in its lowest form
Includes; where dwells enjoyment there is He!

With still a flying point of bliss remote,
A happiness in store afar, a sphere
Of distant glory in full view; thus climbs
Pleasure its heights for ever and for ever!
The centre fire heaves underneath the earth,
And the earth changes like a human face;
The molten ore bursts up among the rocks,
Winds into the stone's heart, out-branches bright
In hidden mines, spots barren river-beds,
Crumbles into fine sand where sunbeams bask –
God joys therein! The wroth sea's waves are edged
With foam, white as the bitten lip of hate,
When, in the solitary waste, strange groups
Of young volcanos come up, cyclops-like,
Strung together with their eyes on flame –
God tastes a pleasure in their uncouth pride!
Then all is still; earth is a wintry clod:
But spring-wind, like a dancing psaltress, passes
Over its breast to waken it, rare verdure

Buds tenderly upon rough banks, between
The withered tree-roots and the cracks of frost,
Like a smile striving with a wrinkled face;
The grass grows bright, the boughs are swoln with blooms
Like chrysalids impatient for the air,
The shining dorrs are busy, beetles run
Along the furrows, ants make their ado;
Above, birds fly in merry flocks, the lark
Soars up and up, shivering for very joy;
Afar the ocean sleeps; white fishing-gulls
Flit where the strand is purple with its tribe
Of nested limpets; savage creatures seek
Their loves in wood and plain – and God renews
His ancient rapture! Thus He dwells in all,
From life's minute beginnings, up at last
To man – the consummation of this scheme
Of being, the completion of this sphere
Of life: whose attributes had here and there
Been scattered o'er the visible world before,
Asking to be combined, dim fragments meant
To be united in some wondrous whole,
Imperfect qualities throughout creation,
Suggesting some one creature yet to make,
Some point where all those scattered rays should meet
Convergent in the faculties of man.
Power – neither put forth blindly, nor controlled
Calmly by perfect knowledge; to be used
At risk, inspired or checked by hope and fear:
Knowledge – not intuition, but the slow
Uncertain fruit of an enhancing toil,
Strengthened by love: love – not serenely pure,
But strong from weakness, like a chance-sown plant
Which, cast on stubborn soil, puts forth changed buds
And softer stains, unknown in happier climes;
Love which endures and doubts and is oppressed
And cherished, suffering much and much sustained,
A blind, oft-failing, yet believing love,
A half-enlightened, often chequered trust: –
Hints and previsions of which faculties,
Are strewn confusedly everywhere about
The inferior natures, and all lead up higher,
All shape out dimly the superior race,
The heir of hopes too fair to turn out false,
And man appears at last. So far the seal
Is put on life; one stage of being complete,
One scheme wound up: and from the grand result

A supplementary reflux of light
Illustrates all the inferior grades, explains
Each back step in the circle. Not alone
For their possessor dawn those qualities,
But the new glory mixes with the heaven
And earth; man, once descried, imprints for ever
His presence on all lifeless things: the winds
Are henceforth voices, in a wail or shout,
A querulous mutter, or a quick gay laugh,
Never a senseless gust now man is born!
The herded pines commune and have deep thoughts,
A secret they assemble to discuss
When the sun drops behind their trunks which glare
Like grates of hell: the peerless cup afloat
Of the lake-lily is an urn, some nymph
Swims bearing high above her head: no bird
Whistles unseen, but through the gaps above
That let light in upon the gloomy woods,
A shape peeps from the breezy forest-top,
Arch with small puckered mouth and mocking eye:
The morn has enterprise, deep quiet droops
With evening, triumph takes the sunset hour,
Voluptuous transport ripens with the corn
Beneath a warm moon like a happy face:
– And this to fill us with regard for man,
With apprehension of his passing worth,
Desire to work his proper nature out,
And ascertain his rank and final place.
For these things tend still upward, progress is
The law of life, man's self is not yet Man!
Nor shall I deem his object served, his end
Attained, his genuine strength put fairly forth,
While only here and there a star dispels
The darkness, here and there a towering mind
O'erlooks its prostrate fellows: when the host
Is out at once to the despair of night,
When all mankind alike is perfected,
Equal in full-blown powers – then, not till then,
I say, begins man's general infancy!
For wherefore make account of feverish starts
Of restless members of a dormant whole,
Impatient nerves which quiver while the body
Slumbers as in a grave? O, long ago
The brow was twitched, the tremulous lids astir,
The peaceful mouth disturbed; half-uttered speech
Ruffled the lip, and then the teeth were set,

The breath drawn sharp, the strong right-hand clenched stronger,
As it would pluck a lion by the jaw;
The glorious creature laughed out even in sleep!
But when full roused, each giant-limb awake,
Each sinew strung, the great heart pulsing fast,
He shall start up and stand on his own earth,
Thence shall his long triumphant march begin,
Thence shall his being date, – thus wholly roused,
What he achieves shall be set down to him! –
When all the race is perfected alike
As Man, that is; all tended to mankind,
And, man produced, all has its end thus far:
But in completed man begins anew
A tendency to God. Prognostics told
Man's near approach; so in man's self arise
August anticipations, symbols, types
Of a dim splendour ever on before
In that eternal circle run by life.
For men begin to pass their nature's bound,
And find new hopes and cares which fast supplant
Their proper joys and griefs; they outgrow all
The narrow creeds of right and wrong, which fade
Before the unmeasured thirst for good: while peace
Rises within them ever more and more.
Such men are even now upon the earth,
Serene amid the half-formed creatures round
Who should be saved by them and joined with them.
Such was my task, and I was born to it –
Free, as I said but now, from much that chains
Spirits, high-dowered but limited and vexed
By a divided and delusive aim,
A shadow mocking a reality
Whose truth avails not wholly to disperse
The flitting mimic called up by itself,
And so remains perplexed and nigh put out
By its fantastic fellow's wavering gleam.
I, from the first, was never cheated thus;
I never fashioned out a fancied good
Distinct from man's; a service to be done,
A glory to be ministered unto,
With powers put forth at man's expense, withdrawn
From labouring in his behalf; a strength
Denied that might avail him. I cared not
Lest his success ran counter to success
Elsewhere: for God is glorified in man,
And to man's glory vowed I soul and limb.

ROBERT BROWNING

Reverie

I know there shall dawn a day
    – Is it here on homely earth?
Is it yonder, worlds away,
    Where the strange and new have birth,
That Power comes full in play?

Is it here, with grass about,
    Under befriending trees,
When shy buds venture out,
    And the air by mild degrees
Puts winter's death past doubt?

Is it up amid whirl and roar
    Of the elemental flame
Which star-flecks heaven's dark floor,
    That, new yet still the same,
Full in play comes Power once more?

Somewhere, below, above,
    Shall a day dawn – this I know –
When Power, which vainly strove
    My weakness to o'erthrow,
Shall triumph. I breathe, I move,

I truly am, at last!
    For a veil is rent between
Me and the truth which passed
    Fitful, half-guessed, half-seen,
Grasped at – not gained, held fast,

I for my race and me
    Shall apprehend life's law:
In the legend of man shall see
    Writ large what small I saw
In my life's tale: both agree.

As the record from youth to age
    Of my own, the single soul –
So the world's wide book: one page
    Deciphered explains the whole
Of our common heritage.

How but from near to far
　Should knowledge proceed, increase?
Try the clod ere test the star!
　Bring our inside strife to peace
Ere we wage, on the outside, war!

So, my annals thus begin:
　With body, to life awoke
Soul, the immortal twin
　Of body which bore soul's yoke
Since mortal and not akin.

By means of the flesh, grown fit,
　Mind, in surview of things,
Now soared, anon alit
　To treasure its gatherings
From the ranged expanse – to-wit,

Nature, – earth's, heaven's wide show
　Which taught all hope, all fear:
Acquainted with joy and woe,
　I could say 'Thus much is clear,
Doubt annulled thus much: I know.

'All is effect of cause:
　As it would, has willed and done
Power: and my mind's applause
　Goes, passing laws each one,
To Omnipotence, lord of laws.'

Head praises, but heart refrains
　From loving's acknowledgement.
Whole losses outweigh half-gains:
　Earth's good is with evil blent:
Good struggles but evil reigns.

Yet since Earth's good proved good –
　Incontrovertibly
Worth loving – I understood
　How evil – did mind descry
Power's object to end pursued –

Were haply as cloud across
　Good's orb, no orb itself:
Mere mind – were it found at loss
　Did it play the tricksy elf
And from life's gold purge the dross?

Power is known infinite:
   Good struggles to be – at best
Seems – scanned by the human sight,
   Tried by the senses' test –
Good palpably: but with right

Therefore to mind's award
   Of loving, as power claims praise?
Power – which finds naught too hard,
   Fulfilling itself all ways
Unchecked, unchanged: while barred,

Baffled, what good began
   Ends evil on every side.
To Power submissive man
   Breathes 'E'en as Thou art, abide!'
While to good 'Late-found, long-sought,

'Would Power to a plenitude
   But liberate, but enlarge
Good's strait confine, – renewed
   Where ever the heart's discharge
Of loving!' Else doubts intrude.

For you dominate, stars all!
   For a sense informs you – brute,
Bird, worm, fly, great and small,
   Each with your attribute
Or low or majestical!

Thou earth that embosomest
   Offspring of land and sea –
How thy hills first sank to rest,
   How thy vales bred herb and tree
Which dizen thy mother-breast –

Do I ask? 'Be ignorant
   Ever!' the answer clangs:
Whereas if I plead world's want,
   Soul's sorrows and body's pangs,
Play the human applicant, –

Is a remedy far to seek?
   I question and find response:
I – all men, strong or weak,
   Conceive and declare at once
For each want its cure. 'Power, speak

'Stop change, avert decay,
   Fix life fast, banish death,
Eclipse from the star bid stay,
   Abridge of no moment's breath
One creature! Hence, Night, hail, Day!'

What need to confess again
   No problem this to solve
By impotence? Power, once plain
   Proved Power, – let on Power devolve
Good's right to co-equal reign!

Past mind's conception – Power!
   Do I seek how star, earth, beast,
Bird, worm, fly, gained their dower
   For life's use, most and least?
Back from the search I cower.

Do I seek what heals all harm,
   Nay, hinders the harm at first,
Saves earth? Speak, Power, the charm!
   Keep the life there unamerced
By change, change, death's alarm!

As promptly as mind conceives,
   Let Power in its turn declare
Some law which wrong retrieves,
   Abolishes everywhere
What thwarts, what irks, what grieves!

Never to be! and yet
   How easy it seems – to sense
Like man's – if somehow met
   Power with its match – immense
Love, limitless, unbeset

By hindrance on every side!
   Conjectured, nowise known,
Such may be: could man confide
   Such would match – were Love but shown
Stript of the veils that hide –

Power's self now manifest!
   So reads my record: thine,
O world, how runs it? Guessed
   Were the purport of that prime line,
Prophetic of all the rest!

'In a beginning God
  Made heaven and earth.' Forth flashed
Knowledge: from star to clod
  Man knew things: doubt abashed
Closed its long period.

Knowledge obtained Power praise.
  Had Good been manifest,
Broke out in cloudless blaze,
  Unchequered as unrepressed,
In all things Good at best –

Then praise – all praise, no blame –
  Had hailed the perfection. No!
As Power's display, the same
  Be Good's – praise forth shall flow
Unisonous in acclaim!

Even as the world its life,
  So have I lived my own –
Power seen with Love at strife,
  That sure, this dimly shown,
– Good rare and evil rife.

Whereof the effect be – faith
  That, some far day, were found
Ripeness in things now rathe,
  Wrong righted, each chain unbound,
Renewal born out of scathe.

Why faith – but to lift the load,
  To leaven the lump, where lies
Mind prostrate through knowledge owed
  To the loveless Power it tries
To withstand, how vain! In flowed

Ever resistless fact:
  No more than the passive clay
Disputes the potter's act,
  Could the whelmed mind disobey
Knowledge the cataract.

But, perfect in every part,
  Has the potter's moulded shape,
Leap of man's quickened heart,
  Throe of his thought's escape,
Stings of his soul which dart

Through the barrier of flesh, till keen
    She climbs from the calm and clear,
Through turbidity all between,
    From the known to the unknown here,
Heaven's 'Shall be,' From Earth's 'Has been'?

Then life is – to wake not sleep,
    Rise and not rest, but press
From earth's level where blindly creep
    Things perfected, more or less,
To the heaven's height, far and steep,

Where, amid what strifes and storms,
    May wait the adventurous quest,
Power is Love – transports, transforms
    Who aspired from worst to best,
Sought the soul's world, spurned the worms'.

I have faith such end shall be:
    From the first, Power was – I knew.
Life has made clear to me
    That, strive but for closer view,
Love were as plain to see.

When see? When there dawns a day,
    If not on the homely earth,
Then yonder, worlds away,
    Where the strange and new have birth,
And Power comes full in play.

Epilogue

At the midnight in the silence of the sleep-time,
    When you set your fancies free,
Will they pass to where – by death, fools think, imprisoned –
Low he lies who once so loved you, whom you loved so,
   – Pity me?

Oh to love so, be so loved, yet so mistaken!
    What had I on earth to do
With the slothful, with the mawkish, the unmanly?
Like the aimless, helpless, hopeless, did I drivel
   – Being – who?

One who never turned his back but marched breast forward,
  Never doubted clouds would break,
Never dreamed, though right were worsted, wrong would triumph,
Held we fall to rise, are baffled to fight better,
  Sleep to wake.

No, at noonday in the bustle of man's work-time
  Greet the unseen with a cheer!
Bid him forward, breast and back as either should be,
'Strive and thrive!' cry 'Speed, – fight on, fare ever
  There as here!'

CHRISTOPHER PEARSE CRANCH

So Far, So Near

Thou, so far, we grope to grasp thee –
Thou, so near, we cannot clasp thee –
Thou, so wise, our prayers grow heedless –
Thou, so loving, they are needless!
In each human soul thou shinest,
Human-best is thy divinest.
In each deed of love thou warmest;
Evil into good transformest.
Soul of all, and moving centre
Of each moment's life we enter.
Breath of breathing – light of gladness –
Infinite antidote of sadness; –
All-preserving ether flowing
Through the worlds, yet past our knowing.
Never past our trust and loving,
Nor from thine our life removing.

Still creating, still inspiring,
Never of thy creatures tiring;
Artist of thy solar spaces;
And thy humble human faces;
Mighty glooms and splendours voicing;
In thy plastic work rejoicing;
Through benignant law connecting
Best with best – and all perfecting,
Though all human races claim thee,
Thought and language fail to name thee,
Mortal lips be dumb before thee,
Silence only may adore thee!

JONES VERY

The Created

There is naught for thee by thy haste to gain;
'Tis not the swift with Me that win the race;
Through long endurance of delaying pain,
Thine opened eye shall see thy Father's face;
Nor here nor there, where now thy feet would turn,
Thou wilt find Him who ever seeks for thee;
But let obedience quench desires that burn,
And where thou art, thy Father, too, will be.
Behold! as day by day the spirit grows,
Thou see'st by inward light things hid before;
Till what God is, thyself, his image shows;
And thou dost wear the robe that first thou wore,
When bright with radiance from his forming hand,
He saw thee Lord of all his creatures stand.

FREDERICK WILLIAM FABER

From The Eternal Word

I

Amid the eternal silences
   God's endless Word was spoken;
None heard but He who always spake,
   And the silence was unbroken.
     Oh marvellous! Oh worshipful!
     No song or sound is heard,
   But everywhere and every hour,
   In love, in wisdom, and in power,
The Father speaks His dear Eternal Word!

II

For ever in the eternal land
   The glorious Day is dawning;
For ever is the Father's Light
   Like an endless outspread morning.
     Oh marvellous! Oh worshipful!
     No song or sound is heard,
   But everywhere and every hour,
   In love, in wisdom, and in power,
The Father speaks His dear Eternal Word!

III

From the Father's vast tranquillity,
   In light co-equal glowing
The kingly consubstantial Word
   Is unutterably flowing.
      Oh marvellous! Oh worshipful!
     No song or sound is heard,
But everywhere and every hour,
In love, in wisdom, and in power,
The Father speaks His dear Eternal Word!

IV

For ever climbs that Morning Star
   Without ascent or motion;
For ever is its daybreak shed
   On the Spirit's boundless ocean.
      Oh marvellous! Oh worshipful!
     No song or sound is heard,
But everywhere and every hour,
In love, in wisdom, and in power,
The Father speaks His dear Eternal Word.

EDWARD CASWALL

The Order of Pure Intuition

Hail, sacred Order of eternal Truth!
   That deep within the soul,
In axiomatic majesty sublime,
   One undivided whole, –

Up from the underdepth unsearchable
   Of primal Being springs,
An inner world of thought, co-ordinate
   With that of outward things!

Hail, Intuition pure! whose essences
   The central core supply
Of conscience, language, science, certitude,
   Art, beauty, harmony!

Great God! I thank Thy majesty supreme,
   Whose all-creative grace
Not in the sentient faculties alone
   Has laid my reason's base;

Not in abstractions thin by slow degrees
    From grosser forms refin'd;
Not in tradition, nor the broad consent
    Of conscious humankind; –

But in th' essential Presence of Thyself,
    Within the soul's abyss;
Thyself, alike of her intelligence
    The fount, as of her bliss;

Thyself, by nurture, meditation, grace,
    Reflexively reveal'd;
Yet ever acting on the springs of thought,
    E'en when from thought conceal'd!

AUBREY DE VERE

The Sun God

I saw the Master of the Sun. He stood
High in his luminous car, himself more bright;
An Archer of immeasurable might:
On his left shoulder hung his quivered load;
Spurned by his Steeds the eastern mountain glowed;
Forward his eager eye, and brow of light
He bent; and, while both hands that arch embowed,
Shaft after shaft pursued the flying Night.
   No wings profaned that godlike form; around
His neck high-held an ever-moving crowd
Of locks hung glistening; while such perfect sound
Fell from his bowstring, that th' ethereal dome
Thrilled as a dewdrop; and each passing cloud
Expanded, whitening like the ocean foam.

AUBREY DE VERE

Implicit Faith

Of all great Nature's tones that sweep
    Earth's resonant bosom, far or near,
Low-breathed or loudest, shrill or deep,
    How few are grasped by mortal ear.

Ten octaves close our scale of sound:
   Its myriad grades, distinct or twined,
Transcend our hearing's petty bound,
   To us as colours to the blind.

In Sound's unmeasured empire thus
   The heights, the depths alike we miss;
Ah, but in measured sound to us
   A compensating spell there is!

In holy music's golden speech
   Remotest notes to notes respond:
Each octave is a world; yet each
   Vibrates to worlds its own beyond.

Our narrow pale the vast resumed;
   Our sea-shell whispers of the sea:
Echoes are ours of angel-plumes
   That winnow far infinity!

Clasp thou of Truth the central core!
   Hold fast that centre's central sense!
An atom there shall fill thee more
   Than realms on Truth's circumference.

That cradled Saviour, mute and small,
   Was God – is God while worlds endure!
Who holds Truth truly holds it all
   In essence, or in miniature.

Know what thou know'st! He knoweth much
   Who knows not many things: and he
Knows most whose knowledge hath a touch
   Of God's divine simplicity.

PHILIP JAMES BAILEY

Knowledge

The knowledge of God is the wisdom of man –
This is the end of Being, wisdom; this
Of wisdom, action; and of action, rest;
And of rest, bliss; that by experience sage
Of good and ill, the diametric powers

Which thwart the world, the thrice-born might discern
That death divine alone can perfect both,
The mediate and initiate; that between
The Deity and nothing, nothing is.

The Atlantean axis of the world
And all the undescribed circumference,
Where earth's thick breath thins off to blankest space
Uniting with inanity, this truth
Confess, the sun-sire and the death-world too,
And undeflected spirit pure from Heaven,
That He who makes, destroying, saves the whole.
The Former and Re-Former of the world
In wisdom's holy spirit all renew.

To know this, is to read the runes of old,
Wrought in the time-outlasting rock; to see
Unblinded in the heart of light; to feel
Keen through the soul, the same essential strain,
Which vivifies the clear and fire-eyed stars,
Still harping their serene and silvery spell
In the perpetual presence of the skies,
And of the world-cored calm, where silence sits
In secret light all hidden; this to know –
Brings down the fiery unction from on high,
The spiritual chrism of the sun,
Which hallows and ordains the regnant soul –
Transmutes the splendid fluid of the frame
Into a fountain of divine delight,
And renovative nature; – shows us earth,
One with the great galactic line of life
Which parts the hemispheral palm of Heaven;
This with all spheres of Being makes concord
As at the first creation, in that peace
Premotional, pre-elemental, prime,
Which is the hope of earth, the joy of Heaven,
The choice of the elect, the grace of life,
The blessing and the glory of our God.
And – as the vesper hymn of time precedes
The starry matins of Eternity,
And daybreak of existence in the Heavens, –
To know this, is to know we shall depart
Into the storm-surrounding calm on high,
The sacred cirque, the all-central infinite
Of that self-blessedness wherein abides
Our God, all-kind, all-loving, all-beloved; –

To feel life one great ritual, and its laws,
Writ in the vital rubric of the blood,
Flow in, obedience, and flow out, command,
In sealike circulation; and be here
Accepted as a gift by Him who gives
An empire as an alms, nor counts it aught,
So long as all His creatures joy in Him,
The great Rejoicer of the Universe,
Whom all the boundless spheres of Being bless.

PHILIP JAMES BAILEY

From The Mystic

God was, alone in unity. He willed
The infinite creation; and it was.
That the creation might exist, His Son,
And that it might return to Him, the Spirit
Disclosed themselves within Him; thus triune
But as the all-made must of necessity
Inferior be to its creator, thus
Arose the infinite imperfect, time,
The spirit-host angelic, heavenly race,
Brute life and vegetive, electric light,
Matter and fleshly form; to human souls
Nine generations from aeternity.
But God, who is Love, decreed it should return
By pure regeneration unto God;
Wherefore was need that He from whom came life
Should taste death, but in tasting swallow up;
That commune with all creatures might be made,
On this hand, and on that, with Deity.
Thus death and evil expiate ends divine;
The Spirit the imperfect hallowing, death
The Son; the soul regenerate hies to God;
And as in radial union with the point
Infinite, both in greatness, place, and power.
Lives with the maker and the all-made in love.

PHILIP JAMES BAILEY

From Festus

I

'God is the sole and self-subsistent one;
From Him, the sun-creator, nature was
Aethereal essences, all elements,
The souls therein indigenous, and man
Symbolic of all being. Out of earth
The matron moon was moulded, and the sea
Filled up the shining chasm; both now fulfil
One orbit and one nature, and all orbs
With them one fate, one universal end.
From light's projective moment, in the earth
The moon was, even as earth i' the sun; the sun
A fiery incarnation of the heavens.
When sun, earth, moon again make one, resumes
Nature her heavenly state; is glorified.'
As, to the sleepless eye, form forth, at last,
The long immeasurable layers of light,
And beams of fire enormous in the east,
The broad foundations of the heaven-domed day
All fineless as the future, so uprose
On mine the great celestial certainty.
The mask of matter fell off, I beheld,
Void of all seeming, the sole substance mind,
The actualized ideal of the world.
An absolutest essence filled my soul;
And superseding all its modes and powers,
Gave to the spirit a consciousness divine;
A sense of vast existence in the skies;
Boundless commune with spiritual light, and proof
Self-shown, of heaven commensurate with all life.
And I to the light of the great spirit's eyes
Mine hungry eyes returned which, past the first
Intensifying blindness, clearlier saw
The words she uttered of triumphant truth.
For truly, and as my vision heightened, lo!
The universal volume of the heavens,
Star-lettered in celestial characters,
Moved musically into words her breath framed forth,
And varied momently; and I perceived
That thus she spake of God: I silent still
And harkening to the sea-swell of her voice:

'From one divine, all permanent unity comes
The many and infinite; from God all just
To himself and others, who to all is love,
Earth and the moon, like syllables of light,
Uttered by him, were with all creatures blessed
By him, and with a sevenfold blessing sealed
To perfect rest, celestial order; all
The double-tabled book of heaven ad earth,
Despite such due deficiency as cleaves
Inevitably to soul, till God resume,
Progressive aye, possessing too all bliss
Elect and universal in the heavens.'

II

And none can truly worship but who have
The earnest of their glory from on high,
God's nature in them. It is the love of God,
The ecstatic sense of oneness with all things,
And special worship towards himself that thrills
Through life's self-conscious chord, vibrant in him,
Harmonious with the universe, which makes
Our sole fit claim to being immortal; that
Wanting nor willing, the world cannot worship.
And whether the lip speak, or in inspired
Silence, we clasp our hearts as a shut book
Of song unsung, the silence and the speech
Is each his; and as coming from and going
To him, is worthy of him and his love.
Prayer is the spirit speaking truth to truth;
The expiration of the thing inspired.
Above the battling rock-storm of this world
Lies heaven's great calm, through which as through a bell,
Tolleth the tongue of God eternally,
Calling to worship. Whoso hears that tongue
Worships. The spirit enters with the sound,
Preaching the one and universal word,
The God-word, which is spirit, life, and light;
The written word to one race, the unwrit
Revealment to the thousand-peopled world.
The ear which hears is pre-attuned in heaven,
The eye which sees prevision hath ere birth.
But the just future shall to many give
Gifts which the partial present doles to few;
To all the glory of obeying God.

EMILY BRONTË

Last Lines

No coward soul is mine,
No trembler in the world's storm-troubled sphere:
    I see heaven's glories shine,
And faith shines equal, arming me from fear.

O God within my breast,
Almighty, ever-present Deity!
    Life – that in me has rest,
As I – undying Life – have power in Thee!

Vain are the thousand creeds
That move men's hearts: unutterably vain;
    Worthless as withered weeds,
Or idlest froth amid the boundless main,

To waken doubt in one
Holding so fast by thine infinity;
    So surely anchor'd on
The steadfast rock of immortality.

With wide-embracing love
Thy Spirit animates eternal years,
    Pervades and broods above,
Changes, sustains, dissolves, creates, and rears.

Though earth and man were gone,
And suns and universes ceased to be,
    And Thou were left alone,
Every existence would exist in Thee.

There is not room for Death,
Nor atom that his might could render void:
    Thou – THOU art Being and Breath,
And what THOU art may never be destroy'd.

EMILY BRONTË

The Philosopher

'Enough of thought, philosopher!
   Too long hast thou been dreaming
Unlightened, in this chamber drear,
   While summer's sun is beaming!
Space-sweeping soul, what sad refrain
Concludes thy musings once again?

'Oh, for the time when I shall sleep
Without identity,
And never care how rain may steep,
Or snow may cover me!
No promised heaven, these wild desires,
Could all, or half fulfil;
No threatened hell, with quenchless fires,
Subdue this quenchless will!'

'So said I, and still say the same;
   Still, to my death, will say –
Three gods, within this little frame,
   Are warring night and day;
Heaven could not hold them all, and yet
   They all are held in me;
And must be mine till I forget
   My present entity!
Oh, for the time, when in my breast
   Their struggles will be o'er!
Oh, for the day, when I shall rest,
   And never suffer more!'

'I saw a spirit, standing, man,
   Where thou dost stand – an hour ago,
And round his feet three rivers ran,
   Of equal depth, and equal flow –
A golden stream – and one like blood;
   And one like sapphire seemed to be,
But, where they joined their triple flood
   It tumbled in an inky sea.
The spirit sent his dazzling gaze
   Down through that ocean's gloomy night
Then, kindling all, with sudden blaze,
   The glad deep sparkled wide and bright –
White as the sun, far, far more fair
   Than its divided sources were!'

'And even for that spirit, seer,
   I've watched and sought my life-time long;
Sought him in heaven, hell, earth, and air –
   An endless search, and always wrong!
Had I but seen his glorious eye
   Once light the clouds that wilder me,
I ne'er had raised this coward cry
   To cease to think, and cease to be;
I ne'er had called oblivion blest,
   Nor, stretching eager hands to death,
Implored to change for senseless rest
   This sentient soul, this living breath –
Oh, let me die – that power and will
   Their cruel strife may close;
And conquered good, and conquering ill
   Be lost in one repose!'

HENRY DAVID THOREAU

I Am a Parcel of Vain Strivings

I am a parcel of vain strivings tied
   By a chance bond together,
  Dangling this way and that, their links
   Were made so loose and wide,
    Methinks,
   For milder weather.

A bunch of violets without their roots,
   And sorrel intermixed,
  Encircled by a wisp of straw
   Once coiled about their shoots,
    The law
   By which I'm fixed.

A nosegay which Time clutched from out
   Those fair Elysian fields,
  With weeds and broken stems, in haste,
   Doth make the rabble rout
    That waste
   The day he yields.

And here I bloom for a short hour unseen,
　　Drinking my juices up,
　With no root in the land
　　　To keep my branches green.
　　　　But stand
　　　In a bare cup.

Some tender buds were left upon my stem
　　In mimicry of life,
　But ah! the children will not know,
　　　Till time has withered them,
　　　　The woe
　　　With which they're rife.

But now I see I was not plucked for naught,
　　And after in life's vase
　Of glass set while I might survive,
　　　But by a kind hand brought
　　　　Alive
　　　To a strange place.

That stock thus thinned will soon redeem its hours,
　　And by another year,
　Such as God knows, with freer air,
　　　More fruits and fairer flowers
　　　　Will bear,
　　　While I droop here.

HENRY DAVID THOREAU

The Moon Now Rises

The moon now rises to her absolute rule,
And the husbandman and hunter
Acknowledge her for their mistress.
Asters and golden reign in the fields
And the life everlasting withers not.
The fields are reaped and shorn of their pride
But an inward verdure still crowns them
The thistle scatters its down on the pool
And yellow leaves clothe the river –
And nought disturbs the serious life of men.
But behind the sheaves and under the sod

There lurks a ripe fruit which the reapers have not gathered
The true harvest of the year – the boreal fruit
Which it bears forever.
With fondness annually watering and maturing it.
But man never severs the stalk
Which bears this palatable fruit.

HENRY DAVID THOREAU

I was Made Erect and Lone

I was made erect and lone
And within me is the bone
Still my vision will be clear
Still my life will not be drear
To the center all is near
Where I sit there is my throne
If age choose to sit apart
If age choose give me the start
Take the sap and leave the heart.

HENRY DAVID THOREAU

For Though the Caves Were Rabitted

For though the caves were rabitted,
    And the well sweeps were slanted,
Each house seemed not inhabited
    But haunted.

The pensive traveller held his way,
    Silent & melancholy,
For every man an idiot was,
    And every house a folly.

WALT WHITMAN

From Song of the Open Road

Here is the efflux of the Soul;
The efflux of the Soul comes from within, through embower'd gates,
    ever provoking questions;
These yearnings, why are they? These thoughts in the darkness, why
    are they?

Why are there men and women that while they are nigh me, the
    sunlight expands my blood?
Why, when they leave me, do my pennants of joy sink flat and lank?
Why are there trees I never walk under, but large and melodious
    thoughts descend upon me?
(I think they hang there winter and summer on those trees, and
    always drop fruit as I pass;)
What is it I interchange so suddenly with strangers?
What with some driver, as I ride on the seat by his side?
What with some fisherman, drawing his seine by the shore, as I walk
    by, and pause?
What gives me to be free to a woman's or man's good-will?
What gives them to be free to mine?
The efflux of the Soul is happiness – here is happiness;
I think it pervades the open air, waiting at all times;
Now it flows unto us – we are rightly charged.

. . .

All parts away for the progress of souls;
All religion, all solid things, arts, governments – all that was or is
    apparent upon this globe or any globe, falls into niches and corners
        before the procession of souls along the grand roads of
        the universe.
Of the progress of the souls of men and women along the grand roads
    of the universe, all other progress is the needed emblem and
    sustenance.

WALT WHITMAN

Grand Is the Seen

Grand is the seen, the light, to me – grand are the sky and stars,
Grand is the earth, and grand are lasting time and space,
And grand their laws, so multiform, puzzling, evolutionary;
But grander far the unseen soul of me, comprehending, endowing all
    those,
Lighting the light, the sky and stars, delving the earth, sailing the sea,
(What were all those, indeed, without thee, unseen soul? of what
    amount without thee?)
More evolutionary, vast, puzzling, O my soul!
More multiform far – more lasting thou than they.

WALT WHITMAN

To See God

Why should I wish to see God better than this day?
I see something of God each hour of the twenty-four, and each
    moment then,
In the faces of men and women I see God and in my own face in
    the glass,
I see letters from God dropped in the street, and every one is signed by
    God's name.

WALT WHITMAN

From Passage to India

O vast Rondure, swimming in space,
Cover'd all over with visible power and beauty,
Alternate light and day and the teeming spiritual darkness,
Unspeakable high processions of sun and moon and countless stars
    above,
Below, the manifold grass and waters, animals, mountains, trees,
With inscrutable purpose, some hidden prophetic intention,
Now first it seems my thought begins to span thee.

. . .

Passage indeed O soul to primal thought,
Not lands and seas alone, thy own clear freshness,
The young maturity of brood and bloom,
To realms of budding bibles.

O soul, repressless, I with thee and thou with me,
Thy circumnavigation of the world begin,
Of man, the voyage of his mind's return,
To reason's early paradise,
Back, back to wisdom's birth, to innocent intuitions,
Again with fair creation.

O we can wait no longer,
We too take ship O soul
Joyous we too launch out on trackless seas,
Fearless for unknown shores on waves of ecstasy to sail,
Amid the wafting winds, (thou pressing me to thee, I thee to me,
　　O soul,)
Caroling free, singing our song of God,
Chanting our chant of pleasant exploration.

With laugh and many a kiss,
(Let others deprecate, let others weep for sin, remorse, humiliation,)
O soul thou pleasest me, I thee.
Ah more than any priest O soul we too believe in God,
But with the mystery of God we dare not dally.

O soul thou pleasest me, I thee,
Sailing these seas or on the hills, or waking in the night,
Thoughts, silent thoughts, of Time and Space and Death, with
　　　waters flowing,
Bear me indeed as through the regions infinite,
Whose air I breathe, whose ripples hear, lave me all over,
Bathe me O God in thee, mounting to thee,
I and my soul to range in range of thee.

O Thou transcendent,
Nameless, the fibre and the breath,
Light of the light, shedding forth universes, thou centre of them,
Thou mightier centre of the true, the good, the loving,
Thou moral, spiritual fountain – affection's source – thou reservoir,
(O pensive soul of me – O thirst unsatisfied – waitest not there?
Waitest not haply for us somewhere there the Comrade perfect?)
Thou pulse – thou motive of the stars, suns, systems,
That, circling, move in order, safe, harmonious,
Athwart the shapeless vastnesses of space,
How should I think, how breathe a single breath, how speak, if,
　　　out of myself,
I could not launch, to those, superior universes?

Swiftly I shrivel at the thought of God,
At Nature and its wonders, Time and Space and Death,
But that I, turning, call to thee O soul, thou actual Me,
And lo, thou gently masterest the orbs,
Thou matest Time, smilest content at Death,
And fillest, swellest full the vastnesses of Space.

Greater than stars or suns,
Bounding O soul thou journeyest forth;
What love than thine and ours could wider amplify?
What aspirations, wishes, outvie thine and ours O soul?
What dreams of the ideal? what plans of purity, perfection, strength?
What cheerful willingness for others' sake to give up all?
For others' sake to suffer all?

Reckoning ahead O soul, when thou, the time achiev'd,
The seas all cross'd, weather'd the capes, the voyage done,
Surrounded, copest, frontest God, yieldest, the aim attain'd,
As fill'd with friendship, love complete, the Elder Brother found,
The Younger melts in fondness in his arms.

Passage to more than India!
Are thy wings plumed indeed for such far flights?
O soul, voyagest thou indeed on voyages like those?
Disportest thou on waters such as those?
Soundest below the Sanscrit and the Vedas?
Then have thy bent unleash'd.

Passage to you, your shores, ye aged fierce enigmas!
Passage to you, to mastership of you, ye strangling problems!
You, strew'd with the wrecks of skeletons, that, living, never
    reach'd you.

Passage to more than India!
O secret of the earth and sky!
Of you O waters of the sea! O winding creeks and rivers!
Of you O woods and fields! of you strong mountains of my land!
Of you O prairies! of you gray rocks!
O morning red! O cloud! O rain and snows!
O day and night, passage to you!

O sun and moon and all you stars! Sirius and Jupiter!
Passage to you!

Passage, immediate passage! the blood burns in my veins!
Away O soul! hoist instantly the anchor!
Cut the hawsers – haul out – shake out every sail!
Have we not stood here like trees in the ground long enough?
Have we not grovel'd here long enough, eating and drinking like
    mere brutes?
Have we not darken'd and dazed ourselves with books long enough?

Sail forth – steer for the deep waters only,
Reckless, O soul, exploring, I with thee, and thou with me,
For we are bound where mariner has not yet dared to go,
And we will risk the ship, ourselves and all.

O my brave soul!
O farther farther sail!
O daring joy, but safe! are they not all the seas of God?
O farther, farther, farther sail!

MATTHEW ARNOLD

From The Buried Life

Fate, which foresaw
How frivolous a baby man would be,
By what distractions he would be possess'd,
How he would pour himself in every strife,
And well-nigh change his own identity –
That it might keep from his capricious play
His genuine self, and force him to obey
Even in his own despite, his being's law,
Bade through the deep recesses of our breast
The unregarded River of our Life
Pursue with indiscernible flow its way;
And that we should not see
The buried stream, and seem to be
Eddying about in blind uncertainty,
Though driving on with it eternally.

But often, in the world's most crowded streets,
But often, in the din of strife,
There rises an unspeakable desire
After the knowledge of our buried life,
A thirst to spend our fire and restless force
In tracking out our true, original course;
A longing to inquire
Into the mystery of this heart that beats
So wild, so deep in us, to know
Whence our thoughts come and where they go.
And many a man in his own breast then delves,
But deep enough, alas, none ever mines!
And we have been on many thousand lines,
And we have shown, on each, spirit and power,

But hardly have we, for one little hour,
Been on our own line, have we been ourselves;
Hardly had skill to utter one of all
The nameless feelings that course through our breast,
But they course on for ever unexpress'd.
And long we try in vain to speak and act
Our hidden self, and what we say and do
Is eloquent, is well – but 'tis not true!

 And then we will no more be rack'd
With inward striving, and demand
Of all the thousand nothings of the hour
Their stupefying power:
Ah yes, and they benumb us at our call:
Yet still, from time to time, vague and forlorn,
From the soul's subterranean depth upborne
As from an infinitely distant land,
Come airs, and floating echoes, and convey
A melancholy into all our day.
Only – but this is rare –
When a beloved hand is laid in ours,
When, jaded with the rush and glare
Of the interminable hours,
Our eyes can in another's eyes read clear,
When our world-deafen'd ear
Is by the tones of a loved voice caress'd –
A bolt is shot back somewhere in our breast,
And a lost pulse of feeling stirs again:
The eye sinks inward, and the heart lies plain,
And what we mean, we say, and what we would, we know.
A man becomes aware of his life's flow,
And hears its winding murmur, and he sees
The meadows where it glides, the sun, the breeze.
And there arrives a lull in the hot race
Wherein he doth for ever chase
That flying and elusive shadow, Rest.
An air of coolness plays upon his face,
And an unwonted calm pervades his breast.
And then he thinks he knows
The Hills where his life rose,
And the Sea where it goes.

MATTHEW ARNOLD

From Empedocles on Etna

Hither and thither spins
The wind-borne, mirroring soul,
A thousand glimpses wins,
And never sees a whole;
Looks once, and drives elsewhere, and leaves its last employ.

The Gods laugh in their sleeve
To watch man doubt and fear,
Who knows not what to believe
Since he sees nothing clear,
And dares stamp nothing false where he finds nothing sure.

Is this, Pausanias, so?
And can our souls not strive,
But with the winds must go,
And hurry where they drive?
Is fate indeed so strong, man's strength indeed so poor?

I will not judge. That man,
Howbeit, I judge as lost,
Whose mind allows a plan,
Which would degrade it most;
And he treats doubt the best who tries to see least ill.

Be not, then, fear's blind slave!
Thou art my friend; to see,
All knowledge that I have,
And skill I wield, are free.
Ask not the latest news of the last miracle,

Ask not what days and nights
In trance Pantheia lay,
But ask how thou such sights
May'st see without dismay;
Ask what most helps when known, thou son of Anchitus!

What? hate, and awe, and shame
Fill thee to see our time;
Thou feelest thy soul's frame
Shaken and out of chime?
What? life and chance go hard with thee too, as with us;

Thy citizens, 'tis said,
Envy thee and oppress,
Thy goodness no men aid,
All strive to make it less;
Tyranny, pride, and lust, fill Sicily's abodes;

Heaven is with earth at strife,
Signs make thy soul afraid,
The dead return to life,
Rivers are dried, winds stay'd;
Scarce can one think in calm, so threatening are the Gods;

And we feel, day and night,
The burden of ourselves –
Well, then, the wiser wight
In his own bosom delves,
And asks what ails him so, and gets what cure he can.

The sophist sneers: Fool, take
Thy pleasure, right or wrong.
The pious wail: Forsake
A world these sophists throng.
Be neither saint nor sophist-led, but be a man!

These hundred doctors try
To preach thee to their school.
We have the truth! they cry;
And yet their oracle,
Trumpet it as they will, is but the same as thine.

Once read thy own breast right,
And thou hast done with fears;
Man gets no other light,
Search he a thousand years.
Sink in thyself! there ask what ails thee, at that shrine!

GEORGE MACDONALD

The Eternal Child

The mortal man, all careful, wise and troubled,
The eternal child in the nursery doth keep.
To-morrow on to-day the man heaps doubled;
The child laughs, hopeful, even in his sleep.
The man rebukes the child for foolish trust;
The child replies, 'Thy care is for poor dust;
Be still and let me wake that thou mayest sleep.'

Till I am one, with oneness magnified,
I must breed contradiction, strife and doubt;
Things tread Thy court, look real – take proving hold –
My Christ is not yet grown to cast them out;
Alas! to me, false-judging, 'twixt the twain,
The *Unseen* oft fancy seems, while, all about,
The *Seen* doth lord it with a mighty train.

But when the Will hath learned obedience royal,
He straight will set the child upon the throne;
To whom the seen things all, grown instant loyal,
Will gather to his feet, in homage prone –
The child their master they have ever known:
Then shall the visible fabric plainly lean
On a Reality that never can be seen.

DANTE GABRIEL ROSSETTI

Soul's Beauty

From The House of Life

Under the arch of Life, where love and death,
   Terror and mystery, guard her shrine, I saw
   Beauty enthroned; and though her gaze struck awe,
I drew it in as simply as my breath.
Hers are the eyes which, over and beneath,
   The sky and sea bend on thee, – which can draw,
   By sea or sky or woman, to one law,
The allotted bondman of her palm and wreath.

This is that Lady Beauty, in whose praise
    Thy voice and hand shake still, – long known to thee
      By flying hair and fluttering hem, – the beat
      Following her daily of thy heart and feet,
    How passionately and irretrievably,
In what fond flight, how many ways and days!

DANTE GABRIEL ROSSETTI

Sudden Light

    I have been here before,
    But when or how I cannot tell:
    I know the grass beyond the door,
    The sweet keen smell,
    The sighing sound, the lights around the shore.

    You have been mine before, –
    How long ago I may not know:
    But just when at that swallow's soar
    Your neck turned so,
    Some veil did fall, – I knew it all of yore.

    Has this been thus before?
    And shall not thus time's eddying flight
    Still with our lives our love restore
    In death's despite,
    And day and night yield one delight once more?

GEORGE MEREDITH

Hymn to Colour

With Life and Death I walked when Love appeared,
And made them on each side a shadow seem.
Through wooded vales the land of dawn we neared,
Where down smooth rapids whirls the helmless dream
To fall on daylight; and night puts away
  Her darker veil for grey.

In that grey veil green grassblades brushed we by;
We came where woods breathed sharp, and overhead
Rocks raised clear horns on a transforming sky:
Around, save for those shapes, with him who led
And linked them, desert varied by no sign
   Of other life than mine.

By this the dark-winged planet, raying wide,
From the mild pearl-glow to the rose upborne,
Drew in his fires, less faint than far descried,
Pure-fronted on a stronger wave of morn:
And those two shapes the splendour interweaved,
   Hung web-like, sank and heaved.

Love took my hand when hidden stood the sun
To fling his robe on shoulder-heights of snow.
Then said: There lie they, Life and Death in one.
Whichever is, the other is: but know,
It is thy craving self that thou dost see,
   Not in them seeing me.

Shall man into the mystery of breath
From his quick beating pulse a pathway spy?
Or learn the secret of the shrouded death,
By lifting up the lid of a white eye?
Cleave thou thy way with fathering desire
   Of fire to reach to fire.

Look now where Colour, the soul's bridegroom, makes
The house of heaven splendid for the bride.
To him as leaps a fountain she awakes,
In knotting arms, yet boundless: him beside,
She holds the flower to heaven, and by his power
   Brings heaven to the flower.

He gives her homeliness in desert air,
And sovereignty in spaciousness; he leads
Through widening chambers of surprise to where
Throbs rapture near an end that aye recedes,
Because his touch is infinite and lends
   A yonder to all ends.

Death begs of Life his blush; Life Death persuades
To keep long day with his caresses graced.
He is the heart of light, the wing of shades,
The crown of beauty: never soul embraced
Of him can harbour unfaith; soul of him
    Possessed walks never dim.

Love eyed his rosy memories: he sang:
O bloom of dawn, breathed up from the gold sheaf
Held springing beneath Orient! that dost hang
The space of dewdrops running over leaf;
They fleetingness is bigger in the ghost
    Than Time with all his host!

Of thee to say behold, has said adieu:
But Love remembers how the sky was green,
And how the grasses glimmered lightest blue;
How saint-like grey took fervour; how the screen
Of cloud grew violet; how thy moment came
    Between a blush and flame.

CHRISTINA ROSSETTI

From Later Life: A Double Sonnet of Sonnets

I

Before the mountains were brought forth, before
    Earth and the world were made, then God was God:
And God will still be God, when flames shall roar
    Round earth and heaven dissolving at His nod:
    And this God is our God, even while His rod
Of righteous wrath falls on us smiting sore:
And this God is our God for evermore
    Thro' life, thro' death, while clod returns to clod.
For tho' He slay us we will trust in Him;
    We will flock home to Him by divers ways:
    Yea, tho' He slay us we will vaunt His praise,
Serving and loving with the Cherubim,
Watching and loving with the Seraphim,
    Our very selves His praise thro' endless days.

V

Lord, Thou Thyself art Love and only Thou;
    Yet I who am not love would fain love Thee;
    But Thou alone being Love canst furnish me
With that same love my heart is craving now.
Allow my plea! for if Thou disallow,
    No second fountain can I find but Thee;
    No second hope or help is left to me,
No second anything, but only Thou.
O Love accept, according my request;
    O Love exhaust, fulfilling my desire;
    Uphold me with the strength that cannot tire,
Nerve me to labour till Thou bid me rest,
    Kindle my fire from Thine unkindled fire,
And charm the willing heart from out my breast.

CHRISTINA ROSSETTI

St Peter

St Peter once: 'Lord, dost Thou wash my feet?' –
    Much more I say: Lord, dost Thou stand and knock
    At my closed heart more rugged than a rock,
Bolted and barred, for Thy soft touch unmeet,
Nor garnished nor in any wise made sweet?
    Owls roost within and dancing satyrs mock.
    Lord, I have heard the crowing of the cock
And have not wept: ah, Lord, thou knowest it.
Yet still I hear Thee knocking, still I hear:
    'Open to Me, look on Me eye to eye,
That I may wring thy heart and make it whole;
And teach thee love because I hold thee dear
    And sup with thee in gladness soul with soul,
And sup with thee in glory by and by.'

CHRISTINA ROSSETTI

From Monna Innominata: A Sonnet of Sonnets

13

'E drizzeremo glí occhi al Primo Amore.'[1]

DANTE

'Ma trovo peso non de la mie braccia.'[2]

PETRARCA

If I could trust mine own self with your fate,
   Shall I not rather trust it in God's hand?
   Without Whose Will one lily doth not stand,
Nor sparrow fall at his appointed date;
   Who numbereth the innumerable sand,
Who weighs the wind and water with a weight,
To Whom the world is neither small nor great,
   Whose knowledge foreknew every plan we planned.
Searching my heart for all that touches you,
   I find there only love and love's goodwill
Helpless to help and impotent to do,
      Of understanding dull, of sight most dim;
      And therefore I commend you back to Him
   Whose love your love's capacity can fill.

[1] And we will direct our eyes to the primal love.
[2] But I find a burden to which my arms suffice not.

CHRISTINA ROSSETTI

To What Purpose is this Waste?

A windy shell singing upon the shore:
A lily budding in a desert place;
Blooming alone
With no companion
To praise its perfect perfume and its grace:
A rose crimson and blushing at the core,
Hedged in with thorns behind it and before:
A fountain in the grass,
Whose shadowy waters pass
Only to nourish birds and furnish food
For squirrels of the wood:
An oak deep in the forest's heart, the house

Of black-eyed tiny mouse;
Its strong roots fit for fuel roofing in
The hoarded nuts, acorns and grains of wheat;
Shutting them from the wind and scorching heat,
And sheltering them when the rains begin:
A precious pearl deep buried in the sea
Where none save fishes be:
The fullest merriest note
For which the skylark strains his silver throat,
Heard only in the sky
By other birds that fitfully
Chase one another as they fly:
The ripest plum down tumbled to the ground
By southern winds most musical of sound.
But by no thirsty traveller found:
Honey of wild bees in their ordered cells
Stored, not for human mouths to taste: –
I said, smiling superior down: What waste
Of good, where no man dwells.

This I said on a pleasant day in June
Before the sun had set, tho' a white moon
Already flaked the quiet blue
Which not a star looked thro'.
But still the air was warm, and drowsily
It blew into my face:
So since that same day I had wandered deep
Into the country, I sought out a place
For rest beneath a tree,
And very soon forgot myself in sleep:
Not so mine own words had forgotten me.
Mine eyes were opened to behold
All hidden things,
And mine ears heard all secret whisperings:
So my proud tongue that had been bold
To carp and to reprove,
Was silenced by the force of utter Love.

All voices of all things inanimate
Join with the song of Angels and the song
Of blessed Spirits, chiming with
Their Hallelujahs. One wind wakeneth
Across the sleeping sea, crisping along
The waves, the brushes thro' the great
Forests and tangled hedges, and calls out
Of rivers a clear sound,

And makes the ripe corn rustle on the ground,
And murmurs in a shell;
Till all their voices swell
Above the clouds in one loud hymn
Joining the song of Seraphim,
Or like pure incense circle round about
The walls of Heaven, or like a well-spring rise
In shady Paradise.

A lily blossoming unseen
Holds honey in its silver cup
Whereon a bee may sup,
Till being full she takes the rest
And stores it in her waxen nest:
While the fair blossom lifted up
On its one stately stem of green
Is type of her, the Undefiled,
Arrayed in white, whose eyes are mild
As a white dove's, whose garment is
Blood-cleansed from all impurities
And earthly taints,
Her robe the righteousness of Saints.

And other eyes than our's
Were made to look on flowers,
Eyes of small birds and insects small:
The deep sun-blushing rose
Round which the prickles close
Opens her bosom to them all.

The tiniest living thing
That soars on feathered wing,
Or crawls among the long grass out of sight,
Has just as good a right
To its appointed portion of delight
As any King.

Why should we grudge a hidden water stream
To birds and squirrels while we have enough?
As if a nightingale should cease to sing
Lest we should hear, or finch leafed out of sight
Warbling its fill in summer light;
As if sweet violets in the spring
Should cease to blow, for fear our path should seem
Less weary or less rough.

So every oak that stands a house
For skilful mouse,
And year by year renews its strength,
Shakes acorns from a hundred boughs
Which shall be oaks at length.

Who hath weighed the waters and shall say
What is hidden in the depths from day?
Pearls and precious stones and golden sands,
Wondrous weeds and blossoms rare,
Kept back from human hands,
But good and fair,
A silent praise as pain is silent prayer.
A hymn, an incense rising toward the skies,
As our whole life should rise;
An offering without stint from earth below,
Which Love accepteth so.

Thus is it with a warbling bird,
With fruit bloom-ripe and full of seed,
With honey which the wild bees draw
From flowers, and store for future need
By a perpetual law.
We want the faith that hath not seen
Indeed, but hath believed His truth
Who witnessed that His work was good:
So we pass cold to age from youth.
Alas for us: for we have heard
And known, but have not understood.

O earth, earth, earth, thou yet shalt bow
Who are so fair and lifted up,
Thou yet shalt drain the bitter cup.
Men's eyes that wait upon thee now,
All eyes shall see thee lost and mean,
Exposed and valued at thy worth,
While thou shalt stand ashamed and dumb. –
Ah, when the Son of Man shall come,
Shall He find faith upon the earth? –

CHRISTINA ROSSETTI
Confluents

As rivers seek the sea,
    Much more deep than they,
So my soul seeks thee
    Far away:
As running rivers moan
On their course alone,
    So I moan
    Left alone.

As the delicate rose
    To the sun's sweet strength
Doth herself unclose,
    Breadth and length;
So spreads my heart to thee
Unveiled utterly,
    I to thee
    Utterly.

As morning dew exhales
    Sunwards pure and free,
So my spirit fails
    After thee:
As dew leaves not a trace
On the green earth's face;
    I, no trace
    On thy face.

Its goal the river knows,
    Dewdrops find a way,
Sunlight cheers the rose
    In her day:
Shall I, lone sorrow past,
Find thee at the last?
    Sorrow past,
    Thee at last?

CHRISTINA ROSSETTI

Resurgam

From depth to height, from height to loftier height,
The climber sets his foot and sets his face,
Tracks lingering sunbeams to their halting-place,
And counts the last pulsations of the light.
Strenuous thro' day and unsurprised by night
He runs a race with Time and wins the race,
Emptied and stripped of all save only Grace,
Will, Love, a threefold panoply of might.
Darkness descends for light he toiled to seek:
He stumbles on the darkened mountain-head,
Left breathless in the unbreathable thin air,
Made freeman of the living and the dead: –
He wots not he had topped the topmost peak,
But the returning sun will find him there.

SIR EDWIN ARNOLD

From The Light of the World, Book I

And Heaven, whate'er betide,
Spreads surely somewhere, on Death's farther side!
This sphere obscure, viewed with dim eyes to match,
This earthly span – gross, brief – wherein we snatch,
Rarely and faintly, glimpses of Times past
Which have been boundless, and of Times to last
Beyond them timelessly; how should such be
All to be seen, all we were made to see?
This flesh fallacious, binding us, indeed,
To sense, and yet so largely leaving freed
That we do know things are we cannot know,
And high and higher on Thought's stairways go
Till each last round leads to some sudden steep
Where Reason swims, and falters; or must leap
Headlong, perforce, into the Infinite,
How should we say outside this shines no light
Of lovelier scenes unseen; of lives which spread
Pleasant and unexpected for the Dead,
As our World, opening to the Babe's wide eyes
New from the Womb, and full of birth's surprise?
How should this prove the All, the Last, the First?

Why shall no inner, under, splendours burst
Once – twice – the Veil? Why put a marvel by
Because too rich with hope? Why quite deny
The Heavenly story, lest our doubtful hearts –
Which mark the stars, and take them for bright parts
Of golden spear beam. Oh, a dream, belike!
Some far-fetched Vision, new to peasant's sleep
Of Paradise stripped bare! – But, why thus keep
Secrets for them? This bar, which doth enclose
Better and nobler souls, why burst for those
Who supped on the parched pulse, and lapped the stream,
And each, at the same hour, dreams the same dream!

. . .

Of boundless Being, ships of life that sail
In glittering argosies – without a tale,
Without a term – or, of that shoreless Sea,
The scattered silver Islets, drifting free
To destinies unmeasured – see, too, there
By help of dead believing eyes, which were,
The peoples of the stars; and listen, meek,
To those vast voices of the stars, which speak –
If ever they shall speak – in each man's tongue?

SIR EDWIN ARNOLD (*trans*)

From With Sa'di in the Garden

A Drop of Rain was falling from forth a summer cloud,
It saw the ocean under it roll billows large and loud;
And, all ashamed and sore dismayed, it whispered 'Woe is me!
By Allah! I am nought! what counts one Rain-drop to the Sea.'

But while it mocked and mourned itself – for littleness forlorn –
Into a sea-shell's opened lips the Drop of Rain was borne,
There many a day and night it lay, until at last it grew
A lovely Pearl of lucent ray, faultless in form and hue;

And God our Lord, who knoweth best how sea-fish made His gem,
Caused those that dive to bring it up; – so in the diadem
Of Persia's King they set that Pearl, and so the Rain-drop came
To be a Sultan's pride and wealth, a jewel of great name!

In that it fell, for loftiness that Rain-drop was designed;
It rose to majesty and worth, because of modest mind!
Oh Sa'di! here thou singeth sooth! Who waits at Door of Fate
With lowly heart and humble voice finds unexpected state.

True, Friends! it is not station, birth, nor wealth,
For power, nor learning, lends us grace to grow
A Pearl upon the Neck-string of the Friend!

SIR EDWIN ARNOLD (*trans*)

From The Light of Asia, Book VI

                              Lo! the Dawn
            Sprang with Buddh's victory! lo! in the East
            Flamed the first fires of beauteous day, poured forth
            Through fleeting folds of Night's black drapery.
            High in the widening blue the herald-star
            Faded to paler silver as there shot
            Brighter and brightest bars of rosy gleam
            Across the grey. Far off the shadowy hills
            Saw the great Sun, before the world was 'ware,
            And donned their crowns of crimson; flower by flower
            Felt the warm breath of Morn and 'gan unfold
            Their tender lids. Over the spangled grass
            Swept the swift footsteps of the lovely Light,
            Turning the tears of Night to joyous gems,
            Decking the earth with radiance, 'broidering
            The sinking storm-clouds with a golden fringe,
            Gilding the feathers of the palms, which waved
            Glad salutation; darting beams of gold
            Into the glades; touching with magic wand
            The stream to rippled ruby; in the brake
            Finding the mild eyes of the antelopes
            And saying 'It is day!' in nested sleep
            Touching the small heads under many a wing
            And whispering, 'Children, praise the light of day!'
            Whereat there piped anthems of all the birds,
            The Koïl's fluted song, the Bulbul's hymn,
            The 'morning, morning' of the painted thrush,
            The twitter of the sunbirds starting forth
            To find the honey ere the bees be out,
            The grey crow's caw, the parrot's scream, the strokes
            Of the green hammersmith, the myna's chirp,

The never-finished love talk of the doves:
Of mirth, the voice of bodiless Prets and Bhuts
Foreseeing Buddh; and Devas in the air
Cried 'It is finished, finished!' and the priests
Stood with the wondering people in the streets
Watching those golden splendours flood the sky,
And saying 'There hath happed some mighty thing.'
Also in Ran and Jungle grew that day
Friendship amongst the creatures; spotted deer
Browsed fearless where the tigress fed her cubs,
And cheetahs lapped the pool beside the bucks;
Under the eagle's rock the brown hares scoured
While his fierce beak but preened an idle wing;
The snake sunned all his jewels in the beam
With deadly fangs in sheath; the shrike let pass
The nestling-finch; the emerald halcyons
Sate dreaming while the fishes played beneath,
Now hawked the merops, though the butterflies –
Crimson and blue and amber – flitted thick
Around his perch; the Spirit of our Lord
Lay potent upon man and bird and beast,
Even while he mused under that Bôdhi-tree,
Glorified with the Conquest gained for all,
And lightened by a Light greater than Day's.

Then he arose – radiant, rejoicing, strong –
Beneath the Tree, and lifting high his voice
Spake this, in hearing of all Times and Worlds:

· · ·

    Many a House of life
Hath held me – seeking ever him who wrought
These prisons of the senses, sorrow-fraught;
    Sore was my ceaseless strife!

    But now,
Thou Builder of this Tabernacle – Thou!
I know Thee! Never shalt Thou build again
    These walls of pain,
Nor raise the roof-tree of deceits, nor lay
    Fresh rafters on the clay;
Broken Thy house is, and the ridge-pole split!
    Delusion fashioned it!
Safe pass I thence – deliverance to obtain.

RICHARD WATSON DIXON

From A Lover's Consolation

. . . There is one way for thee; but one; inform
Thyself of it; pursue it; one way each
Soul hath by which the infinite in reach
Lyeth before him; seek and ye shall find
                                    . . . O joy, joy, joy to fill
The day with leagues! go thy way, all things say,
Thou hast thy way to go, thou hast thy day
To live; thou hast thy need of thee to make
In the heart of others; do thy thing; yea, slake
The world's great thirst for yet another man!
And be thou sure of this; no other can
Do for thee that appointed thee of God . . .

EMILY DICKINSON

He Fumbles at Your Soul

He fumbles at your soul
As players at the keys
Before they drop full music on.
He stuns you by degrees,
Prepares your brittle nature
For the ethereal blow
By fainter hammers further heard,
Then nearer, then so slow
Your breath has time to straighten,
Your brain to bubble cool,
Deals one imperial thunderbolt
That scalps your naked soul.

When winds take forests in their paws
The universe is still.

EMILY DICKINSON

Our Journey Had Advanced

Our journey had advanced,
Our feet were almost come
To that odd fork in being's road,
Eternity by term.

Our pace took sudden awe,
Our feet reluctant led;
Before were cities, but between,
The forest of the dead.

Retreat was out of hope;
Behind, a sealed route,
Eternity's white flag before,
And God at every gate.

EMILY DICKINSON

The Only News I Know

The only news I know
Is bulletins all day
From immortality;

The only shows I see
Tomorrow and today,
Perchance eternity.

The only one I meet
Is God, the only street
Existence; this traversed,

If other news there be
Or admirabler show,
I'll tell it you.

Emily Dickinson

I Taste a Liquor Never Brewed

I taste a liquor never brewed –
From Tankards scooped in Pearl –
Not all the Vats upon the Rhine
Yield such an Alcohol!

Inebriate of Air – am I –
And Debauchee of Dew –
Reeling – thro endless summer days –
From inns of Molten Blue –

When 'Landlords' turn the drunken Bee
Out of the Foxglove's door –
When Butterflies – renounce their 'drams' –
I shall but drink the more!

Emily Dickinson

Safe in their Alabaster Chambers

Safe in their Alabaster Chambers –
Untouched by Morning –
And untouched by Noon –
Lie the meek members of the Resurrection –
Rafter of Satin – and Roof of Stone!

Grand go the Years – in the Crescent – above them –
Worlds scoop their Arcs –
And Firmaments – row –
Diadems – drop – and Doges – surrender –
Soundless as dots – on a Disc of Snow.

Emily Dickinson

Heaven is What I Cannot Reach

Heaven is what I cannot reach.
The apple on the tree,
Provided it do hopeless hang,
That Heaven is to me.

The colour on the cruising cloud,
The interdicted land
Behind the hill, the house behind,
There paradise is found.

Her teazing purples, afternoons,
The credulous decoy,
Enamored of the conjuror
That spurned us yesterday.

Emily Dickinson

Read, Sweet, How Others Strove

Read sweet, how others strove,
Till we are stouter;
What they renounced,
Till we are less afraid;
How many times they bore the faithful witness,
Till we are helped
As if a kingdom cared.

Read then of faith
That shone above the fagot,
Clear strains of hymn.

Emily Dickinson

Bring Me the Sunset in a Cup

Bring me the sunset in a cup,
Reckon the morning's flagons up
And say how many dew,
Tell me how far the morning leaps,
Tell me what time the weaver sleeps
Who spun the breadths of blue.

Write me how many notes there be
In the new robin's exstasy
Among astonished boughs,
How many trips the tortoise makes,
How many cups the bee partakes,
The debauchee of dews.

Also, who laid the rainbow's piers,
Also, who leads the docile spheres
By withes of supple blue?
Whose fingers string the stalactite,
Who counts the wampum of the night
To see that none is due?

Who built this little alban house
And shut the windows down so close
My spirit cannot see?
Who'll let me out some gala day
With implements to fly away,
Passing pomposity?

EMILY DICKINSON

We Thirst at First

We thirst at first – 'tis nature's act –
And later, when we die,
A little water supplicate
Of fingers going by.

It intimates the finer want
Whose adequate supply
Is that great water in the west
Termed Immortality.

JOHN RUSKIN

Mont Blanc

He who looks upon from the vale by night,
When the clouds vanish and the winds are stayed,
For ever finds, in Heaven's serenest height,
A space that hath no stars – a mighty shade –
A vacant form, immovably displayed,
Steep in the unstable vault. The planets droop
Behind it; the fleece-laden moonbeams fade;
The midnight constellations, troop by troop,
Uncomprehended yet, and hardly known
For finite, but by what it takes away
Of the east's purple deepening into day.

Still, for a time, it keeps its awful rest,
Cold as the prophet's pile on Carmel's crest:
Then falls the fire of God. – Far off or near,
Earth and the sea, wide worshipping, descry
That burning altar in the morning sky;
And the strong pines their utmost ridges rear,
Moved like a host, in angel guided fear
And sudden faith. So stands the Providence
Of God around us; mystery of Love!
Obscure, unchanging, darkness and defence, –
Impenetrable and unmoved above
The valley of our watch; but which shall be
The light of Heaven hereafter, when the strife
Of wandering stars, that rules this night of life,
Dies in the Dawning of Eternity.

JOHN GREENLEAF WHITTIER

From The Tent on the Beach

The harp at Nature's advent strung
    Has never ceased to play;
The song the stars of morning sung
    Has never died away.

And prayer is made, and praise is given,
    By all things near and far;
The ocean looketh up to heaven,
    And mirrors every star.

The green earth sends her incense up
    From many a mountain shrine;
From folded leaf and dewy cup
    She pours her sacred wine.

The mists above the morning rills
    Rise white as wings of prayer;
The altar curtains of the hills
    Are sunset's purple air.

The blue sky is the temple's arch,
    Its transept earth and air,
The music of its starry march
    The chorus of a prayer.

JOHN GREENLEAF WHITTIER

The Over-Heart

'For of Him, and through Him, and to Him are
all things: to whom be glory forever!'
                              (*Rom 11:36*)

Above, below, in sky and sod,
   In leaf and spar, in star and man,
   Well might the wise Athenian scan
The geometric signs of God,
   The measured order of His plan.

And India's mystics sang aright,
   Of the One Life pervading all,
   One Being's tidal rise and fall
In soul and form, in sound and sight,
   Eternal outflow and recall.

God is: and man in guilt and fear
   The central fact of Nature owns;
   Kneels, trembling by his altar stones,
And darkly dreams the ghastly smear
   Of blood appeases and atones.

Guilt shapes the Terror: deep within
   The human heart the secret lies
   Of all the hideous deities;
And, painted on a ground of sin,
   The fabled gods of torment rise!

And what is He? The ripe grain nods,
   The sweet dews fall, the sweet flowers blow;
   But darker signs His presence show:
The earthquake and the storm are God's,
   And good and evil interflow.

O hearts of love! O souls that turn
   Like sunflowers to the pure and best!
   To you the truth is manifest:
For they the mind of Christ discern
   Who lean like John upon His breast!

In him of whom the sybil told,
    For whom the prophet's harp was toned,
    Whose need the sage and magian owned,
The loving heart of God behold,
    The hope for which the ages groaned!

Fade, pomp of dreadful imagery
    Wherewith mankind have deified
    Their hate, and selfishness, and pride!
Let the sacred dreamer wake to see
    The Christ of Nazareth at his side!

What doth that holy Guide require?
    No rite of pain, nor gift of blood,
    But man a kindly brotherhood,
Looking, where duty is desire,
    To Him, the beautiful and good.

Gone be the faithlessness of fear,
    And let the pitying heaven's sweet rain
    Wash out the altar's bloody stain;
The law of Hatred disappear,
    The law of Love alone remain.

How fall the idols false and grim!
    And lo! their hideous wreck above
    The emblems of the Lamb and Dove!
Man turns from God, not God from him;
    And guilt, in suffering, whispers Love!

The world sits at the feet of Christ,
    Unknowing, blind, and unconsoled;
    It yet still touch His garment's fold,
And feel the heavenly Alchemist
    Transform its very dust to gold.

The theme befitting angel tongues
    Beyond a mortal's scope has grown.
    O heart of mine! with reverence own
The fulness which to it belongs,
    And trust the unknown for the known.

EDGAR ALLAN POE

A Dream Within a Dream

Take this kiss upon the brow!
And, in parting from you now,
Thus much let me avow –
You are not wrong, who deem
That my days have been a dream;
Yet if Hope has flown away
In a night, or in a day,
In a vision, or in none,
Is it therefore the less *gone?*
All that we see or seem
Is but a dream within a dream.

I stand amid the roar
Of a surf-tormented shore,
And I hold within my hand
Grains of the golden sand –
How few! yet how they creep
Through my fingers to the deep,
While I weep – while I weep!
Oh God! can I not grasp
Them with a tighter clasp?
O God! can I not save
One from the pitiless wave?
Is *all* that we see or seem
But a dream within a dream?

ALGERNON CHARLES SWINBURNE

The Recall

Return, they cry, ere yet your day
   Set, and the sky grow stern:
Return, strayed souls while yet ye may
   Return.

But heavens beyond us yearn;
Yea, heights of heaven above the sway
   Of stars that eyes discern.

The soul whose wings from shoreward stray
   Makes toward her viewless bourne
Through trustless faith and unfaith say,
   Return.

JOHN ADDINGTON SYMONDS

The Prism of Life

All that began with God, in God must end:
   All lives are garnered in His final bliss:
   All wills hereafter shall be one with His:
   When in the sea we sought, our spirits blend.
Rays of pure light, which one frail prism may rend
   Into conflicting colours, meet and kiss
   With manifold attraction, yet still miss
   Contentment, while their kindred hues contend.
Break but that three-edged glass: – inviolate
   The sundered beams resume their primal state,
   Weaving pure light in flawless harmony.
Thus decomposed, subject to love and strife,
   God's thought, made conscious through man's mortal life,
   Resumes through death the eternal unity.

JOHN ADDINGTON SYMONDS

Adventante Deo

Lift up your heads, gates of my heart, unfold
   Your portals to salute the King of kings!
   Behold Him come, borne on cherubic wings
   Engrained with crimson eyes and grail of gold!
Before His path the thunder-clouds withhold
   Their stormy pinions, and the desert sings:
   He from His lips divine and forehead flings
   Sunlight of peace unfathomed, bliss untold.
O soul, faint soul, disquieted how long!
   Lift up thine eyes, for lo, thy Lord is near,
   Lord of all loveliness and strength and song,
The Lord who brings heart-sadness better cheer,
   Scattering those midnight dreams that dote on wrong,
   Purging with heaven's pure rays love's atmosphere!

JOHN ADDINGTON SYMONDS

An Invocation

To God, the everlasting, who abides,
One Life within things infinite that die:
To Him whose unity no thought divides:
Whose breath is breathed through immensity.

Him neither eye hath seen, nor ear hath heard;
Nor reason, seated in the souls of men,
Though pondering oft on the mysterious word,
Hath e'er revealed His Being to mortal ken.

Earth changes, and the starry wheels roll round;
The seasons come and go, moons wax and wane;
The nations rise and fall, and fill the ground,
Storing the sure results of joy and pain:

Slow knowledge widens toward a perfect whole,
From that first man who named the name of heaven,
To him who weighs the planets as they roll,
And knows what laws to every life are given.

Yet He appear not. Round the extreme sphere
Of science still thin ether floats unseen:
Darkness still wraps Him round; and ignorant fear
Remains of what we are, and what have been.

Only we feel Him; and in aching dreams,
Swift intuitions, pangs of keen delight,
The sudden vision of His glory seems
To sear our souls, dividing the dull night:

And we yearn toward Him. Beauty, Goodness, Truth;
These three are one; one life, one thought, one being;
One source of still rejuvenescent youth;
One light for endless and unclouded seeing.

Mere symbols we perceive – the dying beauty,
The partial truth that few can comprehend,
The vacillating faith, the painful duty,
The virtue labouring to a dubious end.

O God, unknown, invisible, secure,
Whose being by dim resemblances we guess,
Who in man's fear and love abidest sure,
Whose power we feel in darkness and confess!

Without Thee nothing is, and Thou art nought
When on Thy substance we gaze curiously:
By Thee impalpable, named Force and Thought,
The solid world still ceases not to be.

Lead Thou me God, Law, Reason, Duty, Life!
All names for Thee alike are vain and hollow –
Lead me, for I will follow without strife;
Or, if I strive, still must I blindly follow.

JAMES RHOADES

From Out of the Silence

Lo! in the vigils of the night, ere sped
The first bright arrows from the Orient shed,
The heart of Silence trembled into sound,
And out of Vastness came a Voice, which said:

I am alone; thou only art in Me:
I am the stream of Life that flows through thee:
I comprehend all substance, fill all space:
I am pure Being, by whom all things be.

I am thy Dawn, from darkness to release:
I am the Deep, wherein thy sorrows cease:
Be still! be still! and know that I am God:
Acquaint thyself with Me, and be at peace!

I am the Silence that is more than sound:
If therewithin thou lose thee, thou art found:
The stormless, shoreless Ocean, which is I –
Thou canst not breathe, but in its bosom drowned.

I am all Love: there is naught else but I:
I am the Power: the rest is phantasy:
Evil, and anguish, sorrow, death, and hell –
These are the fear-flung shadows of a lie.

Arraign not Mine Omnipotence, to say
That aught beside in earth or heaven hath sway!
The powers of darkness are not: that which is
Abideth: these but vaunt them for a day.

Know thou thyself: as thou hast learned of Me,
I made thee three in one, and one in three –
Spirit and Mind and Form, immortal Whole,
Divine and undivided Trinity.

Seek not to break the triple bond assigned:
Mind sees by Spirit: Body moves by Mind:
Divorced from Spirit, both way-wildered fall –
Leader and led, the blindfold and the blind.

Look not without thee: thou hast that within,
Makes whole thy sickness, impotent thy sin:
Survey thy forces, rally to thyself:
That which thou would'st not hath no power to win.

I, God, enfold thee like an atmosphere:
Thou to thyself wert never yet more near:
Think not to shun Me: whither would'st thou fly?
Nor go not hence to seek Me: I am here.

EDWARD DOWDEN

By the Window

Still deep into the West I gazed; the light
Clear. spiritual, tranquil as a bird
Wide-winged that soars on the smooth gale and sleeps,
Was it from sun far-set or moon unrisen?
Whether from moon, or sun, or angel's face
It held my heart from motion, stayed my blood,
Betrayed each rising thought to quiet death
Along the blind charm'd way to nothingness,
Lull'd the last nerve that ached. It was a sky
Made for a man to waste his will upon,
To be received as wiser than all toil,
And much more fair. And what was strife of men?
And what was time?

Then came a certain thing.
Are intimations for the elected soul
Dubious, obscure, of unauthentic power
Since ghostly to the intellectual eye,
Shapeless to thinking? Nay, but are not we
Servile to words and an usurping brain,
Infidels of our own high mysteries,
Until the senses thicken and lose the world,
Until the imprisoned soul forgets to see,
And spreads blind fingers forth to reach the day,
Which once drank light, and fed on angels' food?
It happened swiftly, came and straight was gone.

One standing on some aery balcony
And looking down upon a swarming crowd
Sees one man beckon to him with finger-tip
While eyes meet eyes; he turns and looks again –
The man is lost, and the crowd sways and swarms.
Shall such an one say, 'Thus 'tis proved a dream,
And no hand beckoned, no eyes met my own?'
Neither can I say this. There was a hint,
A thrill, a summons faint yet absolute,
Which ran across the West; the sky was touch'd,
And failed not to respond. Does a hand pass
Lightly across your hair? you feel it pass
Not half so heavy as a cobweb's weight,
Although you never stir; so felt the sky
Not unaware of the Presence, so my soul
Scarce less aware. And if I cannot say

The meaning and monition, words are weak
Which will not paint the small wing of a moth,
Nor bear a subtile odour to the brain,
And much less serve the soul in her large needs.
I cannot tell the meaning, but a change
Was wrought in me; it was not the one man
Who came to the luminous window to gaze forth,
And who moved back into the darkened room
With awe upon his heart and tender hope;
From some deep well of life tears rose; the throng
Of dusty cares, hopes, pleasures, prides fell off,
And from a sacred solitude I gazed
Deep, deep into the liquid eyes of Life.

EDWARD DOWDEN

The Secret of the Universe

I spin, I spin, around, around,
    And close my eyes,
    And let the bile arise
From the sacred region of the soul's Profound;
Then gaze upon the world; how strange! how new!
    The earth and heaven are one,
    The horizon-line is gone,
The sky how green! the land how fair and blue!
Perplexing items fade from my large view,
And thought which vexed me with its false and true
Is swallowed up in Intuition; this,
    This is the sole true mode
    Of reaching God,
And gaining the universal synthesis
Which makes All – One; while fools with peering eyes
Dissect, divide, and vainly analyse.
So round, and round, and round again!
How the whole globe swells within my brain,
The stars inside my lids appear,
The murmur of the spheres I hear
Throbbing and beating in each ear;
Right in my navel I can feel
The centre of the world's great wheel.

Ah peace divine, bliss dear and deep,
    No stay, no stop,
    Like any top
Whirling with swiftest speed, I sleep.
O ye devout ones round me coming,
Listen! I think that I am humming;
    No utterance of the servile mind
With poor chop-logic rules agreeing
    Here shall ye find,
But inarticulate burr of man's unsundered being.
Ah, could we but devise some plan.
Some patent jack by which a man
Might hold himself ever in harmony
With the great whole, and spin perpetually,
    As all things spin
    Without, within,

As Time spins off into Eternity,
And Space into the inane Immensity,
And the Finite into God's Infinity,
    Spin, spin, spin, spin.

EDWARD DOWDEN

Communion

Lord, I have knelt and tried to pray to-night,
But Thy love came upon me like a sleep,
And all desire died out; upon the deep
Of Thy mere love I lay, each thought in light
Dissolving like the sunset clouds, at rest
Each tremulous wish, and my strength weakness, sweet
As a sick boy with soon o'erwearied feet
Finds, yielding him unto his mother's breast
To weep for weakness there. I could not pray,
But with closed eyes I felt Thy bosom's love
Beating toward mine, and then I would not move
Till of itself the joy should pass away;
At last my heart found voice, – 'Take me, O Lord,
And do with me according to Thy word.'

EDWARD DOWDEN

Love's Lord

When weight of all the garner'd years
    Bows me, and praise must find relief
In harvest-song, and smiles and tears
    Twist in the band that binds my sheaf;

Thou known Unknown, dark, radiant sea
    In whom we live, in whom we move,
My spirit must lose itself in Thee,
    Crying a name – Life, Light, or Love.

Edward Dowden

The Initiation

Under the flaming wings of cherubim
  I moved toward that high altar. O, the hour!
And the light waxed intenser, and the dim
  Low edges of the hills and the grey sea
Were caught and captur'd by the present Power,
  My sureties and my witnesses to be.

Then the light drew me in. Ah, perfect pain!
  Ah, infinite moment of accomplishment!
Thou terror of pure joy, with neither wane
  Nor waxing, but long silence and sharp air
As womb-forsaking babes breathe. Hush! the event
  Let him who wrought Love's marvellous things declare.

Shall I who fear'd not joy, fear grief at all?
  I on whose mouth Life laid his sudden lips
Tremble at Death's weak kiss, and not recall
  That sundering from the flesh, the flight from time,
The judgements stern, the clear apocalypse,
  The lightnings, and the Presences sublime.

How came I back to earth? I know not how,
  Nor what hands led me, nor what words were said.
Now all things are made mine, – joy, sorrow; now
  I know my purpose deep, and can refrain;
I walk among the living, not the dead;
  My sight is purged; I love and pity men.

Gerard Manley Hopkins

God's Grandeur

The world is charged with the grandeur of God.
  It will flame out, like shining from shook foil,
  It gathers to a greatness like the ooze of oil
Crushed. Why do men then now not reck His rod?
Generations have trod, have trod, have trod;
  And all is seared with trade; bleared, smeared with toil;
  And bears man's smudge, and shares man's smell; the soil
Is bare now, nor can foot feel being shod.

And for all this, nature is never spent;
   There lives the dearest freshness deep down things;
And though the last lights from the black west went,
   Oh, morning at the brown brink eastwards springs –
Because the Holy Ghost over the bent
   World broods with warm breast, and with, ah, bright wings.

GERARD MANLEY HOPKINS

Hurrahing in Harvest

Summer ends now; now, barbarous in beauty, the stooks rise
Around; up above, what wind-walks! what lovely behaviour
Of silk-sack clouds! has wilder, wilful-wavier
Meal-drift moulded ever and melted across skies?

I walk, I lift up, I lift up heart, eyes,
Down all that glory in the heavens to glean our Saviour;
And, eyes, heart, what looks, what lips yet gave you a
Rapturous love's greeting of realer, of rounder replies?

And the azurous hung hills are his world-wielding shoulder
Majestic – as a stallion stalwart, very-violet-sweet! –
These things, these things were here and but the beholder
Wanting; which two when they once meet,
The heart rears wings bold and bolder
And hurls for him, O half hurls earth for him off under his feet.

GERARD MANLEY HOPKINS

The Windhover

To Christ our Lord

I caught this morning morning's minion, kingdom
   of daylight's dauphin, dapple-dawn-drawn Falcon, in his riding
Of the rolling level underneath him steady air, and striding
High there, how he rung upon the rein of a wimpling wing
In his ecstacy! then off, off forth on swing,
   As a skate's heel sweeps smooth on a bow-bend: the hurl and gliding
   Rebuffed the big wind. My heart in hiding
Stirred for a bird, – the achieve of, the mastery of the thing!

Brute beauty and valour and act, oh, air, pride, plume, here
　　Buckle! AND the fire that breaks from thee then, a billion
Times told lovelier, more dangerous, O my chevalier!

　　No wonder of it: sheer plod makes plough down sillion
Shine, and blue-bleak embers, ah my dear,
　　Fall, gall themselves, and gash gold-vermilion.

GERARD MANLEY HOPKINS

Pied Beauty

Glory be to God for dappled things –
　　For skies of couple-colour as a brinded cow;

　　For rose-moles all in stipple upon trout that swim;
Fresh-firecoal chestnut-falls; finches' wings;
　　Landscape plotted and pieced – fold, fallow, and plough;
　　And all trades, their gear and tackle and trim.

All things counter, original, spare, strange;
　　Whatever is fickle, freckled (who knows how?)
　　With swift, slow; sweet, sour; adazzle, dim;
He fathers-forth whose beauty is past change:
　　　　　　　　　　　　Praise him.

GERARD MANLEY HOPKINS

The Caged Skylark

As a dare-gale skylark scanted in a dull cage,
　　Man's mounting spirit in his bone-house, mean house, dwells –
　　That bird beyond the remembering his free fells;
This in drudgery, day-labouring-out life's age.

Though aloft on turf or perch or poor low stage
　　Both sing sometimes the sweetest, sweetest spells,
　　Yet both droop deadly sometimes in their cells
Or wring their barriers in bursts of fear or rage.

Not that the sweet-fowl, song-fowl, needs no rest –
Why, hear him, hear him babble and drop down to his nest,
   But his own nest, wild nest, no prison.

Man's spirit will be flesh-bound, when found at best,
But uncumbered: meadow-down is not distressed
   For a rainbow footing it nor he for his bones risen.

GERARD MANLEY HOPKINS

The Starlight Night

Look at the stars! look, look up at the skies!
   O look at all the fire-folk sitting in the air!
   The bright boroughs, the circle-citadels there!
Down in dim woods the diamond delves! the elves'-eyes!
The grey lawns cold where gold, where quickgold lies!
   Wind-beat whitebeam! airy abeles set on a flare!
   Flake-doves sent floating forth at a farmyard scare! –
Ah well! it is all a purchase, all is a prize.

Buy then! bid then! – What? – Prayer, patience, alms, vows.
Look, look: a May-mess, like on orchard boughs!
   Look! March-bloom, like on mealed-with-yellow sallows!
These are indeed the barn; withindoors house
The shocks. This piece-bright paling shuts the spouse
   Christ home, Christ and his mother and all his hallows.

GERARD MANLEY HOPKINS

The Dark-Out Lucifer

   The dark-out Lucifer detesting this
      Self-trellises the touch-tree in live green twines
      And loops the fruity boughs with beauty-bines.

GERARD MANLEY HOPKINS

As Kingfishers Catch Fire

As kingfishers catch fire, dragonflies draw flame;
    As tumbled over rim in roundy wells
    Stones ring; like each tucked string tells, each hung bell's
Bow swung finds tongue to fling out broad its name;
Each mortal thing does one thing and the same:
    Deals out that being indoors each one dwells;
    Selves – goes its self; *myself* it speaks and spells,
Crying *What I do is me: for that I came.*

I say more: the just man justices;
    Keeps grace: that keeps all his goings graces;
Acts in God's eye what in God's eye he is –
    Christ. For Christ plays in ten thousand places,
Lovely in limbs, and lovely in eyes not his
    To the Father through the features of men's faces.

EDWARD CARPENTER

Love's Vision

At night in each other's arms,
Content, overjoyed, resting deep deep down in the darkness,
Lo! the heavens opened and He appeared –
Whom no mortal eye may see,
Whom no eye clouded with Care,
Whom none who seeks after this or that, whom none
    who has not escaped from self.
There – in the region of Equality, in the world of
    Freedom no longer limited,
Standing as a lofty peak in heaven above the clouds,
From below hidden, yet to all who pass into that region
    most clearly visible –
He the Eternal appeared.

EDWARD CARPENTER

From By the Shore

The play goes on!
Suddenly I am the great living Ocean itself – the awful
    Spirit of Immensity creeps over my face.

I am in love with it. All night and ages and ages long
    and for ever I pour my soul out to it in love.
I spread myself out broader and broader for ever, that
    I may touch it and be with it everywhere.
There is no end. But ever and anon it maddens me
    with its touch. I arise and sweep away my bounds.

I know but I do not care any longer which my own
    particular body is – all conditions and fortunes
    are mine.
By the ever-beautiful coast-line of human life, by all
    shores, in all climates and countries, by every
    secluded nook and inlet,

Under the eye of my beloved Spirit I glide:
O joy! for ever, ever, joy!
I am not hurried – the whole of eternity is mine;
With each one I delay, with each one I dwell – with you
    I dwell.
The warm breath of each life ascends past me;
I take the thread from the fingers that are weary, and
    go on with the work;
The secretest thoughts of all are mine, and mine are
    the secretest thoughts of all.

All night by the shore;
And the fresh air comes blowing with the dawn,
The mystic night fades – but my joy fades not.
I arise and cast a stone into the water (O sea of faces
    I cast this poem among you) – and turn landward
    over the rustling beach.

EDWARD CARPENTER
So Thin a Veil

So thin a veil divides
   Us from such joy, past words,
Walking in daily life – the business of the hour, each
   detail seen to;
Yet carried, rapt away, on what sweet floods of other
   Being:
Swift streams of music flowing, light far back through
   all Creation shining,
Loved faces looking –
Ah! from the true, the mortal self
So thin a veil divides!

EDWARD CARPENTER
From The World-Spirit

Like soundless summer lightning seen afar,
   A halo o'er the grave of all mankind,
O undefined dream-embosomed star,
   O charm of human love and sorrow twined:

Far, far away beyond the world's bright streams,
   Over the ruined spaces of the lands,
Thy beauty, floating slowly, ever seems
   To shine most glorious; then from out our hands

To fade and vanish, evermore to be
   Our sorrow, our sweet longing sadly borne,
Our incommunicable mystery
   Shrined in the soul's long night before the morn.

. . .

And yet, o'er all, the One through many seen,
   The phantom Presence moving without fail,
Sweet sense of closelinked life and passion keen
   As of the grass waving before the gale.

What art Thou, O that wast and art to be?
    Ye forms that once through shady forest-glade
Or golden light-flood wandered lovingly,
    What are ye? Nay, though all the past do fade

Ye are not therefore perished, ye whom erst
    The eternal Spirit struck with quick desire,
And led and beckoned onward till the first
    Slow spark of life became a flaming fire.

Ye are not therefore perished: for behold
    To-day ye move about us, and the same
Dark murmur of the past is forward rolled
    Another age, and grows with louder fame

Unto the morrow: newer ways are ours,
    New thoughts, new fancies, and we deem our lives
New-fashioned in a mould of vaster powers;
    But as of old with flesh the spirit strives,

And we but head the strife. Soon shall the song
    That rolls all down the ages blend its voice
With our weak utterance and make us strong;
    That we, borne forward still, may still rejoice,

Fronting the wave of change. Thou who alone
    Changeless remainest, O most mighty Soul,
Hear us before we vanish! O make known
    Thyself in us, us in Thy living whole.

EDWARD CARPENTER

In the Deep Cave of the Heart

In the deep cave of the heart, far down,
    Running under the outward shows of the world and of people,
    Running under geographies, continents, under the fields and the
roots of the grasses and trees, under the little thoughts and dreams of
men, and the history of races,
    Deep, far down,
    I see feel and hear wondrous and divine things.
    Voices and faces are there; arms of lovers, known and unknown,
reach forward and fold me;
    Words float, and fragrance of Time ascends, and Life ever circling.

EDWARD CARPENTER

From Towards Democracy

Standing beyond Time,
    As the Earth to the bodies of all men gives footing and free passage,
yet draws them to itself with final overmastering force, and is their
bodies–
    So I their souls.

I am the ground of thy soul;
    And I am that which draws thee unbeknown – veiled Eros,
Visitor of thy long night-time;
    And I that give thee form from ancient ages,
    Thine own – yet in due time to return to Me
    Standing beyond Time.

O gracious Mother, in thy vast eternal sunlight
Heal us, thy foolish children, from our sins;
Who heed thee not, but careless of thy Presence
Turn our bent backs on thee, and scratch and scrabble
In ash-heaps for salvation.

EDWARD CARPENTER

India, the Wisdom-Land

Here also in India – wonderful, hidden – over the sands of miles,
    Through thousands of miles of coco-nut groves, by the winding
banks of immense rivers, over interminable areas of rice-fields,
    On the great Ghauts and Himalayas, through vast jungles tenanted
by wild beasts,
    Under the cloudless glorious sky – the sun terrible in strength and
beauty – the moon so keen and clear among the tree-tops,
    In vast and populous cities, behind colors and creeds and sects and
races and families,
    Behind the interminable close-fitting layers of caste and custom,
    Here also, hidden away, the secret, the divine knowledge.

Ages back, thousands of years lost in the dim past,
    A race of seers over the northern mountains, with flocks and herds,
Into India, the Wisdom-land, descended;
    The old men leading – not belated in the rear –
    Eagle-eyed, gracious-eyed old men, with calm faces, resolute calm
mouths,

Active, using their bodies with perfect command and power –
retaining them to prolonged age, or laying them down in death at will.

These men, retiring rapt – also at will – in the vast open under the
sun or stars,

Having circled and laid aside desire, having lifted and removed from
themselves the clinging veils of thought and oblivion,

Saw, and became what they saw, the imperishable universe.

Within them, sun and moon and stars, within them past and future,

Interiors of objects and of thoughts revealed – one with all being –

Life past, death past – the calm and boundless sea

Of deep, of changeless incommunicable Joy.

And now to-day, under the close-fitting layers of caste and custom,
hidden away,

The same seers, the same knowledge.

All these thousands of years the long tradition kept intact,

Handed down, the sacred lore, from one to another, carefully
guarded,

Beneath the outer conventional shows, beneath all the bonds of
creed and race, gliding like a stream which nothing can detain,

Dissolving in its own good time all bonds, all creeds,

The soul's true being – the cosmic vast emancipated life – Freedom,
Equality –

The precious semen of Democracy.

SAMUEL WADDINGTON

A Persian Apologue

Love came to crave sweet love, if love might be;
    To the Beloved's door he came, and knocked: –
'And who art thou?' she asked, – 'we know not thee!'
Then shyly listened, nor the door unlocked.
Love answered, 'It is I!' 'Nay, thee and me
This house will never hold.' – 'Twas thus she mocked
His piteous quest; and, weeping, home went he,
While thro' the night the moaning plane-tree rocked.
    Three seasons sped, and lo, again Love came;
Again he knocked: again in simple wise,
'Pray, who is there?' she asked, – 'What is thy name?'
But Love had learnt the magic of replies, –
'It is Thyself!' he whispered, and behold,
The door was opened, and love's mystery told.

SAMUEL WADDINGTON

Amiel

Lone wanderer 'mid the loftiest heights of Thought,
 Tired watcher for the Dawn that brings the Light,
Whose spirit, in rapt vision, ever sought
 To view the shadowy realm beyond our sight,
 The powers eternal and the Infinite, –
Say, was thy quest in vain? Was it for nought
 To garner truth thou labour'dst thro' the night,
Thy life unfruitful and thy work unwrought?

Nay, not in vain, – if Hope, and Joy, and Love,
 Together watched thy journey on the way;
Oh, not in vain, – if voices from above,
 Calling thee onward, led thee day by day:
His life alone is vain who never strove, –
 Not theirs who for the Truth still watch and pray.

SAMUEL WADDINGTON

Human

Across the trackless skies thou may'st not wander;
Thou may'st not tread the infinite beyond;
In peace possess thy soul, reflect and ponder,
Full brief thy gaze, tho' Nature's magic wand
Light up an universe, and bid thee wonder!
What thought beyond the sea there may be land
Where grows the vine, where blooms the oleander,
Where verdure gleams amid the desert sand, –
Yet not for thee those foreign, fertile spaces,
Remote, unseen, unknown, though known to be!
Thy home is here, and here beloved faces
Make sweet and fair the home and heart of thee;
Thy home is here, and here thy heart embraces
Life's joy and hope, love, truth, and liberty!

EDMOND GORE ALEXANDER HOLMES

The Creed of My Heart

A flame in my heart is kindled by the might of the morn's pure breath;
A passion beyond all passion; a faith that eclipses faith;
A joy that is more than gladness; a hope that outsoars desire;
A love that consumes and quickens; a soul-transfiguring fire.
My life is possessed and mastered: my heart is inspired and filled.
All other visions have faded: all other voices are stilled.
My doubts are vainer than shadows: my fears are idler than dreams:
They vanish like breaking bubbles, those old soul-torturing themes.
The riddles of life are cancelled, the problems that bred despair:
I cannot guess them or solve them, but I know that they are not there.
They are past, they are all forgotten, the breeze has blown them away;
For life's inscrutable meaning is clear as the dawn of day.
It is there – the secret of Nature – there in the morning's glow;
There in the speaking stillness; there in the rose-flushed snow.
It is here in the joy and rapture; here in my pulsing breast:
I feel what has ne'er been spoken: I know what has ne'er been guessed.
The rose-lit clouds of morning; the sun-kissed mountain heights;
The orient streaks and flushes; the mingling shadows and lights;
The flow of the lonely river; the voice of its distant stream;
The mists that rise from the meadows, lit up by the sun's first beam; –
They mingle and melt as I watch them; melt and mingle and die.
The land is one with the water: the earth is one with the sky.
The parts are as parts no longer: Nature is All and One:
Her life is achieved, completed: her days of waiting are done.
I breathe the breath of the morning. I am one with the one
    World-Soul.
I live my own life no longer, but the life of the living Whole.
I am more than self: I am selfless: I am more than self: I am I.
I have found the springs of my being in the flush of the eastern sky.
I – the true self, the spirit, the self that is born of death –
I have found the flame of my being in the morn's ambrosial breath.
I lose my life for a season: I lose it beyond recall:
But I find it renewed, rekindled, in the life of the One, the All.
I look not forward or backward: the abysses of time are nought.
From pole to pole of the heavens I pass in a flash of thought.
I clasp the world to my bosom: I feel its pulse in my breast, –
The pulse of measureless motion, the pulse of fathomless rest.
Is it motion or rest that thrills me? Is it lightning or moonlit peace?
Am I freer than waves of ether, or prisoned beyond release?
I know not; but through my spirit, within me, around, above,
The world-wide river is streaming, the river of life and love.
Silent, serene, eternal, passionless, perfect, pure; –

I may not measure its windings, but I know that its aim is sure.
In its purity seethes all passion: in its silence resounds all song:
Its strength is builded of weakness: its right is woven of wrong.
I am borne afar on its bosom; yet its source and its goal are mine,
From the sacred springs of Creation to the ocean of love Divine.
I have ceased to think or to reason: there is nothing to ponder or
     prove:
I hope, I believe no longer: I am lost in a dream of love.

EDMOND GORE ALEXANDER HOLMES

Nirvana

Could my heart but see Creation as God sees it, – from within;
     See His grace behind its beauty, see His will behind its force;
See the flame of life shoot upward when the April days begin;
     See the wave of life rush outward from its pure eternal source;

Could I see the summer sunrise glow with God's transcendent hope;
     See His peace upon the waters in the moonlit summer night;
See Him nearer still when, blinded, in the depths of gloom I grope, –
     See the darkness flash and quiver with the gladness of His light;

Could I see the red-hot passion of His love resistless burn
     Through the dumb despair of winter, through the frozen
          lifeless clod; –
Could I see what lies around me as God sees it, I should learn
     That its outward life is nothing, that its inward life is God.

Vain the dream! To spirit only is the spirit-life revealed:
     God alone can see God's glory: God alone can feel God's love.
By myself the soul of Nature from myself is still concealed;
     And the earth is still around me, and the skies are still above.

Vain the dream! I cannot mingle with the all-sustaining soul:
     I am prisoned in my senses; I am pinioned by my pride;
I am severed by my selfhood from the world-life of the Whole;
     And my world is near and narrow, and Gods world is waste
          and wide.

Vain the dream! Yet in the morning, when the eastern skies are red,
     When the dew is on the meadows, when the lark soars up
          and sings, –
Leaps a sudden flame within me from its ashes pale and dead,
     And I see God's beauty burning through the veil of outward things.

Brighter grows the veil and clearer, till, beyond all fear and doubt,
　　I am ravished by God's splendour into oneness with His rest;
And I draw the world within me, and I send my soul without;
　　And God's pulse is in my bosom, and I lie upon God's breast.

Dies the beatific vision in the moment of its birth;
　　Dies, but in its death transfigures all the sequence of my days;
Dies, but dying crowns with triumph all the travail of the earth,
　　Till its harsh discordant murmurs swell into a psalm of praise.

Then a yearning comes upon me to be drawn at last by death,
　　Drawn into the mystic circle in which all things live and move,
Drawn into the mystic circle of the love which is God's breath, –
　　Love creative, love receptive, love of loving, love of love.

God! the One, the All of Being! let me lose my life in Thine;
　　Let me be what Thou hast made me, be a quiver of Thy flame.
Purge my self from self's pollution; burn it into life divine;
　　Burn it till it dies triumphant in the firespring whence it came.

EDMOND GORE ALEXANDER HOLMES

La Vie Profonde

Hemmed in by petty thoughts and petty things,
　　Intent on toys and trifles all my years,
Pleased by life's gauds, pained by its pricks and stings,
　　Swayed by ignoble hopes, ignoble fears;
Threading life's tangled maze without life's clue,
　　Busy with means, yet heedless of their ends,
Lost to all sense of what is real and true,
　　Blind to the goal to which all Nature tends: –
Such is my surface self: but deep beneath,
　　A mighty actor on a world-wide stage,
Crowned with all knowledge, lord of life and death,
　　Sure of my aim, sure of my heritage, –
I – the true self – live on, in self's despite,
That 'life profound' whose darkness is God's light.

EDMOND GORE ALEXANDER HOLMES

The God Within

Life of my life! soul of my inmost soul!
　　Pure central point of everlasting light!
Creative splendour! Fountain-head and goal
　　Of all the rays that make the darkness bright –
　　　　And pierce the gloom of nothing more and more
　　And win new realms from the abyss of night!
　　　　O God, I veil my eyes and kneel before
　　　　Thy shrine of love and tremble and adore.

The unfathomable past is but the dawn
　　Of thee triumphant rising from the tomb;
And could we deem thy lamp of light withdrawn,
　　Back in an instant into primal gloom
　　　　All things that are, all things that time has wrought,
　　All that shall ever yet unseal the womb
　　　　Of elemental Chaos, swift as thought
　　　　Would melt away and leave a world of nought.

We gaze in wonder on the starry face
　　Of midnight skies, and worship and aspire,
Yet all the kingdoms of abysmal space
　　Are less than thy one point of inmost fire:
　　　　We dare not think of time's unending way,
　　Yet present, past, and future would expire,
　　　　And all eternity would pass away
　　　　In thy one moment of intensest day.

Of old our fathers heard thee when the roll
　　Of midnight thunder crashed across the sky:
I hear thee in the silence of the soul –
　　Its very stillness is the majesty
　　　　Of thy mysteries voice, that moves me more
　　Than wrath of tempest as it rushes by,
　　　　Or booming thunder, or the surging roar
　　　　Of seas that storm a never-trodden shore.

And they beheld thee when the lightning shone,
   And tore the leaden slumber of the storm
With vivid flame that was and then was gone,
    Whose blaze made blind, whose very breath was warm: –
      But I, if I would see thee, pray for grace
To veil my eyes to every outward form,
      And in the darkness for a moment's space
      I see the splendour of thy cloudless face.

In thought I climb to Being's utmost brink
   And pass beyond the last imagined star,
And tremble and grow dizzy while I think –
    But thou art yet more infinitely far,
      O God, from me who breathe the air of sin,
And I am doomed to traverse worlds that are
      More fathomless to fancy ere I win
      The central altar of the soul within.

How shall I worship thee? With speechless awe
   Of guilt that shrinks when innocence is near
And veils its face: with faith, that ever saw
    Most when its eyes were clouded with a tear:
      With hope, the breath of spirits that aspire:
Lastly, with love – the grave of every fear,
      The fount of faith, the triumph of desire,
      The burning brightness of thine own white fire . . .

O God that dwellest in transcendent light
   Beyond our dreams, who grope in darkness here,
Beyond imagination's utmost flight, –
    I bless thee most that sometimes when a tear
      Of tender yearning rises unrepressed,
Lo! for an instant thou art strangely near –
      Nearer to my own heart than I who rest.

WILLIAM SHARP

The Mystic's Prayer

Lay me to sleep in sheltering flame,
   O Master of the Hidden Fire!
Wash pure my heart, and cleanse for me
   My soul's desire.

In flame of sunrise bathe my mind,
O Master of the Hidden Fire,
That, when I wake, clear-eyed may be
My soul's desire.

MARGARET DELAND

Life

By one great Heart the Universe is stirred:
By Its strong pulse, stars climb the darkening blue;
It throbs in each fresh sunset's changing hue,
And thrills through low sweet song of every bird:

By It, the plunging blood reds all men's veins;
Joy feels that heart against his rapturous own,
And on It, Sorrow breathes her sharpest groan;
It bounds through gladnesses and deepest pains.

Passionless beating through all Time and Space,
Relentless, calm, majestic in Its march,
Alike, though Nature shake heaven's endless arch,
Or man's heart break, because of some dead face!

'Tis felt in sunshine greening the soft sod,
In children's smiling, as in mother's tears;
And, for strange comfort, through the aching years,
Men's hungry souls have named that great Heart, God!

H P SHASTRI (*trans*)

From Poems of Harischandra

I will devote my whole life to loving Thee.
Patiently will I endure mountains of hardship
And still set my heart on Thee.
In Thy devotion I will suffer rain and storm,
Nor shall I serve any other.
The rest of my life will be passed in Thy love.
Says Harischandra: For the sake of the world I shall not be deterred;
Whatever comes I will endure;
I shall continue to love Thee till my last breath.

. . .

From every pore of my body issues the cry 'I am God!'
O Harischandra, who can describe what the wise feel?
From a drop, he has become the ocean;
He is the tree, the branches, and the leaves.

FRANCIS THOMPSON

The Kingdom of God

In no strange land

O world invisible, we view thee,
O world intangible, we touch thee,
O world unknowable, we know thee,
Inapprehensible, we clutch thee!

Does the fish soar to find the ocean,
The eagle plunge to find the air –
That we ask of the stars in motion
If they have rumour of thee there?

Not where the wheeling systems darken,
And our benumbed conceiving soars! –
The drift of pinions, would we hearken,
Beats at our own clay-shuttered doors.

The angels keep their ancient places; –
Turn but a stone and start a wing!
'Tis ye, 'tis your estrangèd faces,
That miss the many-splendoured thing.

But (when so sad thou canst not sadder)
Cry, – and upon thy so sore loss
Shall shine the traffic of Jacob's ladder
Pitched betwixt Heaven and Charing Cross.

Yea, in the night, my Soul, my daughter,
Cry – clinging Heaven by the hems;
And lo, Christ walking on the water
Not of Gennesareth, but Thames!

FRANCIS THOMPSON

From The Mistress of Vision

Where is the land of Luthany,
Where is the tract of Elenore?
I am bound therefor.

'Pierce thy heart to find the key;
With thee take
Only what none else would keep;
Learn to dream when thou dost wake,
Learn to wake when thou dost sleep.
Learn to water joy with tears,
Learn from fears to vanquish fears;
To hope, for thou dar'st not despair,
Exult, for that thou dar'st not grieve;
Plough thou the rock until it bear;
Know, for thou else couldst not believe;
Lose, that the lost thou may'st receive;
Die, for none other way canst live.
When earth and heaven lay down their veil,
And that apocalypse turns thee pale;
When thy seeing blindeth thee
To what thy fellow-mortals see;
When their sight to thee is sightless;
Their living, death; their light, most lightless;
Search no more –
Pass the gates of Luthany, tread the region Elenore.'

Yet ever and anon a trumpet sounds
From the hid battlements of Eternity;
Those shaken mists a space unsettle, then
Round the half-glimpsèd slowly wash again.
    But not ere him who summoneth
    I first have seen, enwound
With glooming robes purpureal, cypress-crowned;
His name I know, and what his trumpet saith.
Whether man's heart or life it be which yields
    Thee harvest, must Thy harvest-fields
    Be dunged with rotten death?

Now of that long pursuit
    Comes on at hand the bruit;
That Voice is round me like a bursting sea:
    'And is thy earth so marred,
    Shattered in shard on shard?
Lo, all things fly thee, for thou fliest Me!
Strange, piteous, futile thing!
Wherefore should any set thee love apart?
Seeing none but I makes much of naught' (He said),
'And human love needs human meriting:
    How hast thou merited –
Of all man's clotted clay the dingiest clot?
    Alack, thou knowest not
How little worthy of any love thou art!
Whom wilt thou find to love ignoble thee,
    Save Me, save only Me?
All which I took from thee I did but take,
    Not for thy harms,
But just that thou might'st seek it in My arms/
    All which thy child's mistake
Fancies at lost, I have stored for thee at home:
    Rise, clasp My hand, and come!'

Where is the land of Luthany.
And where the region Elenore?
I do faint therefor.

'When to the new eyes of thee
All things by immortal power,
Near or far,
Hiddenly
To each other linkèd are,
That thou canst not stir a flower
Without troubling of a star;
When thy song is shield and mirror
To the fair snake-curlèd Pain,
Where thou dar'st affront her terror
That on her thou may'st attain
Perséan conquest; seek no more,
O seek no more!
Pass the gates of Luthany, tread the region Elenore.'

Risen 'twixt Anteros and Eros,
    Blood and Water, Moon and Sun,
He upbears me, He *Ischyros*,
    I bear Him, the *Athanaton*!'

Where is laid the Lord arisen?
   In the light we walk in gloom;
Though the Sun has burst his prison,
   We know not his biding-room.
Tell us where the Lord sojourneth,
   For we find an empty tomb.
'Whence He sprung, there He returneth,
   Mystic Sun, – the Virgin's Womb.'
     Hidden Sun, His beams so near us,
      Cloud enpillared as He was
     From of old, there He, *Ischyros*,
      Waits our search, *Athanatos*.

'Who will give Him me for brother,
   Counted of my family,
Sucking the sweet breasts of my Mother? –
   I His flesh, and mine is He;
To my Bread myself the bread is,
   And my Wine doth drink me: see.
His left hand beneath my head is,
   His right hand embraceth me!'
     Sweetest Anteros and Eros,'
      Lo, her arms He learns across;
     Dead that we die not, stooped to rear us,
      Thanatos Athanatos.

Who is She, in candid vesture,
   Rushing up from out the brine?
Treading with resilient gesture
   Air, and with that Cup divine?
She in us and we in her are,
   Beating Godward; all that pine,
Lo, a wonder and a terror –
   The Sun hath blushed the Sea to Wine!
     He the Anteros and Eros,
      She the Bride and Spirit; for
     Now the days of promise near us,
      And the Sea shall be no more.

Open wide thy gates, O Virgin.
   That the King may enter thee!
At all gates the clangours gurge in,
   God's paludament lightens, see!
Camp of Angels! Well we even
   Of this thing may doubtful be, –
If thou art assumed to Heaven,
   Or is Heaven assumed to thee!
     Consummatum. Christ the promised,
      Thy maiden realm, is won, O Strong!
     Since to such sweet Kingdom comest,
     Remember me, poor Thief of Song!

Cadent fails the stars along: –
   Mortals, that behold a Woman
     Rising 'twixt the Moon and Sun;
   Who am I the heavens assume? an
   All am I, and I am one.

FRANCIS THOMPSON

Assumpta Maria

'*Mortals, that behold a Woman*
   Rising 'twixt the Moon and Sun;
Who am I the heavens assume? an
   All am I, and I am one.

'Multitudinous ascend I,
   Dreadful as a battle arrayed,
For I bear you whither tend I;
   Ye are I: be undismayed!
I, the Ark that for the graven
   Tables of the law was made;
Man's own heart was one; one, Heaven;
   Both within my womb were laid.
     For there Anteros with Eros,
      Heaven with man, conjoinèd was, –
     Twin-stone of the Law, *Ischyros,*
     Agios Athanatos.

'I, the flesh-girt Paradises
   Gardenered by the Adam new,
Daintied o'er with dear devices
   Which He loveth, for He grew.
I, the boundless strict savannah
   Which God's leaping feet go through;
I. the heaven whence the Manna,
   Weary Israel, slid on you!
     He the Anteros and Eros,
       I the body, He the Cross;
     He upbeareth me, *Ischyros*,
       Agios Athanatos!

'I am Daniel's mystic Mountain,
   Whence the mighty stone was rolled;
I am the four Rivers' Fountain,
   Watering Paradise of old;
Cloud down-raining the Just One am,
   Danae of the Shower of Gold;
I the Hostel of the Sun am;
   He the Lamb, and I the Fold.
     He the Anteros and Eros,
       I the body, He the Cross;
     He is fast to me, *Ischyros*,
       Agios Athanatos!

'I, the presence-hall where Angels
   Do enwheel their placèd King –
Even my thoughts which, without change else,
   Cyclic burn and cyclic sing.
To the hollow of Heaven transplanted,
   I a breathing Eden spring,
Where with venom all outpanted
   Lies the slimed Curse shrivelling.
     For the brazen Serpent clear on
       That old fangèd knowledge shone;
     I to Wisdom rise, *Ischyron*,
       Agion Athanaton!

'Then commanded and spake to me
   He who framed all things that be;
And my Maker entered through me,
   In my tent His rest took He.
Lo! He standeth, Spouse and Brother,
   I to Him, and He to me,
Who upraised me where my mother
   Fell, beneath the apple-tree.'

ELLEN MARY CLERKE

The Building and Pinnacle of the Temple

Not made with hands, its walls began to climb
　　From roots in Life's foundations deeply set,
　　Far down amid primaeval forms, where yet
Creation's Finger seemed to grope in slime.
Yet not in vain passed those first-born of Time,
　　Since each some presage gave of structure met
　　In higher types, lest these the bond forget
That links Earth's latest to the fore-world's prime
　　And living stone on living stone was laid,
　　In scale ascending ever, grade on grade,
To that which in its Maker's eyes seemed good –
　　The Human Form: and in that shrine of thought,
　　By the long travail of the ages wrought,
The Temple of the Incarnation stood.

Through all the ages since the primal ray,
　　Herald of life, first smote the abysmal night
　　Of elemental Chaos, and the might
Of the Creative Spark informed the clay,
From worm to brute, from brute to man – its way
　　The Shaping Thought took upward, flight on flight,
　　By stages which Earth's loftiest unite
Unto her least, made kin to such as they.
　　As living link, or prophecy, or type
　　Of purpose for fulfilment yet unripe,
Each has its niche in the supreme design;
　　Converging to one Pinnacle, whereat
　　Sole stands Creation's Masterpiece – and that
Which was through her – the Human made Divine.

ROBERT BRIDGES

From The Testament of Beauty

　　Beneath the spaceless dome of the soul's firmament
he liveth in the glow of a celestial fire,
fed by whose timeless beams our small obedient sun
is as a cast-off satellite, that borroweth
from the great Mover of all; and in the light of light

man's little works, strewn on the sands of time, sparkle
like cut jewels in the beautitude of God's countenance.
   But heav'nward tho' the chariot be already mounted,
'tis Faith alone can keep the charioteer in heart –

. . .

   This is the supreme ecstasy of the mountaineer,
to whom the morn is bright, when with his goal in sight,
some icepeak high i' the heav'ns, he is soul-bounden for it,
prospecting the uncertain clue of his perilous step
to scale precipices where no foot clomb afore,
for good or ill success to his last limit of strength;
his joy in the doing and his life in his hand
he glorieth in the fortunes of his venturous day;
'mid the high mountain silences, where Poesy
lieth in dream and *the secret strength of things
that governs thought* inhabiteth, where man wandereth
into God's presence.

ROBERT BRIDGES

From A Hymn of Nature

I

Power eternal, power unknown, uncreate:
   Force of force, fate of fate
   Beauty and light are thy seeing,
   Wisdom and right thy decreeing,
   Life of life is thy being.
In the smile of thine infinite starry gleam,
   Without beginning or end,
   Measure or number,
   Beyond time and space,
   Without foe or friend,
In the void of thy formless embrace,
   All things pass as a dream
   Of thine unbroken slumber.

ROBERT BRIDGES

Awake, My Heart, to Be Loved

Awake, my heart, to be loved, awake, awake!
The darkness silvers away, the morn doth break,
It leaps in the sky: unrisen lustres slake
The o'ertaken moon. Awake, O heart, awake!

She too that loveth awaketh and hopes for thee;
Her eyes already have sped the shades that flee,
Already they watch the path thy feet shall take:
Awake, O heart, to be loved, awake, awake!

And if thou tarry from her, – if this could be, –
She cometh herself, O heart, to be loved, to thee;
For thee would unashamèd herself forsake:
Awake to be loved, my heart, awake, awake!

Awake, the land is scattered with light, and see,
Uncanopied sleep is flying from field and tree:
And blossoming boughs of April in laughter shake;
Awake, O heart, to be loved, awake, awake!

Lo, all things wake and tarry and look for thee:
She looketh and saith, 'O sun, now bring him to me.
Come more adored, O adored, for his coming's sake,
And awake my heart to be loved: awake, awake!'

ROBERT BRIDGES

Sonnets from The Growth of Love

VIII

For beauty being the best of all we know
Sums up the unsearchable and secret aims
Of nature, and on joys whose earthly names
Were never told can form and sense bestow:

And man hath sped his instinct to outgo
The step of science; and against her shames
Imagination stakes out heavenly claims,
Building a tower above the head of woe.

Nor is there fairer work for beauty found
Than that she win in nature her release
From all the woes that in the world abound:
Nay, with his sorrow may his love increase,
If from man's greater need beauty redound,
And claim his tears for homage of his peace.

XXXV

All earthly beauty hath one cause and proof,
To lead the pilgrim soul to beauty above:
Yet lieth the greater bliss so far aloof,
That few there be are wean'd from earthly love.
　　Joy's ladder it is, reaching from home to home,
The best of all the work that all was good;
Whereof 'twas writ the angels aye upclomb,
Down sped, and at the top the Lord God stood.

But I my time abuse, my eyes by day
Center'd on thee, by night my heart on fire –
Letting my number'd moments run away –
Nor e'en 'twixt night and day to heaven aspire:
　　So true it is that what the eye seeth not
But slow is loved, and loved is soon forgot.

RAMAKRISHNA (*trans* S Nikhilananda)

Hymns of Ramakrishna

1

Dive deep, O mind, dive deep in the Ocean of God's Beauty;
If you descend to the uttermost depths,
There you will find the gem of Love.

Go seek, O mind, go seek Vrindāvan in your heart.
Where with His loving devotees
Sri Krishna sports eternally,

Light up, O mind, light up true wisdom's shining lamp,
And let it burn with steady flame
Unceasingly within your heart.

Who is it that steers your boat across the solid earth?
It is your guru, says Kubir;
Meditate on his holy feet.

2

Dwell, O mind, within yourself:
Enter no other's home.
If you but seek there, you will find
All you are searching for.

God, the true Philosopher's Stone,
Who answers every prayer.
Lies hidden deep within your heart,
The richest gem of all.

How many pearls and precious stones
Are scattered all about
The outer court that lies before
The chamber of your heart!

3

High in the heaven of the Mother's feet, my mind was soaring like
    a kite,
When came a blast of sin's rough wind that drove it swiftly toward
    the earth.
Māyā disturbed its even flight by bearing down upon one side,
And I could make it rise no more.
Entangled in the twisting string of love for children and for wife,
Alas! my kite was rent in twain.

It lost its crest of wisdom soon and downward plunged as I let it go;
How could it hope to fly again, when all its top was torn away?
Though fastened with devotion's cord, it came to grief in playing here;
Its six opponents worsted it.
Now Nareschandra rues this game of smiles and tears, and thinks
    it better
Never to have played at all.

4

The black bee of my mind is drawn in sheer delight
To the blue lotus flower of Mother Śyāmā's feet
The blue flower of the feet of Kāli, Śiva's Consort;
Tasteless, to the bee, are the blossoms of desire.
My Mother's feet are black, and black, too, is the bee;
Black is made one with black! This much of the mystery
My mortal eyes behold, then hastily retreat.
But Kamalākānta's hopes are answered in the end;
He swims in the Sea of Bliss, unmoved by joy or pain.

O Mother, what a machine is this that Thou hast made!
What pranks Thou playest with this toy
Three and a half cubits high!
Hiding Thyself within, Thou holdest the guiding string;
But the machine, not knowing it,
Still believes it moves by itself.
Whoever finds the Mother remains a machine no more;

5

Thou art my All in All, O Lord! – the Life of my life, the Essence
    of essence;
In the three worlds I have none else but Thee to call my own.
Thou art my peace, my joy, my hope; Thou my support, my wealth,
    my glory;
Thou my wisdom and my strength.

Thou art my home, my place of rest; my dearest friend, my next of kin;
My present and my future, Thou; my heaven and my salvation.
Thou art my scriptures, my commandments; Thou art my ever
    gracious Guru;
Thou the Spring of my boundless bliss.

Thou art the Way, and Thou the Goal; Thou the Adorable One,
    O Lord!
Thou art the Mother tender-hearted; Thou the chastising Father;
Thou the Creator and Protector; Thou the Helmsman who dost steer
My craft across the sea of life.

6

Dance, my heart; O dance to-day with joy!
The hymn of Love filleth the days and the nights with music, and the
    world hearkeneth to the melody.

Mad with joy, Life and Death dance to the rhythm of this music.
The hills and the sea and the earth dance:
The world of man danceth in laughter and tears.

Why put on the robe of the monk, and live aloof from the world in
    lonely pride?

Beyond my heart danceth in the delight of a hundred arts, and the
    Creator is well-pleased.

7

Hallowed be Brahman, the Absolute, the Infinite, the Fathomless!
Higher than the highest, deeper than the deepest depths!
Thou art the Light of Truth, The Fount of Love, the Home of Bliss!
This universe with all its manifold and blessed modes
Is but the enchanting poem of Thine inexhaustible thought;
Its beauty overflows on every side.

O Thou Poet, great and primal, in the rhythm of Thy thought
The sun and moon arise and move toward their setting;
The stars, shining like bits of gems, are the fair characters
In which Thy song is written across the blue expanse of sky;

8

When such delusion veils the world, through Mahāmāyā's spell,
That Brahmā is bereft of sense,
And Vishnu loses consciousness,
What hope is left for men?

The narrow channel first is made, and there the trap is set;
But open though the passage lies,
The fish, once safely through the gate,
Do not come out again.

The silk-worm patiently prepares its closely spun cocoon;
Yet even though a way leads forth,
Encased within its own cocoon,
The worm remains to die.

9

Proclaim the glory of God's name as long as life remains in you;
The dazzling splendour of His radiance floods the universe!
Like nectar streams His boundless love, filling the hearts of men
    with joy:
The very thought of His compassion sends a thrill through every limb!
How can one fittingly describe Him? Through His abounding grace
The bitter sorrows of this life are all forgotten instantly.

On every side – on land below, in sky above, beneath the seas:
In every region of this earth – men seek Him tirelessly,
And as they seek Him, ever ask: Where is His limit, where His end?
True Wisdom's Dwelling-place is He, the Elixir of Eternal Life,
The Sleepless, Ever-wakeful Eye, the Pure and Stainless One:
The vision of His face removes all trace of sorrow from our hearts.

10

Sing, O bird that nestles deep within my heart!
Sing, O bird that sits on the Kalpa-Tree of Brahman!
Sing God's everlasting praise.
Taste, O bird, of the four fruits of the Kalpa-Tree,
Dharma, artha, kāma, moksha.
Sing, O bird, 'He alone is the Comfort of my soul!'
Sing, O bird, 'He alone is my life's enduring Joy!'
O thou wondrous bird of my life,
Sing aloud in my heart! Unceasingly sing, O bird!
Sing for evermore, even as the thirsty chātak
Sings for the raindrop from the cloud.

RĀMA TIRTHA (*trans* A J Alston)

From Poems of Rāma Tirtha

13

I salute you, O my soul.
You are ever Existence, Consciousness and Bliss,
Why undergo delusion, fear and grief?
If no one has come to a house,
How can anyone leave it?
If no one has gone to sleep,
How can anyone awake?
If you have never been born
How can you die?
Give up all error and grief.
You are neither body, mind nor senses.
Wealth, profit and loss cannot affect you
Leave worry and fear behind.
Wake up, my darling,
And enter your eternal happy home.
Rise up like the sun and depart,
Leave all care behind.
Rāma (God) is ever with you.
Laugh, play, why do you grieve?
Stand firm on the high peak of Bliss,
Fill every breath with SO HAM.

31

He who is drunk with the eternal
Does not require wine.
Those who have offered their hearts in sacrifice
Do not seek the odour of roast meat.
Why do You hide Your face,
What is my fault?
We sit together all the time,
So why this veil?
Let Your face emerge,
That I may see what the veil conceals.

32

Those who have not drunk the wine of love
Would gain little if they drank ambrosia
And became immortal.
Those who have not dipped their heads
Beneath the waters of devotion
May live on from age to age,
But it will avail nothing.
You may be famous, learned, eloquent, charitable,
But unless you tread the path of love,
All is vain.
If you preach virtues you do not practise,
If you go on pilgrimage to Mecca
With infidelity in your heart,
All is vain.
You read the Gulistān and the Būstān,
But you did not understand Sa'dī's meaning.
If you knew by heart
All the classics ever written, it would not help.
Unless you have drunk to intoxication
Of the cup of love,
Even to hear the music of the spheres
Would amount to little.
Unless you are drowned in the waters of love,
Bathing in the Ganges, the Jumna and Godāvarī
Will not help.
You may spend the whole day at prayer,
But if there is no love for the Lord
Your purposes will not be realized,
Your tears will be of no avail.

33

If there is love,
If should be love of God.
Lovers of anything else are pitiable.
If you wasted the whole day in dissipation,
At least remember God at night,
Before you pass into sleep.
Whatever seeds you have sown for this world,
You have greedily reaped the harvest.
Now it is time you sowed some seeds
For the life to come.
You were happy to sleep here
On the bed of restlessness.

62

Do you see me? Who am I?
I am the dawning of the Light of God.
I am love, lover and beloved,
Shining everywhere: I alone exist.
As Adam, I am the object
Of the worship of the angels,
The place of manifestation of God.
My position is absence of all position.
I have hidden myself in the veil
To enjoy the spectacle.
Ana'l Haqq is my home,
I am the brilliance in the sun
Of the light of spiritual illumination.
Tell me, brother, whom should I seek?
Whom could I find?
Hidden in the recesses of my own Self,
I alone exist.

VIVEKANANDA

The Living God

He who is in you and outside you,
Who works through all hands,
Who walks on all feet,
Whose body are all ye,
Him worship, and break all other idols!

He who is at once the high and low,
The sinner and the saint,
Both God and worm,
Him worship – visible, knowable, real, omnipresent,
Break all other idols!

In whom is neither past life
Nor future birth nor death,
In whom we always have been
And always shall be one,
Him worship. Break all other idols!

Ye fools! who neglect the living God,
And His infinite reflections with which the world is full.
While ye run after imaginary shadows,
That lead alone to fights and quarrels,
Him worship, the only visible!
Break all other idols!

VIVEKANANDA

Requiescat in Pace

Speed forth, O Soul! upon thy star-strewn path;
Speed, blissful one! where thought is ever free,
Where time and space no longer mist the view,
Eternal peace and blessings be with thee!

Thy service true complete thy sacrifice,
Thy home the heart of love transcendent find;
Remembrance sweet, that kills all space and time.
Like altar roses fill thy place behind!

Thy bonds are broke, thy quest in bliss is found,
And one with That which comes as Death and Life;
Thou helpful one! unselfish e'er on earth,
Ahead! still help with love this world of strife!

VIVEKANANDA

From A Song I Sing to Thee

When all the many movements of the mind
Are, by Thy grace, made one, and unified,
The light of that unfoldment is so great
That, in its splendour, it surpasses far
The brilliance of ten thousand rising suns.
Then, sooth, the sun of Chit reveals itself.
And melt away the sun and moon and stars,
High heaven above, the nether worlds, and all!
This universe seems but a tiny pool
Held in a hollow caused by some cow's hoof.

– This is the reaching of the region which
Beyond the plane of the External lies.

Calmed are the clamours of the urgent flesh,
The tumult of the boastful mind is hushed,
Cords of the heart are loosened and set free,
Unfastened are the bondages that bind,
Attachment and delusion are no more!
   Aye! There sounds sonorous the Sound
Void of vibration. Verily! Thy Voice!
   Hearing that Voice, Thy servant, reverently,
Stands ever ready to fulfil Thy work.

   'I exist.
      When, at Pralaya time
This wondrous universe is swallowed up;
Knowledge, the knower and the known, dissolved;
The world no more distinguishable, now,
No more conceivable; when sun and moon
And all the outspent stars, remain no more –
Then is the state of Maha-Nirvâna
When action, act, and actor, are no more,
When instrumentality is no more;
Great darkness veils the bosom of the dark –
      There I am present.

'I am present!
    At Pralaya time,
When this vast universe is swallowed up,
Knowledge, and knower, and the known
Merged into one. The universe no more
Can be distinguished or can be conceived
By intellect. The sun and moon and stars are not.
Over the bosom of the darkness, darkness moves
Intense. Devoid of all the threefold bonds,
Remains the universe, Gunas are calmed
Of all distinctions. Everything deluged
In one homogeneous mass, subtle,
Pure, of atom-form, indivisible –
   There I am present.

'Once again,
    I unfold Myself – that "I";
Of my "Shakti" the first great change is Om;
The Primal Voice rings through the void;
Infinite Space hears that great vibrant sound.
The group of Primal Causes shakes off sleep,
New life revives atoms interminable;
Cosmis existence heaves and whirls and sways,
Dances and gyrates, moves towards the core,
From distances immeasurably far.

The animate Wind arouses rings of Waves
Over the Ocean of great Elements;
Stirring, falling, surging, that vast range of Waves
Rushes with lightning fury. Fragments thrown
By force of royal resistance, through the path
Of space, rush, endless, in the form of spheres
Celestial, numberless, Planets and stars
Speed swift; the mans' abode, the earth revolves.

'At the Beginning,
    I, The Omniscient One,
I am! The moving and the un-moving,
All this Creation comes into being
By the unfoldment of My power supreme.
I play with My own Maya, My Power Divine.
The One, I become the many, to behold
My own Form.

'At the Beginning,
   I, the Omniscient One,
I am! The moving and the un-moving,
All this Creation comes into being
By the unfoldment of My power supreme.
Perforce of My command, the wild storm blows
On the face of the earth; clouds clash and roar;
The flash of lightning startles and rebounds;
   Softly and gently the Malaya breeze
Flows in and out like calm, unruffled breath;
The moon's rays pour their cooling current forth;
The earth's bare body in fair garb is clothed,
Of trees and creepers multitudinous;
And the flower a-bloom lifts her happy face,
Washed with drops of dew, toward the sun.'

RABINDRANATH TAGORE

From Gitanjali

11

Leave this chanting and singing and
telling of beads! Whom dost thou
worship in this lonely dark corner of a
temple with doors all shut? Open
thine eyes and see thy God is not before thee!

He is there where the tiller is tilling
the hard ground and where the path-
maker is breaking stones. He is with
them in sun and in shower, and his
garment is covered with dust. Put off
thy holy mantle and even like him come
down on the dusty soil!

Deliverance? Where is this deliverance
to be found? Our master himself has
joyfully taken upon him the bonds of
creation; he is bound with us all for ever.

Come out of thy meditations and
leave aside thy flowers and incense!
What harm is there if thy clothes
become tattered and stained? Meet
him and stand by him in toil and in
sweat of thy brow.

49

You came down from your throne and stood at my cottage door.

I was singing all alone in a corner, and the melody caught your ear. You came down and stood at my cottage door.

Masters are many in your hall, and songs are sung there at all hours. But the simple carol of this novice struck at your love. One plaintive little strain mingled with the great music of the world, and with a flower for a prize you came down and stopped at my cottage door.

73

Deliverance is not for me in renunciation. I feel the embrace of freedom in a thousand bonds of delight.

Thou ever pourest for me the fresh draught of thy wine of various colours and fragrance, filling this earthen vessel to the brim.

My world will light its hundred different lamps with thy flame and place them before the altar of thy temple.

No, I will never shut the doors of my senses. The delights of sight and hearing and touch will bear thy delight.

Yes, all my illusions will burn into illumination of joy and all my desires ripen into fruits of love.

74

The day is no more, the shadow is upon the earth. It is time that I go to the stream to fill my pitcher.

The evening air is eager with the sad music of the water. Ah, it calls me out into the dusk. In the lonely lane there is no passer by, the wind is up, the ripples are rampant in the river.

I know not if I shall come back
home. I know not whom I shall
chance to meet. There at the fording
in the little boat the unknown man
plays upon his lute.

Rabindranath Tagore

From On the Sick-Bed

At noon – half awake, half asleep –
I saw as in a dream
The outer shell of my being drop off.
In the stream of the Unknown
Floated away all the gatherings of the miser –
His name, his deeds, his honour, his dishonour,
Remembrances of shame
That bore the seal of passing sweetness!
All these I cannot call back.
The Self that is beyond self, asks:
For what do I sigh most?
It is not for the past spent in joy and suffering,
But for the future, ever unattainable –
In whose heart, Hope
Like the seed in the womb of earth
Dreams through the night
For the light that is not yet come.

25 November 1940

On the way to recovery,
As I received the call of gracious life,
She gave me anew fresh vision
With which to see the world.
This blue expanse bathed in morning light –
The seat of meditation of the *Tapaswi*
Revealed to me the timeless first moment
At the beginning of Creation.
I realized that this birth is strung together
With ever new births –
Like the seven-coloured rays of the sun,
One prospect bears within itself,
Unseen, streams of many creations.

. . .

In the pure light of early dawn
I saw the Universe consecrated with the crown of Peace.
With bowed heads the trees uttered their benediction.
The Peace that is firmly established at the heart of the Universe,
Preserves herself through all the strife and pain of the Ages.
In this distracted world that Peace manifests herself
At the beginning and at the end of the day.
O Poet, the herald of the Good,
You surely have received her invitation.
If ignoring that call,
You become the mouthpiece of despair,
The emissary of the deformed,
And on the broken harp, playing a false tune,
Distort the eternal Truth of the Universe –
Then what purpose was there in your being born?

. . .

Through all the sorrows and sufferings of life,
This message of the sages glows bright
In my heart:
'The Immortal Being manifests himself in Joy.'
To prove the contrary is nothing but empty cleverness,
Trying to belittle the Great.
He who sees Supreme Truth
Beyond Time and Space, in its entirety –
For him alone has life a meaning.

28 November 1940

I have never put trust in my deeds
But only in my self –
For I know the relentless waves of eternal Time
Will wash those deeds away.
Morning and night,
Filling my soul's chalice with divine nectar,
I have drunk it.
The love I have cherished every moment
Has been garnered in that cup –
The burden of sorrow has not cracked it,
Nor the dust blackened its handicraft.
When I leave the stage of life,
I know that season after season
The flowers shall bear witness
How I have loved this world.

This love, this gift of life
Alone is true;
When I depart,
This undying truth shall confute death.

Open the door –
Let the blue sky pour in unhindered,
And the scent of the flowers enter my room.
Let the first rays of the sun
Go up to it and you will not see its head;
Follow behind it and you will not see its rear.
Hold fast to the way of antiquity
In order to keep in control the realm of today.
The ability to know the beginning of antiquity
Is called the thread running through the way.

When carrying on your head your perplexed bodily
    soul can you embrace in your arms the One
And not let go?
In concentrating your breath can you become as
    supple
As a babe?
Can you polish your mysterious mirror
And leave no blemish?
Can you love the people and govern the state
Without resorting to action?
When the gates of heaven open and shut
Are you capable of keeping to the role of the female?
When your discernment penetrates the four quarters
Are you capable of not knowing anything?
It gives them life and rears them.
It gives them life yet claims no possession;
It benefits them yet exacts no gratitude;
It is the steward yet exercises no authority.
Such is called the mysterious virtue.

Heaven and earth are enduring. The reason why
heaven and earth can be enduring is that they do not
give themselves life. Hence they are able to be long-
lived.
    Therefore the sage puts his person last and it comes
        first,
    Treats it as extraneous to himself and it is preserved.
Is it not because he is without thought of self that he
is able to accomplish his private ends?

Bathe my whole being
And lave my nerves.
'I am alive' – this message of welcome
Rustles in the forest leaves –
Let me hear it.
Let the morning wrap me in her veil,
As she wraps the green earth decked in tender grass.
The love that I received in my life –
Her silent voice I hear in the sky,
In the wind.
In her pure waters I take my ablution
And see life's Truth sparkling like a gem
In the heart of the blue.

The flame of consciousness
That burns bright in my heart
Is not a fortuitous prisoner
Within the narrow confines of life.
That flame, which at the beginning
Rises from the Void,
And at the end
Encounters meaningless death.
Illumines the interval
And gives it significance.
This consciousness throbs through the skies
As Supreme Joy –
Its message echoes in my heart
And holds together sun and stars
In constant rhythm
Through the endless festival of Creation!

When I see Man
Helpless within the walls
Of his unbearable suffering,
I do not know
Where he will find consolation.
I know the root of this suffering
Is his riotous living,
Is in his folly.
But this knowledge brings no comfort.
When I know
The Truth that is hidden
In Man's spiritual striving
Is beyond pleasure and pain –
Then do I realize
That those Seekers who make fruitful
This truth in their lives,
Are the ultimate goal of Man's destiny.

RABINDRANATH TAGORE

From Recovery

14 February 1941

'Sweet is the world, sweet the dust of it,'
This great hymn I chant in my heart.
It makes my life significant.
Day after day the gems of truth come to me
As a gift – their loveliness dims not.
Therefore at the border of death, this great hymn –
'Sweet is the world, sweet the dust of it' –
Echoes in the heart of Joy.
When I take with me the last touch of earth,
I shall proclaim:
'The mark of Victory, written in dust, is on my
    brow.'
Behind the *Māyā* of evil
I have seen the light of the eternal.
Truth's loveliness has taken form in earth's dust –
Knowing this, I salute the dust.

Bathed in morning light
All things are made holy and beautiful.
The formless One, the limitless,
With its touchstone creates forms of Joy.
Under the altar of the ever-old
Is consecrated the ever-new.

In sunshine and shadow,
Is woven the cloth of earth
With threads of green and blue.
The leaves dance in rhythm
With the heart-beat of the sky.
From forest to forest,
On the neck of morning
Sparkles the necklace of diamond.
The random songs of birds
Chant their praises to the goddess of life.
The love in the heart of man,
Joined to all these,
Gives them the touch of immortality –
It makes sweet the dust of earth
And spreads over it
The throne of Eternal Man.

. . .

'Begetter of this earth!
In whose glorious light
Man first beheld the veritable form of God –
If full-throated I could chant the Vedic hymns,
Then my praise
Would have mingled with all this light.'
But words fail;
I only gaze at the Far Beyond,
And spread my silence over the pale midday sky.

In this deserted room,
On this silent morn,
I sit before my window.
One hears the song of the green
Pouring out in rhythm.
Under the light of the blue sky
The mind floats on the stream
That flows from the fount of immortality.
To whom shall I send my hymn of praise –
This yearning of my heart?
It seeks voice to give value
To that which is beyond all value –
But it remains silent.
It only says: 'I am happy.'
The rhythm comes to a stop,
But its cadence says: 'I am blest.'

RABINDRANATH TAGORE

From Last Poems

Now has come Man Supreme
Man after God's own heart!
The world is a-tremble with wonder
And the grass quivers.
In heaven resounds the conch,
On earth plays the drum of Victory –
The sacred moment has come
That brings the Great Birth!
The gates guarding the moonless night have fallen,
The hill of sunrise rings with the call 'Fear not'
And ushers in the dawn of a new life!
The heavens thunder the song of Victory:
'Man has come!'

CLIFFORD BAX

Turn Back, O Man

Turn back, O man, forswear thy foolish ways;
Old now is earth, and none may count her days,
Yet thou, her child, whose head is crowned with flame,
Still wilt not hear thine inner God proclaim:
Turn back, O man, forswear thy foolish ways.

Earth might be fair and all men glad and wise.
Age after age their tragic empires rise,
Built while they dream, and in that dreaming weep;
Would man but wake from out his haunted sleep,
Earth might be fair and all men glad and wise.

Earth shall be fair, and all her people one:
Not till that hour shall God's whole will be done;
Now, even now, once more from earth to sky
Peals forth in joy man's old undaunted cry;
Earth shall be fair, and all her folk be one.

CLIFFORD BAX

The Meaning of Man

Take courage; for the race of man is divine.
The Golden Verses

Dear and fair as Earth may be
Not from out her womb are we, –
Like an elder sister only, like a foster-mother, she,
For we come of heavenly lineage, of a pure undying race,
We who took the poppied potion of our life, and quaffing deep
Move enchanted now forever in the shadow world of sleep,
In the vast and lovely vision that is wrought of time and space.

Overhead the sun and moon
Shining as the gates of birth
Give to each a common boon, –
All the joy of earth;
Mountains lit with moving light,
Forest, cavern, cloud and river,
Ebb and flow of day and night
Around the world forever.

These and all the works of man may he who will behold,
Mighty shapes of bygone beauty, songs of beaten gold,
Starlike thoughts that once, in ages gone, were found by seer-sages,
All the throng'd and murmuring Past, the life men loved of old.
Yet sometimes at the birth of night when hours of heat and splendour
Melt away in darkness, and the flaming sun has set
Across the brooding soul will sweep, like music sad and tender,
Sudden waves of almost passionate regret,
For then the hills and meadowlands, the trees and flowerful grasses,
All the world of wonder that our eyes have gazed upon,
Seems remote and mournful, as a rainbow when it passes
Leaves the heart lamenting for the beauty come and gone,
And in the deep that is the soul there surges up a cry
'Whence are all the starry legions traversing the sky?
Whence the olden planets and the sun and moon and earth?
Out of what came all of these and out of what came I?'
And far away within the same unfathomable deep
Comes an answer rolling 'Earth and moon and sun,
All that is, that has been, or that ever time shall reap,
   Is but moving home again, with mighty labours done,
   The Many to the Everlasting One.'

    And this is the meaning of man,
       The task of the soul,
    The labour of worlds, and the plan
       That is set for the whole,
    For the spark of the spirit imprisoned within it,
       In all things one and the same,
    Aeon by aeon and minute by minute,
       Is longing to leap into flame,
To shatter the limits of life and be lost in a glory intense
    and profound
As the soul with a cry goes out into music and seeks to be
    one with the sound.

    For as those that are sunken deep
    In the green dim ocean of sleep,
In a thousand shapes for a thousand ages the one great
   Spirit is bound.
    The air we inhale and the sea,
      The warm brown earth and the sun,
      Came forth at the Word of the One
From the same First Mother as we,
And now, as of old when the world began
The stars of the night are the kindred of man,
For all things move to a single goal,

The giant sun or the thinking soul.
Ah what though the Tree whose rise and fall
Of sap is fed from the Spirit of All,
With suns for blossoms and planets for leaves,
Be vaster yet than the mind conceives?
Earth is a leaf on the boundless Tree,
And the unborn soul of the earth are we.

O man is a hungering exiled people, a host in an unknown land,
A wandering mass in the vast with only a black horizon to face,
Yet still, though we toil for a time in the heat over measureless deserts
    of sand
The longing for beauty that shines in the soul is the guiding-star of
    the race.
    It is this that alone may redeem
    A world ignoble with strife,
    This only brings all that we dream
    From the shattered chaos of life.
And this that forever shall spur us and lead us from peak unto peak on
    the way
Till body and spirit be welded in one and the long Night fall on the Day,
And all the sonorous music of time, the hills and the woods and the
    wind and the sea,
The one great song of the whole creation, of all that is and that yet
    shall be,
Chanted aloud as a paean of joy by the Being whose home is the vast
Shall tremble away in silence, and all be gone at the last,
Save only afar in the Heart of the Singer of whom it was chanted
    and heard
Remembrance left of the music as a sunset-fire in the west,
Remembrance left of the mighty Enchanted Palace that rose at
    His Word,
This, and a joy everlasting, an immense inviolate rest.

MICHAEL FIELD

Renewal

As the young phoenix, duteous to his sire,
    Lifts in his beak the creature he has been,
    And, lifting o'er the corse broad vans for screen,
Bears it to solitudes, erects a pyre,

And, soon as it is wasted by the fire,
   Grids with disdainful claw the ashes clean;
   Then spreading unencumber'd wings serene
Mounts to the aether with renew'd desire:

So joyously I lift myself above
   The life I buried in hot flames to-day.
      The flames themselves are dead: and I can range
Alone through the untarnish'd sky I love,
   And I trust myself, as from the grave I may,
      To the enchanting miracles of change.

MUHAMMAD IQBAL

Make Self Strong, and Thou Wilt Endure

Thou hast being, and art thou afraid of not-being?
O foolish one, thy understanding is at fault.
Since I am acquainted with the harmony of Life,
I will tell thee what is the secret of Life –
To sink into thyself like the pearl,
Then to emerge from thine inward solitude;
To collect sparks beneath the ashes,
And become a flame and dazzle men's eyes.

Move round thyself! Be a circling flame!
What is life but to be freed from moving round others
And to regard thyself as the Holy Temple?
Beat thy wings and escape from the attractions of Earth;
Like birds, be safe from falling.

EVA GORE-BOOTH

Harvest

Though the long seasons seem to separate
Sower and reaper or deeds dreamed and done,
Yet when a man reaches the Ivory Gate
Labour and life and seed and corn are one.

Because thou art the doer and the deed,
Because thou art the thinker and the thought,
Because thou art the helper and the need,
And the cold doubt that brings all things to nought.

Therefore in every gracious form and shape
The world's dear open secret shalt thou find,
From the One Beauty there is no escape
Nor from the sunshine of the Eternal mind.

The patient labourer, with guesses dim,
Follows this wisdom to its secret goal.
He knows all deeds and dreams exist in him,
And all men's God in every human soul.

EVA GORE-BOOTH

The Quest

For years I sought the many in the One,
I thought to find lost waves and broken rays,
The rainbow's faded colours in the sun –
The dawns and twilights of forgotten days.

But now I seek the One in every form,
Scorning no vision that a dewdrop holds,
The gentle Light that shines behind the storm,
The Dream that many a twilight hour enfolds.

PAUL HOOKHAM

A Meditation

'The Self is Peace; that Self am I.
The Self is Strength; that Self am I.'
      What needs this trembling strife
With phantom threats of Form and Time and Space?
      Could once my Life
Be shorn of their illusion, and efface
From its clear heaven that stormful imagery,
      My Self were seen
An Essence free, unchanging, strong, serene.

The Self is Peace. How placid dawns
    The Summer's parent hour
Over the dewy maze that drapes the fields,
    Each drooped wild flower,
Or where the lordship of the garden shields
Select Court beauties and exclusive lawns!
    'Tis but the show
And fitful dream of Peace the Self can know.

The Self is Strength. Let Nature rave,
    And tear her maddened breast,
Now doom the drifting ship, with blackest frown,
    Or now, possessed
With rarer frenzy, wreck the quaking town,
And bury quick beneath her earthy wave –
    She cannot break
One fibre of that Strength, one atom shake,

The Self is one with the Supreme
    Father in fashioning,
Though clothed in perishable weeds that feel
    Pain's mortal sting,
The unlifting care, the wound that will not heal;
Yet these are not the Self – they only seem.
    From faintest jar
Of whirring worlds the true Self broods afar.

Afar he whispers to the mind
    To rest on the Good Law,
To know that naught can fall without its range,
    Nor any flaw
Of Chance disturb its reign, or shadow of Change;
That what can bind the life the Law must bind –
    Whatever hand
Dispose the lot, it is by that Command;

To know no suffering can beset
    Our lives, that is not due,
That is not forged by our own act and will;
    Calmly to view
Whate'er betide of seeming good or ill.
The worst we can conceive but pays some debt
    Or breaks some seal,
To free us from the bondage of the Wheel.

EDWARD WILLIAM THOMSON

From Aspiration

My friend conceived the soul hereafter dwells
In any heaven the inmost heart desires,
The heart, which craves delight, at pain rebels,
And balks, or obeys the soul till life expires.

He deem'd that all the eternal Force contrives
Is wrought to revigorate its own control,
And that its alchemy some strength derives
From every tested and unflagging soul.

He deem'd a spirit which avails to guide
A human heart, gives proof of energy
To be received in That which never bides,
But ever toils for what can never be –

A perfect All – toward which the Eternal strives
To urge for ever every atom's range,
The Ideal, which never unto Form arrives,
Because new concept emanates from change.

He deem'd the inmost heart is what aligns
Man's aspiration, noble or impure,
And that immortal Tolerance assigns
Each soul what Aspiration would secure.

And if it choose what highest souls would rue –
Some endless round of mortal joys inane –
Such fate befits what souls could not subdue
The heart's poor shrinking from the chrism of pain.

. . .

My friend review'd, nigh death, how staunch the soul
Had waged in him a conflict, never done,
To rule the dual self that fought control,
Spirit and flesh inextricably one.

His passionless judgement ponder'd well the past,
Patient, relentless, ere he spoke sincere, –
'Through all the strife my soul prevail'd at last,
It rules my inmost heart's desire here;

'My Will craves not some paradise of zest
Where mortal joys eternally renew,
Nor blank nirvana, nor elysian rest,
Nor palaced pomp to bombast fancy true;

'It yearns no whit to swell some choiring strain
In endless amplitudes of useless praise;
It dares to aspire to share the immortal pain
Of toil in moulding Form from phase to phase.

'To me, of old, such fate some terror bore,
But now great gladness in my spirit glows,
While death clings round me friendlier than before,
To loose the soul that mounts beyond repose.'

. . .

Yet, at the end, from seeming death he stirr'd
As one whose sleep is broke by sudden shine,
And whisper'd *Christ*, as if the soul had heard
Tidings of some exceeding sweet design.

THE HON MAURICE BARING

The Heart of the Lily

She listened to the music of the spheres;
  We thought she did not hear our happy strings;
  Stars diadem'd her hair in misty rings,
And all too late we knew those stars were tears.
Without she was a temple of pure snow,
  Within were piteous flames of sacrifice;
  And underneath the dazzling mask of ice
A heart of swiftest fire was dying slow.

She in herself, as lonely lilies fold
Stiff silver petals over secret gold,
  Shielded her passion and remained afar
From pity. Cast red roses on the pyre!
She that was snow shall rise to Heaven as fire
  In the still glory of the morning star.

LASCELLES ABERCROMBIE

He

                              Yea, here the end
Of love's astonishment! Now know we Spirit,
And Who, for ease of joy, contriveth Spirit.
Now all life's loveliness and power we have
Dissolved in this one moment, and our burning
Carries all shining upward, till in us
Life is not life, but the desire of God,
Himself desiring and himself accepting.
Now what was prophecy in us is made
Fulfilment: we are the hour and we are the joy,
We in our marvellousness of single knowledge,
Of Spirit breaking down the room of fate
And drawing into his light the greeting fire
Of God, – God known in ecstasy of love
Wedding himself to utterance of himself.

FRANK KENDON

The Flower

All's in this flower . . .
Times, seasons, losses, all the fruits of woe,
Beauty's fragility, and death's bare gain,
Pluck'd in passing by, five minutes ago.

All's in this flower, the war of life and death,
God's character and purpose written down,
The force of love, the proof and power of faith –
All's here, and all unknown.

ANDREW LANG

From Song by the Subconscious Self

I know not what my secret is,
    I know but it is mine,
I know to dwell with it were bliss,
    To die for it divine.
I cannot yield it in a kiss,
    Nor breathe it in a sigh;
Enough that I have lived for this,
    For this, my love, I die.

JAMES H COUSINS

The Quest

They said: 'She dwelleth in some place apart,
    Immortal Truth, within whose eyes
    Who looks may find the secret of the skies
And healing for life's smart!'

I sought Her in loud caverns underground, –
    On heights where lightnings flashed and fell;
    I scaled high Heaven; I stormed the gates of Hell,
But Her I never found.

Till thro' the tumults of my Quest I caught
    A whisper: 'Here, within thy heart,
    I dwell; for I am thou: behold, thou art
The Seeker – and the Sought.'

JAMES H COUSINS

Vision

When I from life's unrest had earned the grace
Of utter ease beside a quiet stream;
When all that was had mingled in a dream
To eyes awakened out of time and place;
Then in the cup of one great moment's space
Was crushed the living wine from things that seem;
I drank the joy of very Beauty's gleam,
And saw God's glory face to shining face.

Almost my brow was chastened to the ground,
But for an inner Voice that said: 'Arise!
Wisdom is wisdom only to the wise:
Thou art thyself the Royal thou hast crowned:
In Beauty thine own beauty thou hast found,
And thou hast looked on God with God's own eyes.'

JOHN SPENCER MUIRHEAD

Quiet

There is a flame within me that has stood
    Unmoved, untroubled through a mist of years,
    Knowing nor love nor laughter, hope nor fears,
Nor foolish throb of ill, nor wine of good.
I feel no shadow of the winds that brood,
    I hear no whisper of a tide that veers,
    I weave no thought of passion, nor of tears,
Unfettered I of time, of habitude.
I know no birth, I know no death that chills;
    I fear no fate nor fashion, cause nor creed,
I shall outdream the slumber of the hills,
    I am the bud, the flower, I the seed:
    For I do know that in whate'er I see
    I am the part and it the soul of me.

ELSA BARKER

The Slumberer

O Thou mysterious One, lying asleep
Within the lonely chamber of my soul!
Thou art my life's true goal,
Thine is the only altar that I keep.
Rapt in the contemplation of thy repose,
I see in thy still face that Mystic Rose
Whose perfume is my soul's imaginings,
And Beauty at whose awesomeness I weep
With over-plentitude of ecstasy.
Thy slumber is the great world-mystery.

ELSA BARKER

Microprosopos

Behind, the orient darkness of thine eyes,
The eyes of God interrogate my soul
   With whelming love. The luminous waves that roll
Over thy body are His dream. It lies
On thee as the moon-glamour on the skies;
   And all around – the yearning aureole
   Of His effulgent being – broods the whole
Rapt universe, that our love magnifies.

O thou, through whom for me Infinity
   Is manifest! Bitter and salt, thy tears
   Are the heart-water of the passionate spheres,
With all their pain. I drink them thirstily!
While in thy smile is realized for me
   The flaming joys of archangelic years.

ELSA BARKER

He Who Knows Love

He who knows Love – becomes Love, and his eyes
Behold Love in the heart of everyone,
   Even the loveless: as the light of the sun
Is one with all it touches. He is wise
With undivided wisdom, for he lies
   In Wisdom's arms. His wanderings are done,
   For he has found the Source whence all things run –
The guerdon of the quest, that satisfies.

He who knows Love becomes Love, and he knows
   All beings are himself, twin-born of Love.
Melted in Love's own fire, his spirit flows
   Into all earthly forms, below, above;
He is the breath and glamour of the rose,
   He is the benediction of the dove.

The paradigm of all the latent things
That in their distined hour Time magnifies:
Its emblems are the intimate hush that lies
Over the moonlit lake;
The wonder and the ache
Of unborn love that trembles in its sleep;
The hope that thrills the heavy earth
With presage of becoming, and vast birth;
The secret of the caverns of the deep.

ELSA BARKER

The Mystic Rose

I, woman, am that wonder-breathing rose
That blossoms in the garden of the King.
    In all the world there is no lovelier thing,
And the learned stars no secret can disclose
Deeper than mine – that almost no one knows.
    The perfume of my petals in the spring
    Is inspiration to all bards that sing
Of love, the spirit's lyric unrepose.

Under my veil is hid the mystery
    Of unaccomplished aeons, and my breath
    The Master-Lover's life replenisheth.
The mortal garment that is worn by me
The loom of Time renews continually;
    And when I die – the universe knows death.

ALFRED NOYES

From Creation

In the beginning, there was nought
    But heaven, one Majesty of Light,
Beyond all speech, beyond all thought,
    Beyond all depth, beyond all height,
Consummate heaven, the first and last,
    Enfolding in its perfect prime
No future rushing to the past,
    But one rapt Now, that knew not Space or Time.

Formless it was, being gold on gold,
    And void – but with that complete Life
Where music could no wings unfold
    Till lo, God smote the strings of strife!
'Myself unto Myself am Throne,
    Myself unto Myself am Thrall!
I that am All am all alone.'
    He said, 'Yea, I have nothing, having all.'

ELLA DIETZ

Emanation

Out of the depths of the Infinite Being eternal,
Out of the cloud more bright than the brightness of sun,
Out of the inmost the essence of spirit supernal,
    We issued as one.

First essence electric, concentric, revolving, subduing,
We throbbed through the ether, a part of the infinite germ,
Dissolving, resolving, absorbing, reforming, renewing,
    The endless in term.

Through forms multifarious onward and ever advancing,
Progressing through ether from molecule to planet and star,
Forms infinitestimal revealed by the sunbeam while dancing,
    Controlled from afar.

Then part of the elements swayed by invisible forces,
The spirit of flame interchangeably water and air,
And matter more gross, still moulded by stars in their courses,
    To forms new and rare.

Part of the salt of the sea – of the fathomless ocean –
Part of the growth of the earth, and the light hid within,
The Boundless and Endless revealed in each varying motion
    Unknown yet to sin.

The breath of all life, harmonious, ductile, complying,
Obedient lapsed in the force of the Infinite Will,
Untiring, unresting, incessant, unknowing, undying,
    Love's law we fulfil.

Spirit of growth in the rocks, and the ferns, and the mosses,
Spirit of growth in the trees, and the grasses, and flowers,
Rejoicing in life, unconscious of changes or losses,
    Of days or of hours.

Spirit of growth in the bird and the bee, ever tending
To form more complex its beauty and use thus combined,
Adapted perfection, the finite and infinite blending,
    One gleam from One Mind.

Thus spirally upward we come from the depths of creation,
The man and the woman – the garden of Eden have found,
And joined by the Lord in an endless and holy relation
    Ensphered and made round.

The innermost law of their being fulfilling, obeying,
The King and the Queen, perfected, companioned, are crowned,
The Incomprehensible thus in expression conveying
    Its ultimate bound.

Obedience still is the law of each fresh emanation,
The prayer to the Father, 'Not my will, but Thy will be done.'
Then deathless, immortal, we pass through all forms of creation,
    The twain lost in One.

Ella Dietz

The King's Daughter

I am beloved of the Prince of the garden of pleasure, I am beloved;
I am his pearl, and his dove, and his heart's hidden treasure, I am
    approved;
To-day he has given his love, oh! his love without measure,
    Which can never be moved.

He has called me 'Beloved of my soul', and my heart beats, repeating
    'Beloved of my soul',
And my blood dances swift through my veins in a musical beating;
    The twin currents roll,
Pouring forth their wild love, then again to their centre retreating
    Under righteous control.

O king of my life's hidden spring! O lord of my being!
    Beloved of my heart;

Our lips breathed one prayer, and our souls, in a sudden, agreeing,
　　Knit, joining each part
Of the long-severed Word that the prophets beheld in their seeing –
　　Belovèd thou art.

The long-severed name of the Lord we are loving and fearing;
　　Our Sabbaths of rest
Do welcome the Son; the Redeemed hail the Bridegroom's appearing –
　　His Name ever blest;
The Word in our hearts spoken now, in soft accents endearing,
　　With joy is confest.

Yea! Imrah – the Word, the Redeemed, the Bride of the Morning,
　　The joy of the earth;
O Imrah, beloved, whom the world had outcast in its scorning,
　　Rejoice in thy birth;
Ten thousands shall bless thee and bring thee thy gems of adorning,
　　And comfort thy dearth.

HAROLD MONRO

God

Once, long before the birth of time, a storm
Of white desire, by its own ardour hurled,
Flashed out of infinite Desire, took form,
Strove, won, survived: and God became the world.

Next, some internal force began to move
Within the bosom of that latest earth:
The spirit of an elemental love
Stirred outward from itself, and God was birth.

Then outward, upward, with heroic thew,
Savage from young and bursting blood of life,
Desire took form, and conquered, and anew
Strove, conquered, and took form: and God was strife

Thus, like a comet, fiery flight on flight;
Flash upon flash, and purple morn on morn:
But always out of agony – delight;
And out of death – God evermore reborn,

Till, waxing fair and subtle and supreme,
Desiring his own spirit to possess,
Man of the bright eyes and the ardent dream
Saw paradise, and God was consciousness.

He is that one Desire, that life, that breath,
That Soul which, with infinity of pain,
Passes through revelation and through death
Onward and upward to itself again.

Out of the lives of heroes and their deeds,
Out of the miracle of human thought,
Out of the songs of singers, God proceeds;
And of the soul of them his Soul is wrought.

Nothing is lost: all that is dreamed or done
Passes unaltered the eternal way,
Immerging in the everlasting One,
Who was the dayspring and who is the day.

Kahlil Gibran (*trans* Anthony Rizcallah Ferris)

Song of the Wave

The strong shore is my beloved
And I am his sweetheart.
We are at last united by love, and
Then the moon draws me from him.
I go to him in haste and depart
Reluctantly, with many
Little farewells.

I steal swiftly from behind the
Blue horizon to cast the silver of
My foam upon the gold of his sand, and
We blend in melted brilliance.

I quench his thirst and submerge his
Heart; he softens my voice and subdues
My temper.
At dawn I recite the rules of love upon
His ears, and he embraces me longingly.

At eventide I sing to him the song of
Hope, and then print smooth kisses upon
His face; I am swift and fearful, but he
Is quiet, patient, and thoughtful. His
Broad bosom soothes my restlessness.

As the tide comes we caress each other,
When it withdraws, I drop to his feet in
Prayer.

Many times have I danced around mermaids
As they rose from the depths and rested
Upon my crest to watch the stars;
Many times have I heard lovers complain
Of their smallness, and I helped them to sigh.

Many times have I teased the great rocks
And fondled them with a smile, but never
Have I received laughter from them;
Many times have I lifted drowning souls
And carried them tenderly to my beloved
Shore. He gives them strength as he
Takes mine.

Many times have I stolen gems from the
Depths and presented them to my beloved
Shore. He takes in silence, but still
I give for he welcomes me ever.

In the heaviness of night, when all
Creatures seek the ghost of Slumber, I
Sit up, singing at one time and sighing
At another. I am awake always.

Alas! Sleeplessness has weakened me!
But I am a lover, and the truth of love
Is strong.
I may weary, but I shall never die.

KAHLIL GIBRAN (*trans* Anthony Rizcallah Ferris)

The Life of Love

Spring

Come, my beloved; let us walk amidst the knolls,
For the snow is water, and Life is alive from its
Slumber and is roaming the hills and valleys.
Let us follow the footprints of Spring into the
Distant fields, and mount the hilltops to draw
Inspiration high above the cool green plains.

Dawn of Spring has unfolded her winter-kept garment
And placed it on the peach and citrus trees; and
They appear as brides in the ceremonial custom of
The Night of Kedre.

The sprigs of grapevine embrace each other like
Sweethearts, and the brooks burst out in dance
Between the rocks, repeating the song of joy;
And the flowers bud suddenly from the heart of
Nature, like foam from the rich heart of the sea.

Come, my beloved; let us drink the last of Winter's
Tears from the cupped lilies, and soothe our spirits
With the shower of notes from the birds, and wander
In exhilaration through the intoxicating breeze.
Let us sit by that rock, where violets hide; let us
Pursue their exchange of the sweetness of kisses.

Summer

Let us go into the fields, my beloved, for the
Time of harvest approaches, and the sun's eyes
Are ripening the grain.
Let us tend the fruit of the earth, as the
Spirit nourishes the grains of Joy from the
Seeds of Love, sowed deep in our hearts.
Let us fill our bins with the products of
Nature, as life fills so abundantly the
Domain of our hearts with her endless bounty.
Let us make the flowers our bed, and the
Sky our blanket, and rest our heads together
Upon pillows of soft hay.
Let us relax after the day's toil, and listen
To the provoking murmur of the brook.

Autumn

Let us go and gather the grapes of the vineyard
For the winepress, and keep the wine in old
Vases, as the spirit keeps Knowledge of the
Ages in eternal vessels.

Let us return to our dwelling, for the wind has
Caused the yellow leaves to fall and shroud the
Withering flowers that whisper elegy to Summer.

Come home, my eternal sweetheart, for the birds
Have made pilgrimage to warmth and left the chilled
Prairies suffering pangs of solitude. The jasmine
And myrtle have no more tears.

Let us retreat, for the tired brook has
Ceased its song; and the bubblesome springs
Are drained of their copious weeping; and
The cautious old hills have stored away
Their colourful garments.

Come, my beloved; Nature is justly weary
And is bidding her enthusiasm farewell
With quiet and contented melody.

Winter

Come close to me, oh companion of my full life;
Come close to me and let not Winter's touch
Enter between us. Sit by me before the hearth,
For fire is the only fruit of Winter.

Speak to me of the glory of your heart, for
That is greater than the shrieking elements
Beyond our door.
Bind the door and seal the transoms, for the
Angry countenance of the heaven depresses my
Spirit, and the face of our snow-laden fields
Makes my soul cry.

Feed the lamp with oil and let it not dim, and
Place it by you, so I can read with tears what
Your life with me has written upon your face.

Bring Autumn's wine. Let us drink and sing the
Song of remembrance to Spring's carefree sowing,
And Summer's watchful tending, and Autumn's
Reward in harvest.

Come close to me, oh beloved of my soul; the
Fire is cooling and fleeing under the ashes.
Embrace me, for I fear loneliness; the lamp is
Dim, and the wine which we pressed is closing
Our eyes. Let us look upon each other before
They are shut.
Find me with your arms and embrace me; let
Slumber then embrace our souls as one.
Kiss me, my beloved, for Winter has stolen
All but our moving lips.

You are close by me, My Forever.
How deep and wide will be the ocean of Slumber;
And how recent was the dawn!

GEORGE WILLIAM RUSSELL (Æ)

Krishna

I paused beside the cabin door and saw the King
    of Kings at play,
Tumbled upon the grass I spied the little heavenly
    runaway.
The mother laughed upon the child made gay by its
    ecstatic morn,
And yet the sages spake of It as of the Ancient and
    Unborn.
I heard the passion breathed amid the honeysuckle
    scented glade,
And saw the King pass lightly from the beauty that he had
    betrayed.
I saw him pass from love to love; and yet the pure
    allowed His claim
To be the purest of the pure, thrice holy, stainless,
    without blame.
I saw the open tavern door flash on the dusk a ruddy
    glare,
And saw the King of Kings outcast reel brawling through
    the starlit air.

And yet He is the Prince of Peace of whom the ancient
    wisdom tells,
And by their silence men adore the lovely silence where
    He dwells.
I saw the King of Kings again, a thing to shudder at and
    fear,
A form so darkened and so marred that childhood fled
    if it drew near.
And yet He is the Light of Lights whose blossoming is
    Paradise,
That Beauty of the King which dawns upon the seers'
    enraptured eyes.
I saw the King of Kings again, a miser with a heart
    grown cold,
And yet He is the Prodigal, the Spendthrift of the Heavenly
    Gold,
The largesse of whose glory crowns the blazing brows
    of cherubim,
And sun and moon and stars and flowers are jewels
    scattered forth by Him.
I saw the King of Kings descend the narrow doorway to
    the dust
With all his fires of morning still, the beauty, bravery,
    and lust.
And yet He is the life within the Ever-living Living Ones,
The ancient with eternal youth, the cradle of the infant
    suns,
The fiery fountain of the stars, and He the golden urn
    where all
The glittering spray of planets in their myriad beauty fall.

GEORGE WILLIAM RUSSELL (Æ)

Unity

One thing in all things have I seen:
One thought has haunted earth and air:
Clangoar and silence both have been
Its palace chambers. Everywhere

I saw the mystic vision flow
And live in men and woods and streams,
Until I could no longer know
The stream of life from my own dreams.

Sometimes it rose like fire in me
Within the depths of my own mind,
And spreading to infinity,
It took the voices of the wind.

WILLIAM BUTLER YEATS

The Lake Isle of Innisfree

I will arise and go now, and go to Innisfree,
And a small cabin build there, of clay and wattles made;
Nine bean-rows will I have there, a hive for the honey-bee,
    And live alone in the bee-loud glade.

And I shall have some peace there, for peace comes dropping slow,
Dropping from the veils of the morning to where the cricket sings;
There midnight's all a glimmer, and noon a purple glow,
    And evening full of the linnet's wings.

I will arise and go now, for always night and day
I hear lake-water lapping with low sounds by the shore;
While I stand on the roadway, or on the pavements gray,
    I hear it in the deep heart's core.

WILLIAM BUTLER YEATS

To the Secret Rose

Far off, most secret, and inviolate Rose,
Enfold me in my hour of hours; where those
Who sought thee at the Holy Sepulchre,
Or in the wine-vat, dwell beyond the stir
And tumult of defeated dreams; and deep
Among pale eyelids heavy with the sleep
Men have named beauty. Your great leaves enfold
The ancient beards, the helms of ruby and gold
Of the crowned Magi; and the king whose eyes
Saw the Pierced Hands and Rood of Elder rise
In druid vapour and make the torches dim;
Till vain frenzy awoke and he died; and him
Who met Fand walking among flaming dew,
By a grey shore where the wind never blew,
And lost the world and Emir for a kiss;

And him who drove the gods out of their liss
And till a hundred morns had flowered red
Feasted, and wept the barrows of his dead;
And the proud dreaming king who flung the crown
And sorrow away, and calling bard and clown
Dwelt among wine-stained wanderers in deep woods;
And him who sold tillage and house and goods,
And sought through lands and islands numberless years
Until he found with laughter and with tears
A woman of so shining loveliness,
That men threshed corn at midnight by a tress,
A little stolen tress. I too await
The hour of thy great wind of love and hate.
When shall the stars be blown about the sky,
Like the sparks blown out of a smithy, and die?
Surely thine hour has come, thy great wind blows,
Far off, most secret, and inviolate Rose?

WILLIAM BUTLER YEATS

From Sailing to Byzantium

III

O sages standing in God's holy fire
As in the gold mosaic of a wall,
Come from the holy fire, perne in a gyre,
And be the singing-masters of my soul.
Consume my heart away; sick with desire
And fastened to a dying animal
It knows not what it is; and gather me
Into the artifice of eternity.

IV

Once out of nature I shall never take
My bodily form from any natural thing
But such a form as Grecian goldsmiths make
Of hammered gold and gold enamelling
To keep a drowsy Emperor awake;
Or set upon a golden bough to sing
To lords and ladies of Byzantium
Of what is past, or passing, or to come.

JOHN MASEFIELD

From Sonnets and Poems

XII

What am I, Life? A thing of watery salt
held in cohesion by unresting cells
Which work they know not why, which never halt,
Myself unwitting where their master dwells.
I do not bid them, yet they toil, they spin;
A world which uses me as I use them,
Nor do I know which end or which begin,
Nor which to praise, which pamper, which condemn.
So, like a marvel in a marvel set,
I answer to the vast, as wave by wave
The sea of air goes over, dry or wet,
Or the full moon comes swimming from her cave,
Or the great sun comes north, this myriad I
Tingles, not knowing how, yet wondering why.

XIII

If I could get within this changing I,
This ever altering thing which yet persists,
Keeping the features it is reckoned by,
While each component atom breaks or twists,
If, wandering past strange groups of shifting forms,
Cells at their hidden marvels hard at work,
Pale from much toil, or red from sudden storms,
I might attain to where the Rulers lurk.
If, pressing past the guards in those grey gates,
The brain's most folded, intertwisted shell,
I might attain to that which alters fates,
The King, the supreme self, the Master Cell;
Then, on Man's earthly peak, I might behold
The unearthly self beyond, unguessed, untold.

XXVIII

You are more beautiful than women are,
Wiser than men, stronger than ribbed death,
Juster than Time, more constant than the star,
Dearer than love, more intimate than breath,
Having all art, all science, all control
Over the still unsmithied, even as Time
Cradles the generations of man's soul.
You are the light to guide, the way to climb.

So, having followed beauty, having bowed
To wisdom and to death, to law, to power,
I like a blind man stumble from the crowd
Into the darkness of a deeper hour,
Where in the lonely silence I may wait
The prayed-for gleam – your hand upon the gate.

XXXII

So beauty comes, so with a failing hand
She knocks, and cries, and fails to make me hear,
She who tells futures in the falling sand,
And still, by signs, makes hidden meanings clear;
She, who behind this many peopled smoke,
Moves in the light and struggles to direct,
Through the deaf ear and by the baffled stroke,
The wicked man, the honoured architect.
Yet at a dawn before the birds begin,
In dreams, as the horse stamps and the hound stirs,
Sleep slips the bolt and beauty enters in
Crying aloud those hurried words of hers,
And I awake and, in the birded dawn,
Know her for Queen, and own myself a pawn.

XXXIII

You will remember me in days to come,
With love, or pride, or pity, or contempt,
So will my friends (not many friends, yet some),
When this my life will be a dream out-dreamt;
And one, remembering friendship by the fire,
And one, remembering love time in the dark,
And one, remembering unfulfilled desire.
Will sigh, perhaps, yet be beside the mark;
For this my body with its wandering ghost
Is nothing solely but an empty grange,
Dark in a night that owls inhabit most,
Yet when the King rides by there comes a change;
The windows gleam, the cresset's fiery hair
Blasts the blown branch and beauty lodges there.

EZRA POUND

The Garret

Come, let us pity those who are better off than we are.
Come, my friend, and remember
   that the rich have butlers and no friends,
And we have friends and no butlers.
Come, let us pity the married and the unmarried.

Dawn enters with little feet
   like a gilded Pavlova,
And I am near my desire.
Nor has life in it aught better
Than this hour of clear coolness,
   the hour of waking together.

EZRA POUND

Ortus

How have I laboured?
How have I not laboured
To bring her soul to birth,
To give these elements a name and a centre!
She is beautiful as the sunlight, and as fluid.
She has no name, and no place.
How have I laboured to bring her soul into separation
To give her a name and her being!

Surely you are bound and entwined,
You are mingled with the elements unborn;
I have loved a stream and a shadow.

I beseech you enter your life.
I beseech you learn to say 'I',
When I question you;
For you are no part, but a whole,
No portion, but a being.

EZRA POUND

Ballad for Gloom

For God, our God, is a gallant foe
That playeth behind the veil.

I have loved my God as a child at heart
That seeketh deep bosoms for rest,
I have loved my God as maid to man,
But lo, this thing is best:

To love your God as a gallant foe
    that plays behind the veil,
To meet your God as the night winds meet
    beyond Arcturus' pale.

I have play'd with God for a woman,
I have staked with my God for truth,
I have lost to my God as a man, clear eyed,
    His dice be not of ruth.

For I am made as a naked blade,
    But hear ye this thing in sooth:

Who loseth to God as man to man
    Shall win at the turn of the game.
I have drawn my blade where the lightnings meet,
    But the ending is the same:
Who loseth to God as the sword blades lose
    Shall win at the end of the game.

For God, our God, is a gallant foe
    that playeth behind the veil,
Whom God deigns not to overthrow
    Hath need of triple mail.

D H LAWRENCE

Song of a Man Who Has Come Through

Not I, not I, but the wind that blows through me!
A fine wind is blowing the new direction of Time.
If only I let it bear me, carry me, if only it carry me!
If only I am sensitive, subtle, oh, delicate, a winged gift!
If only, most lovely of all, I yield myself and am borrowed
By the fine, fine wind that takes its course through the chaos
     of the world
Like a fine, an exquisite chisel, a wedge-blade inserted;
If only I am keen and hard like the sheer tip of a wedge
Driven by invisible blows,
The rock will split, we shall come at the wonder, we shall find
     the Hesperides.

Oh, for the wonder that bubbles into my soul,
I would be a good fountain, a good well-head,
Would blur no whisper, spoil no expression.

What is the knocking?
What is the knocking at the door in the night?
It is somebody wants to do us harm.

No, no, it is the three strange angels.
Admit them, admit them.

D H LAWRENCE

The Ship of Death

I

Now it is autumn and the falling fruit
and long journey towards oblivion.

The apples falling like great drops of dew
to bruise themselves an exit from themselves.

And it is time to go, to bid farewell
to one's own self, and find an exit
from the fallen self.

II

Have you built your ship of death, O have you?
O build your ship of death, for you will need it.

The grim frost is at hand, when the apples will fall
thick, almost thundrous, on the hardened earth.

And death is on the air like a smell of ashes!
Ah! can't you smell it?

And in the bruised body, the frightened soul
finds itself shrinking, wincing from the cold
that blows upon it through the orifices.

III

And can a man his own quietus make
with a bare bodkin?

With daggers, bodkins, bullets, man can make
a bruise or break of exit for his life;
but is that a quietus, O tell me, is it quietus?

Surely not so! for how could murder, even self-murder
even a quietus make?

IV

O let us talk of quiet that we know,
that we can know, the deep and lovely quiet
of a strong heart at peace!

How can we this, our own quietus, make?

V

Build then the ship of death, for you must take
the longest journey, to oblivion.
And die the death, the long and painful death
that lies between the old self and the new.

Already our bodies are fallen, bruised, badly bruised,
already our souls are oozing through the exit
of the cruel bruise.

Already the dark and endless ocean of the end
is washing in through the breaches of our wounds,
already the flood is upon us.

Oh build your ship of death, your little ark
and furnish it with food, with little cakes, and wine
for the dark flight down oblivion.

VI

Piecemeal the body dies, and the timid soul
has her footing washed away, as the dark flood rises.

We are dying, we are dying, we are all of us dying
and nothing will stay the death-flood rising within us
and soon it will rise on the world, on the outside world.

We are dying, we are dying, piecemeal our bodies are dying
and our strength leaves us,
and our soul cowers naked in the dark rain over the flood,
cowering in the last branches of the tree of our life.

VII

We are dying, we are dying, so all we can do
is now to be willing to die, and to build the ship
of death to carry the soul on the longest journey.

A little ship, with oars and food
and little dishes, and all accoutrements
fitting and ready for the departing soul.

Now launch the small ship, now as the body dies
and life departs, launch out, the fragile soul
in the fragile ship of courage, the ark of faith
with its store of food and little cooking pans

and change of clothes,
upon the flood's black waste
upon the waters of the end
upon the sea of death, where still we sail
darkly, for we cannot steer, and have no port.

There is no port, there is nowhere to go
only the deepening black darkening still
blacker upon the soundless, ungurgling flood
darkness at one with darkness, up and down
and sideways utterly dark, so there is no direction any more.
And the little ship is there; yet she is gone.
She is not seen, for there is nothing to see her by.
She is gone! gone! and yet
somewhere she is there.
Nowhere!

VIII

And everything is gone, the body is gone
completely under, gone, entirely gone.
The upper darkness is heavy on the lower,
between them the little ship
is gone
she is gone.
It is the end, it is oblivion.

IX

And yet out of eternity, a thread
separated itself on the blackness,
a horizontal thread
that fumes a little with pallor upon the dark.
Is it illusion? or does the pallor fume
A little higher?
Ah wait, wait, for there's the dawn,
the cruel dawn of coming back to life
out of oblivion.

Wait, wait, the little ship
drifting, beneath the deathly ashy grey
of a flood-dawn.

Wait, wait! even so, a flush of yellow
and strangely, O chilled wan soul, a flush of rose.

A flush of rose, and the whole thing starts again.

X

The flood subsides, and the body, like a worn sea-shell
emerges strange and lovely.
And the little ship wings home, faltering, and lapsing
on the pink flood,
and the frail soul steps out, into her house again
filling the heart with peace.

Swings the heart renewed with peace
even of oblivion.

Oh build your ship of death, oh build it!
for you will need it.
For the voyage of oblivion awaits you.

T S ELIOT

From Little Gidding

IV

The dove descending breaks the air
With flame of incandescent terror
Of which the tongues declare
The one discharge from sin and error.
The only hope, or else despair
   Lies in the choice of pyre or pyre –
   To be redeemed from fire by fire.

Who then devised the torment? Love.
Love is the unfamiliar Name
Behind the hands that wove
The intolerable shirt of flame
Which human power cannot remove.
   We only live, only suspire
   Consumed by either fire or fire.

. . .

V

With the drawing of this Love and the voice of this Calling

We shall not cease from exploration
And the end of all our exploring
Will be to arrive where we started
And know the place for the first time.
Through the unknown, remembered gate
When the last of earth left to discover
Is that which was the beginning;
At the source of the longest river
The voice of the hidden waterfall
And the children in the apple-tree
Not known, because not looked for
But heard, half-heard, in the stillness
Between two waves of the sea.
Quick now, here, now, always –
A condition of complete simplicity
(Costing not less than everything)
And all shall be well and
All manner of thing shall be well
When the tongues of flames are in-folded
Into the crowned knot of fire
And the fire and the rose are one.

V S DE PINTO

The Fountain

In the midst of darkness there is a bright Fountain,
tossing always its splendour high towards heaven;
sometimes it seems a slender shaft, a tall column,
then changes to a flower, a golden lily of light,
then a slim nymph unveiling shining breast and thigh,
always changing a quenchless spring of loveliness.

I was born in darkness among the shadow folk;
I am only a shadow in the old dim forest
that sleeps around the Fountain, yet I have dreamt that I
one day might dare to leave this world of death and night,
might dare to plunge into the living spring of light.

I have dreamt that I came forth a radiant shape endu'd
with the life-giving beauty of the shining waters.
I came into the forest, and as I shook bright drops
out of my hair a trail of light ran through the gloom
and spread like a flood of fire up to the murky sky
turning it to heavenly blue, and on the old dry boughs
a million green and golden shoots flamed and a choir
of all the birds of the world burst into starry song,
and children with bright hair ran laughing thro' the glades
among a wilderness of dewy delicate flowers,
moonlight colour'd and silver, purple, azure and gold.

This is only a dream, and I am still a shadow
among the shadow folk in the dead dark forest.

but the Fountain is no dream. Still in virgin splendour
it proudly shines, and I still see and adore its presence,
always changing, a quenchless spring of loveliness.

V S DE PINTO

From A Song of Life

My body is not this little parcel of flesh,
This bundle of nerves and tissues, these chalky bones;
My body is a wide and blossoming meadow,
My body is a mountain with wild torrents and rainbright stones.

My hair is not this little tuft of fur,
My hair is the leaves of the forests, green, golden and red;
My blood is not these few poor drops in my veins,
My blood is the wine of the world from a million vineyards shed.

I do not only look from these two dim windows,
I look from the countless eyes of heaven, the crowded stars;
And the risen sun is my great and glowing Eye,
And the setting sun that beholds the world through crimson bars.

J KRISHNAMURTI

From The Song of Life

V

A thousand eyes with a thousand views,
A thousand hearts with a thousand loves,
Am I.

As the sea that receiveth
The clean and the impure rivers
And heedeth not,
So am I.

Deep is the mountain lake,
Clear are the waters of the spring,
And my love is the hidden source of things.

Ah, come hither and taste of my love;
Then, as of a cool evening
The lotus is born,
Shalt thou find thy heart's own secret desire.

The scent of the jasmine fills the night air;
Out of the deep forest
Comes the call of a passing day.

The Life of my love is unburdened;
The attainment thereof is the freedom of fulfillment.

VI

Love is its own divinity.
If thou shalt follow it,
Putting aside the weary burden
Of a cunning mind,
Thou shalt be free of the fear
Of anxious love.

Love is not hedged about
By space and time,
By joyless things of the mind.

Such love delights in the heart
Of him who has richly wandered
In the confusion of love's own pursuits.

The Self, the Beloved,
The hidden loveliness of all things,
Is love's immortality.

O, why needst thou seek further,
Why further, friend?
In the dust of careless love
Lies Life's endless journey.

VII

Love Life.
Neither the beginning nor the end
Knows whence it comes.
For it has no beginning and no end.
Life is.

In the fulfilling of Life there is no death,
Nor the ache of great loneliness.
The voice of melody, the voice of desolation,
Laughter and the cry of sorrow,
Are but Life on its way to fulfillment.

Look into the eyes of thy neighbor
And find thyself with Life;
Therein is immortality,
Life eternal, never changing.

For him who is not in love with Life,
There is the anxious burden of doubt
And the lone fear of solitude;
For him there is but death.

Love Life, and thy love shall know of no corruption.
Love Life, and thy judgment shall uphold thee.
Love Life; thou shalt not wander away
From the path of understanding.

As the fields of the earth are divided,
Man makes a division of Life
And thereby creates sorrow.

Worship not the ancient gods
With incense and flowers,
But Life with great rejoicing;
Shout in the ecstasy of joy
There is no entanglement in the dance of Life.

I am of that Life, immortal, free;
The Eternal Source.
Of that Life I sing.

VIII

Seek not the perfume of a single heart
Nor dwell in its easeful comfort;
For therein abides
The dear of loneliness.

I wept,
For I saw
The loneliness of a single love.

In the dancing shadows
Lay a withered flower.

The worship of many in the one
Leads to sorrow.
But the love of the one in many
Is everlasting bliss.

IX

How easily
The tranquil pool is disturbed
By the passing winds.

. . .

XI

As out of the deep womb of a mountain
Is born a swift-running stream;
So out of the arching depths of my heart
Has come forth joyous love,
The perfume of the world.

Through the sunlit valleys rush the waters,
Entering lake upon lake,
Ever wandering, never still;
So is my love,
Emptying itself from heart to heart.

As the waters move sadly
Through the dark, cavernous valley;
So has my love become dull
Through the shame of easy desire.

As the tall trees are destroyed
By the strong rush of waters
That have nourished their deep roots
So has my love torn cruelly
The heart of its rejoicing.

I have shattered the very rock on which I grew.
And as a wide river
Now escapes to the dancing sea, whose waters know no bondage;
So is my love in the perfection of its freedom.

High among the rocks
An eagle is building his nest.
All things are great with Life.
O friend,
Life fills the world.
Thou and I are in eternal union.

Life is as the waters
That satisfy the thirst of kings and beggars alike:
The golden vessel for the king,
For the beggar the potter's vessel
Which breaks to pieces at the fountain.
Each holds his vessel dear.

There is loneliness,
There is fear of solitude,
The ache of a dying day,
The sorrow of a passing cloud.

Life, destitute of love,
Wanders from house to house,
With none to declare its loveliness.

Out of the granite rock
Is fashioned a graven image
Which men hold sacred;
But they tread carelessly the rock
On the way
That leads to the temple.

O friend,
Life fills the world.
Thou and I are in eternal union.

XV

I have no name;
I am as the fresh breeze of the mountains.
I have no shelter;
I am as the wandering waters.
I have no sanctuary, like the dark gods;
Nor am I in the shadow of deep temples.
I have no sacred books,
Nor am I well-seasoned in tradition.

AUROBINDO GHOSE

Surrender

O Thou of whom I am the instrument,
  O secret Spirit and Nature housed in me,
Let all my mortal being now be blent
  In Thy still glory of divinity.

I have given my mind to be dug Thy channel mind,
  I have offered up my will to be Thy will:
Let nothing of myself be left behind
  In our union mystic and unutterable.

My heart shall throb with the world-beats of Thy love,
  My body become Thy engine for earth-use;
In my nerves and veins Thy rapture's streams shall move;
  My thoughts shall be hounds of Light for Thy power to loose.

Keep only my soul to adore eternally
And meet Thee in each form and soul of Thee.

AUROBINDO GHOSE

The Divine Worker

I face earth's happenings with an equal soul;
　　In all are heard Thy steps: Thy unseen feet
Tread Destiny's pathways in my front. Life's whole
　　Tremendous theorem is Thou complete.

No danger can perturb my spirit's calm:
　　My acts are Thine; I do Thy works and pass;
Failure is cradled on Thy deathless arm,
　　Victory is Thy passage mirrored in Fortune's glass.

In this rude combat with the fate of man
　　Thy smile within my heart makes all my strength;
Thy Force in me labours at its grandiose plan,
　　Indifferent to the Time-snake's crawling length.

No power can slay my soul; it lives in Thee.
Thy presence is my immortality.

AUROBINDO GHOSE

The Bliss of Brahman

I am swallowed in a foam-white sea of bliss,
　　I am a curving wave of God's delight,
　　A shapeless flow of happy passionate light,
A whirlpool of the streams of Paradise.
I am a cup of His felicities,
　　A thunderblast of His golden ecstasy's might,
　　A fire of joy upon creation's height;
I am His rapture's wonderful abyss.

I am drunken with the glory of the Lord,
　　I am vanquishes by the beauty of the Unborn;
　　　I have looked, alive, upon the Eternal's face.
My mind is cloven by His radiant sword,
　　My heart by His beatific touch is torn,
　　　My life is a meteor-dust of His flaming Grace.

AUROBINDO GHOSE

From Savitri

From Book I, Canto IV

A hyphen must connect Matter and Mind,
The narrow isthmus of the ascending soul:
We must renew the secret bond in things,
Our hearts recall the lost divine Idea,
Reconstitute the perfect word, unite
The Alpha and the Omega in one sound;
Then shall the Spirit and Nature be at one.
Two are the ends of the mysterious plan.
In the wide signless ether of the Self,
In the unchanging Silence white and nude,
Aloof, resplendent like gold dazzling suns
Veiled by the Ray no mortal eye can bear,
The Spirit's free and absolute potencies
Burn in the solitude of the thoughts of God.
A rapture and a radiance and a hush
Delivered from the approach of wounded hearts,
Denied to the Idea that looks at grief,
Remote from the Force that cries out in its pain,
In his inalienable bliss they live.
Immaculate in self-knowledge and self-power,
Calm they repose on the eternal Will.
Only his law they count and him obey;
They have no goal to reach, no aim to serve.
Implacable in their timeless purity,
All barter or bribe of worship they refuse;
Unmoved by cry of revolt and ignorant prayer
They reckon not our virtue and our sin,
They bend not to the voices that implore,
They hold no traffic with error and its reign:
They are guardians of the silence of the Truth,
They are keepers of the immutable decree.
A deep surrender is their source of might,
A still identity their way to know,
Motionless is their action like a sleep.
At peace, regarding the trouble beneath the stars,
Deathless, watching the works of Death and Chance,
Immobile, seeing the millenniums pass,
Untouched while the long map of Fate unrolls,
They look on our struggle with impartial eyes,
And yet without them cosmos could not be.

From Book I, Canto V

One-pointed to the immaculate Delight,
Questing for God as for a splendid prey,
He mounted burning like a cone of fire.
To a few is given that godlike rare release.
One among many thousands never touched,
Engrossed in the external world's design.
Is chosen by a secret witness Eye
And driven by a pointing hand of Light
Across his soul's unmapped immensitudes.
A pilgrim of the everlasting Truth,
Our measures cannot hold his measureless mind;
He has turned from the voices of the narrow realm
And left the little lane of human Time.
In the hushed precincts of a vaster plan
He treads the vestibules of the Unseen,
Or listens following a bodiless Guide
To a lonely cry in boundless vacancy.
All the deep cosmic murmur falling still,
He lives in the hush before the world was born,
His soul left naked to the timeless One.
Far from compulsion of created things
Thought and its shadowy idols disappear,
The moulds of form and person are undone.
The ineffable Wideness knows him for its own.
A lone forerunner of the Godward earth,
Among the symbols of yet unshaped things
Watched by closed eyes, mute faces of the Unborn,
He journeys to meet the Incommunicable,
Hearing the echo of his single steps
In the eternal courts of Solitude.
A nameless Marvel fills the motionless hours.
His spirit mingles with Eternity's heart
And bears the silence of the Infinite.
In a divine retreat from mortal thought,
In a prodigious gesture of soul-sight,
His being towered into pathless heights,
Naked of its vesture of humanity.
As thus it rose, to meet him bare and pure
A strong Descent leaped down. A Might, a Flame,
A Beauty half-visible with deathless eyes,
A violent Ecstasy, a Sweetness dire,
Enveloped him with its stupendous limbs
And penetrated nerve and heart and brain
That thrilled and fainted with the epiphany:

His nature shuddered in the Unknown's grasp.
In a moment shorter than Death, longer than Time,
By a power more ruthless than Love, happier than Heaven,
Taken sovereignly into eternal arms,
Haled and coerced by a stark absolute bliss,
In a whirlwind circuit of delight and force
Hurried into unimaginable depths,
Upborne into immeasurable heights,
It was torn out from its mortality
And underwent a new and bourneless change.
An Omniscient knowing without sight or thought,
An indecipherable Omnipotence,
A mystic Form that could contain the worlds,
Yet make one human breast its passionate shrine,
Drew him out of his seeking loneliness
Into the magnitudes of God's embrace.
As when a timeless Eye annuls the hours
Abolishing the agent and the act,
So now his spirit shone out wide, blank, pure:
His wakened mind became an empty slate
On which the Universal and Sole could write.
All that represses our fallen consciousness
Was taken from him like a forgotten load:
A fire that seemed the body of a god
Consumed the limiting figures of the past
And made large room for a new self to live.

From Book II, Canto II

All we attempt in this imperfect world,
Looks forward or looks back beyond Time's gloss
To its pure idea and firm inviolate type
In an absolute creation's flawless skill.
To seize the absolute in shapes that pass,
To feel the eternal's touch in time-made things,
This is the law of all perfection here.
A fragment here is caught of heaven's design;
Else could we never hope for greater life
And ecstasy and glory could not be
Even in the littleness of our mortal state,
Even in this prison-house of outer form,
A brilliant passage for the infallible Flame
Is driven through gross walls of nerve and brain,
A Splendour presses or a Power breaks through,
Earth's great dull barrier is removed awhile,

The inconscient seal is lifted from our eyes
And we grow vessels of creative might.
The enthusiasm of a divine surprise
Pervades our life, a mystic stir is felt.

From Book III, Canto III

Thrilled with the hidden Transcendent's joy and peace,
There was no more division's endless scroll;
One grew the Spirit's secret unity,
All nature felt again the single bliss;
There was no cleavage between soul and soul,
There was no barrier between world and God.
Overpowered were form and memory's limiting line;
The covering mind was seized and torn apart;
It was dissolved and now no more could be,
The one Consciousness that made the world was seen;
All now was luminosity and force.
Abolished in its last thin fainting trace
The circle of the little self was gone;
The separate being could no more be felt;
It disappeared and knew itself no more,
Lost in the Spirit's wide identity.
His nature grew a movement of the All,
Exploring itself to find that all was He,
His soul was a delegation of the All
That turned from itself to join the one Supreme.
Transcended was the human formula;
Man's heart that had obscured the Inviolable
Assumed the mighty beating of a god's;
His seeking mind ceased in the Truth that knows;
His life was a flow of the universal life.
He stood fulfilled on the world's highest line
Awaiting the ascent beyond the world,
Awaiting the Descent the world to save.
A Splendour and a Symbol wrapped the earth,
Serene epiphanies looked and hallowed vasts
Surrounded, wise infinitudes were close
And bright remotenesses leaned near and kin.
Sense failed in that tremendous lucency:
Ephemeral voices from his hearing fell
And Thought potent no more sank large and pale
Like a tired god into mysterious seas.
The robes of mortal thinking were cast down
Leaving his knowledge bare to absolute sight;
Fate's driving ceased and Nature's sleepless spur:

The athlete heavings of the will were stilled
In the Omnipotent's unmoving peace.
Life in his members lay down vast and mute;
Naked, unwalled, unterrified it bore
The immense regard of Immortality.
The last movement died and all at once grew still.
A weight that was the unseen Transcendent's hand
Laid on his limbs the spirit's measureless seal,
Infinity swallowed him into shoreless trance.

From Book XI, Canto I

My dreadful hands laid on thy bosom shall force
Thy being bathed in fiercest longings' streams.
Thou shalt discover the one and quivering note
And cry, the harp of all my melodies,
And roll, my foaming wave in seas of love.
Even my disasters' clutch shall be to thee
The ordeal of my rapture's contrary shape:
In pain's self shall smile on thee my secret face:
Thou shalt bear my ruthless beauty unabridged
Amid the world's intolerable wrongs,
Trampled by the violent misdeeds of Time
Cry out to the ecstasy of my rapture's touch.
All beings shall be to thy life my emissaries;
Drawn to me on the bosom of thy friend,
Compelled to meet me in thy enemy's eyes,
My creatures shall demand me from thy heart.
Thou shalt not shrink from any brother soul.
Thou shalt be attracted helplessly to all.
Men seeing thee shall feel my hands of joy,
In sorrow's pangs feel steps of the world's delight,
Their life experience its tumultuous shock
In the mutual craving of two opposites.
Hearts touched by thy love shall answer to my call,
Discover the ancient music of the spheres
In the revealing accents of thy voice,
And nearer draw to me because thou art:
Enamoured of thy spirit's loveliness
They shall embrace my body in thy soul,
Hear in thy life the beauty of my laugh,
Know the thrilled bliss with which I made the worlds.
All that thou hast, shall be for others' bliss,
All that thou art, shall to my hands belong.
I will pour delight from thee as from a jar,
I will whirl thee as my chariot through the ways,

I will use thee as my sword and as my lyre,
I will play on thee my minstrelsies of thought.
And when thou art vibrant with all ecstasy,
And when thou liv'st one spirit with all things,
Then will I spare thee not my living fires,
But make thee a channel for my timeless force.
My hidden presence led thee unknowing on
From thy beginning in earth's voiceless bosom
Through life and pain and time and will and death,
Through outer shocks and inner silences
Along the mystic roads of Space and Time
To the experience which all Nature hides.
Who hunts and seizes me, my captive grows:
This shalt thou henceforth learn from thy heart-beats.
For ever love, O beautiful slave of God!
O lasso of my rapture's widening noose,
Become my cord of universal love.
The spirit ensnared by thee force to delight
Of creation's oneness sweet and fathomless.

RAMANA MAHARSHI (*trans* A W Chadwick)

Song of the *Poppadum*

No need about the world to roam
And suffer from depression;
Make *poppadum* within the home
According to the lesson
Of 'Thou art That', without compare,
The Unique Word, unspoken
Of Him who is the Adept-Sage,
The great Apotheosis.
With his eternal heritage
That Being-Wisdom-Bliss is.

Make *poppadum* and after making fry;
Eat, so your cravings you may satisfy.

The grain which is the black gram's yield.
The so-called self or ego,
Grown in the body's fertile field
Of five-fold sheaths, put into
The roller-mill made out of stone,
Which is the search for Wisdom,

The 'Who am I?' 'Tis thus alone
The Self will gain its freedom.
This must be crushed to finest dust
And ground up into fragments
As being the non-self, so must
We shatter out attachments.

    Make *poppadum* . . .

Mix in the juice of square-stemmed vine,
This is association
With Holy Men. With this combine,
Within the preparation,
Some cummin-seed of mind-control
And pepper of restraining
The wayward senses, with them roll
That salt which is remaining
Indifferent to the world we see,
With condiment of leanings
Towards a virtuous unity.
These are their different meanings.

    Make *poppadum* . . .

The mixture into dough now blend
And on the stone then place it
Of mind, by tendencies hardened,
And without ceasing paste it
With heavy strokes of the 'I-I'
Delivered with the pestle
Of introverted mind. Slowly
The mind will cease to wrestle.
Then roll out with the pin of peace
Upon the slab of Brahman,
Continue efforts without cease
With energetic élan.

    Make *poppadum* . . .

The *poppadum* or soul's now fit
To put into the fry-pan,
The one infinite symbol it
Of the great Silence, which can
Be first prepared by putting in
Some clarified fresh butter
Of the Supreme. And now begin

To hear it till it sputter,
On Wisdom's self-effulgent flame
Fry *poppadum*, 'I' as That.
Enjoying all alone the same;
Which Bliss we ever aim at.

Make *poppadum* of self and after eat;
Of Perfect Peace then you will be replete.

RAMANA MAHARSHI (*trans* Kapila Sastry)

From Sat Darshan

As in a well of water deep,
Dive deep with Reason cleaving sharp.
With speech, mind and breath restrained,
Exploring thus mayest thou discover
    the real source of ego-self.
The mind through calm in deep plunge enquires.
That alone is real quest for the Self.

RAMANA MAHARSHI (*trans* Br Sarvatma Chaitanya and Om Sadhu)

Bridal Garland of Letters to Sri Arunachala*

1

You root out the ego
Of those who in their heart
Dwell on You, O
Arunachala!

2

May I and You be one
Not to be unjoined like
Azhahu and Sundaram,
Arunachala!

3

Lo! Entering my home
You did drag me out and
In your heart-cave fettered me,
Arunachala!

* Arunachala, a sacred hill in S. India, symbol of the self.

4

For whose sake did you take me?
Now if you forsake me
The world will blame you,
Arunachala!

5

Do escape this blame!
Why then make me think of you?
Who can leave the other now,
Arunachala!

6

You who give love greater
Than one's own mother's,
Is this your love,
Arunachala!

7

Firmly stand upon
My mind lest she
Run away fooling you,
Arunachala!

8

Do reveal your beauty
So the world-roaming mind
Sees you ever and is stilled,
Arunachala!

9

Is this your bravery
If you don't unite now
With me destroying me,
Arunachala!

10

O why do you sleep
When all else drags me?
Does this become you,
Arunachala!

11

When the thieves, the five senses,
Intrude into my heart,
Are you not in my heart,
Arunachala!

12

You, the only one that is;
Who can enter but you?
'tis your jugglery indeed,
Arunachala!

13

Quintessence of Om,
Unrivalled, unsurpassed,
Who can comprehend you,
Arunachala!

14

'tis your duty to give me
Your love like a mother
And to keep me in your care,
Arunachala!

15

Eye of the eye you *are*!
Who can see you who sees
Eyelessly? O see me,
Arunachala!

16

Magnet and iron wise
Never cease attracting me
And be one with me,
Arunachala!

17

Ocean of mercy
In the form of a mount
Do have mercy on me,
Arunachala!

18

Gem of light that shines below
Above and everywhere,
My baseness do destroy,
Arunachala!

19

Shining as my guru's form,
My evils do destroy
And virtuous make me,
Arunachala!

20

Stand by me lest I fall
Prey to the tortures
Of the sharp cutting snares,
Arunachala!

21

Though I beg and beg
You cheat me and yield not,
Assure me: Fear not!
Arunachala!

22

Do not mar your taintless fame
Of giving unasked,
Be gracious to me,
Arunachala!

23

O fruit in my hand!
Let me drink your real essence
And be drunk with bliss,
Arunachala!

24

How can I survive after
Embracing you who with flag
Raised kill your devotees,
Arunachala!

25

You of nature angerless!
What have I done to be
The target of your wrath,
Arunachala!

26

Great mount of mercy
Glorified by Gautama!
Glance at me and make me yours,
Arunachala!

27

All engulfing
Sun of bright rays!
Make my mind-lotus bloom,
Arunachala!

28

Is it merely for food
That I came to you
As a mendicant!
Arunachala!

29

Moon of grace! Your cooling rays
Place on my mind and reveal
Your words of nectar,
Arunachala!

30

Of all vainglory strip me,
Lay me bare and enfold me
In the glory of your grace,
Arunachala!

31

Join me quietly, there
Where speech and thought subside
And the sea of bliss surges,
Arunachala!

32

O try me no more by
Playing tricks but show me
Your form of light,
Arunachala!

33

'Stead of teaching me
Jugglery to cheat the world,
Teach me abidance in Self,
Arunachala!

34

If you won't unite with me
My body'll melt away,
I'll be lost in a flood of tears,
Arunachala!

35

If you do spurn me
Karmas will only burn me
How then shall I be saved
Arunachala!

36

Without speaking you said:
'Just be without speech!'
And then you stayed still,
Arunachala!

37

What will befall me now
If you sleep lazily
Absorbed in bliss, say
Arunachala!

38

You remain still as if
Full of valour you had
My evils destroyed,
Arunachala!

39

How can I who
Am worse than a dog
Seek you and reach you,
Arunachala!

40

Grant that I may know you
So my weary longing
Of not knowing you leaves me,
Arunachala!

41

How can even you hover
Before me like a bee,
Saying: You have not bloomed!
Arunachala!

42

Though I know no principle,
You've become accessible;
What a gracious principle,
Arunachala!

43

Indeed Self is
The principle supreme:
Reveal this yourself to me,
Arunachala!

44

'Turn ever Self-ward,
Look with the mind's eye and
It'll be known!' you said, my
Arunachala!

45

Seeking Self, weak of mind
I returned frustrated;
Gracious help me,
Arunachala!

46

Of what use this birth
Without pure knowledge!
Do come and fulfill it,
Arunachala!

47

In your real Self fix me
Where only the pure in
Mind and speech dwell, my
Arunachala!

48

When I approached you
As my only god,
You annihilated me,
Arunachala!

49

Treasure of divine grace
Obtained unsought,
My mind's bewilderment end,
Arunachala!

50

Coming boldly to your real
Home, nothing more was needed.
Such is your grace, O
Arunachala!

51

Unless with your hands of grace
You touch 'n embrace me,
I'll be lost; have mercy,
Arunachala!

52

Unite with me so I
May be blissful ever;
Be gracious, flawless one,
Arunachala!

53

Don't mock me who's sought you
Be just and bejewel me
With your grace and then look,
Arunachala!

54

Turning to you of my own
O single one, you stood
Unmoved. Have you no shame,
Arunachala!

55

Shower your soothing grace
Ere the fire of longing
For you burns me to ashes,
Arunachala!

56

Grant the eternal state
Of bliss by the union
Free of feeling 'I and you',
Arunachala!

57

When will thoughts cease
So I may attain you
Who are subtler than space,
Arunachala!

58

Without knowledge am I
And know no scriptures,
My wrong knowledge dispel
Arunachala!

59

Melting more and more with longing
I took refuge in you,
There itself you stood revealed,
Arunachala!

60

You aroused attraction
In me who loved you not,
Now do not cheat me,
Arunachala!

61

Spoilt fruit is of no use;
Behold, it's only right
To eat it when it's ripe,
Arunachala!

62

Do not be Lord Yama,
Give yourself and take me
Without torturing me,
Arunachala!

63

With your look and your thought,
With your touch mature me
And make me yours, O
Arunachala!

64

Let your grace pervade me
Ere maya's poison seize me
And reaching my head kills me,
Arunachala!

65

See, unless you glance at me
Shattering delusion,
Who else can plead for me,
Arunachala!

66

Freeing me from that madness
You made me mad like you;
Now cure this madness too,
Arunachala!

67

O fearless one!
Why fear to take me
Who came to you without fear,
Arunachala!

68

Of what account a pure
Or impure mind, say
When grace is got, pray
Arunachala!

69

Wholly wed me so the mind
Full of wordly leanings
May gain those to be whole,
Arunachala!

70

When I thought of your name
You grabbed and dragged me away;
Who can gauge your glory, my
Arunachala!

71

Like an unriddable ghost
You possessed me, made me ghost
So my ghostlines goes, my
Arunachala!

72

Uphold me as support
To cling to lest I droop
Like a tender creeper,
Arunachala!

73

With powder bewitching me
You stole my egoity
And showed your reality,
Arunachala!

74

Reveal the battle of grace
In ether, the substrate
Of going or coming void,
Arunachala!

75

Your splendour let me gain
Casting out attachment to
The body of elements,
Arunachala!

76

Mountain of medicine!
Why hesitate to give the
Med'cine ending confusion
Arunachala!

77

Unattached you shine
Slaying the ego of those
Who with attachment come,
Arunachala!

78

Low of wit, I pray only
When with sorrows overwhelmed
But withhold not your grace,
Arunachala!

79

Protect me lest I be
Like a storm-tossed ship
Without a helmsman,
Arunachala!

80

Isn't it your duty
To fix me in that state
The ends of which weren't found,
Arunachala!

81

Be not like a mirror
Held to a noseless man
But raise and embrace me,
Arunachala!

82

In Self, let us merge
On the floral bed of mind
In the house of the body,
Arunachala!

83

How great You unite
With those mellow ones
Who're humble ever more,
Arunachala!

84

With your magic salve of grace
You dispelled my delusion
And swayed me to your truth,
Arunachala!

85

You shaved me clean, O wonder!
And did dance your dance
In sheer heart-space,
Arunachala!

86

Fulfill my one desire
To be rid of delusion
And madly crave for you, my
Arunachala!

87

If you stay silent
Unresponding like stone,
Will such silence befit you,
Arunachala!

88

Who was it that ruined
My life by throwing
Mud into my mouth,
Arunachala!

89

Who was it that lured me
Unknown to anyone
And robbed me of my mind
Arunachala!

90

Since you are my beloved
I spoke out, be not piqued;
Come and gladden me
Arunachala!

91

Come, let us revel
In the house of void space
Free of night and day,
Arunachala!

92

Taking aim at me you
Hurled your shaft of grace and
Devoured me and my life-force,
Arunachala!

93

What did you, O gain supreme,
Gain by gaining me who gained
Naught in this nor other worlds,
Arunachala!

94

Did you not call me: Come!
Now do suffer your fate
Of providing for me,
Arunachala!

95

Calling me, ent'ring my heart
You granted your life 'n lo!
I lost mine; how gracious,
Arunachala!

96

If forsaken I'll be wretched,
Let me not loose hold of you
When I leave this life,
Arunachala!

97

Dragging me from home by stealth
Ent'ring the home of my heart
You revealed it as your home,
Arunachala!

98

I've exposed your doings
Be not angry, but save me
Openly granting your grace,
Arunachala!

99

Confer on me the essence
Of Vedas which shines without
A second in Vedanta,
Arunachala!

100

Take my slander as praise,
Accept me in your kingdom
Of grace and forsake me not,
Arunachala!

101

As ice in water melts
Melt me as love
In you the form of love,
Arunachala!

102

When I thought of Arunai
I was caught in grace's mesh;
Will your net ever fail,
Arunachala!

103

Resolved to ensnare me in
Grace, like a spider you
Bound me and fed on me,
Arunachala!

104

May I be devoted
To the devotees of those
Who with love hear your name,
Arunachala!

105

Shine forever saving
The helpless ones like me
So they may attain bliss,
Arunachala!

106

May your ears that hear the sweet
Songs that melt the bones
Hear my poor strains too,
Arunachala!

107

Bear with my mean words,
Take them as fine praises and
Give as you will, Mount of patience
Arunachala!

108

Arunachala-Ramana!
Give me your bridal garland,
Wear my garland of letters,
Arunachala!

Arunachala Siva, Arunachala Siva,
Arunachala Siva, Arunachala!

Arunachala Siva, Arunachala Siva,
Arunachala Siva, Arunachala!

Glory to Arunachala!
Glory to his devotees!
Glory to this Bridal Garland!

SRI MURUGANAR

Ramana the Magician

Both male and female, far yet near,
Mountain-huge and atom-small,
Pure Awareness he, whose sidelong glance
Has made me see
The Truth invisible
And hear
The dancing music of his Feet,
For he has caught within his heart
And carries in his cosmic dance
This midget! What extravagance
Of grace to hold me in this bliss,
Both mine and his
Together and apart!

Awareness wherein brightly shine
These many forms of persons, places, time,
All separate-seeming though in substance one,
Into that same Awareness he transmuted
This 'I' of mine. Now, nothing to be known,
My past undone, my being his,
I stand, unruffled bliss, a rock
Untouched by any shock.
Lord Siva Vēnkatesha, King of kings,
Came conquering
And made me his alone.

What is this 'I' that rises from within?
Only a thought that like a bubble floats
Up to the troubled surface of Awareness.
In sleep the sea is still, no bubble rises,
Then too you are and are aware you are.
You're not the 'I' that rises and sets,
You are the sole Awareness in the All,
The eternal, uncreated light of Being.

Wallace Stevens

From An Ordinary Evening in New Haven

VII

Professor Eucalyptus said, 'The search
For reality is as momentous as
The search for god.' It is the philosopher's search

For an interior made exterior
And the poet's search for the same exterior made
Interior: breathless things broodingly abreath

With the inhalations of original cold
And of original earliness. Yet the sense
Of cold and earliness is a daily sense,

Not the predicate of bright origin.
Creation is not renewed by images
Of lone wanderers. To recreate, to use

The cold and earliness and bright origin
Is to search. Likewise to say of the evening star,
The most ancient light in the most ancient sky,

That it is wholly an inner light, that it shines
From the sleepy bosom of the real, recreates,
Searches a possible for its possibleness.

WALLACE STEVENS

From Credences of Summer

VI

The rock cannot be broken. It is the truth.
It rises from land and sea and covers them.
It is a mountain half way green and then,
The other immeasurable half, such rock
As placid air becomes. But it is not

A hermit's truth nor symbol in hermitage.
It is the visible rock, the audible,
The brilliant mercy of a sure repose,
On this present ground, the vividest repose,
Things certain sustaining us in certainty.

It is the rock of summer, the extreme,
A mountain luminous half way in bloom
And then half way in the extremest light
Of sapphires flashing from the central sky,
As if twelve princes sat before a king.

VII

Far in the woods they sang their unreal songs,
Secure. It was difficult to sing in face
Of the object. The singers had to avert themselves
Or else avert the object. Deep in the woods
They sang of summer in the common fields.

They sang desiring an object that was near,
In face of which desire no longer moved,
Nor made of itself that which it could not find . . .
Three times the concentred self takes hold, three times
The thrice concentred self, having possessed

The object, grips it in savage scrutiny,
Once to make captive, once to subjugate
Or yield to subjugation, once to proclaim
The meaning of the capture, this hard prize,
Fully made, fully apparent, fully found.

VIII

The trumpet of morning blows in the clouds and through
The sky. It is the visible announced,
It is the more than visible, the more
Than sharp, illustrious scene. The trumpet cries
This is the successor of the invisible.

This is its substitute in stratagems
Of the spirit. This, in sight and memory,
Must take its place, as what is possible
Replaces what is not. The resounding cry
Is like ten thousand tumblers tumbling down.

To share the day. The trumpet supposes that
A mind exists, aware of division, aware
Of its cry as clarion, its diction's way
As that of a personage in a multitude:
Man's mind grown venerable in the unreal.

WALLACE STEVENS

Design

I found a dimpled spider, fat and white,
On a white heal-all, holding up a moth
Like a white piece of rigid satin cloth –
Assorted characters of death and blight
Mixed ready to begin the morning right,
Like the ingredients of a witches' broth –
A snow-drop spider, a flower like a froth,
And dead wings carried like a paper kite.

What had that flower to do with being white,
The wayside blue and innocent heal-all?
What brought the kindred spider to that height,
Then steered the white moth thither in the night?
What but design of darkness to appall? –
If design govern in a thing so small.

WALLACE STEVENS

To the One of Fictive Music

Sister and mother and diviner love,
And of the sisterhood of the living dead
Most near, most clear, and of the clearest bloom,
And of the fragrant mothers the most dear
And queen, and of diviner love the day
And flame and summer and sweet fire, no thread
Of cloudy silver sprinkles in your gown
Its venom of renown, and on your head
No crown is simpler than the simple hair.

Now, of the music summoned by the birth
That separates us from the wind and sea,
Yet leaves us in them, until earth becomes,
By being so much of the things we are,
Gross effigy and simulacrum, none
Gives motion to perfection more serene
Than yours, out of our imperfections wrought,
Most rare, or ever of more kindred air
In the laborious weaving that you wear.

For so retentive of themselves are men
That music is intensest which proclaims
The near, the clear, and vaunts the clearest bloom,
And of all vigils musing the obscure,
That apprehends the most which sees and names,
As in your name, an image that is sure,
Among the arrant spices of the sun,
O bough and bush and scented vine, in whom
We give ourselves our likest issuance.

PART 8:
Twentieth Century

OCTAVIO PAZ (*trans* J M Cohen)
Certainty

If the white light of this lamp
is real, and real
the hand that writes,
are the eyes real
that look at what I write?

One word follows another.
What I saw vanishes.
I know that I am alive,
and living between two parentheses.

RAINER MARIA RILKE (*trans* J B Leishman)
From The Book of Hours

34

The day is coming when from God the Tree
a bough unlike that over Italy
in summer-ripe annunciance shall glisten;
here in a country where the people listen,
and everyone is solitary like me.

For only solitaries shall behold
the mysteries, and many of that mould
far more than any narrow one shall gain.
For each shall see a different God made plain,
till they acknowledge, near to crying,
that through their so diverse descrying,
through their affirming and denying,
unitingly diversifying,
one God rolls ever-flowingly.

This the conclusive hymn shall be
which then the seers will be singing:
Fruit out of God the Root is springing,
go, smash those bells that you were ringing;
we've reached that quieter season, bringing
the hour to full maturity.
Fruit out of God the Root is springing.
Be grave and see.

RAINER MARIA RILKE (*trans* J B Leishman)

Shatter Me, Music

Shatter me, music, with rhythmical fury!
Lofty reproach, lifted against the heart
that feared such surge of perception, sparing itself. My heart,
   – there:
behold your glory! Can you remain contented
with less expansive beats, when the uppermost arches
are waiting for you to fill them with organing impulse?
Why do you long for the face withheld, for the far beloved?
For, oh, if your longing lacks breath to extort resounding
   storms
from the trumpet an angel blows on high at the end of the
   world,
she also does not exist, nowhere, will never be born,
she whom you parchingly miss . . .

RAINER MARIA RILKE (*trans* J B Leishman)

Exposed on the Heart's Mountains

Exposed on the heart's mountains. Look, how small there!
look, the last hamlet of words, and, higher,
(but still how small!) yet one remaining
farmstead of feeling: d'you see it?
Exposed on the heart's mountains. Virgin rock
under the hands. Though even here
something blooms: from the dumb precipice
an unknowing plant blooms singing into the air.
But what of the knower? Ah, he began to know
and holds his peace, exposed on the heart's mountains.
While, with undivided mind,
many, maybe, many well-assured mountain beasts,
pass there and pause. And the mighty sheltered bird
circles the summits' pure refusal. – But, oh,
no longer sheltered, here on the heart's mountains . . .

TEILHARD DE CHARDIN (*trans* Blanche Gallagher)

From Meditation

Love
is the free and imaginative outflowing
of the Spirit over all unexplored paths.
It links those
who love in bonds that unite,
but do not destroy, causing them to discover in their mutual contact
an exaltation capable of stirring in the very core
   of their being all that they possess
      of 'uniqueness' and 'creative' power.
Love alone
can unite living beings
so as to complete and fulfill them,
for it alone joins them by what is deepest
   in themselves. All we need
is to imagine our ability to love
developing until it embraces the totality
      of the people of the Earth.

. . .

Theoretically,
this transformation of love is quite possible.
What paralyzes life is failure to believe
     and failure to dare.
The day will come when,
after harnessing space,
   the winds,
     the tides,
       and gravitation,
we shall harness for God the energies of love.
And, on that day, for the second time
in the history of the world,
     we shall have discovered fire.

. . .

Do not brace yourself against suffering.
Try to close your eyes and surrender yourself,
   as if to a great loving energy.
This attitude is neither weak nor absurd,
it is the only one that cannot lead us astray.
Try to 'sleep,' with that *active* sleep of confidence
   which is that of the seed in the fields in winter.

         ...

To love
is to discover and complete one's self
in someone other than oneself,
an act impossible of general realization on Earth
so long as each can see in the neighbor no more than
a closed fragment following its own course
   through the world.
It is precisely
this state of isolation that will end
if we begin to discover in each other
not merely the elements of one and the same thing,
but of a single Spirit in search of itself.
The existence of such a power
becomes possible in the curvature of a world
   capable of noogenesis.

E E CUMMINGS

i thank You God for most this amazing

i thank You God for most this amazing
day: for the leaping greenly spirits of trees
and a blue true dream of sky; and for everything
which is natural which is infinite which is yes

(i who have died am alive again today,
and this is the sun's birthday; this is the birth
day of life and of love and wings: and of the gay
great happening illimitably earth)

how should tasting touching hearing seeing
breathing any – lifted from the no
of all nothing – human merely being
doubt unimaginable You?

(now the ears of my ears awake and
now the eyes of my eyes are opened)

W H Auden
Anthem

Let us praise our Maker, with true passion extol Him.
Let the whole creation give out another sweetness,
Nicer in our nostrils, a novel fragrance
From cleansed occasions in accord together
As one feeling fabric, all flushed and intact,
Phenomena and numbers announcing in one
Multitudinous œcumenical song
Their grand givenness of gratitude and joy,
Peaceable and plural, their positive truth
An authoritative This, an unthreatened Now
When, in love and in laughter, each lives itself,
For, united by His Word, cognition and power,
System and Order, are a single glory,
And the pattern is complex, their places safe.

W H Auden
Prime

Simultaneously, as soundlessly,
    Spontaneously, suddenly
As, at the vaunt of the dawn, the kind
    Gates of the body fly open
To its world beyond, the gates of the mind,
    The horn gate and the ivory gate
Swing to, swing shut, instantaneously
    Quell the nocturnal rummage
Of its rebellious fronde, ill-favored,
    Ill-natured and second-rate,
Disenfranchised, widowed and orphaned
    By an historical mistake:
Recalled from the shades to be a seeing being,
    From absence to be on display,
Without a name or history I wake
    Between my body and the day.

Holy this moment, wholly in the right,
    As, in complete obedience
To the light's laconic outcry, next
    As a sheet, near as a wall,
Out there as a mountain's poise of stone,
    The world is present, about,
And I know that I am, here, not alone
    But with a world and rejoice.

Unvexed, for the will has still to claim
    This adjacent arm as my own,
The memory to name me, resume
    Its routine of praise and blame,
And smiling to me is this instant while
    Still the day is intact, and I
The Adam sinless in our beginning,
    Adam still previous to any act.

I draw breath; that is of course to wish
    No matter what, to be wise,
To be different, to die and the cost,
    No matter how, is Paradise
Lost of course and myself owing a death:
    The eager ridge, the steady sea.
The flat roofs of the fishing village
    Still asleep in its bunny.
Though as fresh and sunny still, are not friends
    But things to hand, this ready flesh
No honest equal, but my accomplice now.
    My assassin to be, and my name
Stands for my historical share of care
    For a lying self-made city.
Afraid of our living task, the dying
    Which the coming day will ask.

THEODORE ROETHKE

The Waking

I wake to sleep, and take my waking slow.
I feel my fate in what I cannot fear.
I learn by going where I have to go.

We think by feeling. What is there to know?
I hear my being dance from ear to ear.
I wake to sleep, and take my waking slow.

Of those so close beside me, which are you?
God bless the Ground! I shall walk softly there,
And learn by going where I have to go.

Light takes the Tree; but who can tell us how?
The lowly worm climbs up a winding stair;
I wake to sleep, and take my waking slow.

Great Nature has another thing to do
To you and me; so take the lively air,
And, lovely, learn by going where to go.

This shaking keeps me steady. I should know.
What falls away is always. And is near.
I wake to sleep, and take my waking slow.
I learn by going where I have to go.

THEODORE ROETHKE

Meditation at Oyster River

1

Over the low, barnacled, elephant-colored rocks,
Come the first tide-ripples, moving, almost without sound, toward me,
Running along the narrow furrows of the shore, the rows of dead clam
    shells;
Then a runnel behind me, creeping closer,
Alive with tiny striped fish, and young crabs climbing in and out of
    the water.
No sound from the bay. No violence.
Even the gulls quiet on the far rocks,
Silent, in the deepening light,
Their cat-mewing over,
Their child-whimpering.
At last one long undulant ripple,
Blue-black from where I am sitting,
Makes almost a wave over a barrier of small stones,
Slapping lightly against a sunken log.
I dabble my toes in the brackish foam sliding forward,
Then retire to a rock higher up on the cliff-side.
The wind slackens, light as a moth fanning a stone:

A twilight wind, light as a child's breath
Turning not a leaf, not a ripple.
The dew revives on the beach-grass;
The salt-soaked wood of a fire crackles;
A fish raven turns on its perch (a dead tree in the rivermouth),
Its wings catching a last glint of the reflected sunlight.

2

The self persists like a dying star,
In sleep, afraid. Death's face rises afresh,
Among the shy beasts, the deer at the salt-lick,
The doe with its sloped shoulders loping across the highway,
The young snake, poised in green leaves, waiting for its fly,
The hummingbird, whirring from quince-blossom to morning-glory –
With these I would be.
And with water: the waves coming forward, without cessation,
The waves, altered by sand-bars, beds of kelp, miscellaneous
    driftwood.
Topped by cross-winds, tugged at by sinuous undercurrents
The tide rustling in, sliding between the ridges of stone,
The tongues of water, creeping in, quietly.

3

In this hour,
In this first heaven of knowing,
The flesh takes on the pure poise of the spirit,
Acquires, for a time, the sandpiper's insouciance,
The hummingbird's surety, the kingfisher's cunning –
I shift on my rock, and I think:
Of the first trembling of a Michigan brook in April,
Over a lip of stone, the tiny rivulet;
And that wrist-thick cascade tumbling from a cleft rock,
Its spray holding a double rain-bow in early morning,
Small enough to be taken in, embraced, by two arms, –
Or the Tittebawasee, in the time between winter and spring,
When the ice melts along the edges in early afternoon.
And the midchannel begins cracking and heaving from the
    pressure beneath,
The ice piling high against the iron-bound spiles,
Gleaming, freezing hard again, creaking at midnight –
And I long for the blast of dynamite,
The sudden sucking roar as the culvert loosens its debris of branches
    and sticks,
Welter of tin cans, pails, old bird nests, a child's shoe riding a log,
As the piled ice breaks away from the battered spiles,
And the whole river begins to move forward, its bridges shaking.

THEODORE ROETHKE

The Minimal

I study the lives on a leaf: the little
Sleepers, numb nudgers in cold dimensions,
Beetles in caves, newts, stone-deaf fishes,
Lice tethered to long limp subterranean weeds,
Squirmers in bogs,
And bacterial creepers
Wriggling through wounds
Like elvers in ponds,
Their wan mouths kissing the warm sutures,
Cleaning and caressing,
Creeping and healing.

THEODORE ROETHKE

It Was Beginning Winter

It was beginning winter,
An in-between time,
The landscape still partly brown:
The bones of weeds kept swinging in the wind,
Above the blue snow.

It was beginning winter,
The light moved slowly over the frozen field,
Over the dry seed-crowns,
The beautiful surviving bones
Swinging in the wind.

Light traveled over the wide field;
Stayed.
The weeds stopped swinging.
The mind moved, not alone,
Through the clear air, in the silence.

THEODORE ROETHKE

The Right Thing

Let others probe the mystery if they can.
Time-harried prisoners of *Shall* and *Will* –
The right thing happens to the happy man.

The bird flies out, the bird flies back again;
The hill becomes the valley, and is still;
Let others delve that mystery if they can.

God bless the roots! – Body and soul are one!
The small become the great, the great the small;
The right thing happens to the happy man.

Child of the dark, he can out leap the sun,
His being single, and that being all:
The right thing happens to the happy man.

Or he sits still, a solid figure when
The self-destructive shake the common wall;
Takes to himself what mystery he can,

And, praising change as the slow night comes on,
Wills what he would, surrendering his will
Till mystery is no more: No more he can.
The right thing happens to the happy man.

THEODORE ROETHKE

Was it Light?

Was it light?
Was it light within?
Was it light within light?
Stillness becoming alive,
Yet still?

A lively understandable spirit
Once entertained you.
It will come again.
Be still.
Wait.

THEODORE ROETHKE

Now in this Waning of Light

Now, in this waning of light,
I rock with the motion of morning;
In the cradle of all that is,
I'm lulled into half-sleep
By the lapping of water,
Cries of the sandpiper.
Water's my will, and my way,
And the spirit runs, intermittently,
In and out of the small waves,
Runs with the intrepid shorebirds –
How graceful the small before danger!

In the first of the moon,
All's a scattering,
A shining.

ROBERT FROST

Bereft

Where had I heard this wind before
Change like this to a deeper roar?
What would it take my standing there for,
Holding open a restive door,
Looking down hill to a frothy shore?
Summer was past and day was past.
Sombre clouds in the west were massed.
Out in the porch's sagging floor,
Leaves got up in a coil and hissed,
Blindly struck at my knee and missed.
Something sinister in the tone
Told me my secret must be known:
Word I was in the house alone
Somehow must have gotten abroad,
Word I was in my life alone,
Word I had no one left but God.

ROBERT FROST

Trial by Existence

And from a clifftop is proclaimed
The gathering of the souls for birth . . .

And none are taken but who will,
Having first heard the life read out
That opens earthward, good and ill,
Beyond the shadow of a doubt;
And very beautifully God limns,
And tenderly, life's little dream,
But naught extenuates or dims,
Setting the thing that is supreme.

Nor is there wanting in the press
Some spirit to stand simply forth,
Heroic in its nakedness,
Against the uttermost of earth.
The tale of earth's unhonoured things
Sounds nobler there than 'neath the sun;
And the mind whirls and the heart sings,
And a shout greets the daring one . . .

And so the choice must be again,
But the last choice is still the same;
And the awe passes wonder then,
And a hush falls for all acclaim.
And God has taken a flower of gold
And broken it, and used therefrom
The mystic link to bind and hold
Spirit to matter till death come . . .

ROBERT DUNCAN

From Poetry, a Natural Thing

Neither our vices nor our virtues
further the poem. 'They came up
and died
just like they do every year
on the rocks.'

The poem
feeds upon thought, feeling, impulse,
    to breed itself,
a spiritual urgency at the dark ladders leaping.

This beauty is an inner persistence
    toward the source
striving against (within) down-rushet of the river,
    a call we heard and answer
in the lateness of the world
    primordial bellowings
from which the youngest world might spring.

salmon not in the well where the
    hazelnut falls
but at the falls battling, inarticulate,
    blindly making it.

HART CRANE

Meditation

I have drawn my hands away
Toward peace and the grey margins of the day.
The andante of vain hopes and lost regret
Falls like slow rain that whispers to forget –
Like a song that neither questions nor replies
It laves with coolness tarnished lips and eyes.

I have drawn my hands away
At last to touch the ungathered rose. O stay,
Moment of dissolving happiness! Astir
Already in the sky, night's chorister
Has brushed a petal from the jasmine moon,
And the heron has passed by, alas, how soon!

I have drawn my hands away
Like ships for guidance in the lift and spray
Of stars that urge them toward an unknown goal.
Drift, O wakeful one, O restless soul,
Until the glittering white open hand
Of heaven thou shalt read and understand.

HART CRANE

Hieroglyphics

From 10 Unpublished Poems

IX

Did one look at what one saw
Or did one see what one looked at?

HART CRANE

The Hurricane

Lo, Lord, Thou ridest!
Lord, Lord, Thy swifting heart

Nought stayeth, nought now bideth
But's smithereened apart!

Ay! Scripture flee'th stone!
Milk-bright, Thy chisel wind

Rescindeth flesh from bone
To quivering whittlings thinned –

Swept, whistling straw! Battered,
Lord, e'en boulders now outleap

Rock sockets, levin-lathered!
Nor, Lord, may worm outdeep

Thy drum's gambade, its plunge abscond!
Lord God, while summits crashing

Whip sea-kelp screaming on blond
Sky-seethe, dense heaven dashing –

Thou ridest to the door, Lord!
Thou bidest wall nor floor, Lord!

HART CRANE

From Atlantis

O Thou steeled Cognizance whose leap commits
The agile precincts of the lark's return;
Within whose lariat sweep encinctured sing
In single chrysalis the many twain, –
Of stars Thou art the stitch and stallion glow
And like an organ, Thou, with sound of doom –
Sight, sound and flesh Thou leadest from time's realm
As love strikes clear direction for the helm.

Swift peal of secular light, intrinsic Myth
Whose fell unshadow is death's utter wound, –
O River-throated – iridescently upborne
Through the bright drench and fabric of our veins;
With white escarpments swinging into light,
Sustained in tears the cities are endowed
And justified conclamant with ripe fields
Revolving through their harvests in sweet torment.

Forever Deity's glittering Pledge, O Thou
Whose canticle fresh chemistry assigns
To wrapt inception and beatitude, –
Always through blinding cables, to our joy,
Of thy white seizure springs the prophecy:
Always through spiring cordage, pyramids
Of silver sequel, Deity's young name
Kinetic of white choiring wings . . . ascends.

Migrations that must needs void memory,
Inventions that cobblestone the heart, –
Unspeakable Thou Bridge to Thee, O Love.
Thy pardon for this history, whitest Flower,
O Answerer of all, – Anemone, –
Now while thy petals spend the suns about us, hold –
(O Thou whose radiance doth inherit me)
Atlantis, – hold thy floating singer late!

So to thine Everpresence, beyond time,
Like spears ensanguined of one tolling star
That bleeds infinity – the orphic strings,
Sidereal phalanxes, leap and converge:
– One Song, one Bridge of Fire! Is it Cathay,
Now pity steeps the grass and rainbows ring
The serpent with the eagle in the leaves . . . ?
Whispers antiphonal in azure swing.

ROBERT LOWELL

The Day

It's amazing
the day is still here
like lightning on an open field,
terra firma and transient
swimming in variation,
fresh as when man first broke
like the crocus all over the earth.

From a train, we saw cows
strung out on a hill
at differing heights,
one sex, one herd,
replicas in hierarchy –
the sun had turned
them noonday bright.

They were child's daubs in a book
I read before I could read.

They fly by like a train window:
flash-in-the-pan moments
of the Great Day,
the *dies illa*,
when we lived momently
together forever
in love with our nature –

as if in the end,
in the marriage with nothingness,
we could ever escape
being absolutely safe.

RICHARD EBERHART

The Eclipse

I stood out in the open cold
To see the essence of the eclipse
Which was its perfect darkness.

I stood in the cold on the porch
And could not think of anything so perfect
As man's hope of light in the face of darkness.

KATHLEEN RAINE

Self

Who am I, who
Speaks from the dust,
Who looks from the clay?

Who hears
For the mute stone,
For fragile water feels
With finger and bone?

Who for the forest breathes the evening,
Sees for the rose,
Who knows
What the bird sings?

Who am I, who for the sun fears
The demon dark,
In order holds
Atom and chaos?

Who out of nothingness has gazed
On the beloved face?

KATHLEEN RAINE

Night Sky

There came such clear opening of the night sky,
The deep glass of wonders, the dark mind
In unclouded gaze of the abyss
Opened like the expression of a face.
I looked into that clarity where all things are
End and beginning, and saw
My destiny there: 'So', I said, 'no other
'Was possible ever. This
'Is I. The pattern stands so for ever.'

What am I? Bound and bounded,
A pattern among the stars, a point in motion
Tracing my way. I am my way: it is I
I travel among the wonders.
Held in that gaze and known
In the eye of the abyss,
'Let it be so', I said,
And my heart laughed with joy
To know the death I must die.

KATHLEEN RAINE

Natura Naturans

Veil upon veil
Petal and shell and scale
The dancer of the whirling dance lets fall.

Visible veils the invisible
Reveal, conceal
In bodies that most resemble
The fleeting mind of nature never still.

A young princess
Sealed in the perfect signature of what she was
With her grave lips of silent dust imparts a mystery
Hidden two thousand years under the Appian Way.

A frond in the coal,
An angel traced upon a crumbling wall,
Empty chrysalids of that bright ephemerid the soul.

KATHLEEN RAINE

To the Sun

1

Sun, great giver of all that is,
Once more I return from dream to your times and places
As geese wing over London in this morning's dawn
Before the human city invades your immaculate spaces.
Sun, greatest of givers, your speeding rays
Weave again familiar quotidian things, epiphanies
Of trees, leaves, wings, jewelled rain, shining wonders.
Your golden mask covers the unknown
Presence of the awakener of all eyes
On whose blinding darkness none can gaze.
Clouds and hills and gardens and forests and seas,
High-rise buildings, dust and ordure, derelict and broken things
Receive alike from holiest, purest source
Meaning and being, messages each morning brings
To this threshold where I am.
Old, I marvel that I have been, have seen
Your everything and nothing realm, all-giving sun.

2

How address you, greatest of givers,
God, angel, these words served once, but no longer
Apollo's chariot or Surya's horses imaged in stone
Of Konarak, glorious metaphor of the advancing power
Of the unwearied sun from the eternal East. My time
Has other symbols, speeding light waves, light-years, rays
Cycling for ever the boundless sphere of space,
Vast emptiness of what is or is not,
Unsolid matter's equivocal seeming –
Science only another grandiose myth we have dreamed,
Ptolemaic or Copernican, or Einstein's paradigm
Less real than those magnificent stone horses
As light triumphs over darkness for yet one more day.
But no myth, as before our eyes you are, or seem!
In your numinous glory I have seen you rise
From beyond the Farne Isles casting your brilliance
Over cold northern seas, or over the seas of Greece,
Have seen your great rim rising from India's ocean.
As you circle the earth birds sing your approach each morning,
New flowers open in wilderness, gardens, waste-places,

All life your retinue, as before all eyes you summon,
Greatest of givers, your heavens outspread
Our earth's vast and minute spaces, to each the whole,
And today I receive yet again from your inexhaustible treasury
Of light, this room, this green garden, my boundless universe.

3

Ancestral sun, do you remember us,
Children of light, who behold you with living eyes?
Are we as you, are you as we? It seems
As if you look down on us with living face:
Who am I who see your light but the light I see,
Held for a moment in the form I wear, your beams.

I have stood on shores of many seas,
Of lakes and rivers, and always over the waters,
Across those drowning gulphs of fear
Your golden path has come to me
Who am but one among all who depart and return.

Blinding sun, with your corona of flames, your chasms of fire,
Presence, terrible theophany,
Am I in you, are you in me,
Infinite centre of your unbounded realm
Whose multitudes sing Holy, Holy, Holy?
Do you go into the dark, or I?

4

Not that light is holy, but that the holy is the light –
Only by seeing, by being, we know,
Rapt, breath stilled, bliss of the heart.
No microscope nor telescope can discover
The immeasurable: not in the seen but in the seer
Epiphany of the commonplace.
A hyacinth in a glass it was, on my working-table,
Before my eyes opened beyond beauty light's pure living flow.
'It is I', I knew, 'I am that flower, that light is I,
'Both seer and sight'.
Long ago, but for ever; for none can un-know
Native Paradise in every blade of grass.
Pebble, and particle of dust, immaculate.
'It has been so and will be always', I knew,

KATHLEEN RAINE

The World

It burns in the void,
Nothing upholds it.
Still it travels.

Travelling the void
Upheld by burning
Nothing is still

Burning it travels.
The void upholds it.
Still it is nothing.

Nothing it travels
A burning void
Upheld by stillness.

STEVIE SMITH

The Airy Christ

(After reading Dr Rieu's translation of St Mark's Gospel)

Who is this that comes in splendour, coming from the blazing East?
This is he we had not thought of, this is he the airy Christ.

Airy, in an airy manner in an airy parkland, walking,
Others take him by the hand, lead him, do the talking.

But the Form, the airy One, frowns an airy frown,
What they say he knows must be, but he looks aloofly down,

Looks aloofly at his feet, looks aloofly at his hands,
Knows they must, as prophets say, nailèd be to wooden bands.

As he knows the words he sings, that he sings so happily
Must be changed to working laws, yet sings he ceaselessly.

Those who truly hear the voice, the words, the happy song,
Never shall need working laws to keep from doing wrong.

Deaf men will pretend sometimes they hear the song, the words,
And make excuse to sin extremely; this will be absurd.

Heed it not. Whatever foolish men may do the song is cried
For those who hear, and the sweet singer does not care that he
   was crucified.

For he does not wish that men should love him more than anything
Because he died; he only wishes they would hear him sing.

RICHARD WILBUR

Mind

Mind in its purest play is like some bat
That beats about in caverns all alone,
Contriving by a kind of senseless wit
Not to conclude against a wall of stone.

It has no need to falter or explore;
Darkly it knows what obstacles are there,
And so may weave and flitter, dip and soar
In perfect courses through the blackest air.

And has this simile a like perfection?
The mind is like a bat. Precisely. Save
That in the very happiest intellection
A graceful error may correct the cave.

JOHN GILLESPIE MAGEE JR

High Flight

Oh! I have slipped the surly bonds of Earth
And danced the skies on laughter-silvered wings;
Sunward I've climbed, and joined the tumbling mirth
Of sun-split clouds – and done a hundred things
You have not dreamed of – wheeled and soared and swung
High in the sunlit silence. Hov'ring there,
I've chased the shouting wind along, and flung
My eager craft through footless halls of air . . .
Up, up the long, delirious, burning blue
I've topped the wind-swept heights with easy grace.
Where never lark, or even eagle, flew;
And, while with silent, lifting mind I've trod
The high untrespassed sanctity of space,
Put out my hand, and touched the feet of God.

ROBERT BLY

Waking from Sleep

Inside the veins there are navies setting forth,
Tiny explosions at the water lines,
And seagulls weaving in the wind of the salty blood.

It is the morning. The country has slept the whole winter.
Window seats were covered with fur skins, the yard was full
Of stiff dogs, and hands that clumsily held heavy books.

Now we wake, and rise from bed, and eat breakfast! –
Shouts rise from the harbor of the blood,
Mist, and masts rising, the knock of wooden tackle in the sunlight.

Now we sing, and do tiny dances on the kitchen floor.
Our whole body is like a harbor at dawn;
We know that our master has left us for the day.

ARTHUR OSBORNE

Arunachala[1]

I sought to devour Thee;
Come now and devour me,
Then there will be peace, Arunachala

You bade me give all for you –
Take now the giver too,
Survive alone, Arunachala!

Let now the deception end.
There was no lover or friend
Apart from Thyself, Arunachala!

Now that at last I know
All this a magic show,
Let it dissolve in Thee, Arunachala!

[1] Red Mountain (lit): a symbol of the blissful self in Southern Shivaism.

ARTHUR OSBORNE

Be Still

Thou art? – I am? – Why argue? – Being is.
Keep still and be. Death will not still the mind.
Nor argument, nor hopes of after-death.
This world the battle-ground, yourself the foe
Yourself must master. Eager the mind to seek.
Yet oft astray, causing its own distress
Then crying for relief, as though some God
Barred from it jealously the Bliss it sought
But would not face.

Till in the end,
All battles fought, all earthly loves abjured,
Dawn in the East, there is no other way
But to be still. In stillness then to find
The giants all were windmills, all the strife
Self-made, unreal; even he that strove
A fancied being, as when that good knight
Woke from delirium and with a loud cry
Rendered his soul to God.

Mind, then, or soul?
Break free from subtle words. Only be still,
Lay down the mind, submit, and Being then
Is Bliss, Bliss Consciousness: and That you are.

ARTHUR OSBORNE

The Dance

Away, away!
Into the sky I dance!
Bending, swaying lightfoot leaping,
Tireless staying, rhythm keeping,
Up in the air!
The rhythm and sway
Now here, now there!
Swift and smooth as a maiden's glance,
I sway and I glide
And nimbly I ride,

With never a care,
As inly I throb to the cosmic tide:
No outer step, no body stride.
Thus the rhythm keeps its track
In a stiff old body with arthritic back.

ARTHUR OSBORNE

Death

'He hath revenge on Death, for he died well,'
A poet wrote in life's far distant spring,
Stumbling on truth. Death's fabled heaven and hell
And drearier prospect yet the new times brings
Of a blank nothingness hedge like a ring
The seeming self whose lifelong passing bell
Tolls in his ears, although the mind may cling
To fragile hopes the gathering years dispel.

But 'Die before you die' the Prophet said:
Give up the seeming self that from the world
Falls into death; remains that Self instead
Wherein earth, heaven and hell like dreams are furled.

The world in you, not you in it, has died,
For That you are and nothing else beside.

ARTHUR OSBORNE

The Few

No argument can pierce the shuttered mind.
Let truth shine forth resplendent as the sun,
Still, crouched in their dark corner, will they find
Some guttering candle till life's day be done.
Even though we sang like angels in their ear
    They would not hear.

Those only in whose heart some inkling dwells,
Grown over though it be, crushed down, denied,
Will greet the pealing of the golden bells
And welcome truth when all around deride.
Yet sight has laid a debt upon their will
    Not all fulfil.

For even of those who see, only a few
Will have the intrepid wisdom to arise
And barter time's false values for the true,
Making their life a valiant enterprise
To vindicate their heritage long lost,
    Nor count the cost.

And out of that so noble fellowship
Questing the Grail upon the mountain peaks,
Well is it if it meet the expectant lip
Of even one persistently who seeks.
Yet is this quest the glory and the goal
    Of the awakened soul.

ANGELA MORGAN

Work

A Song of Triumph

Work!
Thank God for the might of it,
The ardour, the urge, the delight of it –
Work that springs from the heart's desire,
Setting the brain and the soul on fire –
Oh, what is so good as the heat of it,
And what is so glad as the beat of it,
And what is so kind as the stern command,
Challenging brain and heart and hand?

Work!
Thank God for the pride of it,
For the beautiful, conquering tide of it,
Sweeping the life in its furious flood,
Thrilling the arteries, cleansing the blood,
Mastering stupor and dull despair,
Moving the dreamer to do and dare.
Oh, what is so good as the urge of it,
And what is so glad as the surge of it,
And what is so strong as the summons deep,
Rousing the torpid soul from sleep?

Work!
Thank God for the pace of it,
For the terrible, keen, swift race of it;
Fiery steeds in full control,
Nostrils a-quiver to greet the goal.
Work, the Power that drives behind,
Guiding the purposes, taming the mind,
Holding the runaway wishes back,
Reining the will to one steady track,
Speeding the energies faster, faster,
Triumphing over disaster.
Oh, what is so good as the pain of it,
And what is so great as the gain of it?
And what is so kind as the cruel goad,
Forcing us on through the rugged road?

Work!
Thank God for the swing of it,
For the clamouring, hammering ring of it,
Passion and labour daily hurled
On the mighty anvils of the world.
Oh, what is so fierce as the flame of it?
And what is so huge as the aim of it?
Thundering on through dearth and doubt,
Calling the plan of the Maker out.
Work, the Titan; Work, the friend,
Shaping the earth to a glorious end,
Draining the swamps and blasting the hills,
Doing whatever the Spirit wills –

Rending a continent apart,
To answer the dream of the Master heart.
Thank God for a world where none may shirk –
Thank God for the splendour of work!

R S THOMAS

Kyrie

From Mass for Hard Times

Because we cannot be clever and honest
and are inventors of things more intricate
than the snowflake – Lord have mercy.

Because we are full of pride
in our humility, and because we believe
in our disbelief – Lord have mercy.

Because we will protect ourselves
from ourselves to the point
of destroying ourselves – Lord have mercy.

And because on the slope to perfection,
when we should be half-way up,
we are half-way down – Lord have mercy.

R S THOMAS

Sure

Where the lamb died
a bird sings.
Where a soul perishes
what music? The cross

is an old-fashioned
weapon, but its bow
is drawn unerringly
against the heart.

R S THOMAS

Target

I look up at the sky at night
and see the archer, Sagittarius,
with his bow drawn, and realise
man is the arrow speeding,

not as some think infinitely
on, but because space is curved,
backwards towards the bowman's heart
to deal him his unstanched wound.

SYLVIA PLATH

Black Rook in Rainy Weather

On the stiff twig up there
Hunches a wet black rook
Arranging and rearranging its feathers in the rain.
I do not expect miracle
Or an accident

To set the sight on fire
In my eye, nor seek
Any more in the desultory weather some design,
But let spotted leaves fall as they fall,
Without ceremony, or portent.

Although, I admit, I desire,
Occasionally, some backtalk
From the mute sky, I can't honestly complain:
A certain minor light may still
Leap incandescent

Out of kitchen table or chair
As if a celestial burning took
Possession of the most obtuse objects now and then –
Thus hallowing an interval
Otherwise inconsequent

By bestowing largesse, honour,
One might say love. At any rate, I now walk
Wary (for it could happen
Even in this dull, ruinous landscape); sceptical,
Yet politic; ignorant

Of whatever angel may choose to flare
Suddenly at my elbow. I only know that a rook
Ordering its black feathers can so shine
As to seize my senses, haul
My eyelids up, and grant

A brief respite from fear
Of total neutrality. With luck,
Trekking stubborn through this season
Of fatigue, I shall
Patch together a content

Of sorts. Miracles occur,
If you care to call those spasmodic
Tricks of radiance miracles. The wait's begun again,
The long wait for the angel,
For that rare, random descent.

HAROLD MORLAND

For Kathleen

I saw a hawk in the air. Its wings
Were still.
               And the lark that sings
As it climbs God's stair
Dropped like a stone.
                   Suddenly alone
With the breathing hills around
I needed a sound.
               I wanted to hear
A human echo. And you came
So quietly that the hawk seemed tame
And I listened to the ladybird's rustle
On the hairy leaf.
               So infinitely small
Yet all.

HAROLD MORLAND

From The Unquenchable Fire

If God is infinite
unlimited in time and space
and nearest universal Light,
must I not be as infinite-in-variety
to all these scattered minds
– being pole, or zenith, tangent to a thought
and all these things at once –
but centre only to myself?
Dear God, allow me Your infinity
and I am all in multitude
but not coherent,
one,

a cloud of finities to every seeing mind
in all the limits of this world and life?
For if I make myself God's centre
I with my own point of thought
encompass Him,
describe and circumscribe
His boundaries no matter where
if He be still the matter . . .

And this ignorance is truth,
this little-everything my all
that sees Him whole;
for even the sum of all men's God
is mere appearance.
God made manifest
is God defined,
a local truth,
            and being in time
is the history of prayer.

HAROLD MORLAND

From The Elements of Life

'. . . when each single atom
                breaks
and returns
to the primal energy from which it sprang,
till creation come again
                and the ultimate darkness
is pricked with a first, new spark of light
that dies in the looking
                and another. Then another.
I have been waiting.'
    Then his laughter broke. 'Look,' he said,
'the ants.'
            A long procession,
workers, soldiers, and those that would be queens
filed across the floor.
    'Why do you laugh at the ants?'
    'Not ants, great King of the Gods. All these are Indras.
In their human life they worked and worshipped,
and one with so much zeal he was translated

and became a spirit of the air,
a god. Then Indra.
But even the gods have frailties
one after another
and his soul
became no bigger than the soul an ant can use
to trudge or scurry
living on corruption.
These are Indras, every one.
Would you wish to count them?'

'What then must I do?'
The Boy replied, 'You must always
answer your own question.
And if no great meteor blinds the sky,
why not kindle a taper?'

. . .

'A man must live in the holiness of delight,
and delight is ritual
                    and art is liturgy
that may not scorn the least of human minutes
which manifest the only light from heaven
our human eye can see,
our sole reflection of eternity.
    And yet the terror is we know
we never know eternity,
and ever move towards the ultimate light
in deeper darkness.'
    Hari closed the book.
'The tumult of this flesh,' he said,
'may be the body's wisdom of itself.'

A E I FALCONAR

Diving

In meditation it is possible to dive –
deeper and deeper into the mind
to a place where there is no disturbance
and there is absolute solitude.
It is at this point in the profound stillness
that the sound of the mind can be heard.
It is like the sea breaking on a far off reef,

and it lulls the being into extreme calm.
Like the sea it is a music primeval
and here is no storm,
only the silken waves soughing.
When I listen to the sound of this sea,
I sense that I am a voyager
and this sound is a wind
in the sails of a ship.
But this sound is not of this world
for other sounds are heard distinctly
and cause this sound to die –,
though it returns with the silence.
Sometimes I think it as a transcendent sound –
which speaks of unknown powers,
of cosmic storms and sun winds
sighing in the brain.
This is no earthly voyage,
and I see visions of ships that sail on no earthly sea.
Our ships sail on upon a silent sea;
no wind, there is no sound
but we move on.

ALLEN GINSBERG

Sunflower Sutra

I walked on the banks of the tincan banana dock and sat down under
the huge shade of a Southern Pacific locomotive to look at the
sunset over the box house hills and cry.

Jack Kerouac sat beside me on a busted rusty iron pole, companion, we
thought the same thoughts of the soul, bleak and blue and sad-eyed,
surrounded by the gnarled steel roots of trees of machinery.

The oily water on the river mirrored the red sky, sun sank on top of
final Frisco peaks, no fish in that stream, no hermit in those mounts,
just ourselves rheumy-eyed and hung-over like old bums on the
riverbank, tired and wily.

Look at the Sunflower, he said, there was a dead gray shadow against
the sky, big as a man, sitting dry on top of a pile of ancient sawdust –

– I rushed up enchanted – it was my first sunflower, memories of Blake
– my visions – Harlem

and Hells of the Eastern rivers, bridges clanking Joes Greasy Sand-
wiches, dead baby carriages, black treadless tires forgotten and
unretreaded, the poem of the riverbank, condoms & pots, steel
knives, nothing stainless, only the dank muck and the razor-sharp
artifacts passing into the past –

and the gray Sunflower poised against the sunset, crackly bleak and
dusty with the smut and smog and smoke of olden locomotives in its
eye –

corolla of bleary spikes pushed down and broken like a battered crown,
seeds fallen out of its face, soon-to-be-toothless mouth of sunny air,
sunrays obliterated on its hairy head like a dried wire spiderweb,

leaves stuck out like arms out of the stem, gestures from the sawdust
root, broke pieces of plaster fallen out of the black twigs, a dead fly in
its ear,

Unholy battered old thing you were, my sunflower O my soul, I loved
you then!

The grime was no man's grime but death and human locomotives,

all that dress of dust, that veil of darkened railroad skin, that smog of
cheek, that eyelid of black mis'ry, that sooty hand or phallus or
protuberance of artificial worse-than-dirt – industrial – modern – all
that civilization spotting your crazy golden crown –

and those blear thoughts of death and dusty loveless eyes and ends
and withered roots below, in the home-pile of sand and sawdust,
rubber dollar bills, skin of machinery, the guts and innards of the
weeping coughing car, the empty lonely tincans with their rusty
tongues slack, what more could I name, the smoked ashes of some
cock cigar, the cunts of wheelbarrows and the milky breasts of cars,
wornout asses out of chairs & sphincters of dynamos – all these

entangled in your mummied roots – and you there standing before me
in the sunset, all your glory in your form!

A perfect beauty of a sunflower! a perfect excellent lovely sunflower
existence! a sweet natural eye to the new hip moon, woke up alive and
excited grasping in the sunset shadow sunrise golden monthly breeze!

How many flies buzzed round you innocent of your grime, while you
cursed the heavens of the railroad and your flower soul?

Poor dead flower? when did you forget you were a flower! when did
you look at your skin and decide you were an impotent dirty old
locomotive? the ghost of a locomotive? the specter and shade of a
once powerful mad American locomotive?

You were never no locomotive, Sunflower, you were a sunflower!

And you Locomotive, you are a locomotive, forget me not!

So I grabbed up the skeleton thick sunflower and stuck it at my side
like a scepter,

and deliver my sermon to my soul, and Jack's soul too, and anyone
who'll listen,

– We're not our skin of grime, we're not our dread bleak dusty image-
less locomotives, we're all golden sunflowers inside, blessed by our
own seed & hairy naked accomplishment-bodies growing into mad
black formal sunflowers in the sunset, spied on by our eyes under
the shadow of the mad locomotive riverbank sunset Frisco hilly
tincan evening sitdown vision.

BUSINESS REPLY MAIL
FIRST-CLASS MAIL PERMIT NO. 11 ROCKPORT MA

POSTAGE WILL BE PAID BY ADDRESSEE

Element Books
**PO BOX 830
ROCKPORT MA 01966-9930**

**BUSINESS REPLY SERVICE
LICENCE NO SA386**

ELEMENT BOOKS LIMITED
LONGMEAD
SHAFTESBURY
DORSET SP7 8BR

MARK STRAND

The Coming of Light

Even this late it happens:
the coming of love, the coming of light.
You wake and the candles are lit as if by themselves,
stars gather, dreams pour into your pillows,
sending up warm bouquets of air.
Even this late the bones of the body shine
and tomorrow's dust flares into breath.

MARK STRAND

Keeping Things Whole

In a field
I am the absence
of field.
This is
always the case.
Wherever I am
I am what is missing.

When I walk
I part the air
and always
the air moves in
to fill the spaces
where my body's been.

We all have reasons
for moving.
I move
to keep things whole.

The Child

Sometimes it is inconceivable that I should be the age I am
Almost always it is at a dry point in the afternoon
I cannot remember what
I am waiting for and in my astonishment I
Can hear the blood crawling over the plains
Hurrying on to arrive before dark
I try to remember my faults to make sure
One after the other but it is never
Satisfactory the list is never complete

At times night occurs to me so that I think I have been
Struck from behind I remain perfectly
Still feigning death listening for the
Assailant perhaps at last
I even sleep a little for later I have moved
I open my eyes the lanternfish have gone home in darkness
On all sides the silence is unharmed
I remember but I feel no bruise

Then there are the stories and after a while I think something
Else must connect them besides just this me
I regard myself starting the search turning
Corners in remembered metropoli
I pass skins withering in gardens that I see now
Are not familiar
And I have lost even the thread I thought I had

If I could be consistent even in destitution
The world would be revealed
While I can try to repeat what I believe
Creatures spirits not this posture
I do not believe in knowledge as we know it
But I forget

This silence coming at intervals out of the shell of names
It must be all one person really coming at
Different hours for the same thing
If I could learn the word for yes it could teach me questions
I would see that it was itself every time and I would
Remember to say take it up like a hand
And go with it this is at last
Yourself

The child that will lead you

MICHAEL DILLON

Sonnet on a Sleeping World

Awake and yet asleep! The whole world lies
Unconscious of its own unconscious state;
Destructive of itself and blind to fate,
Ignoring all the warnings of the wise.
For here and there a man may waken, rise,
Shake off the shackles ere it be too late,
His mind to master, anger, greed and hate
Drive out and penetrate the veiled guise
Of man mechanical – his nature true –
Which he perceives, his helplessness he knows;
All others cling to dreams that they can do
Whate'er they will – themselves mere puppet shows,
Their strings worked by events, nor do they heed
The call to rouse as slaves from fetters freed.

MICHAEL DILLON

Happiness

E'en as the butterfly upon a twig
Forestalls the hunter's net and flits away,
Alighting on a leaf beyond his grasp,
Until the hunter, scratched and labouring, climbs,
The net once more aloft and ready to descend –
Too late again, the butterfly is gone!
So man pursues what he deems Happiness,
Elusive, hov'ring, always out of reach,
A wisp of light that acts as a decoy
To lure men to the fens of discontent
Which suck them down in unfulfilled desires,
The lust for luxury and ease of life
Which they mistake for happiness of mind.
Yet in the world this lesson has been taught
Through all the years by those whom Heaven sent:
Desires breed desires, when from them free
Man only then becomes what Man should be.

MICHAEL DILLON

Who Is I?

1

So diligent in search, no stone unturned,
He strove to find the Truth for which he yearned;
And when at last a Teacher he descried:
'I want to know' . . . 'I have long sought' . . . he cried,
'I heard some say' . . . 'I read somewhere of this . . .'
'I long to find the path to perfect bliss . . .'
Amid the clamour loud the Teacher gave a sigh,
Then quietly he asked the question: 'Who is I?'

2

The speaker stopped and gaped a moment, then
He thumped his chest and raised his voice again:
'I am Aloysius Smith, from far I come,
'I left my family and friends and home,
'I search for Truth; this pearl of price I seek,
'If you can help I beg you now to speak.'
He paused and in the hush there came a second sigh,
Again he heard the quiet question: 'Who is I?'

3

His parted lips this time no sound came through,
At last his teeming brain had caught the clue;
He dropped his eyes before the Teacher's gaze,
His hands hung limp, no longer could he raise
His head, but sank upon one knee, bowed low,
As one who had received a stunning blow.
His pride was pierced, he gave a heartfelt sigh
And, softly speaking, said: 'Sir, show me, who is I?'

MICHAEL DILLON

Old Wineskins

How hard it is for narrow-visioned man
To break away from long-held, fond ideas,
To overthrow the teachings of his youth,
To burst asunder Personality
And launch himself upon the Sea of Truth,
And walk upon the waters, free of fears,

Aware this is the only way he can
Make any progress in the realm of Thought,
Or open up the channels of the mind,
At present blocked by so much wordly lore,
By prejudice, convention and the rest
That education and example store
In him with precepts, all which make him blind
And hide from him the fact of knowing naught.

MICHAEL DILLON

Atonement

Not for the faint of heart the search for Truth,
Not for the weak of will or dull intent;
Beset with troubles from the very start,
Pulled back by shackles, torn apart by doubts,
Until from perseverance, from the dark
A tiny ray of light shines down the Way,
To show a single step ahead – no more.
And if the eyes by then are not too blind,
By lengthy struggle with the written word;
And if the ears at last are not too deaf,
From listening to the sounds of argument;
And if the teeming brain is not too dulled
To grasp the Truth, so long and hardly sought;
Then all materialism falls in place,
A true perspective of the world is grasped,
Where earthly lusts and wants no longer count
For more than they are worth, in proper place;
All merged together in the true Desire
Which rises over all and with it brings
The sense of Happiness, because the feet
Are set upon the rightful Way to God,
To reach At-onement with the Trinity
Of Beauty, Truth and Love eternally.

MICHAEL DILLON

Adversity

Look in, not out! So seek we not to blame
Another for our anger, grief or shame.
It matters not how much we have been tried,
By no event can we be justified.
While we may feel some cause for what we do,
We have a Right NOT to be wrathful, too.
This Right is one that few can realise
And fewer still will try to exercise.
How strange it is we like to feel abused,
In pity of ourselves so hardly used!
A pleasure false which cunningly deludes
And chance of real happiness precludes;
Were we but willing just to pay the price
And this, our suffering, to sacrifice,
No longer like to feel mistreated so,
Immeasurably in stature we would grow:
No brooding on our wrongs, no inner strife,
We would be Masters of ourselves – and Life.

MICHAEL DILLON

Reincarnation

Can any think this is the end of all,
That this one life determines each his fate,
That deeds of violence, thoughts so full of hate
And all the wickedness that from the Fall
Of Man hath filled the world with bitter gall,
With pain and suffering – the common state
Throughout mankind which years cannot abate
One whit – that from such depths is no recall,
No chance that by experience each may learn
And live again to test himself anew,
Correct mistakes, or fail to discern
The error of his ways or lusts subdue?
Must life on life not come ere we can win
To Perfect Good, or sink beneath our Sin?

TED HUGHES
Fire-Eater

Those stars are the fleshed forebears
Of these dark hills, bowed like labourers,

And of my blood.

The death of a gnat is a star's mouth: its skin,
Like Mary's or Semele's, thin

As the skin of fire:
A star fell on her, a sun devoured her.

My appetite is good
Now to manage both Orion and Dog

With a mouthful of earth, my staple.
Worm-sort, root-sort, going where it is profitable.

A star pierces the slug,

The tree is caught up in the constellations.
My skull burrows among antennae and fronds.

TED HUGHES
Crag Jack's Apostasy

The churches, lord, all the dark churches
Stooped over my cradle once:
I came clear, but my god's down
Under the weight of all that stone:
Both my power and my luck since
Have kicked at the world and slept in ditches.

I do not desire to change my ways,
But now call continually
On you, god or not god, who
Come to my sleeping body through
The world under the world; pray
That I may see more than your eyes

In an animal's dreamed head; that I shall –
Waking, dragged suddenly
From a choir-shaken height
By the world, lord, and its dayfall –
Keep more than the memory
Of a wolf's head, of eagles' feet.

TED HUGHES

The Perfect Forms

Here is Socrates, born under Pisces,
Smiling, complacent as a phallus,
Or Buddha, whose one thought fills immensity:

Visage of Priapus: the undying tail-swinging
Stupidity of the donkey
That carries Christ. How carefully he nurses

This six-day abortion of the Absolute –
No better for the fosterings
Of fish, reptile and tree-leaper throughout

Their ages of Godforsaken darkness –
This monstrous-headed difficult child!
Of such is the kingdom of heaven.

SEAMUS HEANEY

From Seeing Things

II

Claritas. The dry-eyed Latin word
Is perfect for the carved stone of the water
Where Jesus stands up to his unwet knees
And John the Baptist pours out more water
Over his head: all this in bright sunlight
On the façade of a cathedral. Lines
Hard and thin and sinuous represent
The flowing river. Down between the lines
Little antic fish are all go. Nothing else.

And yet in that utter visibility
The stone's alive with what's invisible:
Waterweed, stirred sand-grains hurrying off,
The shadowy, unshadowed stream itself.
All afternoon, heat wavered on the steps
And the air we stood up to our eyes in wavered
Like the zig-zag hieroglyph for life itself.

SEAMUS HEANEY

From Lightenings

viii

The annals say: when the monks of Clonmacnoise
Were all at prayers inside the oratory
A ship appeared above them in the air.

The anchor dragged along behind so deep
It hooked itself into the altar rails
And then, as the big hull rocked to a standstill,

A crewman shinned and grappled down the rope
And struggled to release it. But in vain.
'This man can't bear our life here and will drown,'

The abbot said, 'unless we help him.' So
They did, the freed ship sailed, and the man climbed back
Out of the marvellous as he had known it.

xii

And lightening? One meaning of that
Beyond the usual sense of alleviation,
Illumination, and so on, is this:

A phenomenal instant when the spirit flares
With pure exhilaration before death –
The good thief in us harking to the promise!

So paint him on Christ's right hand, on a promontory
Scanning empty space, so body-racked he seems
Untranslatable into the bliss

Ached for at the moon-rim of his forehead,
By nail-craters on the dark side of his brain:
This day thou shalt be with Me in Paradise.

SEAMUS HEANEY

From Squarings

xxxvii

In famous poems by the sage Han Shan,
Cold Mountain is a place that can also mean
A state of mind. Or different states of mind

At different times, for the poems seem
One-off, impulsive, the kind of thing that starts
I have sat here facing the Cold Mountain

For twenty-nine years, or *There is no path*
That goes all the way – enviable stuff,
Unfussy and believable.

Talking about it isn't good enough
But quoting from it at least demonstrates
The virtue of an art that knows its mind.

SEAMUS HEANEY

From Settings

xxiv

Deserted harbour stillness. Every stone
Clarified and dormant under water,
The harbour wall a masonry of silence.

Fullness. Shimmer. Laden high Atlantic
The moorings barely stirred in, very slight
Clucking of the swell against boat boards.

Perfected vision: cockle minarets
Consigned down there with green-slicked bottle glass,
Shell-debris and a reddened bud of sandstone.

Air and ocean known as antecedents
Of each other. In apposition with
Omnipresence, equilibrium, brim.

ROBERT GOSLIN

Brahman

I sought Thee in the timeless halls of space
I sought Thee in the spaceless halls of time
But found that time and space do not exist.
I wondered 'Who am I?' and 'Who art Thou?'
And then I found Thee. Thou in me and I in Thee.
'Twas then I knew that I do not exist.
For I am nothing; yet am everything
For evermore . . . and so we cannot die.

ROBERT GOSLIN

Advaita

When you have calmed the furies of the mind
Forgotten greed and all ambition's snare;
When you have banished all intruding thought
And scotched the Ego lurking in its lair;
When you have come to nothing and seek nought
But less than nothing – in your earthly quest,
You will be ALL at last – and more than nothing,
For nothing will be more than all the rest.

ROBERT GOSLIN

Atman

Never dare presume to say,
'I am This' or 'I am That.'
'I did This' or 'I did That.'
Better lay claim to nothing.
All the gifts you have are lent,
Subtle, rare, and transient.
Fostered in an earthly shell.
For you, yourself, are nothing
But extension of the Light,
Which emanates from Oneness,
And is screened from human sight;
But when your shell is broken
And your light returns to source
To bask in warmth eternal,
You will know yourself at last.

ROBERT GOSLIN
Stillness

Tormented friend, why do you still enquire
And thirst to know the sum of things entire?
The more you strive, the less you will succeed;
The mind cannot fulfil the spirit's need.
Striving too hard begets a troubled mind
And those who strive will always stay confined.
For you are not the body, not the mind
But LIGHT IMMORTAL, mortally enshrined.

So live in bliss – enjoy the simple task;
Seek not to know, and do not dare to ask
Why you are here, or what your fate will be.
Be still and listen to the symphony
Which your surroundings play in unity.
The part cannot exist without the whole;
The whole cannot exist without the part;
And reason has no place in cosmic art.

When stillness reigns, you are the sum of things;
The Nothing and the All that Oneness brings.
When stillness reigns, you are Infinity
And sense the nearness of Divinity.
Just as the pigeon navigates in flight
And homeward speeds before a hint of night;
So too, the soul, will homeward soar one day
Without a mind to guide it on its way.

ZBIGNIEW HERBERT (*trans* Czeslaw Milosz)
Revelation

Two perhaps three
times
I was sure
I would touch the essence
and would know

the web of my formula
made of allusions as in the Phaedo
had also the rigour
of Heisenberg's equation

I was sitting immobile
with watery eyes
I felt my backbone
fill with quiet certitude

earth stood still
heaven stood still
my immobility
was nearly perfect

the postman rang
I had to pour out the dirty water
prepare tea

Siva lifted his finger
the furniture of heaven and earth
started to spin again

I returned to my room
where is that perfect peace
the idea of a glass
was being spilled all over the table

I sat down immobile
with watery eyes
filled with emptiness
i.e. with desire

If it happens to me once more
I shall be moved neither by the postman's bell
nor by the shouting of angels

I shall sit
immobile
my eyes fixed
upon the heart of things

a dead star

a black drop of infinity

OLEG MOGILEVER (*trans* Nadhia Sutara)

Inquiry into the 'I'

A Garland of Sonnets

I

In the Cave of the Heart dwells the True I,
The Source of glory, abiding eternally –
Immortal, limitless Dawn,
The call of the Eternal, the joy of humanity.

Here are destroyed the illusions of existence
In the baring of the Ultimate Truth –
All that is false is consumed in It.
Marvellous is the shift from 'I' to I.

When the star of personality arises,
With 'me' and 'mine' repeating incessantly,
Then the Source of Being can be traced.

Nature, Knowledge, Bliss:
Onto the Path, Adept!
Pursue the Self, knowing that Its legacy
Radiates alone with a subtle Light.

II

Radiating alone with a subtle Light
Is HE – the Atman – concealed by the trinity of bodies . . .
Fearless, dispassionate, beyond reproach.
Permanent is the victory of the one who attains Him.

–'That great Healing, is it far off?' –
–'Avert thy gaze from outer affairs,
Turn thy longing eye within –
That healing frontier eternally awaits thee:

'Where the Goal is inestimable, and Totality the only Substance;
In the flaming Cave ends the Way,
Where complete is the deliverance from bondage.

'When the Light alone absorbs all diversity,
And all dualities resolve,
That single Essence shines forth without defect.'

III

Its Essence shining forth without defect,
It welcomes home the seeker –
The unbroken thread from age to age,
Bestowed through the Wisdom Eternal.

O, Reality! Source and Substance of the Stream of Life Divine!
O, imperishable seed of perishable life!
O, THOU, the ruling depths within,
Everything is only THEE, everywhere THEE Alone!

O, grant Thou the strength to renounce the glitter of the world,
To cast aside the ever-arising *vasanas*,
To free from the body the feeling of Thee – the I!

To THEE I hasten, to my Self – to the refuge of the Heart –
To discern my Self in THEE, eternally subsistent:
Blissful Consciousness of Being.

IV

Blissful Consciousness of Being,
Sat-Chit-Ananda – Triune Oneness,
Gift of Wisdom in the death of self,
The draught that grants resurrection.

O, Being of the Eternal Flame
That burns with the stillness of the Primal Cause,
That pulsates with the breath of 'I-I' –
Thou art Thyself . . . Where art Thou, my birthright, my heritage?!

Arming myself with the Guru's Covenant –
Holy Ramana, like unto the Light of the World –
I set off on the Quest, my begging bowl full to the brim with Him.

This immemorial calling is unattainable
So long as the One is not realised:
Brahman is the sole Reality – THAT is the Truth itself.

V

Brahman is the sole Reality – THAT is the Truth Itself,
Bottomless abysses beyond all sounding,
The countless names and forms of creation,
Are but a mere deception in the universal Mist.

'Everything is THAT, everything is THAT' – here is the passage
    across the Fog.
'Who am I? Who am I?' – here is the sword that cuts through
    the shadows.
And 'THAT – WHICH – IS' shall arise and consume thee,
Alone, without another, without a mind . . .

O, Radiance! Eternally youthful moment
O, Ocean that knows no shore!
One and one only!
Into which all the rivers shall merge!

And the rest – is it a grand Joke or a Game?
Enough of theories! It is time to realise:
The world of duality is the magic of the Source.

VI

The world of duality is the magic of the Source,
The fruit of miraculous Maya, its mysterious power:
No sooner does *tamas* conceal Reality,
Than *rajas* gives rise to name and form.

And the I-sense forsakes its Source,
Forgetting THAT – the Ground of all Being –
And thus giving birth to 'I', 'my', 'they', and the rest –
Good and evil, diversity, distinctions and judgements of all kinds.

Here self-sense celebrates the banquet macabre of personality:
Armed with the scourge of logic,
This vampire, a master of deceit, accustoms himself to the
    realm of space and time.

All the contents of innumerable vessels
Can't quench his unslakable thirst,
The object of the ego, longing for blood.

VII

The object of the ego, athirst for blood,
Through layer upon layer in the onion of sheaths,
Where the life-streams converge
That drag the helpless *jiva* into incarnation.

There the five-headed hungers suffer cruelly,
Suckling madly at the body of the world:
Taste, sight, touch, smell, and hearing –
Not only *jnanendriyas* but also *karmendriyas*:

Speech, hands, feet, generation and excretion –
The five-fold *pranas* complete the scene;
Alas, not only with flowers is my begging bowl full . . .

Yet within sits the *antaryami*,
And the entire Universe is only its bauble, its toy,
The plaything of the restless mind.

VIII

The plaything of the restless mind
Is this whole forest of creation: the vast multitude of forms,
Unquenchable desires, eternally arising yearnings,
Are all drawn together by the action of the reasoning mind.

Like the prodigal son, who has forgotten his Home,
Which he neither can forsake, not yet find another place to
    rest his head,
The I-sense wanders lost and forlorn, though born out of
    the Heart of Brahman,
And heir to the Immutable, the Omnipresent and Eternal.

Thus the poor *jiva*, whose essence is the True I.
Suffers the restrictions of the cycle of rebirth
In the ego's incarnations from life to life.

It does not see that there is a Pathway Home
To its original Freedom, a Return to its own True Self . . .
A direct path to one's immutable Nature.

IX

There is a direct path to one's immutable Nature,
That is beyond all causes and beginnings.
The limitlessness of the Absolute is that Mooring,
To which cling the souls who call out for their birthright.

This mystic Pole-Star of the ages
That dissolves the imprint of *samsara*
Beckons true seekers, the effloresence of the race,
Extolled alike by scriptures and sages.

Of all religions, of all the spiritual paths,
It is the ultimate Goal from the very genesis of Time,
Though each must find his own way there.

Among the many paths that lead to Brahman,
The most direct, like an arrow, is the one straight route
Laid open by Sri Ramana, the omnipresent Guru.

X

Laid open by Sri Ramana, the omnipresent Guru,
Who, when but 17, vanquished the fear of Death
By realising that the body is not I, but only fuel for the funeral pyre:
With this knowledge He attained Enlightenment.

He forsook the place of His birth
For Arunachala, His true native place . . .
The earthly embodiment of the Light of the Heart,
Issuing a silent call to the Quest for the I.

In cave and in ashram, at the summit of Being,
He is everywhere, formless and One –
The affirmation and witness of the scriptures.

Satguru, instructing the adepts through Silence,
He teaches from all eternity the direct path to Brahman:
Only realize that the ego is a phantom without substance.

XI

Only realize that the ego is a phantom without substance,
The formless spirit, weary of form:
Samsara, body, the restless mind –
Everything is a reflection of the Light, and no more . . .

The world of sensations but feeds the illusion
And pampers the stronghold of separateness:
The ego, masquerading as the one true Self,
Disgorges itself with the eruptions of self-sense.

Where is the mouth of this volcano
Whose eruptions project us into the world of name and form,
And veil us with the illusion of the loss of Eternity?

In order to regain our lost Estate,
The scriptures have shown us the Way:
Find the Source of thought in the Cave of the Heart.

XII

Find the Source of thought in the Cave of the Heart –
There where its death is inevitable.
The profane shall vanish into the Heart of Being,
Never again to arise: the Shore has been reached!

To cross the surging sea of Samsara, is there another way?
'I' and 'mine' are far too heavy weights;
Unless one makes this all-embracing sacrifice
How can one enter the Greater Life?

Direct the attention steadily within
To the Lotus of the Heart two digits to the right.
O, Satguru, grant Thy Grace!

One will tame the wild beast that the ego becomes
When it arrogates to itself the feeling of I, thus creating the world
    of maya,
By holding firmly to the Self-Enquiry, 'Who am I?'

XIII

Holding firmly to the Self-Enquiry, 'Who am I?'
And stalking unwaveringly the little 'I',
The adept shall reach the subtle Flame
In the Lotus of the Heart, in the Cave foreordained.

On this death-bed of self, immolated,
He shall rise again made new like the Phoenix.
Alike in both loss and in gain
Once the ego disappears in the Flame.

Sri Ramana! O Master! I beseech Thy Grace, Thy celestial Prasad:
To make this enquiry unceasingly,
And never to lose my way in the fog.

Thy disciple cherishes only this dream,
Arising in Thy Light so miraculous:
To enter, behold, and to master the way!

XIV

To enter, behold, and to master the way!
Who? Whose? Whither? Whence? Unity, duality –
All doubts have fallen away; only the Truth pulsates:
Sat-Chit-Ananda, Being-Awareness-Bliss.

Tat-Tvam-Asi . . . The road is ended.
The goal of Life – Oneness, Liberation – achieved.
The primal Bliss of Being at last is regained
As all fetters fall away from Awareness.

The Jnani has devoured all obstacles, yet sees all within Himself;
The fiery Witness, ever peaceful and poised,
Is He, the incarnation of the Glory of Being.

He is THAT, He is Brahman, the Subtle Effulgence of the One.
He Himself – the sacred object of worship –
Dwells in the Cave of the Heart as the True I.

XV

In the Cave of the Heart, the True I
Radiates alone with a subtle Light:
The one Essence shining forth without defect –
Blissful Consciousness of Being.

Brahman is the sole Reality – THAT is the Truth Itself:
The world of duality is the magic of the Source,
The object of the ego athirst for blood,
The plaything of the restless mind.

There is a direct Path to one's immutable Nature,
Laid open by Sri Ramana, the omnipresent Guru:
Only realise that the ego is a phantom without substance.

Find the Source of thought in the Cave of the Heart,
Holding firmly to the Self-Enquiry, 'Who am I?'
Thus enter, behold, and master the Way!

Index of Poem Titles

Extracts are indicated by the abbreviation 'extr'.

Index of Poets and Translators